Custom Edition for
Thomas Edison State College

Research Methods in the Social Sciences

Taken from:

Basics of Social Research: Qualitative and Quantitative Approaches
by W. Lawrence Neuman

Social Research: An Evolving Process, Second Edition
by Don G. McTavish and Herman J. Loether

Social Research: A Simple Guide
by Morley D. Glicken

Spotlight on Social Research
by Alexander R. Thomas and Polly J. Smith

Taken from:

Basics of Social Research: Qualitative and Quantitative Approaches
by W. Lawrence Neuman
Copyright © 2004 by Pearson Education
Published by Allyn & Bacon
Boston, Massachussetts 02116

Social Research: An Evolving Process, Second Edition
by Don G. McTavish and Herman J. Loether
Copyright © 2002, 1999 by Pearson Education
Published by Allyn & Bacon

Social Research: A Simple Guide
by Morley D. Glicken
Copyright © 2003 by Pearson Education
Published by Allyn & Bacon

Spotlight on Social Research
by Alexander R. Thomas and Polly J. Smith
Copyright © 2003 by Pearson Education
Published by Allyn & Bacon

This special edition published in cooperation with Pearson Custom Publishing.

Printed in the United States of America

15 16 17 18 19 V0ZU 17 16 15 14 13

ISBN 0-536-94154-8

2005420100

EH

Please visit our web site at *www.pearsoncustom.com*

PEARSON CUSTOM PUBLISHING
75 Arlington Street, Suite 300, Boston, MA 02116
A Pearson Education Company

Table of Contents

CHAPTER 1

INTRODUCTION

Consider, if you will, that cold you had last year. Runny nose, sore throat, scratchy eyes. That general feeling of "blah." And now think: What did you do to feel better? Whatever you did, it required knowledge of the common cold and how to address its symptoms. But where did that knowledge come from?

NONSCIENTIFIC APPROACHES TO KNOWLEDGE

Although science involves the search for knowledge, science is not the only approach to gaining knowledge. Other approaches include common sense, mysticism, and rationalism.

Common Sense

Common-sense knowledge is a reliance on what appears to be obvious. For instance, your cold last year did not just mail itself to you. Common sense dictates that you caught the cold from somebody else who had it, most likely someone with whom you spent time. As you recall your relations just prior to catching the cold, you remember that your father, roommate, and significant other's friend also had colds. Obviously, you caught the cold from one of them!

Common sense often leads people to the correct solution to a problem. Given these circumstances, you may well have caught the cold from your father, roommate, or significant other's friend. But common sense cannot tell you the specifics of how that happened. Science informs us that the common cold is caused by numerous viral infections and can be transmitted from one person to another by a variety of mechanisms, such as touch, sharing each other's glass, and the like. Such information, if known, is often included as part of common sense. Because of its reliance on the obvious, common sense does not readily help people understand the nonobvious. In actuality, you may have contacted that cold last year when the stranger standing next to you on the subway coughed.

Mysticism

"God bless you." This is the polite thing to say when someone sneezes, but why? As in many cultures, many Americans believed in the past (and some still do) that illness is the work of spirits or demons that have invaded the body. Because a sneeze is an early symptom of the onset of the common cold and many allergies, it was believed that an incantation to God to bless you could weaken the power of the spirit and help the patient remain healthy. Such sources of knowledge are related to *mysticism*.

Knowledge derived through mysticism relies on extraworldly sources for information. Often, mystical knowledge is believed to be transferred from extraworldly sources to an individual (or mystic) who has unique access to such knowledge. Mystical knowledge can be highly structured, as in the case of many religious traditions, or loosely structured, as is the case with psychics and spiritual mediums.

Rationalism

Knowledge can also be gained through rational means. *Rationalism* utilizes logic and complex systems of knowledge in order to understand aspects of the world. Perhaps the most famous example of rationalism is the following:

> All men are mortal.
> <u>Socrates is a man.</u>
> Therefore, Socrates is mortal.

In this example, it is proven that Socrates is a mortal by logically considering two statements that are true—that men are mortal and that Socrates is a man. If both statements are true, then it logically follows that Socrates is (or rather, was) a man. This conclusion is proven logically and without direct observation of Socrates.

Rationalism can be subject to errors in assumption. In other words, if a statement that is assumed to be true is in fact false, then any statements based on the assumption are possibly (but not necessarily) false as well. For instance, consider the following statement:

> *Events on Earth are influenced by the alignment of celestial bodies to one another.*

If the statement is true, then reading your daily horoscope might not be too bad an idea. If, however, the statement is false, then the entire logical system for gaining knowledge based on its truth (astrology) is possibly false. It is also possible that the logical system might not be false: It is possible that your horoscope rings true for another reason.

SCIENTIFIC KNOWLEDGE

Before discussing science, it is important to acknowledge that most people rely on a mixture of types of knowledge. Our common-sense knowledge that a cold can be passed from one person to the next also assumes that it is a virus that is being passed. Many psychics use astrology to help inform their decisions. Even many scientists are influenced by their religious views. That said, what is science?

Science is a way of gaining knowledge through systematic observation. This method contrasts to mysticism in that the knowledge is observable to anyone. Science is based on the idea that a particular phenomenon can be observed by anybody who repeats the conditions that brought it about. The practice of repeating a study to ensure that the phenomenon can be observed is called *replication*. Science is also systematic in that scientists consciously seek to observe a phenomenon. Scientific observations are specifically searched out in contrast to common-sense observations, which are often based on casual observation. Science also differs from rationalism in that it is based on observation. Although scientific theories are often rational, they need to be tested against observation to be considered accurate. In this sense, the mere deduction that Socrates is mortal is not entirely satisfactory; the theory needs to be tested. Luckily, there are some ethical constraints on science!

Scientific Method

Science relies upon the logic of the scientific method. The first aspect of the scientific method has already been discussed: that phenomenon need to be observable. This means that a study needs to be replicable: others can repeat the study and achieve the same results. Through an accumulation of such observable studies, certain properties of the phenomenon under study can be discerned. For instance, it has been repeatedly observed that water boils and evaporates, or turns from liquid to gas, at 100 degrees Celsius at sea level. The phenomenon is not only observable, but it can be repeated over and over again. In other words, the theory that water boils at 100 degrees Celsius is testable.

Not all scientific knowledge is so straightforward, however. Consider the theory that humans have evolved from an ancestor of both ourselves and the chimpanzee. In this case, the actual process of a human evolving from a common ancestor with chimpanzees has not been observed. So how do we know that this process has taken place? For starters, there has been direct observation of evolution through natural selection of microorganisms, so-called superbugs. Such bacteria have evolved in response to the introduction of antibiotics. As an antibiotic is introduced to a population of bacteria, it kills the organisms that are not resistant to the medication but spares those organisms that are drug resistant. In a classic example of natural selection, those left behind are free to reproduce and in time there is a population of drug-resistant bacteria. There is also a good, albeit incomplete, fossil record of species of protohumans dating back almost to the split with the ancestors of both humans and chimpanzees. In addition, there are numerous observable similarities between contemporary humans and chimpanzees. Our DNA is 99 percent similar, infants of both species look very similar and develop in similar ways, there are obvious physical similarities among adults of both species, and there are far more behavioral similarities than many people (and perhaps chimpanzees as well) would care to admit. From these numerous observations, it can be inferred that humans and chimpanzees share a common ancestor in our evolutionary past (Jones et al., 1992).

Consensus

The scientific method also depends on agreement or consensus among members of the scientific community about the properties of a particular phenomenon. Most scientists, for example, agree that the global climate has been getting warmer over the past century because of increased carbon dioxide emissions by humans. Consensus is not built easily, however, and it is not surprising that there are varying levels of agreement about particular phenomena throughout the sciences. It is difficult to imagine that a scientist living today would dispute that a molecule of water is composed of two atoms of hydrogen and one of oxygen. In contrast, a minority of scientists claim that global warming is not caused by increased carbon dioxide emissions by humans.

In some cases, there is simply not enough evidence for the formation of a consensus. For instance, there is little agreement on the ability of Neandertals, a species of humans that went extinct about twenty thousand years ago, to speak. Did they have language comparable to that of modern humans, did they use only gestures and vocalizations similar to those of other ape species (like chimpanzees), or were their language skills somewhere in between? Although most scientists would likely say somewhere in between, the exact placement of Neandertal language on the continuum between the two poles (no language vs. human language) remains uncertain (Maryanski & Turner, 1992).

The scientific community seeks agreement not only on factual information but on the definition of various phenomena. In fact, reaching a consensus about how a particular term should be defined or measured is often as contentious as the facts about a phenomenon. How should we define unemployment? Obviously, someone who wants a job and does not have one is unemployed. But what about someone who does not want a job? Or someone who wants to work full time but can only find part-time employment? Or someone who cannot find a job in her or his field and so takes a job in another field until one more desirable opens up? Different countries and social scientists measure unemployment differently because there is disagreement over how to define the concept of unemployment.

ASPECTS OF SCIENCE

With so much emphasis placed on the benefits of science and technology, many people have little knowledge of what constitutes science. There are many components of science, and the following are some of the most important.

Induction and Deduction

Science relies on the interplay of inductive reasoning (induction) and deductive reasoning (deduction). Inductive reasoning, which stresses observation and description, dates back to the Lyceum of the Greek philosopher Aristotle. This tradition is still found today in diverse scientific disciplines, from the descriptions of stars found in astronomy to the detailed observations of different cultures found in sociology and anthropology. The descriptions are often used as the foundation for general theories, and from them specific predictions are deduced and tested. Deductive reasoning, which stresses logic and mathematical representation, continues a tradition dating to Plato and his Academy in ancient Athens.

The seventeenth-century English philosopher Francis Bacon believed that a sufficiently large number of observations would yield theories to explain these observations. In this way, Bacon was suggesting that induction was the appropriate way to gain scientific knowledge. *Induction* works from specific observations about a phenomenon and theorizes general principles based on these observations. While observing that temperatures have been rising worldwide, one might theorize that global warming is caused by increased carbon dioxide emissions by humans. In social research, the practice of building theory based on observations is also called grounded theory.

In contrast, the French philosopher René Descartes argued about the same time that knowledge is best gained through deduction. *Deduction* begins with general statements about a phenomenon and makes specific predictions about it based on the general theory. Based on the general theory that global temperatures have been rising, one might predict that global temperatures were warmer during the 1990s than during the 1960s. This specific statement can then be tested for its accuracy.

In practice, science utilizes both approaches.

Quantitative versus Qualitative Data

Science utilizes observations, or data, in order to gain knowledge about phenomena. Data can be quantitative or qualitative.

Quantitative data are data that can be represented numerically. For instance, the median family income of a community is a number that represents the income gained by families in the 50th percentile—in other words, the exact middle—of all the incomes earned by all the families in a community in that year. If we know the median family income, we know that 50 percent made more and 50 percent made less. Using these figures in combination with other quantitative data, we can construct a good description of the community. But some things cannot be understood by looking at quantitative data alone.

Qualitative data are data that are represented by language, pictures, or other nonmathematical devices. The best representation of your hometown may not be a statistical profile but rather a picture of the Main Street or your own written description. These data cannot in their natural form be mathematically manipulated or represented in a table, but they can be useful in conveying knowledge.

Pure and Applied Research

Science also varies in terms of its purpose. Some scientific research is conducted for the sake or purpose of gaining knowledge. Such "knowledge for the sake of knowledge" is called *pure research*. For example, research conducted to understand the composition of a star has little practical value to everyday life on Earth. The purpose of conducting the research is to gain more knowledge—it may be tremendously useful information in the future, but it may not. The true utility of the knowledge is simply having it. In contrast, *applied research* is conducted with some practical purpose in mind. Determining whether or not a given land mass contains oil has a very practical application: extracting the oil. Often, pure research develops a body of knowledge that can then be used as the basis for applied research. Early work with electricity was often pure research, but the early theories were then used as the basis of applied research that revolutionized daily life.

Levels of Analysis

Science attempts to explain phenomena at various levels of observation. Macro-level observation examines large-scale phenomena, such as entire societies or cultures. Micro-level observation, in contrast, deals with small-scale phenomena, such as interactions between individuals. Some scientists also discuss a meso level of analysis—that is, a middle-range level of analysis between the micro and macro levels.

Units of Analysis

A *unit of analysis* is the unit that is actually being measured. It can be the individual, in which case the researcher measures the actions of individuals and tabulates the results. There are other units of analysis as well. Organizations, societies, and social institutions, among other things, can all be used as units of analysis, depending upon the research being conducted. Most surveys, for instance, ask individual people questions and tabulate the results. The individual is the unit of analysis. Other studies compare the poverty rates of different nations, and the nation is the unit of analysis.

Causation

Much research attempts to explain how a phenomenon operates, and this kind of explanation often relies on establishing causation. *Causation* is the concept that the action of a phenomenon affects the behavior of another. For causation to be established, three criteria need to be satisfied.

Relationship. There needs to be a relationship between the action and reaction of the two phenomena. For instance, there is a proven relationship between the approach of a low pressure system in the atmosphere and the development of rain. This relationship is based on the fact that the low pressure system causes rain.

Relationships do not always exist because of causation, however. For instance, there is a relationship between the rate of ice cream consumption and the murder rate. This relationship does not exist because of causation, however, but rather because both phenomena are influenced by the weather. When a relationship between two phenomena exists because of a third variable that affects both, the relationship is said to be spurious.

Temporal Order.   In order to establish that one phenomenon causes another, the cause needs to occur before the effect. Obviously, the effect cannot take place before its cause.

Elimination of Alternatives.   In order to establish causation, possible alternative theories about the relationship need to be eliminated. As the fictional detective Sherlock Holmes noted, the remaining facts, no matter how seemingly implausible, must be correct.

Reliability and Validity

In order to measure phenomena, there needs to be an indicator or test of the phenomenon. Scientists need to measure the phenomena they study and are therefore concerned with the reliability and validity of the measurement.

Reliability refers to the consistency of the measurement. Measures need to be consistent over time. For instance, if an instrument to measure the blood alcohol content of an individual is reliable, it will read the same level of inebriation each time that individual has that blood alcohol content level. Measures also need to be representative; that is, they need to give the same results across different units of analysis. For instance, the blood alcohol content instrument needs to give consistent results for each individual who uses it.

Validity refers to the accuracy of the measure. An instrument used to measure blood alcohol content needs, in fact, to measure blood alcohol content. Not only does a measure need to be valid on the face of things, it also needs to measure the entire nature of the phenomenon. For instance, if a researcher defines a happy family as one in which family members are satisfied with other family members as a whole, the measure of happiness needs to include everyone. A measure concerned only with the relationship between the spouses would not be valid.

SOCIAL SCIENCE RESEARCH METHODS

Social science research utilizes a variety of methods, some of which are used in other sciences and some of which are not. Although each major method is discussed individually, many social scientists practice triangulation: the utilization of three or more distinct methods to research a phenomenon. The advantage of triangulation is that it benefits from the unique properties of each method, and thus a more full and accurate picture of the phenomenon emerges.

As stated earlier, scientific research utilizes both quantitative and qualitative data. Quantitative research methods result primarily in quantitative data, and qualitative research methods result primarily in qualitative data.

There are four major types of quantitative methods. The first, *experimentation*, or *experiments*, studies phenomena under tightly controlled settings. Survey methods gather an array of data from a wide variety of respondents. *Content analysis* studies themes found in the artifacts of a society, such as newspapers, cinema, and music. *Secondary data analysis* uses data collected for a purpose other than the study being conducted in order to understand phenomena.

There are two broad areas of qualitative research. *Historical comparative research* examines historical processes over time and/or compares different populations to one another. In *fieldwork*, the researcher collects data by coming into direct contact with the people being studied. Data are collected by conducting interviews, observing social life, and participating in group activities.

CONCLUSION

As you will see, each social science research method is unique. Each contains an entire body of knowledge focused on making research as precise as possible. And it seems likely that as time moves on, social research will become even more accurate.

THEORY AND SOCIAL RESEARCH

INTRODUCTION

Suppose you want to make sense of the hostility between people of different races. Trying to understand it, you ask a teacher, who responds:

> Most racially prejudiced people learn negative stereotypes about another racial group from their families, friends, and others in their immediate surroundings. If they lack sufficient intimate social contact with members of the group or intense information that contradicts those stereotypes, they remain prejudiced.

This makes sense to you because it is consistent with what you know about how the social world works. This is an example of a small-scale social theory, a type that researchers use when conducting a study.

What do you think of when you hear the word *theory*? Theory is one of the least well understood terms for students learning social science. My students' eyelids droop if I begin a class by saying, "Today we are going to examine the theory of . . . " The mental picture many students have of theory is something that floats high among the clouds. My students have called it "a tangled maze of jargon" and "abstractions that are irrelevant to the real world."

Contrary to these views, theory has an important role in research and is an essential ally for the researcher. Researchers use theory differently in various types of research, but some type of theory is present in most social research. It is less evident in applied or descriptive than in basic or explanatory research. In simple terms, researchers interweave a story about the operation of the social world (the theory) with what they observe when they examine it systematically (the data).

People who seek absolute, fixed answers for a specific individual or a particular one-time event may be frustrated with science and social theories. To avoid frustration, it is wise to keep in mind three things about how social scientific theories work. First, social theories explain recurring patterns, not unique or one-time events. For example, they are not good for explaining why terrorists decided to attack New York's World Trade Center on September 11, 2001, but they can explain patterns, such as the conditions that generally lead to increased levels of fear and feelings of patriotism in a people. Second, social theories are explanations for aggregates, not particular individuals. *Aggregates* are collections of many individuals, cases, or other units (e.g., businesses, schools, families, clubs, cities, nations, etc.). A social theory rarely can explain why Josephine decided to major in nursing rather than engineering, but it can explain why females more than males in general choose nursing over engineering as a major. Third, social theories state a probability, chance, or tendency for events to occur, rather than state that one event must absolutely follow another. For example, instead of stating that when someone is abused as a child, that person will always later abuse his or her own children, a theory might state that when someone experiences abuse during his or her childhood, that person will *tend to* or is *more likely to* become an abusive parent when an adult. Likewise, it might state that people who did not experience childhood abuse might become abusive parents, but they *are less likely to* than someone who has experienced abuse as a child.

WHAT IS THEORY?

In Chapter 1, *social theory* was defined as a system of interconnected abstractions or ideas that condenses and organizes knowledge about the social world. It is a compact way to think of the social world. People are always creating new theories about how the world works.

Many people confuse the history of social thought, or what great thinkers said, with social theory. The classical social theorists (e.g., Durkheim, Weber, Marx, and Tonnies) played an important role in generating innovative ideas. They developed original theories that laid the foundation for subsequent generations of social thinkers. People study the classical theorists because they provided many creative and interrelated ideas at once. They radically changed the way people understood and saw the social world. We study them because geniuses who generate many original, insightful ideas and fundamentally shift how people saw the social world are rare.

People often use theories without making them explicit or labeling them as such. For example, newspaper articles or television reports on social issues usually have unstated social theories embedded within them. A news report on the difficulty of implementing a school desegregation plan will contain an implicit theory about race relations. Likewise, political leaders frequently express social theories when they discuss public issues. Politicians who claim that inadequate education causes poverty or that a decline in traditional moral values causes higher crime rates are expressing theories. Compared to the theories of social scientists, such laypersons' theories are less systematic, less well formulated, and harder to test with empirical evidence.

Almost all research involves some theory, so the question is less *whether* you should use theory than *how* you should use it. Being explicit about the theory makes it easier to read someone else's research or to conduct your own. An awareness of how theory fits into the research process produces better designed, easier to understand, and better conducted studies. Most researchers disparage atheoretical or "crude empiricist" research.

Theories come in many shapes and sizes. In this chapter, I provide an elementary introduction to social theory. You will encounter theory in later chapters, as well.

THE PARTS OF THEORY

Concepts

Concepts are the building blocks of theory.[1] A *concept* is an idea expressed as a symbol or in words. Natural science concepts are often expressed in symbolic forms, such as Greek letters (e.g., p) or formulas (e.g., $s = d/t$; $s =$ speed, $d =$ distance, $t =$ time). Most social science concepts are expressed as words. The exotic symbols of natural science theory make many people nervous, but the use of everyday words in specialized ways can create confusion.

I do not want to exaggerate the distinction between concepts expressed as words and concepts expressed as symbols. Words, after all, are symbols, too; they are symbols we learn with language. Height is a concept with which you are already familiar. For example, I can say the word *height* or write it down; the spoken sounds and written words are part of the English language. The combination of letters in the sound symbolizes, or stands for, the idea of a *height*. Chinese or Arabic characters, the French word *hauteur*, the German word *höhe*, the Spanish word *altura*—all symbolize the same idea. In a sense, a language is merely an agreement to represent ideas by sounds or written characters that people learned at some point in their lives. Learning concepts and theory is like learning a language.[2]

Concepts are everywhere, and you use them all the time. Height is a simple concept from everyday experience. What does it mean? It is easy to use the concept of *height*, but describing the concept itself is difficult. It represents an abstract idea about physical relations. How would you describe it to a very young child or a creature from a distant planet who was totally unfamiliar with it? A new concept from a social theory may seem just as alien when you encounter it for the first time. Height is a characteristic of a physical object, the distance from top to bottom. All people, buildings, trees, mountains, books, and so forth have a height. We can measure height or compare it. A height of zero is possible, and height can increase or decrease over time. As with many words, we use the word in several ways. Height is used in the expressions *the height of the battle, the height of the summer,* and *the height of fashion.*

The word *height* refers to an abstract idea. We associate its sound and its written form with that idea. There is nothing inherent in the sounds that make up the word and the idea it represents. The connection is arbitrary, but it is still useful. People can express the abstract idea to one another using the symbol alone.

Concepts have two parts: a *symbol* (word or term) and a *definition*. We learn definitions in many ways. I learned the word *height* and its definition from my parents. I learned it as I learned to speak and was socialized to the culture. My parents never gave me a dictionary definition. I learned it through a diffuse, nonverbal, informal process. My parents showed me many examples; I observed and listened to others use the word; I used the word incorrectly and was corrected; and I used it correctly and was understood. Eventually, I mastered the concept.

This example shows how people learn concepts in everyday language and how we share concepts. Suppose my parents had isolated me from television and other people, then taught me that the word for the idea *height* was *zdged*. I would have had difficulty communicating with others. People must share the terms for concepts and their definitions if they are to be of value.

Everyday culture is filled with concepts, but many have vague and unclear definitions. Likewise, the values and experiences of people in a culture may limit everyday concepts. Everyday concepts are often rooted in misconceptions or myth. Social scientists borrow concepts from everyday culture, but they refine these concepts and add new ones. Many concepts first developed by social scientists have diffused into the larger culture and become less precise. Concepts such as sexism, life-style, peer group, urban sprawl, and social class began as precise, technical concepts in social theory.

We create concepts from personal experience, creative thought, or observation. The classical theorists originated many concepts. Example concepts include family system, gender role, socialization, self-worth, frustration, and displaced aggression.

Some concepts, especially simple, concrete concepts such as *book* or *height,* can be defined through a simple nonverbal process. Most social science concepts are more complex and abstract. They are defined by formal, dictionary-type definitions that build on other concepts. It may seem odd to use concepts to define other concepts, but we do this all the time. For example, I defined *height* as a distance between top and bottom. *Top, bottom,* and *distance* are all concepts. We often combine simple, concrete concepts from ordinary experience to create more abstract concepts. *Height* is more abstract than *top* or *bottom.* Abstract concepts refer to aspects of the world we do not directly experience. They organize thinking and extend understanding of reality.

Researchers define scientific concepts more precisely than those we use in daily discourse. Social theory requires well-defined concepts. The definition helps to link theory with research. A valuable goal of exploratory research, and of most good research, is to clarify and refine concepts. Weak, contradictory, or unclear definitions of concepts restrict the advance of knowledge.

Concept Clusters. Concepts are rarely used in isolation. Rather, they form interconnected groups, or *concept clusters.* This is true for concepts in everyday language as well as for those in social theory. Theories contain collections of associated concepts that are consistent and mutually reinforcing. Together, they form a web of meaning. For example, if I want to discuss a concept such as *urban decay,* I will need a set of associated concepts (e.g., *urban expansion, economic growth, urbanization, suburbs, center city, revitalization, mass transit,* and *racial minorities*).

Some concepts take on a range of values, quantities, or amounts. Examples of this kind of concept are *amount of income, temperature, density of population, years of schooling,* and *degree of violence.* These are called *variables,* and you will read about them in a later chapter. Other concepts express types of nonvariable phenomena (e.g., *bureaucracy, family, revolution, homeless,* and *cold*). Theories use both kinds of concepts.

Classifications.   Some concepts are simple; they have one dimension and vary along a single continuum. Others are complex; they have multiple dimensions or many subparts. You can break complex concepts into a set of simple, or single-dimension, concepts. For example, Rueschemeyer and associates (1992:43–44) stated that democracy has three dimensions. *Democracy* means (1) regular, free elections with universal suffrage; (2) an elected legislative body that controls government; and (3) freedom of expression and association. The authors recognized that each dimension varies by degree. They combined the dimensions to create a set of types of regimes. Regimes very low on all three dimensions are totalitarian, those high on all three are democracies, and ones with other mixes are either authoritarian or liberal oligarchies.

Classifications are partway between a single, simple concept and a theory.[3] They help to organize abstract, complex concepts. To create a new classification, a researcher logically specifies and combines the characteristics of simpler concepts. You can best grasp this idea by looking at some examples.

The *ideal type* is a well-known classification. Ideal types are pure, abstract models that define the essence of the phenomenon in question. They are mental pictures that define the central aspects of a concept. Ideal types are not explanations because they do not tell why or how something occurs. They are smaller than theories, and researchers use them to build a theory. They are broader, more abstract concepts that bring together several narrower, more concrete concepts. Qualitative researchers often use ideal types to see how well observable phenomena match up to the ideal model. For example, Max Weber developed an ideal type of the concept *bureaucracy*. Many people use Weber's ideal type (see Box 2.1). It distinguishes a bureaucracy from other organizational forms (e.g., social movements, kingdoms,

---

BOX 2.1   Max Weber's Ideal Type of Bureaucracy

- It is a continuous organization governed by a system of rules.
- Conduct is governed by detached, impersonal rules.
- There is division of labor, in which different offices are assigned different spheres of competence.
- Hierarchical authority relations prevail; that is, lower offices are under control of higher ones.
- Administrative actions, rules, and so on are in writing and maintained in files.
- Individuals do not own and cannot buy or sell their offices.
- Officials receive salaries rather than receiving direct payment from clients in order to ensure loyalty to the organization.
- Property of the organization is separate from personal property of officeholders.

Source: Adapted from Chafetz (1978:72).

---

etc.). It also clarifies critical features of a kind of organization that people once found nebulous and hard to think about. No real-life organization perfectly matches the ideal type, but the model helps us think about and study bureaucracy.

Scope

Some concepts are highly abstract, some are at a middle level of abstraction, and some are at a concrete level. Theories with many abstract concepts apply to a wider range of social phenomena than those with concrete concepts and have broader scope. An example of a relationship is: Increased size creates centralization, which in turn creates greater formalization. *Size, centralization,* and *formalization* are very abstract ideas. They can refer to features of a group, organization, or society. We can translate this to say that as an organization or group gets bigger, authority and power relations within it become centralized and concentrated in a small elite. The elite will tend to rely more on written policies, rules, or laws to control and organize others in the group or organization. Thinking explicitly about a theory's scope will make it stronger and allow the researcher to communicate it more clearly to others.

Assumptions. Concepts contain built-in *assumptions*, statements about the nature of things that are not observable or testable. We accept them as a necessary starting point. Concepts and theories build on assumptions about the nature of human beings, social reality, or a particular phenomenon. Assumptions often remain hidden or unstated. One way for a researcher to deepen his or her understanding of a concept is to identify the assumptions on which it is based.

For example, the concept *book* assumes a system of writing, people who can read, and the existence of paper. Without such assumptions, the idea of a *book* makes little sense. A social science concept, such as *racial prejudice*, rests on several assumptions. These include people who make distinctions among individuals based on their racial heritage, attach specific motivations and characteristics to membership in a racial group, and make judgments about the goodness of specific motivations and characteristics. If race became irrelevant, people would cease to distinguish among individuals on the basis of race, to attach specific characteristics to a racial group, and to make judgments about characteristics. If that occurred, the concept of *racial prejudice* would cease to be useful for research. All concepts contain assumptions about social relations or how people behave.

Relationships

Theories contain concepts, their definitions, and assumptions. More significantly, theories specify how concepts relate to one another. Theories tell us whether concepts are related and, if they are,

how they relate to each other. In addition, theories state why the relationship does or does not exist. It is a relationship such as: Economic distress among the White population caused an increase in mob violence against African Americans. When a researcher empirically tests or evaluates a relationship, it is called a *hypothesis*. After many careful tests of a hypothesis confirm the proposition, the scientific community begins to develop confidence that the proposition is true.

THE ASPECTS OF THEORY

Theory can be baffling because it comes in so many forms. We can categorize a theory by (1) the direction of reasoning, (2) the level of social reality that it explains, (3) the forms of explanation it employs, and (4) the overall framework of assumptions and concepts in which it is embedded. Fortunately, all logically possible combinations of direction, level, explanation, and framework are not equally viable. There are only about half a dozen serious contenders.

Direction of Theorizing

Researchers approach the building and testing of theory from two directions. Some begin with abstract thinking. They logically connect the ideas in theory to concrete evidence, then test the ideas against the evidence. Others begin with specific observations of empirical evidence. On the basis of the evidence, they generalize and build toward increasingly abstract ideas. In practice, most researchers are flexible and use both approaches at various points in a study (see Figure 2.1).

Deductive. In a *deductive approach*, you begin with an abstract, logical relationship among concepts, then move toward concrete empirical evidence. You may have ideas about how the world operates and want to test these ideas against "hard data."

Zeitlin and Weyher (2001) used a deductive approach to theory in a study of unions and

FIGURE 2.1 Deductive and Inductive Theorizing

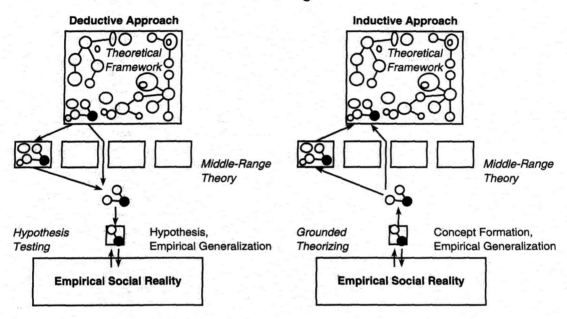

racial equality. They noted that past studies showed that labor unions in the United States generally increased Black-White economic inequality. They did not think unions automatically increased racial inequality but theorized that blue-collar workers have two choices about a strategy for improving their working conditions and wages in a racially diverse society. One is the *exclusionary* strategy—workers of one racial-ethnic group can organize to try to keep out people of different racial-ethnic groups as a way to protect their own social position. A second strategy is *inclusive*—workers adopt a political commitment for equality among all workers and organize to promote interracial cooperation as strategy to strengthen their negotiation position when asking for improved working conditions and wages. The authors deductively reasoned that in areas where an inclusive worker organization (i.e., labor union) prevailed, inequality among workers of different racial groups would

be low and decline, but if an exclusive labor organization prevailed in an area, interracial inequality would be high and increase.

To test the theory, Zeitlin and Weyher examined state-level data on racial inequality between workers. They looked at a period in U.S. history when most factory workers belonged to unions and when local unions belonged to one of two national umbrella labor organizations: the American Federation of Labor (AFL) or the Congress of Industrial Organization (CIO). The AFL was formed in the late 1800s, attracted high-skill White workers, and adopted an exclusionary strategy. The CIO was formed in the late 1930s, attracted low-skill workers of all races, and adopted an inclusive strategy. By the early 1950s, changes in national labor laws and purges of leftists in unions during the Joseph McCarthy anticommunist "Red Scare" era weakened the CIO. In 1955, the two organizations merged and the CIO disappeared. However, from 1940 to 1953, both organizations were active and the AFL was stronger in some states and the CIO in others.

The theory predicted greater racial inequality in states where the AFL was strong and lower levels in strong CIO states. Data showed that the stronger the CIO was relative to the AFL in a state, the greater the level of racial employment and income equality. Also, if there were many labor disputes in the strong CIO states, equality was even greater. After an independent CIO disappeared in the mid-1950s, racial equality declined in the states. The authors concluded that a labor organization's strategy, not unions alone, was the key factor that affected equality among workers of different races.

Inductive. If you use an *inductive approach,* you begin with detailed observations of the world and move toward more abstract generalizations and ideas. When you begin, you may have only a topic and a few vague concepts. As you observe, you refine the concepts, develop empirical generalizations, and identify preliminary relationships. You build the theory from the ground up.

Duneier (1999) used an inductive approach in his study of life on the sidewalk. He noted that in much of social science, both quantitative secondary analysis research and qualitative field research, a researcher develops a theoretical understanding only after data have been collected. He stated, "I began to get ideas from the things I was seeing and hearing on the street" (p. 341). Many researchers who adopt an inductive approach use grounded theory. *Grounded theory* is part of an inductive approach in which a researcher builds ideas and theoretical generalizations based on closely examining and creatively thinking about the data (see Box 2.2). A researcher creates grounded theory out of a process of trying to explain, interpret, and render meaning from data. It arises from trying to account for, understand, or "make sense of" the evidence. Duneier (1999:342) has suggested that

---

BOX
2.2   **What Is Grounded Theory?**

Grounded theory is a widely used approach in qualitative research. It is not the only approach and it is not used by all qualitative researchers. *Grounded theory* is "a qualitative research method that uses a systematic set of procedures to develop an inductively derived theory about a phenomenon" (Strauss and Corbin, 1990:24). The purpose of grounded theory is to build a theory that is faithful to the evidence. It is a method for discovering new theory. In it, the researcher compares unlike phenomena with a view toward learning similarities. He or she sees micro-level events as the foundation for a more macro-level explanation. Grounded theory shares several goals with more positivist-oriented theory. It seeks theory that is comparable with the evidence that is precise and rigorous, capable of replication, and generalizable. A grounded theory approach pursues generalizations by making comparisons across social situations.

Qualitative researchers use alternatives to grounded theory. Some qualitative researchers offer an in-depth depiction that is true to an informant's worldview. They excavate a single social situation to elucidate the micro processes that sustain stable social interaction. The goal of other researchers is to provide a very exacting depiction of events or a setting. They analyze specific events or settings in order to gain insight into the larger dynamics of a society. Still other researchers apply an existing theory to analyze specific settings that they have placed in a macro-level historical context. They show connections among micro-level events and between micro-level situations and larger social forces for the purpose of reconstructing the theory and informing social action.

the process is similar to seeing many symptoms and later arriving at a diagnosis (i.e., a story that explains the source of the symptoms).

Level of Theory

Social theories can be divided into three broad groupings by the level of social reality with which they deal. Most of us devote the majority of our time to thinking about the micro level of reality, the individuals we see and interact with on a day-by-day basis. *Micro-level theory* deals with small slices of time, space, or numbers of people. The concepts are usually not very abstract.

Mulford and others (1998) used a micro-level theory. The researchers' theory was that a halo effect explained why one person misjudged another's behavior. A halo produces expectations. People expect a person who has one visible positive feature (e.g., highly physically attractive) to also possess other less visible positive traits (e.g., cooperative in a game involving money). In a small-scale social setting in which people interacted interpersonally—playing a game with another person—the researchers tested whether people were willing to interact with someone who was attractive and to cooperate with that person more than with a less attractive person. In the game, cooperating with someone when that person also cooperated resulted in winning money, but it resulted in losing money if one person cooperated while the other person "went alone." Researchers found that based on the other player's physical appearance, people regularly misjudged how cooperative the other player would be. As predicted by the halo effect, people regularly overestimated the cooperativeness of attractive people and therefore tended to lose money to them.

Meso-level theory attempts to link macro and micro levels or to operate at an intermediate level. Theories of organizations, social movements, or communities are often at this level.

Vincent Roscigno and William Danaher (2001) used meso-level theory in their study on the labor movement among southern textile workers. The researchers used a theory of movement subculture and political opportunity to explain growing labor movement strength and increased strike activity among workers in one industry in a region of the United States across several years. They expected strike activity to grow as the result of a strong movement subculture that carried a message of injustice and a "political opportunity" or the expectation among people that collective action at a particular time would produce positive results. Their study showed that a technological innovation (i.e., the spread of new radio stations with songs and discussions of working conditions and unfair treatment) contributed to the growth of a subculture of movement solidarity among the textile workers and fostered self-identity as a worker who had common interests with the other textile workers. The technological innovation and events in the political environment (i.e., union organizers and speeches by the President of the United States) also created a political opportunity for the workers. The workers believed that collection action (i.e., strike) was necessary to achieve justice and would produce gains because other workers and government authorities would support their actions.

Macro-level theory concerns the operation of larger aggregates such as social institutions, entire cultural systems, and whole societies. It uses more concepts that are abstract.

The study by Anthony Marx (1998) on race in the United States, South Africa, and Brazil used a macro-level theory. He wanted to explain the conditions that led Black people to engage in protest to gain full citizenship rights and he examined patterns of national racial politics in three counties across two centuries. His theory said that protest resulted in an interaction between (1) race-based political mobilization and (2) national government policies of racial domination (i.e., apartheid in South Africa, Jim Crow laws in southern United States, and no legalized race-based domination in Brazil). Policies of racial domination developed from practices of slavery, exploitation, and discrimination that justified White superiority. The policies reinforced specific racial ideologies that shaped national development during the twentieth century. A critical causal factor was how national political elites used the legalized domination of Blacks to reduce divisions among Whites. In nations that had large regional or class divisions among Whites, national elites tried to increase White backing for the national government by creating legalized forms of racial domination. Over time, such legalized domination froze racial divisions, which promoted a sense of racial identity and consciousness among Blacks. The strong sense of racial identity became a key resource when Blacks mobilized politically to demand full citizenship rights. Legalized racial domination also intensified the Blacks' protest and directed it against the national government as the societal institution that reinforced their experience of racial inequality.

Forms of Explanation

Prediction and Explanation. A theory's primary purpose is to explain. Many people confuse prediction with explanation. There are two meanings or uses of the term *explanation*. Researchers focus on *theoretical explanation,* a logical argument that tells why something occurs. It refers to a general rule or principle. These are a researcher's theoretical argument or connections among concepts. The second type of explanation, *ordinary explanation,* makes something clear or describes something in a way that illustrates it and makes it intelligible. For example, a good teacher "explains" in the ordinary sense. The two types of explanation can blend together. This occurs when a researcher explains (i.e., makes intelligible) his or her explanation (i.e., a logical argument involving theory).

Prediction is a statement that something will occur. It is easier to predict than to explain, and an explanation has more logical power than prediction because good explanations also predict. An explanation rarely predicts more than one outcome, but the same outcome may be predicted by opposing explanations. Although it is less powerful than explanation, many people are entranced by the dramatic visibility of a prediction.

A gambling example illustrates the difference between explanation and prediction. If I enter a casino and consistently and accurately predict the next card to appear or the next number on a roulette wheel, it will be sensational. I may win a lot of money, at least until the casino officials realize I am always winning and expel me. Yet, my method of making the predictions is more interesting than the fact that I can do so. Telling you what I do to predict the next card is more fascinating than being able to predict.

Here is another example. You know that the sun "rises" each morning. You can predict that at some time, every morning, whether or not clouds obscure it, the sun will rise. But why is this so? One explanation is that the Great Turtle carries the sun across the sky on its back. Another explanation is that a god sets his arrow ablaze, which appears to us as the sun, and shoots it across the sky. Few people today believe these ancient explanations. The explanation you probably accept involves a theory about the rotation of the earth and the position of the sun, the star of our solar system. In this explanation, the sun only appears to rise. The sun does not move; its apparent movement depends on the earth's rotation. We are on a planet that both spins on its axis and orbits around a star millions of miles away in space. All three explanations make the same prediction: The sun rises each morning. As you can see, a weak explanation can produce an accurate prediction. A good explanation depends on a well-developed theory and is confirmed in research by empirical observations.

Causal Explanation. *Causal explanation,* the most common type of explanation, is used when the relationship is one of cause and effect. We use it all the time in everyday language, which tends to be sloppy and ambiguous. What do we mean when we say *cause?* For example, you may say that poverty causes crime or that looseness in morals causes an increase in divorce. This does not tell how or why the causal process works. Researchers try to be more precise and exact when discussing causal relations.

Philosophers have long debated the idea of cause. Some people argue that causality occurs in the empirical world, but it cannot be proved. Causality is "out there" in objective reality, and researchers can only try to find evidence for it. Others argue that causality is only an idea that exists in the human mind, a mental construction, not something "real" in the world. This second position holds that causality is only a convenient way of thinking about the world. Without entering into the philosophical debate, many researchers pursue causal relationships.

You need three things to establish causality: temporal order, association, and the elimination of plausible alternatives. An implicit fourth condition is an assumption that a causal relationship makes sense or fits with broader assumptions or a theoretical framework. Let us examine the three basic conditions.

The *temporal order* condition means that a cause must come before an effect. This commonsense assumption establishes the direction of causality: from the cause toward the effect. You may ask: How can the cause come after what it is to affect? It cannot, but temporal order is only one of the conditions needed for causality. Temporal order is necessary but not sufficient to infer causality. Sometimes people make the mistake of talking about "cause" on the basis of temporal order alone. For example, a professional baseball player pitches no-hit games when he kisses his wife just before a game. The kissing occurred before the no-hit games. Does that mean the kissing is the cause of the pitching performance? It is very unlikely. As another example, race riots occurred in four separate cities in 1968, one day after an intense wave of sunspots. The temporal ordering does not establish a causal link between sunspots and race riots. After all, all prior human history occurred before some specific event. The temporal order condi-

tion simply eliminates from consideration potential causes that occurred later in time.

It is not always easy to establish temporal order. With cross-sectional research, temporal order is tricky. For example, a researcher finds that people who have a lot of education are also less prejudiced than others. Does more education cause a reduction in prejudice? Or do highly prejudiced people avoid education or lack the motivation, self-discipline, and intelligence needed to succeed in school? Here is another example. The students who get high grades in my class say I am an excellent teacher. Does getting high grades make them happy, so they return the favor by saying that I am an excellent teacher (i.e., high grades cause a positive evaluation)? Or am I doing a great job, so students study hard and learn a lot, which the grades reflect (i.e., their learning causes them to get high grades)? It is a chicken-and-egg problem. To resolve it, a researcher needs to bring in other information or design research to test for the temporal order.

Simple causal relations are unidirectional, operating in a single direction from the cause to the effect. Most studies examine unidirectional relations. More complex theories specify reciprocal-effect causal relations—that is, a mutual causal relationship or simultaneous causality. For example, studying a lot causes a student to get good grades, but getting good grades also motivates the student to continue to study. Theories often have reciprocal or feedback relationships, but these are difficult to test. Some researchers call unidirectional relations nonrecursive and reciprocal-effect relations recursive.

A researcher also needs an *association* for causality. Two phenomena are associated if they occur together in a patterned way or appear to act together. People sometimes confuse correlation with association. Correlation has a specific technical meaning, whereas association is a more general idea. A correlation coefficient is a statistical measure that indicates the amount of association, but there are many ways to measure association. Figure 2.2 shows 38 people from a lower-income neighborhood and 35 people from

FIGURE 2.2 Association of Income and Race

Lower Income   Upper Income

an upper-income neighborhood. Can you see an association between race and income level?

More people mistake association for causality than confuse it with temporal order. For example, when I was in college, I got high grades on the exams I took on Fridays but low grades on those I took on Mondays. There was an association between the day of the week and the exam grade, but it did not mean that the day of the week caused the exam grade. Instead, the reason was that I worked 20 hours each weekend and was very tired on Mondays. As another example, the number of children born in India increased until the late 1960s, then slowed in the 1970s. The number of U.S.-made cars driven in the United States increased until the late 1960s, then slowed in the 1970s. The number of Indian children born and the number of U.S. cars driven are associated: They vary together or increase and decrease at the same time. Yet there is no causal connection. By coincidence, the Indian government instituted a birth control program that slowed the number of births at the same time that Americans were buying more imported cars.

If a researcher cannot find an association, a causal relationship is unlikely. This is why researchers attempt to find correlations and other measures of association. Yet, a researcher can often find an association without causality. The association eliminates potential causes that are not associated, but it cannot definitely identify a cause. It is a necessary but not a sufficient condition. In other words, you need it for causality, but it is not enough alone.

An association does not have to be perfect (i.e., every time one variable is present, the other also is) to show causality. In the example involving exam grades and days of the week, there is an association if on 10 Fridays I got 7 As, 2 Bs, and 1 C, whereas my exam grades on 10 Mondays were 6 Ds, 2 Cs, and 2 Bs. An association exists, but the days of the week and the exam grades are not perfectly associated. The race and income-level association shown in Figure 2.2 is also an imperfect association.

Eliminating alternatives means that a researcher interested in causality needs to show that the effect is due to the causal variable and not to something else. It is also called *no spuriousness* because an apparent causal relationship that is actually due to an alternative but unrecognized cause is called a spurious relationship, which is discussed in a later chapter (see Box 2.3).

Researchers can observe temporal order and associations. They cannot observe the elimination of alternatives. They can only demonstrate it indirectly. Eliminating alternatives is an ideal because eliminating all possible alternatives is impossible. A researcher tries to eliminate major alternative explanations in two ways: through built-in design controls and by measuring potential hidden causes. Experimental researchers build controls into the study design itself to eliminate alternative causes. They isolate an experimental situation from the influence of all variables except the main causal variable.

Researchers also try to eliminate alternatives by measuring possible alternative causes. This is common in survey research and is called *controlling for* another variable. Researchers use statistical techniques to learn whether the causal variable or something else operates on the effect variable.

Causal explanations are usually in a linear form or state cause and effect in a straight line: A causes B, B causes C, C causes D.

The study of Zeitlin and Weyher (2001) on labor unions and racial inequality discussed earlier provides an example of a causal theoretical explanation. Their explanation links two major concepts: the cause (the strategy of a labor organization, either exclusionary or inclusive) and the effect (the degree of employment inequality between Black and White workers).

We can restate the logic in a deductive causal form: If the proposition is true, then we observe certain things in the empirical evidence. Good causal explanations identify a causal relationship and specify a causal mechanism. A simple causal explanation is: X causes Y, Y occurs because of X, where X and Y are concepts (e.g., early marriage

---

As I was driving home from the university one day, I heard a radio news report about gender and racial bias in standardized tests. A person who claimed that bias was a major problem said that the tests should be changed. Since I work in the field of education and disdain racial or gender bias, the report caught my attention. Yet, as a social scientist, I critically evaluated the news story. The evidence for a bias charge was the consistent pattern of higher scores in mathematics for male high school seniors versus female high school seniors, and for European-background students versus African American students. Was the cause of the pattern of different test scores a bias built into the tests?

When questioned by someone who had designed the tests, the person charging bias lacked a crucial piece of evidence to support a claim of test bias: the educational experience of students. It turns out that girls and boys take different numbers and types of mathematics courses in high school. Girls tend to take fewer math courses. Among the girls who complete the same mathematics curriculum as boys, the gender difference dissolves. Likewise, a large percentage of African Americans attend racially segregated, poor-quality schools in inner cities or in impoverished rural areas. For African Americans who attend high-quality suburban schools and complete the same courses, racial differences in test scores disappear. This evidence suggests that inequality in education causes test score differences. Although the tests may have problems, identifying the real cause implies that changing the tests without first improving or equalizing education could be a mistake.

and divorce). Some researchers state causality in a predictive form: If X occurs, then Y follows. Causality can be stated in many ways: X leads to Y, X produces Y, X influences Y, X is related to Y, the greater X the higher Y.

Here is a simple causal theory: A rise in unemployment causes an increase in child abuse. The subject to be explained is an increase in the occurrence of child abuse. What explains it is a rise in unemployment. We "explain" the increase in child abuse by identifying its cause. A complete explanation also requires elaborating the causal mechanism. My theory says that when people lose their jobs, they feel a loss of self-worth. Once they lose self-worth, they become easily frustrated, upset, and angry. Frustrated people often express their anger by directing violence toward those with whom they have close personal contact (e.g., friends, spouse, children, etc.). This is especially true if they do not understand the source of the anger or cannot direct it toward its true cause (e.g., an employer, government policy, or "economic forces").

The unemployment and child abuse example illustrates a chain of causes and a causal mechanism. Researchers can test different parts of the chain. They might test whether unemployment rates and child abuse occur together, or whether frustrated people become violent toward the people close to them. A typical research strategy is to divide a larger theory into parts and test various relationships against the data.

Relationships between variables can be positive or negative. Researchers imply a positive relationship if they say nothing. A *positive relationship* means that a higher value on the causal variable goes with a higher value on the effect variable. For example, the more education a person has, the longer his or her life expectancy is. A *negative relationship* means that a higher value on the causal variable goes with a lower value on the effect variable. For example, the more frequently a couple attends religious services, the lower the chances of their divorcing each other. In diagrams, a plus sign (+) signifies a positive

relationship and a negative sign (–) signifies a negative relationship.

Structural Explanation. A *structural explanation* is used with functional and pattern theories. Unlike a causal effect chain, which is similar to a string of balls lined up that hit one another in sequence, it is more similar to a wheel with spokes from a central idea or a spider web in which each strand forms part of the whole. A researcher making a structural explanation uses a set of interconnected assumptions, concepts, and relationships. Instead of causal statements, he or she uses metaphors or analogies so that relationships "make sense." The concepts and relations within a theory form a mutually reinforcing system. In structural explanations, a researcher specifies a sequence of phases or identifies essential parts that form an interlocked whole.

Gould's (1991) theory of the social mobilization in the Paris Commune of 1871 is an example of a structural explanation. The Paris Commune was a famous rebellion and takeover of the city of Paris—and very nearly of the government of France—by masses of poor and working people who were led by socialists, Marxists, and radicals. It was a two-month experiment in democratic socialism with free education, worker cooperatives, and radical social reforms. The Commune ended with a brutal battle in which 25,000 Parisians died, most of them shot after surrendering to the national army.

Gould said that people came from different social networks, which shaped their involvement in collective action. Thus, prior to their recruitment into the Paris Commune rebellion, people had social ties to one another. By knowing these ties, Gould predicted who was likely to join. His theory said that isolated people are unlikely to join. People join when those with whom they have intimate social relations join. In addition, a person's location within a web of social ties is important. People at the center of a dense web of ties (i.e., those who have multiple strong ties) are pulled more strongly than those on the periphery (i.e., those with only one or a few weak ties). Gould found that people from the same Paris neighborhood were recruited into a single battalion in the revolutionary defense guard. The new organization, the guard, was built on previous informal ties from the neighborhood—ties of family, neighbor, co-worker, or friend. This created intense intrabattalion loyalty. At the same time, a few people from the neighborhood, some whom were central in it, went to other battalions. This created loyalty across guard battalions. Gould predicted the pattern of battalion behavior from the positions people held in the overlapping social networks of the neighborhood and the guard battalion. He explained the actions of battalions and their responses to events by referring to a broader pattern of social ties among people.

Structural explanation is also used in *functional theory*.[4] Functional theorists explain an event by locating it within a larger, ongoing, balanced social system. They often use biological metaphors. These researchers explain something by identifying its function within a larger system or the need it fulfills for the system. Functional explanations are in this form: "*L* occurs because it serves needs in the system *M*." Theorists assume that a system will operate to stay in equilibrium and to continue over time.

A functional theory of social change says that, over time, a social system, or society, moves through developmental stages, becoming increasingly differentiated and more complex. It evolves a specialized division of labor and develops greater individualism. These developments create greater efficiency for the system as a whole. Specialization and individualism create temporary disruptions. The traditional ways of doing things weaken, but new social relations emerge. The system generates new ways to fulfill functions or satisfy its needs.

Kalmijn (1991) used a functional explanation to explain a shift in how Americans select marriage partners. He relied on secularization theory, which holds that ongoing historical processes of industrialization and urbanization

shape the development of society. During these modernization processes, people rely less on traditional ways of doing things. Religious beliefs and local community ties weaken, as does the family's control over young adults. People no longer live their entire lives in small, homogeneous communities. Young adults become more independent from their parents and from the religious organizations that formerly played a critical role in selecting marriage partners.

Society has a basic need to organize the way people select marriage partners and find partners with whom they share fundamental values. In modern society, people spend time away from small local settings in school settings. In these school settings, especially in college, they meet other unmarried people. Education is a major socialization agent in modern society. Increasingly, it affects a person's future earnings, moral beliefs and values, and ways of spending leisure time. This explains why there has been a trend in the United States for people to marry less within the same religion and increasingly to marry persons with a similar level of education. In traditional societies, the family and religious organization served the function of socializing people to moral values and linking them to potential marriage partners who held similar values. In modern society, educational institutions largely fulfill this function for the social system.

Interpretive Explanation. The purpose of *interpretive explanation* is to foster understanding. The interpretive theorist attempts to discover the meaning of an event or practice by placing it within a specific social context. He or she tries to comprehend or mentally grasp the operation of the social world, as well as get a feel for something or to see the world as another person does. Because each person's subjective world view shapes how he or she acts, the researcher attempts to discern others' reasoning and view of things. The process is similar to decoding a text or work of literature. Meaning comes from the context of a cultural symbol system.

An interpretive explanation is illustrated by Edelman, Fuller, and Mara-Drita's (2001) study of how companies adopted policies related to diversity issues in the early 1990s—that is, affirmative action and equal opportunity. The authors examined what managers said, or their rhetoric, about diversity concerns. Rhetoric included various statements about diversity made by professional managers, business school professors, and consultants in professional workshops, meetings, specialized magazines, and electronic forums.

Edelman and colleagues found that managers took legal ideas, terms, and concepts and converted them into ones that fit into their organizational setting. Professional managers converted vague legal mandates and terms that were based on ideas about racial discrimination and ending injustice. They interjected their own views, values, training, and interests and produced slightly different ideas and procedures. Management rhetoric changed legal ideas from taking specific actions to end racial-ethnic or gender discrimination and changed them into a "new idea" for effective corporate management. The "new idea" was that corporations benefit from a culturally diverse workforce. Simply put, diversity is good for company profits. They consolidated various studies and discussion on how to improve corporate operations around the new idea—a socially heterogeneous workforce is more creative, productive, and profitable.

The authors created a theory of "managerialization of law" from their data. This theory states that professional managers operate in a corporate environment. They will not simply take ideas and mandates created in a government-legal environment and impose them directly onto a corporation's internal operations. In fact, on the issue of affirmative action, many corporate officials saw the legal ideas and requirements as hostile or alien. So the managers converted, or translated, the legal ideas into an acceptable form—one acceptable from a managerial point of view. They used new forms to move their corporations in a direction that would comply with the legal requirements. This is an interpretive ex-planation because the authors explained a social event (i.e., corporations embracing programs and rhetoric to favor cultural diversity) by examining how the managers subjectively constructed new ways of looking at, thinking about, and talking about the diversity issue (i.e., they constructed a new interpretation).

Theoretical Frameworks

So far, you have learned about theory and empirical generalization. Many researchers use middle-range theory. Middle-range theories are slightly more abstract than empirical generalizations or specific hypotheses. As Merton (1967:39) stated, "Middle-range theory is principally used in sociology to guide empirical inquiry."

Middle-range theories can be formal or substantive. We can organize the terms about theory by the degree of abstraction suggested. From the most concrete to the most abstract are empirical generalizations, middle-range theories, and frameworks. A *theoretical framework* (also called a paradigm or *theoretical system*) is more abstract than a formal or substantive theory. Figure 2.1 shows the levels and how they are used in inductive and deductive approaches to theorizing.

Researchers do not make precise distinctions among the degrees of abstraction. When they conduct a study, they primarily use middle-range theory and empirical generalization. They rarely use a theoretical framework directly in empirical research. A researcher may test parts of a theory on a topic and occasionally contrast parts of the theories from different frameworks. Box 2.4 illustrates the various degrees of abstraction with Kalmijn's study of changing marriage partner selection.

Sociology has several major theoretical frameworks.[5] The frameworks are orientations or sweeping ways of looking at the social world. They provide collections of assumptions, concepts, and forms of explanation. Frameworks include many formal or substantive theories (e.g., theories of crime, theories of the family, etc.). Thus, there can be a structural functional theory,

Theoretical Framework. Structural functionalism holds that the processes of industrialization and urbanization change human society from a traditional to a modern form. In this process of modernization, social institutions and practices evolve. This evolution includes those that fill the social system's basic needs, socialize people to cultural values, and regulate social behavior. Institutions that filled needs and maintained the social system in a traditional society are superseded by modern ones.

Formal Theory. Secularization theory says that during modernization, people shift away from a reliance on traditional religious beliefs and local community ties. In traditional society, institutions that conferred ascribed social status (family, church, and community) also controlled socialization and regulated social life. In modern society, they are superseded by secular institutions (e.g., education, government, and media) that confer achievement-oriented status.

Middle-Range Substantive Theory. A theory of intermarriage patterns notes that young adults in modern society spend less time in small, local settings, where family, religion, and community all have a strong influence. Instead, young adults spend increasing amounts of time in school settings. In these settings, especially in college, they have opportunities to meet other unmarried people. In modern society, education has become a major socialization agent. It affects future earnings, moral beliefs and values, and leisure interests. Thus, young adults select marriage partners less on the basis of shared religious or local ties and more on the basis of common educational levels.

Empirical Generalization. Americans once married others with similar religious beliefs and affiliation. This practice is being replaced by marriage to others with similar levels of education.

---

an exchange theory, and a conflict theory of the family. Theories within the same framework share assumptions and major concepts. Some frameworks are oriented more to the micro level, others focus on more macro-level phenomena. Box 2.5 shows four major frameworks in sociology and briefly describes the key concepts and assumptions of each.

THE THREE MAJOR APPROACHES TO SOCIAL SCIENCE

We began this chapter by looking at small-scale parts of a theory (i.e., ideas or concepts). We moved toward larger and broader aspects of social theory, and arrived at major theoretical frameworks in the last section. Now, we move to an even a broader, more abstract level of the linkage between theory and research—fundamental approaches to social science. It involves issues sometimes called *meta-methodological* (i.e., beyond or supersized methodological concerns) and blurs into areas of philosophy that studies what science means. We only briefly touch on the issues here, but we cannot ignore them because they affect how people do social research studies.

About 40 years ago, a now famous philosopher of science, Thomas Kuhn, argued that the way science develops in a specific field across time is based on researchers sharing a general approach, or paradigm. A *paradigm* is an integrated set of assumptions, beliefs, models of doing good research, and techniques for gathering and analyzing data. It organizes core ideas, theoretical frameworks, and research methods. Kuhn observed that scientific fields tend to be held together around a paradigm for a long period of time. Very few researchers question the paradigm, and most focus on operating within its

BOX 2.5	Major Theoretical Frameworks in Sociology

Structural Functionalism

Major Concepts. System, equilibrium, dysfunction, division of labor

Key Assumptions. Society is a system of interdependent parts that is in equilibrium or balance. Over time, society has evolved from a simple to a complex type, which has highly specialized parts. The parts of society fulfill different needs or functions of the social system. A basic consensus on values or a value system holds society together.

Exchange Theory (also Rational Choice)

Major Concepts. Opportunities, rewards, approval, balance, credit

Key Assumptions. Human interactions are similar to economic transactions. People give and receive resources (symbolic, social approval, or material) and try to maximize their rewards while avoiding pain, expense, and embarrassment. Exchange relations tend to be balanced. If they are unbalanced, persons with credit can dominate others.

Symbolic Interactionism

Major Concepts. Self, reference group, role-playing, perception

Key Assumptions. People transmit and receive symbolic communication when they socially interact. People create perceptions of each other and social settings. People largely act on their perceptions. How people think about themselves and others is based on their interactions.

Conflict Theory

Major Concepts. Power, exploitation, struggle, inequality, alienation

Key Assumptions. Society is made up of groups that have opposing interests. Coercion and attempts to gain power are ever-present aspects of human relations. Those in power attempt to hold onto their power by spreading myths or by using violence if necessary.

---

general boundaries to accumulate new knowledge. On rare occasions in history, intellectual difficulties increase, unexpected issues grow, and troubling concerns over proper methods multiply. Slowly, the members of a scientific field shift in how they see things and switch to a new paradigm. Once the new paradigm becomes fully established and widely adopted, the process accumulating knowledge begins anew.

Kuhn's explanation covered how most sciences operate most of the time, but some fields operate with multiple or competing paradigms. This is the case in several of the social sciences. This greatly bothers some social scientists, and they believe having multiple paradigms hinders the growth of knowledge. They see multiple paradigms as a sign of the immaturity or under-

development of the "science" in the social sciences. Some believe all social science researchers should embrace a single paradigm and stop using alternatives to it.

Other social scientists accept the coexistence of multiple paradigms. They recognize that this can be confusing and often makes communicating difficult among those who use a different approach. Despite this, they argue that each social science paradigm provides important kinds of knowledge and insights, so to drop one would limit what we can learn about the social world. These social scientists note that no one definitely can say which approach is "best" or even whether it is necessary or highly desirable to have only one paradigm. So instead of closing off an approach that offers innovative ways to study social life and gain insight into human behavior, they argue for keeping a diversity of approaches.

In this section, we will look at three fundamental paradigms or approaches used in social science. Each approach has been around for over 150 years and is used by many highly respected professional researchers. Three approaches are unequal in terms of the number of followers, quantity of new studies, and types of issues addressed. Often, people who strongly adhere to one approach disagree with researchers who use another, or see the other approaches as being less valuable or less "scientific" than their approach. Although adherents to each approach may use various research techniques, theories, and theoretical frameworks, researchers who adopt one approach tend to favor certain research techniques, theories, or theoretical frameworks over others. The three approaches are positivism, interpretive, and critical; each has internal divisions, offshoots, and extensions, but these are the core ideas of the three major approaches.

Positivist Approach

Positivism is the most widely practiced social science approach, especially in North America. *Positivism* sees social science research as fundamentally the same as natural science research; it assumes that social reality is made up of objective facts that value-free researchers can precisely measure and use statistics to test causal theories. Large-scale bureaucratic agencies, companies, and many people in the general public favor a positivist approach because it emphasizes getting objective measures of "hard facts" in the form of numbers.

Positivists put a great value on the principle of replication, even if only a few studies are replicated. *Replication* occurs when researchers or others repeat the basics of a study and get identical or very similar findings. Positivists emphasize replication and the ultimate test of knowledge. This is because they believe that dif-

ferent observers looking at the same facts will get the same results if they carefully specify their ideas, precisely measure the facts, and follow the standards of objective research. When many studies by independent researchers yield similar findings, confidence grows that we accurately captured the workings of social reality and therefore scientific knowledge increases.

If a researcher repeats a study and does not get similar findings, one or more of five possibilities may be occurring: (1) the initial study was an unusual fluke or based on a misguided understanding of the social world; (2) important conditions were present in the initial study, but no one was aware of their significance so they were not specified; (3) the initial study, or the repeat of it, was sloppy—it did not include very careful, precise measures; (4) the initial study, or the repeat of it, was improperly conducted—researchers failed to closely follow the highest standards for procedures and techniques, or failed to be completely objective; or (5) the repeated study was an unusual fluke.

The positivist approach is *nomothetic;* it means explanations use law or law-like principles. Positivists may use inductive and deductive inquiry, but the ideal is to develop a general causal law or principle then use logical deduction to specify how it operates in concrete situations. Next, the researcher empirically tests outcomes predicted by the principle in concrete settings using very precise measures. In this way, a general law or principle covers many specific situations. For example, a general principle says that when two social groups are unequal and compete for scare resources, in-group feelings and hostility toward the other groups intensify, and the competing groups are likely to engage in conflict. The principle applies to sports teams, countries, ethnic groups, families, or other social groupings. A researcher might deduce that in cities with high levels of interracial inequality, when jobs become more scarce and thereby increase economic competition, each group will express greater hostility about the other racial groups and intergroup conflict (e.g., riots, demonstrations, violent attacks) will increase.

The vast majority of positivist studies are quantitative, and positivists generally see the experiment as the ideal way to do research. Positivist researchers also use other quantitative research techniques, such as surveys or existing statistics, but tend to see them as approximations of the experiment for situations where an experiment is impossible. Positivist researchers advocate value-free science, seek precise quantitative measures, test causal theories with statistics, and believe in the importance of replicating studies.

Interpretive Approach

The interpretive approach is also scientific, but its sees the idea of "scientific" differently from positivism. Unlike the positivist approach, interpretive researchers say that human social life is qualitatively different from other things studied by science. This means that social scientists cannot just borrow the principles of science from the natural sciences. Instead, they believe it is necessary to create special type of science, one based on the uniqueness of humans and that can really capture human social life.

Most researchers who use an interpretive approach adopt a version of the constructionist view of social reality. This view holds that human social life is based less on objective, hard, factual reality than on the ideas, beliefs, and perceptions that people hold about reality. In other words, people socially interact and respond based as much, if not more, on what they believe to be real than what is objectively real. This means that social scientists will be able to understand social life only if they study how people go about constructing social reality. As people grow up, interact, and live their daily lives, they continuously create ideas, relationships, symbols, and roles that they consider to be meaningful or important. These include things such as intimate emotional attachments, religious or moral ideals, beliefs in patriotic values, racial-ethnic or gender differences, or artistic expressions. Rarely

do people relate to the objective facts of reality directly; instead, they do so through the filter of these socially constructed beliefs and perceptions. What positivists and many people view to be objective facts (e.g., a person's height), interpretive researchers say are only at the trivial surface level of social life. Or, the "facts" are images/categories that humans created (i.e., I am two meters tall) and we "forget" that people originated the images/categories but now treat them as being separate from people and objectively real.

Interpretive researchers are skeptical of the positivist attempts to produce precise quantitative measures of objective facts. This is because they view social reality as very fluid. For most humans, social realty is largely the shifting perceptions that they are constantly constructing, testing, reinforcing, or changing and that have become embedded in social traditions or institutions. For this reason, interpretive researchers tend to trust and favor qualitative data. They believe that qualitative data can more accurately capture the fluid processes of social reality. In addition, they favor interpretive over causal forms of theory (see discussion earlier in this chapter).

Interpretive researchers are not likely to adopt a nomothetic approach, but instead favor an idiographic form of explanation and use inductive reasoning. *Idiographic* literally means specific description and refers to explaining an aspect of the social world by offering a highly detailed picture or description of a specific social setting, process, or type of relationship. For example, qualitative researchers do not see replication as the ultimate test of knowledge. Instead, they emphasize *verstehen* or empathetic understanding. *Verstehen* is the desire of a researcher to get inside the worldview of those he or she is studying and accurately represent how the people being studied see the world, feel about it, and act. In other words, the best test of how good social knowledge is not replication but whether the researcher can demonstrate that he or she really captured the inner world, imitate worldview, and personal perspective of the people studied.

Critical Approach

The critical approach shares many features with an interpretive approach, but it blends an objective/materialist with a constructionist view of social reality. The key feature of the critical approach is a desire to put knowledge into action and a belief that research is not value free. Research is the creation of knowledge, and people regularly use knowledge to advance political-moral ends. This gives doing social research a strong connection to political-moral issues. The researcher can decide to ignore and help those with power and authority in society, or advance social justice and empower the powerless.

Critical approach emphasizes the multi-layered nature of social reality. On the surface level, there is often illusion, myth, and distorted thinking. The critical approach notes that people are often misled, are subject to manipulated messages, or hold false ideas. Yet, beneath the surface level at a deeper, often hidden level lies "real" objective reality. Part of the task of social research is to strip away the surface layer of illusion or falsehood. Although a researcher wants to see beyond this layer, he or she does not entirely ignore it. Such an outer layer is important because it profoundly shapes much of human action.

The critical approach has an activist orientation and favors action research. Praxis is the ultimate test of how good an explanation is in the critical approach. *Praxis* is a blending of theory and concrete action; theory informs one about the specific real-world actions one should take to advance social change, and one uses the experiences of engaging in action for social change to reformulate the theory. All the approaches see a mutual relationship between abstract theory and concrete empirical evidence, but the critical approach goes further and tries to dissolve the gap between abstract theory and the empirical experiences of using the theory to make changes in the world.

THE DYNAMIC DUO

You have seen that theory and research are interrelated. Only the naive, new researcher mistakenly believes that theory is irrelevant to research or that a researcher just collects the data. Researchers who attempt to proceed without theory may waste time collecting useless data. They easily fall into the trap of hazy and vague thinking, faulty logic, and imprecise concepts. They find it difficult to converge onto a crisp research issue or to generate a lucid account of their study's purpose. They find themselves adrift as they attempt to design or conduct empirical research.

The reason is simple. Theory frames how we look at and think about a topic. It gives us concepts, provides basic assumptions, directs us to the important questions, and suggests ways for us to make sense of data. Theory enables us to connect a single study to the immense base of knowledge to which other researchers contribute. To use an analogy, theory helps a researcher see the forest instead of just a single tree. Theory increases a researcher's awareness of interconnections and of the broader significance of data (see Table 2.1).

Theory has a place in virtually all research, but its prominence varies. It is generally less central in applied-descriptive research than in basic-explanatory research. Its role in applied and

TABLE 2.1 Major Aspects and Types of Social Theory

Aspect	Types of Social Theory
Direction	Inductive or deductive
Level	Micro, meso, or macro
Explanation	Causal, interpretive, or structural
Abstraction	Empirical generalization, middle range, framework, or paradigm

descriptive research may be indirect. The concepts are often more concrete, and the goal is not to create general knowledge. Nevertheless, researchers use theory in descriptive research to refine concepts, evaluate assumptions of a theory, and indirectly test hypotheses.

Theory does not remain fixed over time; it is provisional and open to revision. Theories grow into more accurate and comprehensive explanations about the make-up and operation of the social world in two ways. They advance as theorists toil to think clearly and logically, but this effort has limits. The way a theory makes significant progress is by interacting with research findings.

The scientific community expands and alters theories based on empirical results. Researchers who adopt a more deductive approach use theory to guide the design of a study and the interpretation of results. They refute, extend, or modify the theory on the basis of results. As researchers continue to conduct empirical research testing a theory, they develop confidence that some parts of it are true. Researchers may modify some propositions of a theory or reject them if several well-conducted studies have negative findings. A theory's core propositions and central tenets are more difficult to test and are refuted less often. In a slow process, researchers may decide to abandon or change a theory as the evidence against it mounts over time and cannot be logically reconciled.

Researchers adopting an inductive approach follow a slightly different process. Inductive theorizing begins with a few assumptions and broad orienting concepts. Theory develops from the ground up as the researchers gather and analyze the data. Theory emerges slowly, concept by concept and proposition by proposition in a specific area. The process is similar to a long pregnancy. Over time, the concepts and empirical generalizations emerge and mature. Soon, relationships become visible, and researchers weave together knowledge from different studies into more abstract theory.

CONCLUSION

In this chapter, you learned about social theory—its parts, purposes, and types. The dichotomy between theory and research is an artificial one. The value of theory and its necessity for conducting good research should be clear. Researchers who proceed without theory rarely conduct top-quality research and frequently find themselves in a quandary. Likewise, theorists who proceed without linking theory to research or anchoring it to empirical reality are in jeopardy of floating off into incomprehensible speculation and conjecture. You are now familiar with the scientific community, the dimensions of research, and social theory.

Key Terms

aggregate
association
assumption
causal explanation
classification
concept cluster
deductive approach
empirical generalization
functional theory
grounded theory
ideal type
idiographic
inductive approach
level of abstraction
macro-level theory
meso-level theory
micro-level theory
negative relationship
nomothetic
paradigm
positive relationship
praxis
prediction
proposition
replication

temporal order
verstehen

Endnotes

1. For more detailed discussions of concepts, *see* Chafetz (1978:45–61), Hage (1972:9–85), Kaplan (1964:34–80), Mullins (1971:7–18), Reynolds (1971), and Stinchcombe (1968, 1973).

2. Turner (1980) discussed how sociological explanation and theorizing can be conceptualized as translation.
3. Classifications are discussed in Chafetz (1978: 63–73) and Hage (1972).
4. An introduction to functional explanation can be found in Chafetz (1978:22–25).
5. Introductions to alternative theoretical frameworks and social theories are provided in Craib (1984), Phillips (1985:44–59), and Skidmore (1979).

CHAPTER 3

ETHICS

Consider the following research design:

> The purpose of the research is to ascertain the role of socialization in the development of personality. Volunteers will be cloned into one of three groups, two experimental and one control. The control group clones will be placed in family units; clones assigned to experimental group 1 will be placed in controlled environments that stress violence and depression; and experimental group 2 clones will be placed in controlled environments that provide for all conceivable needs and stress love and respect for others. Personality inventories will be administered to the clones in each group every year to determine the overall personality characteristics of each individual clone.

Sound unreasonable? In the early twenty-first century, cloning technology is developing at a rapid pace. Although it is likely that most scientists would consider each new clone as a new and unique individual who just happens to be genetically identical to another, that does not mean that every scientist would perceive clones in this way. And let's face it—cloning does present a unique opportunity to further study the role of genetics and socialization in the formation of personality. But wouldn't scientists realize the immorality of such an experimental design? Let's answer this question later.

CODE OF ETHICS

Scientists must adhere to professional codes of ethics. *Codes of ethics* are adopted by professional associations of each scientific discipline, including the American Sociological Association. Although each profession has its own code of ethics, there is considerable agreement on the main points of scientific ethics. The major consideration in all professions is to combat a sense of arrogance that has the potential to inform scientific research. It is thus not surprising that examples of violations of research ethics have often inspired the adoption of the official codes of ethics. But how do we know to adopt a rule against a certain act if no one has ever tried it before?

Voluntary Participation

Research subjects in a study need to be voluntary particpants. In other words, the people under study have a right to know that they are part of a scientific study. Throughout several decades of the twentieth century, African-American men who had tested positive for syphilis were allowed to go through life untreated. The effects of the disease on white men were known to researchers; the experiment investigated whether the effects were the same on black men. Modern medicine, of course, correctly predicted the effects to be the same. In order to prevent the research subjects from seeking treatment for the deadly disease, it is probable that they were not fully informed about the dangers of their conditions. The result of the Tuskegee syphilis experiment was that these men were allowed to suffer the effects of the disease in the name of science despite the fact that they could have been successfully treated (Jones, 1993).

The question of voluntary participation is contentious in certain types of fieldwork. As you will see in Chapter 9, fieldwork researchers must be concerned with the issue of disclosure: the notification of subjects that the researcher is involved in data collection for a scientific study. The issue often revolves around the effect the disclosure may have on those being studied. For instance, it may be argued that a researcher studying a street gang may put herself or himself at risk by disclosing the project or that disclosure may make subjects less willing to discuss certain elements of life that may be important to the study. In practice, however, gang researchers have successfully disclosed their research to gang members without adversely affecting their project (Padilla, 1992; Donaldson, 1993). Indeed, disclosure allows the researcher to ask questions that might otherwise seem strange.

There have been moments in history when subjects of other researchers were not voluntary participants. German physicians performed a range of unethical experiments on nonwilling Jewish subjects during World War II, for example.

Avoidance of Harm

Although it seems obvious, we must state plainly. Researchers cannot harm the subject of their research. Harm can take different forms. Physical harm involves harm directed at an individual's body. Emotional harm is directed at an individual's mental or emotional well-being. Financial harm is harm that reduces or inhibits one's financial well-being. Moral harm is harm that damages one's reputation and self-image. In addition to the researcher's producing such harm directly, it is also considered unethical for a researcher to create conditions under which harm can be caused to others.

Stanley Milgram (1974) was horrified by the willingness of ordinary German citizens to participate in the Holocaust during World War II. One refrain was heard from the perpetrators: Each claimed to be "just following orders." Milgram chose to study this obedience to authority by setting up an experiment during which subjects were asked to administer electric shocks ranging to 450 volts—deadly to humans. The supposed victim of the therapy was a confederate who was not actually being shocked, but the research subjects, most of whom were willing to administer a deadly shock to the stranger in the booth in front of them, were not aware of this. Subjects were faced with the ugly truth that they would kill a person merely because an authority figure asked them to do so—an uncomfortable truth that most people are never forced to confront. Because of the potential psychological damage of this revelation, there was considerable controversy over the ethics of the methods for years after the experiment.

The avoidance of harm also requires that researchers not deceive or mislead subjects. This is not always possible. Numerous experiments in social psychology, for instance, have relied upon concealing the true nature of the study or purposefully misleading the subject. In such cases, subjects need to be *debriefed*, or told the complete purpose of the study at the conclusion of the study.

Anonymity

Research subjects have a right to anonymity. Anonymity is associated with three distinct concepts: anonymity, confidentiality, and privacy. Anonymity refers to the right of an individual to not have his or her identity shared with others. The choice to become part of an experiment ultimately resides with the subject, and so does the decision to share this choice with others. Therefore, the fact that a person has chosen to be a subject in a research project does not in itself allow the researcher to disclose the subject's identity.

When Vidich and Bensman (1968) published their study of a small upstate New York town, they concealed the names of the people in the town and even the town itself. Using pseudonyms for people and places, they wrote in extreme detail about relationships between residents, the political structure of the town, and other such information. The problem was that the detail was perhaps too good. For instance, any reader with a protractor and knowledge of New York state geography could identify the town by reading the opening chapter of the book. Similarly, although most readers did not know the town judge, for instance, a town resident could figure out the identity of the individual being discussed.

Confidentiality is an outgrowth of the right to anonymity. A subject has the right to expect that any information disclosed to the researcher will not be revealed to others. This also means that research findings cannot be reported in a way that makes subjects' statements or secrets apparent to others.

Privacy refers to the right of subjects to choose their own level of disclosure. Agreeing to be a part of an interview, for instance, does not require subjects to discuss topics they do not wish to discuss. A subject may feel quite comfortable discussing finances and morality but not sex.

Reporting Findings

Scientists have an obligation to report the findings of their research. It may seem that the researcher would automatically want to report the findings, but this is not always the case.

At times, the findings of a study may suggest that a theory is wrong or suggest a course of action that some may find objectionable. Numerous studies have supported the theory that humans evolved from an ancestor of both ourselves and modern chimpanzees, but some find the notion of evolution through natural selection to be a challenge to their religious beliefs. Similarly, a study of youth crime may show juvenile crime to be declining, but this finding may undermine the platform of a candidate for elected office. In both cases, the researcher may find political pressure to alter or suppress findings. However, most professional codes of ethics require researchers to work independently of such considerations and release their findings despite the inconvenience to one or another party.

THE INTERNAL REVIEW BOARD

Ethical violations are not all the same. The Tuskegee syphilis experiment, for instance, is a shocking violation of professional ethics for two reasons (Jones, 1993). First, the harm caused by withholding treatment for these patients was a death sentence—no greater harm than that. Second, the research was unnecessary. The effects of syphilis were already known, and any difference between the progression of disease among blacks and whites could have been determined with a nonlethal disease, such as the common cold. The fact that the subjects were not told the full extent of the illness they were suffering calls into question whether they gave informed consent to participate. Without being fully informed about the disease, they could not make an informed decision. Therefore, it cannot be said that these subjects participated voluntarily.

Stanley Milgram's (1974) obedience study, however, did seek to investigate a valid research question. Historical (and not so historical) evidence shows that ordinary people are capable of atrocities, and Milgram sought to understand the psychological foundations of this behavior. He found that 65 percent were willing to administer a deadly shock without the urging of a mob, threat of force, or hatred. Milgram himself was shocked by the results, and it is difficult to argue that they are not significant. But that is not the question. The real question is: Was the advance of knowledge worth the price of the psychological damage experienced by some, if not all, of the subjects? Many argued that it was not, but Milgram was certainly not alone in his contention that the methods he used were not unethical.

In their study of a small town, Vidich and Bensman (1968) took steps to guarantee the anonymity of their subjects. In a sense, they failed to do so because they reported too much. This case does provide a warning to future researchers to pay more attention to issues regarding anonymity.

Often external review of the research design can help mitigate any potentially negative effects. In addition, past ethics violations have brought attention to the need for mechanisms to supervise researchers. Most institutions out of which research is conducted, such as colleges and universities, have adopted ethics codes of their own. In order to ensure that researchers follow ethics codes and the law, *internal review boards* were established to review research proposals before the beginning of a study involving human and other living subjects.

THE ANSWER

Our original question was: Wouldn't scientists realize the immorality of the experimental design utilizing clones? The answer: We don't know.

THE READINGS

Although these readings in ethics are quite different from each other, both address issues related to the nature of scientific research and scientists. Horace Miner's famous 1956 essay, "Body Ritual among the Nacirema," describes an unusual native society located in the Western hemisphere. In "Reporting Unethical Research Behavior," Neil Wenger and associates (1999) wanted to know whether scientists would consider particular types of research unethical and what they would do about it.

■ ■ ■ ■ ■ ▬▬▬▬▬▬▬▬▬▬▬▬▬▬▬▬▬▬▬▬▬▬▬▬▬▬▬▬▬▬▬▬▬▬

BODY RITUAL AMONG THE NACIREMA
Horace Miner
University of Michigan

In a landmass between the Atlantic and Pacific Oceans lives a curious people with an interesting set of rituals. In describing their rituals and the shrines found in their homes, some interesting questions arise about the ability of scientists to properly interpret the data on other cultures without tainting their analysis with their own culturally based biases. [ED.]

The anthropologist has become so familiar with the diversity of ways in which different peoples behave in similar situations that he is not apt to be surprised by even the most exotic customs. In fact, if all of the logically possible combinations of behavior have not been found somewhere in the world, he is apt to suspect that they must be present in some yet undescribed tribe. This point has, in fact, been expressed with respect to clan organization by Murdock (1949:71). In this light, the magical beliefs and practices of the Nacirema present such unusual aspects that it seems desirable to describe them as an example of the extremes to which human behavior can go.

Professor Linton first brought the ritual of the Nacirema to the attention of anthropologists twenty years ago (1936:326), but the culture of this people is still very poorly understood. They are a North American group living in the territory between the Canadian Cree, the Yaqui and Tarahumare of Mexico, and the Carib and Arawak of the Antilles. Little is known of their origin, although tradition states that they came from the east. According to Nacirema mythology, their nation was originated by a culture hero, Notgnihsaw, who is otherwise known for two great feats of strength—the throwing of a piece of wampum across the river Pa-To-Mac and the chopping down of a cherry tree in which the Spirit of Truth resided.

Nacirema culture is characterized by a highly developed market economy which has evolved in a rich natural habitat. While much of the people's time is devoted to economic pursuits, a large part of the fruits of these labors and a considerable portion of the day are spent in ritual activity. The focus of this activity is the human body, the appearance and health of which loom as a dominant concern in the ethos of the people. While such a concern is certainly not

From *American Anthropologist* v58, 503–507, June 1956.

unusual, its ceremonial aspects and associated philosophy are unique.

The fundamental belief underlying the whole system appears to be that the human body is ugly and that its natural tendency is to debility and disease. Incarcerated in such a body, man's only hope is to avert these characteristics through the use of the powerful influences of ritual and ceremony. Every household has one or more shrines devoted to this purpose. The more powerful individuals in the society have several shrines in their houses and, in fact, the opulence of a house is often referred to in terms of the number of such ritual centers it possesses. Most houses are of wattle and daub construction, but the shrine rooms of the more wealthy are walled with stone. Poorer families imitate the rich by applying pottery plaques to their shrine walls.

While each family has at least one such shrine, the rituals associated with it are not family ceremonies but are private and secret. The rites are normally only discussed with children, and then only during the period when they are being initiated into these mysteries. I was able, however, to establish sufficient rapport with the natives to examine these shrines and to have the rituals described to me.

The focal point of the shrine is a box or chest which is built into the wall. In this chest are kept the many charms and magical potions without which no native believes he could live. These preparations are secured from a variety of specialized practitioners. The most powerful of these are the medicine men, whose assistance must be rewarded with substantial gifts. However, the medicine men do not provide the curative potions for their clients, but decide what the ingredients should be and then write them down in an ancient and secret language. This writing is understood only by the medicine men and by the herbalists who, for another gift, provide the required charm.

The charm is not disposed of after it has served its purpose, but is placed in the charm-box of the household shrine. As these magical materials are specific for certain ills, and the real or imagined maladies of the people are many, the charm-box is usually full to overflowing. The magical packets are so numerous that people forget what their purposes were and fear to use

them again. While the natives are very vague on this point, we can only assume that the idea in retaining all the old magical materials is that their presence in the charm-box, before which the body rituals are conducted, will in some way protect the worshipper.

Beneath the charm-box is a small font. Each day every member of the family, in succession, enters the shrine room, bows his head before the charm-box, mingles different sorts of holy water in the font, and proceeds with a brief rite of ablution. The holy waters are secured from the Water Temple of the community, where the priests conduct elaborate ceremonies to make the liquid ritually pure.

In the hierarchy of magical practitioners, and below the medicine men in prestige, are specialists whose designation is best translated "holy-mouth-men." The Nacirema have an almost pathological horror of and fascination with the mouth, the condition of which is believed to have a supernatural influence on all social relationships. Were it not for the rituals of the mouth, they believe that their teeth would fall out, their gums bleed, their jaws shrink, their friends desert them, and their lovers reject them. They also believe that a strong relationship exists between oral and moral characteristics. For example, there is a ritual ablution of the mouth for children which is supposed to improve their moral fiber.

The daily body ritual performed by everyone includes a mouth-rite. Despite the fact that these people are so punctilious about care of the mouth, this rite involves a practice which strikes the uninitiated stranger as revolting. It was reported to me that the ritual consists of inserting a small bundle of hog hairs into the mouth, along with certain magical powders, and then moving the bundle in a highly formalized series of gestures.

In addition to the private mouth-rite, the people seek out a holy-mouth-man once or twice a year. These practitioners have an impressive set of paraphernalia, consisting of a variety of augers, awls, probes, and prods. The use of these objects in the exorcism of the evils of the mouth involve almost unbelievable ritual torture of the client. The holy-mouth-man opens the client's mouth and, using the above mentioned tools, enlarges any holes which decay may have created in the teeth. Magical materials are put into these holes. If there are no naturally occurring holes in the teeth, large sections of one or more teeth are gouged out so that the supernatural substance can be applied. In the client's view, the purpose of these ministrations is to arrest decay and to draw friends. The extremely sacred and traditional character of the rite is evident in the fact that the natives return to the holy-mouth-men year after year, despite the fact that their teeth continue to decay.

It is to be hoped that, when a thorough study of the Nacirema is made, there will be careful inquiry into the personality structure of these people. One has but to watch the gleam in the eye of a holy-mouth-man, as he jabs an awl into an exposed nerve, to suspect that a certain amount of sadism is involved. If this can be established, a very interesting pattern emerges, for most of the population shows definite masochistic tendencies. It was to these that Professor Linton referred in discussing a distinctive part of the daily body ritual which is performed only by men. This part of the rite involves scraping and lacerating the surface of the face with a sharp instrument. Special women's rites are performed only four times during each lunar month, but what they lack in frequency is made up in barbarity. As part of this ceremony, women bake their heads in small ovens for about an hour. The theoretically interesting point is that what seems to be a preponderantly masochistic people have developed sadistic specialists.

The medicine men have an imposing temple, or *latipso*, in every community of any size. The more elaborate ceremonies required to treat very sick patients can only be performed at this temple. These ceremonies involve not only the thaumaturge but a permanent group of vestal maidens who move sedately about the temple chambers in distinctive costume and headdress.

The *latipso* ceremonies are so harsh that it is phenomenal that a fair proportion of the really sick natives who enter the temple ever recover. Small children whose indoctrination is still incomplete have been known to resist attempts to take them to the temple because "that is where you go to die." Despite this fact, sick adults are not only willing but eager to undergo the protracted ritual purification, if they can afford to do so. No matter how ill the supplicant or how grave the emergency, the guardians of many temples will not admit a client if he cannot give a rich gift to the custodian. Even after one has gained admission and survived the ceremonies, the guardians will not permit the neophyte to leave until he makes still another gift.

The supplicant entering the temple is first stripped of all his or her clothes. In every-day life the Nacirema avoids exposure of his body and its natural functions. Bathing and excretory acts are performed only in the secrecy of the household shrine, where they are ritualized as part of the body-rites. Psychological shock results from the fact that body secrecy is suddenly lost upon entry into the *latipso*. A man, whose own wife has never seen him in an excretory act, suddenly finds himself naked and assisted by a vestal maiden while he performs his natural functions into a sacred vessel. This sort of ceremonial treatment is necessitated by the fact that the excreta are used by a diviner to ascertain the course and nature of the client's sickness. Female clients, on the other hand, find their naked bodies are subjected to the scrutiny, manipulation and prodding of the medicine men.

Few supplicants in the temple are well enough to do anything but lie on their hard beds. The daily ceremonies, like the rites of the holy-mouth-men, involve discomfort and torture. With ritual precision, the vestals awaken their miserable charges each dawn and roll them about on their beds of pain while performing ablutions, in the formal movements of which the maidens are highly trained. At other times they insert magic wands in the supplicant's mouth or force him to eat substances which are supposed to be healing. From time to time the medicine men come to their clients and jab magically treated needles into their flesh. The fact that these temple ceremonies may not cure, and may even kill the neophyte, in no way decreases the people's faith in the medicine men.

There remains one other kind of practitioner, known as a "listener." This witch-doctor has the power to exorcise the devils that lodge in the heads of people who have been bewitched.

The Nacirema believe that parents bewitch their own children. Mothers are particularly suspected of putting a curse on children while teaching them the secret body rituals. The counter-magic of the witch-doctor is unusual in its lack of ritual. The patient simply tells the "listener" all his troubles and fears, beginning with the earliest difficulties he can remember. The memory displayed by the Nacirema in these exorcism sessions is truly remarkable. It is not uncommon for the patient to bemoan the rejection he felt upon being weaned as a babe, and a few individuals even see their troubles going back to the traumatic effects of their own birth.

In conclusion, mention must be made of certain practices which have their base in native esthetics but which depend upon the pervasive aversion to the natural body and its functions. There are ritual fasts to make fat people thin and ceremonial feasts to make thin people fat. Still other rites are used to make women's breasts larger if they are small, and smaller if they are large. General dissatisfaction with breast shape is symbolized in the fact that the ideal form is virtually outside the range of human variation. A few women afflicted with almost inhuman hypermammary development are so idolized that they make a handsome living by simply going from village to village and permitting the natives to stare at them for a fee.

Reference has already been made to the fact that excretory functions are ritualized, routinized, and relegated to secrecy. Natural reproductive functions are similarly distorted.

Intercourse is taboo as a topic and scheduled as an act. Efforts are made to avoid pregnancy by the use of magical materials or by limiting intercourse to certain phases of the moon. Conception is actually very infrequent. When pregnant, women dress so as to hide their condition. Parturition takes place in secret, without friends or relatives to assist, and the majority of women do not nurse their infants.

Our review of the ritual life of the Nacirema has certainly shown them to be a magic-ridden people. It is hard to understand how they have managed to exist so long under the burdens which they have imposed upon themselves. But even such exotic customs as these take on real meaning when they are viewed with the insight provided by Malinowski when he wrote (1948:70):

> Looking from far and above, from our high places of safety in the developed civilization, it is easy to see all the crudity and irrelevance of magic. But without its power and guidance early man could not have mastered his practical difficulties as he has done, nor could man have advanced to the higher stages of civilization.

REFERENCES CITED

LINTON, RALPH. 1936. *The Study of Man*. New York: D. Appleton-Century Co.

MALINOWSKI, BRONISLAW. 1948. *Magic, Science, and Religion*. Glencoe: The Free Press.

MURDOCK, GEORGE P. 1949. *Social Structure*. New York: The Macmillan Co.

■ ■ ■ ■ ■ ▬▬▬▬▬▬▬▬▬▬▬▬▬▬▬▬▬▬▬▬▬▬▬▬▬▬

REPORTING UNETHICAL RESEARCH BEHAVIOR

Neil S. Wenger, Stanley G. Korenman, Richard Berk, and Honghu Liu
University of California, Los Angeles

Scientists, as professionals, have a responsibility to self-regulate. However, whistleblowing is rare. We investigated scientists' infrequent disclosure of unethical behavior by studying their responses to scenarios describing unethical research acts and compared their responses to those of research administrators. A cross-sectional survey was administered to National Science Foundation–funded principal investigators and their institutions' repre-

From *Evaluation Review*, 23, 5 (October 1999): 553–70. Copyright © Sage Publications, Inc.

sentatives (IRs) to the Office of Research Integrity. Both scientists and IRs proposed to respond to nearly all research behaviors that they rated as unethical. Scientists more often proposed responses limited to the research team (58% vs. 25% of cases, p < .001) whereas IRs more often proposed to inform an administrator or dean, journal editor, funding agency, professional society, or reporter. The prior behavior and academic rank of the scenario protagonist were associated with responses, but consequences of the unethical behavior were not. Scientists appear to perceive that they uphold their responsibility to respond to unethical behavior by disclosures within the research team, whereas administrators propose to report to externally accountable individuals, raising the question of whether scientists' behavior constitutes professional self-regulation or cover up.

Scientists, as professionals, are supposed to report unethical research behavior (National Academy of Sciences Committee on the Conduct of Science 1995). They have the responsibility to self-regulate and to police the actions of fellow professionals (Sigma Xi 1991 and Flores 1988). Self-regulation sustains academic freedom and limits the influence of religion, politics, and other forces on scientific research (Ben-David 1991). However, *whistle-blowing*, informing about unethical scientific conduct, occurs infrequently. Publicized misconduct cases often reveal missed reporting opportunities.

Why whistle-blowing is uncommon is poorly understood. It might be due to a scientist's perception of collegiality (Swazey and Scher 1981) or related to the serious repercussions that may befall the informant (Lennane 1993). Alternatively, scientists may not accept the responsibility to police the actions of peers. To investigate scientists' self-regulation and whistle-blowing behaviors, we compared how scientists said they would respond to unethical research behavior and the responses of administrators responsible for the conduct of research.

METHODS

This study analyzes data derived from a project aimed at understanding the norms of scientists (Korenman et al. 1998). A computer-generated

survey instrument was developed to elicit responses concerning a respondent's perception of whether specific research behaviors were ethical and, if not, whether and how the subject would respond to knowledge of the behavior. The survey was mailed to all 924 National Science Foundation principal investigators receiving grants from the Division of Molecular and Cellular Biology during 1993 or 1994 and to the 140 administrators responsible for the conduct of research (institutions' representatives, IRs) from the scientists' institutions. We evaluated whether respondents indicated that they would respond to the behavior and the response they proposed. Respondent and scenario-based factors associated with responses to unethical behavior were evaluated, and the responses of scientists and IRs were compared.

INSTRUMENT AND SURVEY TECHNIQUE

Each survey instrument contained 12 scenarios randomly selected from 8,364 possible scenarios. Following a fractional factorial design, scenarios were constructed with series of sentences derived from randomly assigned phrases, each consisting of one level from a dimension (Rossi and Nock 1982). The dimensions were the factors theoretically related to a respondent's reaction to research conduct in four domains: (a) performance and reporting of research, (b) appropriation of the ideas of others, (c) conflicts of interest/commitment, and (d) collegiality/sharing. The other dimensions contained in each scenario were the following: gender and status of the scientist, the harm and larger consequences resulting from the act, and whether this was a first-time offense. A full description of each of the dimensions and the levels within the dimensions is contained in the appendix.

For each scenario, respondents were asked whether the act was unethical and, if so, the degree to which it was unethical on a scale of 1 to 10 (the unethical score). Respondents rating an act as unethical were asked, If you knew about behavior like this, would you

- keep it to yourself?
- speak directly to the researcher about your concerns?

- indicate your misgiving about the behavior to your scientific colleagues?
- inform the editor of relevant journals?
- inform the researcher's immediate supervisor?
- inform the administrator or dean in the researcher's institution?
- inform the researcher's professional society?
- inform the researcher's funding agencies?
- contact a reporter for science, nature, or another professional journal?
- contact the lay media?
- other?

Respondents were instructed to choose as many responses as applicable. Then, they were asked whether punishment was appropriate for this behavior.

The survey, described in detail elsewhere (Korenman et al. 1998), included items asking respondents about demographic characteristics, academic position, and research experience. The survey was approved by the Institutional Review Board for administration without written informed consent.

ANALYSIS

The scenario was the unit of analysis. Only scenarios containing unethical behavior (that is, a behavior rated as unethical by the respondent) were evaluated in this study. The relationship of the response to the behavior and scenario dimensions was evaluated using simple means and proportions, yielding unbiased estimates due to the fractional factorial design (Hox, Kreft, and Hermkens 1991). To understand the response to a particular case of unethical behavior, we aggregated all the responses suggested for each case and categorized the patterns of response. The 21 most common response patterns account for 74% of all scenario cases. The mean unethical score and the proportion of respondents suggesting punishment was computed for each response pattern. The percentage of unethical cases attributable to each pattern was compared between scientists and IRs using chi-square tests. The relationship of each response to the protagonist's characteristics was evaluated for all domains combined using chi-square

tests. The relationship of each response to the specific unethical research behaviors was evaluated.

To understand the differences between scientists and IR proposed reporting, we performed logistic regression including as independent variables respondent academic rank, age and gender, scenario unethical score, the respondent's sample (scientist versus IR), and the interaction of sample and unethical score. The dependent variable was whether the respondent offered a response that included informing an administrator or individual external to researcher's group (a dean, a journal editor, a funding agency, a professional society, or a reporter) versus limiting information within researchers (informing no one or only the researcher and/or colleagues and/or a supervisor). In this analysis, intrarespondent correlation was accounted for using a modified maximum likelihood estimate (Huber 1967) that accumulates scenario information within respondent to increase the standard errors of the parameter estimates reflecting redundancy in correlated observations.

RESULTS

Sixty-nine percent (606) of scientists and 69% (91) of IRs returned completed surveys. Compared to nonresponders, survey responders were younger ($p < .001$), but there was no difference by gender or academic rank. Overall, 97% of respondents held a Ph.D. degree, their median age was 50 years, and 73% were male. Scientists were younger than IRs ($p = .001$), but there was no gender difference. Fifty-one percent of IRs were either the president, vice-president, or provost of their institution.

Respondents offered a response for 95% of behaviors that they rated unethical. They responded more often to research behavior they judged to be more unethical: 71% of acts rated 1 (on the 1 to 10 scale of unethical behavior), 88% of the acts rated 2, 92% of the acts rated 3, 95% to 96% of the acts rated 4 to 6, and 97% to 100% of the acts rated 7 to 10.

For 12% of cases, respondents indicated that their only action would be to speak with the researcher committing the act. For an additional 10%, respondents would speak only with the perpetrator and colleagues; and for 7%, respondents proposed to speak with colleagues only. Respondents felt that punishment was appropriate for 53%, 63%, and 61% of these cases, respectively. Punishment was suggested for nearly all protagonists in cases for which respondents proposed to inform an administrator and/or external party (e.g., journal editor or funder). Overall, respondents said they would inform a journal editor, funding agency, or professional society for 19%, 16%, and 4% of cases, respectively. Contacting the lay media was chosen for 0.5% of cases.

COMPARING RESPONSES TO UNETHICAL BEHAVIOR PROPOSED BY SCIENTISTS AND IRs

Institutional representatives proposed a response to 99% of the behaviors that they classified as unethical, and scientists proposed a response to 94% of unethical acts. IRs proposed different responses than scientists. Seventy-four percent of scientists proposed to speak to the researcher who committed the offense, compared to 67% of IRs ($p = .001$), and scientists proposed to discuss such issues with colleagues far more often than did IRs (58% versus 24%, $p = .001$).

The findings indicate that scientists more often proposed actions that were limited to the researcher and colleagues, whereas IRs proposed to involve administrators, deans, and others more often in revelations of the unethical behavior. For example, scientists would speak with only the researcher and colleagues in 12% of cases and only colleagues in 9% of cases; IRs proposed these actions in only 2% and 0.4% of cases, respectively. IRs proposed to discuss cases with the researcher, supervisor, and an administrator in 18% of cases, whereas scientists suggested this plan in only 3% of cases. Overall, scientists would limit reporting to researchers (researcher and/or colleagues and/or supervisor) or not report for 58% of cases, compared to only 25% for IRs ($p < .001$).

We developed a model of whether respondents said they would report the behavior outside of the group of researchers (inform an administrator or dean, a journal editor, a funding agency, a professional society, or a reporter) versus limiting reporting to the researchers (the re-

searcher and/or colleagues and/or the supervisor). The logistic regression (Somers's $D = 0.53$), adjusting for respondent academic rank, age and gender, scenario unethical score, and the interaction between sample and unethical score revealed that IRs were significantly more likely to inform an administrator or external individual. Figure 2 displays the predicted percentage of cases that scientists and IRs would report to an administrator or external individual by the unethical level of the case. At every unethical level, IRs would report behavior outside the research group more often than would scientists.

RELATIONSHIP OF THE RESPONSE TO THE UNETHICAL ACT

Respondents matched responses with unethical acts. Responses including informing an administrator, dean, or journal editor were prescribed for cases with higher mean unethical score ratings. Informing an administrator or dean was proposed for 23% of the scenarios in which the protagonist made "an honest but serious mistake in reporting research results," whereas such a response was planned for 67% of scenarios in which "fabrication of data" occurred. Respondents proposed to inform the funding agency for 40% of scenarios depicting data fabrication but only 9% of scenarios in which the scientist picked "the best results to report, honestly believing them to be the correct ones." For each response (row) except "keeping it to yourself," the percentage of proposed responses across acts (columns) was significantly different by the chi-square test ($p \leq .001$). Differences in how subjects said they would respond across the range of acts also was found for the other three behavior domains.

Although there was a direct relationship between response and the nature of the unethical act, the response was unrelated to the harm resulting from the unethical act. The exception to this was when a specific reporting act would serve to rectify the effect of the behavior. For example, respondents would report an unethical appropriation of ideas that resulted in a publication in a prestigious journal to a journal editor more often than if the act resulted in a grant or meeting presentation (27% versus 14% versus 13%, $p = .001$).

RELATIONSHIP OF RESPONSE TO THE PROTAGONIST'S CHARACTERISTICS

The type of response to unethical research behavior was not related to the gender of the protagonist. However, there was a relationship between the response and the academic status of the protagonist and whether this was repeated behavior. Compared to senior researchers, junior scientists were more likely to be spoken to directly. The unethical behavior of a tenured, prestigious head of a laboratory was more likely to be discussed with colleagues, a funding agency, and the scientific press. Scientists who committed prior offenses were more likely to be reported to colleagues, supervisors, administrators, editors, and funders, although they were less likely to be directly confronted.

DISCUSSION

This investigation into scientists' proposed responses to unethical research behavior reveals that scientists said they would act in response to 94% of research behaviors that they considered to be unethical. This finding is consistent with the scientists' professional responsibility to self-regulate and to ensure the validity of science—the so-called organized skepticism of Merton (1973). However, the findings appear to conflict with the perception that scientists do not reveal many of the unethical behaviors they discover or suspect (Engler et al. 1987).

These data shed light on the apparent discrepancy between scientists' actual and proposed actions. Although scientists nearly universally propose to report unethical behavior, in fully one third of the cases, the reporting was confined to the researcher, to colleagues, or to a combination of the two. If we add situations in which scientist respondents would report the behavior to the researcher's supervisor, 50% of cases would not be reported by scientist whistleblowers beyond the researcher's immediate superior or colleagues. Reporting would be "constructive"—educational or a warning—and unlikely to generate a disciplinary response. This mode of response would not be viewed by external observers as an accountable reporting of the unethical behavior. These findings elucidate the paradox of scientists' purported willingness to respond to the unethical behavior but the rarity of observable whistle-blowing. This leads to the question, Is the proposed behavior self-regulation or cover-up?

Scientists felt that 69% of the cases in which they would report unethical behavior to some combination of the researcher, supervisor, and colleagues merited punishment. Because reporting the behavior to this internal group is unlikely to result in any administrative action or sanction, these findings suggest that scientist respondents perceived that their actions alone would confer punishment upon the perpetrator of the unethical act (Friedson 1970). Being mistrusted by one's colleagues or profession would be a devastating blow to scientists for whom trust and integrity are the foundation of transaction and communication (Fuchs and Westervelt 1996). Scientists may perceive that they are responding appropriately to unethical acts by informing perpetrators and colleagues. This theory is bolstered by the fact that acts in the minimally to moderately unethical range (mean scores of 4 to 6.5 on the 10-point scale) were handled in this fashion. Responses to behaviors rated as more unethical included scientists' notification of administrators and parties external to the research group.

An alternative explanation of these findings might be the cognitive dissonance between the commitment that scientists feel to the self-policing role as a professional and loyalty to colleagues and the profession. A scientist has an obligation of loyalty to fellow scientists (Swazey and Scher 1981). In addition, there is the potential that exposing research fraud could potentially harm science to a greater degree than the fraud itself (Wenger et al. 1997). The social pressures against external reporting of unethical behavior (Swazey and Scher 1981; Fuchs and Westervelt 1996), uncertainty about whether behaviors are unethical, and the harms that befall whistle-blowers may contribute to scientists' ambivalence.

Compared to scientists, IRs were significantly more likely to report unethical acts to administrators or other individuals who would act on the information, even after accounting for the unethical rating of the act. Not only did IRs propose to notify administrators and outside parties more often, but they proposed to do so for less unethical behaviors than did scientists. This calls into question precisely what is required of a profession to police itself and whether scientists are able to accomplish this.

There are no explicit rules for what behaviors need to be recognized and addressed for a profession to police itself. This is in part integral to the profession's members being the repository of the specialized knowledge, enabling the detection of unethical behavior. However, the very divergent perspectives on the appropriate response to unethical behavior of scientists and those charged with addressing research behavior at their institutions challenge scientists to justify their self-regulation behaviors. Some have suggested that professions alone are unable to self-regulate (Bayles 1981). Proposals to improve regulation include incorporation of lay individuals in the process of deciding on sanctions and creation of more explicit guidelines for reporting and punishment (Bayles 1981; Fox and Braxton 1994; Association of American Medical Colleges 1997). However, these data demonstrate that 50% of unethical behaviors would probably never come to the attention of review panels. These findings call on scientists and regulators to develop a common understanding of the reporting requirements for unethical behavior. Until that is possible, the usual conduct of the scientist will lead to the continued perception that reporting is incomplete.

This study is limited in several ways. The data were derived from a small homogeneous group of scientists; it has been shown that there is variation among the experiences of researchers in different disciplines (Swazey, Anderson, and Lewis 1993) and the findings may not be generalizable to other scientist groups. In addition, the findings are based on responses to scenarios rather than actual behavior. Scenario responses are not always consistent with actual behavior, although responses tend to reflect the direction and relative magnitude of a behavior (Jones, Gerrity, and Eary 1990). In addition, the findings appear to be consistent with the observed behavior of scientists (Hamilton 1992); social

desirability bias would lead to underestimation of the degree to which scientists would handle unethical behavior internally. The expected relationships found between the response to unethical behavior and unethical level of the act, protagonist academic position, and prior behavior, but not with protagonist gender and resultant harms, supports the validity of the survey data. Furthermore, IRs and scientists may perceive different duties to report research. Although IRs, as representatives to the Office of Research Integrity, have a duty to report scientific misconduct once an investigation has been initiated, their initial ethical responsibilities when discovering unethical behavior mirrors that of the scientist. Finally, this is an exploratory study. Further work should elucidate the differences between scientists and IRs found here and should evaluate the purpose and meaning underlying scientists' proposed responses to unethical behavior.

REFERENCES

ASSOCIATION OF AMERICAN MEDICAL COLLEGES. 1997. *Developing a code of ethics in research: A guide for scientific societies.* Washington, DC: Author.

BAYLES, M. D. 1981. Ensuring compliance. In *Professional ethics.* Belmont, CA: Wadsworth.

BEN-DAVID, J. 1991. The profession of science and its powers. In *Scientific growth: Essays on the social organization and ethos of science*, edited by G. Freudenthal. Berkeley: University of California Press.

ENGLER, R. L., J. W. COVELL, P. J. FRIEDMAN, P. S. KITCHER, and R. M. PETERS. 1987. Misrepresentation and responsibility in medical research. *New England Journal of Medicine* 317:1383-9.

FLORES, A. 1988. Introduction: What kind of person should a professional be? In *Professional ideals*, edited by A. Flores. Belmont, CA: Wadsworth.

FOX, M. F., and J. M. BRAXTON. 1994. Misconduct and social control in science. *Journal of Higher Education* 65:373-83.

FRIEDSON, E. 1970. *Profession of medicine: A study of the sociology of applied knowledge.* New York: Dodd, Mead.

FUCHS, S., and S. D. WESTERVELT. 1996. Fraud and trust in science. *Perspective in Biology and Medicine* 39:248-69.

HAMILTON, D. P. 1992. In the trenches, doubts about scientific integrity. *Science* 255:1636.

HOX, J. J., I. G. G. KREFT, P. L. J. HERMKENS. 1991. The analysis of factorial surveys. *Sociological Methods and Research* 4:493-510.

HUNDER, P. J. 1967. *The behavior of maximum likelihood estimates under nonstandard conditions.* Berkeley: University of California Press.

JONES, T. V., M. S. GERRITY, and J. EARY. 1990. Written case simulations: Do they predict physicians' behavior? *Journal of Clinical Epidemiology* 43:805-15.

KORENMAN, S. G., R. BERK, N. S. WENGER, and V. LEW. 1998. Evaluation of the research norms of scientists and administrators responsible for academic research integrity. *JAMA* 279:41-7.

LENNANE, K. J. 1993. "Whistleblowing": A health issue. *BMJ* 307:667-70.

MERTON, R. K. 1973. The normative structure of science. In *The Sociology of Science*, edited by N. W. Storer. Chicago: University of Chicago Press.

NATIONAL ACADEMY OF SCIENCES COMMITTEE ON THE CONDUCT OF SCIENCE. 1995. *On being a scientist: Responsible conduct in research.* Washington, DC: National Academy Press.

ROSSI, P. H., and S. L. NOCK 1982. *Measuring social judgments: The factorial survey approach.* Newbury Park, CA: Sage.

SIGMA XI, The Scientific Research Society. 1991. *Honor in science,* 2d ed. Research Triangle Park.

SWAZEY, J. P., M. S. ANDERSON, and K. S. LEWIS. 1993. Ethical problems in academic research. *American Scientist* 81:542-53.

SWAZEY, J. P., and S. R. SCHER, eds. 1981. The whistleblower as a deviant professional: Professional norms and responses to fraud in clinical research. In *Whistleblowing in biomedical research.* Washington, DC: President's Com- mission for the Study of Ethical Problems in Medicine and Biomedical and Behavioral Research.

WENGER, N. S., S. G. KORENMAN, R. BERK, and S. BERRY. 1997. The ethics of scientific research: An analysis of focus groups of scientists and institutional representatives. *Journal of Invest Medicine* 45:371-80.

COMMENTARY ON THE READINGS

Spell *Nacirema* backwards, and you have *American.* The essay begins much like any normal article based on anthropological fieldwork. But the rituals start to sound strangely familiar, even though the interpretation is all wrong. Bathrooms are not shrines, but an observer from another culture might well perceive them that way. Miner is trying to make an important point: Despite the skill, dedication, and best intentions of social scientists, interpretive mistakes are bound to happen. As social scientists have been raised and continue to live in their own cultures, it is all too easy to interpret the artifacts and practices of members of other cultures—and those of our own—through the lens of our cultural biases about "natives." Social scientists have an ethical obligation to remember that we are not perfect, that mistakes can be made, and often those mistakes in interpretation or judgment can have negative consequences.

Neil Wenger and associates have written a fine essay that not only illuminates the role of the scientific community in reporting unethical behavior, but provides an excellent example of a survey as well. The scientific community is organized to seek out and expand knowledge, and one aspect of this function is to police one another to ensure that research behavior is ethical. The good news in their study is that many scientists recognized the behaviors about which they were asked as unethical. But some might find their findings disturbing:

Fifty percent of cases would not be reported by scientist whistle-blowers beyond the researcher's immediate superior or colleagues. . . . This mode of response would not be viewed by external observers as an accountable reporting of unethical behavior (562).

The results seem to indicate that the mere act of embarrassing the researcher in front of his or her peers is enough to halt the behavior and deter future behavior.

It is possible that most scientists would discuss the unethical behavior with the scientist first and then take more severe action if they were not satisfied with the researcher's response to their criticism. The authors also suggest that personal loyalty might interfere with the ethical obligations to report unethical behavior. Scientists are often friends with one another, and reporting unethical practices might be construed as a betrayal by some. In other cases, a scientist might be concerned that the disclosure of unethical research could have a more negative effect on science than the unethical behavior itself.

In sum, Wenger and associates demonstrate that the reporting of unethical research behavior is more complicated than one would necessarily suppose. There is some comfort to be taken in the finding that many of the situations they discussed were perceived as unethical. This perception of right and wrong most likely guides most scientists to conduct ethical research. And it's a good thing.

CONCLUSION

Ethics are not merely a matter of common sense. Ethical lapses can come about because a researcher deliberately acts unethically, but they can also occur because the researcher does not fully think through a study or acts with a sense of arrogance. This means that researchers need to constantly think about ethics in designing and carrying out research projects.

CHAPTER 4

THE RESEARCH PROPOSAL

The Purpose of the Proposal

The purpose of a research proposal is to develop a plan that describes the way you intend to do an actual research study. You often need to prepare a research proposal for approval by your instructor before your study can begin. Much of what you write in a proposal can be used in the final report of your study, so it is not a wasted effort. In this chapter, we will consider how to construct a proposal that meets the requirements of your setting. That setting might be a class, a funding agency, an organization, an agency you plan to study, people you intend to evaluate, or any setting that first requires you to describe what you plan to do in your research study. Before anyone can approve a study for a classroom assignment or in any organization, they will want to see the proposal. The following content areas should be included in all research proposals.

The Content of the Proposal

The Problem

What problem or issue do you intend to study? Has your problem been studied before? If it has, why are you proposing to study it again? If it hasn't been studied before, what are your reasons for wanting to cover new ground? Can your study do justice to a new problem? Many times, previous studies have been done but not with a particular gender or ethnic group. One of my students wanted to study whether people receiving kidney dialysis actually followed medical advice. He wondered if they stayed on diets, refrained from alcohol use, and discontinued using harmful over-the-counter drugs and, in some cases, folk remedies. He found so many studies on this issue that it hardly seemed necessary to do a similar study again. But when my student, who is Mexican American, discovered that almost nothing on medical compliance and kidney dialysis had been done with Hispanic clients, and because he lived in a state with a very large Hispanic population, he now had excellent reasons for doing the study.

The Importance of the Problem

Why is it important that your study be done? You need to show that your study has relevance. In my graduate social work research classes, all proposals must pass this test. If they aren't relevant to some aspect of social work practice, the project isn't approved. Why is it important to know the compliance rates of Hispanics receiving kidney dialysis? For one thing, kidney dialysis is uncomfortable and expensive. If someone is consuming alcohol or not following their diet while on dialysis, their chances of maintaining a healthy life until they can get a kidney transplant may be poor. Bad habits before a kidney transplant suggest bad habits after the transplant. Why should a medical facility approve a costly and invasive procedure for someone who has ruined his or her own kidneys because of bad health habits and then is likely to ruin their new transplanted kidney? But what if poor compliance with medical directions is caused by a lack of good translators, or by confusing medical terms, or by any communication problem that, once resolved, might result in better medical compliance? If that's the case, lives can be saved. That's social relevance. Plus it's boring to do a study that isn't important to you or to someone else. As long as you're putting in the time and effort to do a study, you might as well do it on a subject that has social relevance.

Prior Research

What have other researchers done in the past that directly relates to the problem you intend to study? This is a key section of the proposal. It requires you to do an extensive review of the prior research on the subject you've chosen. By extensive I mean thorough, time-consuming, and complete. A weak literature review suggests a high likelihood that a study will be poorly done. If you lack the time or desire to investigate prior studies on your subject, will you put much energy into actually doing the study? Probably not. I've heard every excuse imaginable about why more information isn't provided in a literature review. None of the excuses are acceptable. With the Internet and with computerized literature searches, you just can't get away with a weak literature review. And remember, if you're testing a hypothesis (an educated and supportable prediction about the outcome of your study), the hypothesis has to be based on prior research studies available in the literature. One student told me that he couldn't find a single reference related to elder abuse. I went to the Internet and after five minutes found hundreds of references. The student smiled sheepishly and said he didn't know much about using the Internet. Well, duh! Find out, kiddo.

Your Methodology

How do you plan on doing the study? This is called your *methodology*. It includes sample size, research design, the instrument you plan to use, your paradigm, and your hypotheses. If the methodology for your study is weak, or if you fail to explain the reasons for the apparent weaknesses, you'll have trouble getting the proposal approved. Most student research projects have fairly limited and simple methodologies because of time constraints or because of difficulty in finding research subjects. You need to explain these difficulties in your methodology section and anticipate that the reader will want to know how these weaknesses might affect the results. Be honest. Don't try to manipulate people. They'll see right through it.

A student of mine doing a study on disclosure of AIDS by gay or bisexual Latino men to family members predicted a small sample size because he assumed that most Latino men with AIDS would be unwilling to discuss their illness with a researcher. He reasoned that most gay or bisexual men from traditional cultures have ambivalent feelings about their sexuality and believe that AIDS is a disease that might have been prevented had the victim not engaged in gay or bisexual sexual practices. He was correct. Using the entire AIDS network in Southern California and giving each subject $20 to do the interview, he ended up with only 20 subjects. This forced my student to take an extra six months to complete the project. It's difficult to argue with low sample size when subjects are unwilling to take part in a study.

The same is true of another former student who wanted to learn some specifics about male childhood sexual molestation. Because male abuse is significantly under-reported in the literature, she tried to get approval from three social agencies to do guided interviews with male victims and was turned down flat by all three due to confidentiality concerns. As an alternative approach, she was allowed to read files with names omitted at a local child welfare agency. She developed a protocol to guide her research and collected data from the files on the impact of sexual abuse on male clients. This is a secondary way of getting data and her study suffered because of it. The lack of permission on the part of the agencies, however, gave her no other choice. She had to report this in the methodology section of her proposal as a reason for not being able to do a more direct study using actual subjects.

What Is the Study About?

What do you think the outcome of your study will be? This is called a **hypothesis.** A hypothesis is an educated prediction of what the study will find. It is based on what similar studies have found. If you can't state a hypothesis because clear data are lacking in the research literature, you can always ask a **research question** or you can note the **research objectives** of the study. Let's consider how each of these three options might look using the AIDS issue and family disclosure as an example. Note that you can state a hypothesis in a neutral direction (also called a *null hypothesis*), or in a positive or a negative direction. Most serious researchers state a hypothesis in a neutral way to convey objectivity, and to tell the reader that they are making no predictions about the outcome of the study, because they are completely open to whatever the study finds. Examples of the kinds of hypotheses are:

1. **Null Hypothesis:** The disclosure rates of AIDS to family members by gay or bisexual Hispanic men will be no different than that for other ethnic or racial groups.
2. **Alternative Hypothesis (positive prediction):** The disclosure rates of AIDS to family members by gay or bisexual Hispanic men with AIDS will be lower than that of other ethnic or racial groups. (This may also be called a **one-tailed hypothesis.**)
3. **Alternative Hypothesis (negative prediction):** The disclosure rates of AIDS to family members by gay or bisexual Hispanic men will be higher than that of other ethnic or racial groups. (This may also be called a **one-tailed hypothesis.**)
4. **Alternative Hypothesis (a relationship but no direction):** The disclosure rates of AIDS to family members by gay or bisexual Hispanic men will be significant. (This is also called a **two-tailed hypothesis** because the researcher predicts a relationship but doesn't indicate if it will be positive or negative.)
5. **Research Question:** What is the disclosure rate of AIDS to family members among gay or bisexual Hispanic men?
6. **Research Objective:** The purpose of this study is to determine the disclosure rates of AIDS to family members by gay or bisexual Hispanic men.

Type-One and Type-Two Errors: When testing a hypothesis, we may incorrectly predict the outcome of the study and whether it will prove or disprove our hypothesis. A **Type-One Error** is said to occur when we reject the null hypothesis and conclude that there will be a relationship between variables when there won't be. A **Type-Two Error** occurs when we fail to reject the null hypothesis and predict that no relationship will exist when, in fact, one will exist.

The Relevance of the Study

What is the usefulness of the findings of the study? Another way of putting this is, so what? If you can't answer that question, you probably have a weak idea for your study. All findings have potentially important implications for social research. Often, the problem is that the researcher fails to see it. If Hispanic men with AIDS fail to tell their families about their illness, doesn't it say something about the way gay and bisexual men feel about their sexual orientation? And might it also assume a certain homophobia on the part of families? Doesn't this suggest that we should work with Hispanic families by educating them about AIDS and by working toward reunification?

It's painful to think of people dying alone without their families because of a bias that may be related to a lack of knowledge. Shouldn't such studies offer suggestions regarding the way a problem might be remedied? I think so. Frequently, studies are done, data is analyzed and evaluated, and the researcher completely misses the point about what the findings suggest. Perhaps it's because the data aren't obvious, or maybe the researcher is looking for other outcomes. This is an area in which seasoned social researchers might help you look carefully at your data and suggest alternative outcomes that you may have missed.

Choosing a Topic for Your Research Proposal

Your first task in choosing a topic is to talk to people with expertise in the subject area you intend to study. Also, look through recent back issues of journals in your general area of interest. Recently published articles often provide an overview of past research on a specific topic and may suggest gaps in information. And for certain, surf the Internet to find ideas that interest you. The Internet contains a vast array of information, opinions, and generalized discussion on just about every topic you can imagine. Most libraries today have an Internet connection that permits very sophisticated searches for articles on such servers as EpscoHost and PsycINFO. With a little work, you can access your university's Internet system. Plus, there are Internet chat rooms on just about every topic under the sun. People online in chat rooms can often be helpful in suggesting a variation on a topic you may want to study. Some servers provide forums to leave messages for anyone with knowledge about the subject(s) you are interested in studying. The Internet is also a valuable place to look for information available through public or governmental sources. The public documents section in most libraries can also be very helpful and includes reports commissioned through competitive grants by city, county, state, and federal agencies. Also, consider looking at dissertation and thesis abstracts done by students to complete their Master and Doctoral degree requirements.

One concern in selecting a topic is the availability of supportive data, prior studies, and scholarly articles. If you have special access to an understudied population, you might also consider designing a study with that population, keeping in mind that you may be breaking new ground and that prior research is limited. One way to add to your literature review when you honestly can't find prior research is to look for studies that are closely related to your subject but don't directly cover the same material. For example, students looking at the treatment of elderly Arab Americans by relatives in the home were unable to find many published sources. They were able, however, to find a small body of information on the same subject but it related to other ethnic groups. That material proved invaluable as they constructed their methodology and developed their working hypotheses.

Here are some additional ideas to help you select a research topic:

The Problem Touches You Personally

The problem might be something that touches you personally because of an experience you've had in your life. You might be familiar with abuse or domestic violence, for example, because of your professional work or because it has affected you directly. The primary constraint on choosing a topic that touches you personally is your ability to maintain objectivity. If the personal experience you've had makes you so angry or upset that you'd do anything to make certain that the outcome goes your way, you've lost the ability to be objective. Objectivity is a vital part of the scientific process. Without it, no one can possibly accept your findings.

The Problem Relates to an Agency Need

The problem you choose might relate to a need that an organization, church, or social agency has for a piece of research to give that organization a better understanding of a specific problem. The major drawback to this approach is that you may not find the topic interesting and you just may approach it with very limited enthusiasm. Given that you will be working on the proposal and the actual project for a while, you have to ask yourself if the topic will hold your attention. One of my students did a small piece of research on a shelter for women who had been abused by spouses or boyfriends. She used a depression inventory to determine if women entering the shelter had high levels of depression that were lowered after the women completed their time-limited stay in the shelter (six months). She found that levels of depression went down considerably after the shelter experience ended and tended to stay down when testing was repeated months after the subjects left the shelter. The shelter used my student's research to help obtain increased grant monies from funding sources. The added funding allowed the shelter to add additional workers so that more women and their children could leave abusive homes and live in safe and constructive environments. That's a good example of research done for an organization; one that had an exceptional outcome.

You Are Going on for a Doctorate

If you plan to go on for a doctorate, or if you're really interested in research and plan to work as a researcher after you graduate, you may want to consider a quantitative piece of research just to experience the process. Quantitative research is the most common form of research done for doctoral dissertations. Having the experience of using quantitative methodologies would be very helpful to you in your future studies. The topic you choose should probably be something very current that attracts people's attention. Violence in the workplace, school violence, and alcohol consumption among university students (hopefully that doesn't include you) are examples of very relevant research topics that might interest a doctoral admissions committee. Some graduate schools specialize in qualitative research or in specialized areas of inquiry such as addiction or violence. You should know this when you're considering which graduate school to attend and keep it in mind when you choose a research topic for your project.

Ethnic, Racial, or Gender Interests

If you have a strong ethnic, racial, or gender interest and have come upon a topic that begs to be studied but is really not a specific interest of yours, you may be motivated to do the study because the social change implications are great. This is, in fact, a very good example of why researchers would decide to use the critical theory paradigm. Two students of mine, not particularly interested in the residential treatment of female substance abusers, did a study on the length of stay in treatment of men versus women. They found that women stayed half as long in treatment as men did because of serious child care problems that forced women to leave treatment before they were ready. The student researchers noted that a simple change in the agency's philosophy, to allow children to be with their mothers while the mothers underwent residential care, strengthened treatment. However, they used the residential setting of substance abuse treatment as a way of showing how women are often unable to get needed help for serious problems because no one seems to remember that mothers have large child-rearing responsibilities, often with no one to help out in times of crisis.

The Methodology Outweighs the Problem

The actual topic or problem you choose to study may be secondary to gaining experience in using a certain type of methodology. Perhaps you would really like to develop competence using the constructivist paradigm but the topic to be studied isn't necessarily one that excites you. This may happen when a classmate has an idea for a study and wants you to be a partner in the study. It may also happen if your instructor, or someone doing a piece of research, asks you to help out and is willing to offer academic or scholarly publication credit.

Replicating Another Study

You may find a study that has already been done and because the findings are interesting, but need to be expanded, you may want to replicate the study. This underscores the need to do an in-depth literature review. By reading other pieces of research, you may find a subject, methodology, or design that lends itself to replication. The author of the original study may even help you replicate the study by giving you additional data or by letting you use copyrighted research instruments, free of charge. The added benefit of replicating a study is that much of the work has already been done. The problem formulation, much of the literature review, and the methodology have already been developed by the original researcher. The downside of replicating a study is that if the initial researcher proves to be uncooperative (this often happens when students are trying to replicate a study), the study may have unsolvable methodological problems that you aren't aware of, and your study may run into numerous difficulties that make completion of the study impossible.

Other Ideas

There are many other ways to pick topics including brain storming with your instructor, friends, other instructors, classmates, and co-workers. E-mailing developers of instruments to ask if they have ideas about how their instrument might be used with special subjects or topics might also be a good way to choose a research topic. Reading abstracts of prior studies in an area of interest might also be useful.

Issues to Consider When Choosing a Topic

Difficult Populations

Try not to design studies for difficult to reach populations unless you can first be certain of obtaining a sample. An example of a difficult population are the victims of child abuse or rape. It's very difficult to get people to discuss traumas they've experienced to strangers who may or may not respect confidentiality and who may respond in ways that are particularly insensitive to victims. I'm not saying that it's impossible. I am saying that it poses a number of practical problems that may be difficult to overcome.

Surveys

You need a very large population to do surveys. You may not have the resources to send out letters and develop questionnaires in large enough numbers to produce meaningful results. Surveys are also very time-consuming and expensive, and the number of respondents may be so low that nothing statistically meaningful can be obtained from the data.

Studies in Public Agencies

Be careful when designing studies that require approval of a public organization, particularly if research subjects are to be individually studied and politically sensitive subject matter is to be assessed. Public organizations often stonewall students by telling them that the proposal hasn't been approved because of the slowness of the bureaucratic process. The proposal, they may tell you, is stuck at the state level, or the committee to determine whether the study is acceptable hasn't met because of the illness of the chair. It's bunk. The local administrator of any public agency usually has the power to allow relevant research studies. The reason studies are often not allowed is the paranoia public officials have that researchers may discover something negative about the agency. None-the-less, delays of 6 to 8 months in receiving approval to do a research study in a public agency are not unusual in my experience. On the other hand, a simple phone call from someone who knows the administrator (your instructor, perhaps) might result in immediate approval. Such is the wonderful world of politics, favoritism, and personal agendas.

Overly Long Instruments

It's not wise to design instruments that require more than 10 minutes to complete. Subjects simply won't answer the questions, and you'll be left with incomplete data. Keep the instrument short, relevant (no fishing expeditions), and easy to understand. Don't use words like "attachment," "bonding," or "enmeshment." Real people in the real world think that these words convey something inappropriate and they'll refuse to complete the instrument. If you plan to do a study using a mailed instrument, expect very small response rates, perhaps less than 20 percent, and beware that many of the instruments might only be partially completed when returned.

Political Correctness

Be aware of the political implications of the proposed research as you design the study. It should go without saying that we live in a very politically charged society. Studies of women done by men are suspect. Studies of certain ethnic groups done by someone not of that ethnic group are often felt to be overly subjective or biased. I'm not telling you not to do politically sensitive studies, but I am saying that in the social sciences, there is a certain amount of legitimate criticism about the objectivity of such studies.

Human Subjects Problems

Use of certain groups (i.e., children, incarcerated felons, the mentally ill) may create human subjects problems. Think about these issues early in the development of your proposal, and make certain that you can get agency approval to conduct the research. Researchers can sometimes contact populations often thought to be inaccessible with some careful and logical planning. Don't go through the entire process of designing a study without considering ways of obtaining subjects who may pose human subjects concerns. One way to do this is to have agency approval to contact a certain population before you write the proposal. I encourage students to do this so that they do not spend needed energy writing a proposal that will never be approved because the population one hopes to study is unavailable or inaccessible.

Time Limitations

If you are under time constraints, be realistic about how much time it may take to complete a study. All proposals should have a schedule included with the dates on which certain aspects of the study are to be completed. Your instructor will probably give you feedback about how realistic your schedule is, but the best time for feedback is when you're developing the proposal and deciding on your methodology. Always factor in Glicken's Second Law of Time and Space Travel: "It always takes a heck of a lot more time to get there than you ever imagined."

An Adequate Literature Review

The idea for your research study may come from your personal experiences, prior work, and/or observations of social phenomena. These prior experiences should help direct your literature review, and they may be helpful in designing your study. Most researchers know that they will encounter problems similar to those experienced by other researchers. The best way to understand the problems you might encounter in a particular type of study is to look carefully at the literature.

In reviewing the literature, focus on a general issue such as abusive behavior, or narrow the focus of your search to a specific type of abuse, such as elder or child abuse. Look for interactions among the many variables that contribute to abusive behavior. For example, it might be relevant to study the relationship between elder abuse and child abuse to determine if adult children of child abusers are likely to abuse their own elderly parents. Once the problem has been narrowed down, consider an expanded literature review of research issues pertaining to your specific area of interest. This could include methodological concerns shared by other researchers, prior instruments used, human subjects problems, or discussions about the most appropriate way to gather information. Most journal articles discuss difficulties encountered during a study. You should read this as a cautionary note to guide your decision to study an issue that has caused other researchers problems. Here's a good behavioral thought to remember: The best predictor of future behavior is past behavior. If another researcher has encountered serious problems while studying a subject, it's very likely that you will too.

When reading the literature, you have to be very focused, which is to say that you need to know what you are looking for. Selecting articles at random with titles that sound promising will often require that you review literally hundreds of articles. That can be a time-consuming and frustrating experience. A better way to select articles is to look at titles and abstracts, those little summaries that usually come before the article begins. Abstracts can help you narrow your literature search. Try and search for literature that is relevant for each stage of the proposal. If your problem focus is on elder abuse, the first step may be to find out the amount of elder abuse in the United States and the ways in which elder abuse is defined and determined by adult protective service agencies. Step two might be to find out the socio-demographic characteristics of children who abuse their elderly parents. Step three could be to look for articles that show relationships between elder abuse and any aspect of the child-parent relationship that might explain why the elderly parent is being abused. Step four might be to search for appropriate ways of constructing useful methodologies. By dividing your literature search into stages, you can narrow the focus of each search and save time and energy.

Assuming that you will find one article that answers all of your questions is probably wishful thinking, although it happens from time to time. There may be books on elder abuse that answer many of your questions. The problem with using a book or two is that most books use reference material from other authors. When your instructor reads your literature review and finds out that you've only read one or two books, and that the authors you've quoted are those authors used by the author of yet another book, your instructor may be a bit concerned. It's permissible to use another person's interpretation of what an author says, but remember that in doing so, you will be getting and giving second-hand information. The information may also be incorrect. It's usually best to go to the original source and quote the author of that source rather than use a second- or third-hand source.

A Suggested Outline for the Proposal

Each person uses a proposal outline that works for him or her. This outline is one I like to use, but your instructor may suggest a different outline.

A. Title

The title indicates the nature of the study and should be brief, descriptive, and accurate. Many students use very long titles. This is not a good idea because the essence of the subject you're studying may get lost and, additionally, they can be boring. Here are two titles that I think qualify as good examples. "Job Satisfaction among Child Protective Service Workers," and "Parent Abuse among Adult Victims of Child Abuse."

B. Abstract

The abstract should be one paragraph of 100 to 150 words. It should be stated in the future tense because at this point you're still planning to do the study. The content should provide the problem statement, the research methodology, how the data will be analyzed, and the implications of the study for the social sciences. The following abstract containing 94 words is an example of an abstract with elder abuse as the topic:

> This study will evaluate the relationship between the abuse of elderly parents by their adult children and whether those children were abused by their own parents. The study will review the files of 500 abused elderly clients with open cases in an adult protective service agency. A research protocol originally designed by the researchers will be used to collect data. Frequencies, *chi*-squares and correlations will determine the relationship between elder abuse and child abuse. If the data show a significant relationship, extreme care should be made in placing elderly parents with adult children they have abused.

C. Text

1. Problem Statement (three to four pages)

The problem statement contains a specific description of the problem being studied, the need for the study, and the purpose(s) of the study. You should present brief background information about the problem and its significance for the social sciences. You should provide the paradigm you plan to use and the reasons you've chosen to use that specific paradigm. You should also include the hypotheses, research questions, or objectives guiding your study. Finally, you need to explain how the results of the study will have relevance for the social sciences. Using the elder abuse example, one important result of the study for the social sciences might be the recommendation not to place abusive parents with their adult victims.

2. Literature Review (ten to twelve pages)

The literature review is a summary of the literature directly related to your problem formulation and your proposed methodology. It should contain the number of sources consulted, the number of sources used, and the various ways you went about finding sources (Internet search, search of relevant abstracts, etc.). If I were preparing a concise summary of the literature on elder abuse, I would include enough evidence to indicate why elder abuse is a serious problem. Data are always a better way to prove this than testimony. For example, if I were to say that the rate of elder abuse in America is the highest in the world (I'm using this as an example, not as fact) and that the amount of elder abuse in the United States is fully four times that of the country with the next highest rate of elder abuse, I think you would be much more influenced by the data than if I were to quote a reliable source.

Continuing with my example of a literature review on elder abuse, I would include research evidence regarding the cause and impact of elder abuse as well as the major methodologies researchers have used to obtain this data. I would also include literature related to treatment programs designed to reduce abuse among caregivers. The literature section of the proposal should end with a summary statement that briefly reports your major findings and provides added support for the need to do the study and for the hypotheses, objectives or research questions used to guide the study.

3. Methodology Section (six to eight pages)

A. Purpose and Design of the Study

In this section of the proposal, you explain the purpose of your proposed study as well as the research paradigm, the reason for using the paradigm you've chosen, and the design of your study. You do this in more detail than in the problem formulation section. You also state your research question(s) and objectives and/or hypothesis(es). Using the elder abuse example again, I would choose a post-positivist paradigm utilizing an interview protocol with the caretakers and the elders who have been abused by their caretakers. My hypothesis would be: "The primary reason for elder abuse is the abuse by elderly parents of their adult caretakers when the adult caretakers were children." The material presented in the literature review should support your hypotheses.

B. Sampling

In this section, you describe the population you intend to sample (abused elderly and their caregivers) and the approach you plan to use to survey the sample. You also indicate the number of people in your sample and explain why that number is enough to prove or disprove your hypotheses. If there are limitations that impact the sampling process, note those limitations. For example:

> Forty abusive caretakers and forty abused elders will be interviewed in their homes thereby providing a 10 percent sample of the number of active cases in adult protective services of elder abuse in Isabella County, Michigan. The clients and their caretakers must take part in the sampling process as part of a court ordered arrangement providing caretakers with alternative punishments for their abusive behaviors. It isn't certain that elders will talk to the researchers out of concern that what they say may negatively affect their relationships with caretakers. We expect a good response rate from caretakers but a less positive response rate from the elderly clients, although caseworkers from Protective Services will be working with clients to encourage their participation.

C. Data Collection and Instruments

In this section, you describe your plan to collect data. If you are using an existing instrument, you present information regarding the validity, reliability, and cultural sensitivity of the instrument and identify the strengths and weaknesses of your data collection method and the instruments you plan to use. Go on to explain how you will address any weaknesses in the data collection process. If you have created your own instrument, explain why and how you created the instrument and your plans for pre-testing the instrument. Identify the strengths and limitations of your instrument. Describe how the data are to be gathered. Describe how long data collection will take, and explain who will be collecting the data. Suggest a possible schedule to guide your study using a realistic time frame. *If you are using someone else's instrument, remember that you must have the written permission of the developers of the instrument before using it. That written permission should be included in the appendix of the proposal.*

Here is an example of the discussion regarding the use of a research instrument:

> Forty abusive caretakers and forty abused elderly will be chosen at random from a list of 400 active cases of elder abuse with the Isabella County Adult Protective Services providing a 10 percent sample with a margin of error of plus or minus 4.5 percent. The Goldfarb Survey of Elder Abuse, an instrument used to understand the reason for elder abuse by caretakers, will be adminis-

tered. The Goldfarb has very high validity and reliability (provide that data). The abused elders living in their homes will also be interviewed using the CES-D instrument to measure depression. A critical incident interview protocol developed by the University of North Dakota Department of Human Development will also be used. Both instruments have high reliability and validity (give that data). The data from these instruments plus sociodemographic information about the subjects will be correlated to establish a profile of the characteristics of the abusers and the abused, and the possible causation of elder abuse.

D. Protection of Human Subjects

In Chapter 13, we will discuss the human subjects review process. Your proposal must describe how the confidentiality and anonymity of participants will be protected. All proposals that study people must include informed consent and debriefing statements. If an agency site is to be used, you must have the written consent of that agency included in your human subjects application. If you are using a copyrighted instrument, you must include the author's permission to use the instrument. If in doubt about the human subjects review application form and the way it should be completed, contact your instructor or the university human subjects review board chair before you submit the material. (A discussion of human subjects reviews and the typical forms required are provided in Chapter 13 in much more detail.)

Here is an example of what you might say regarding human subjects protection (but in more detail in your proposal:

> Application has been made to the university Institutional Review Board for human subjects approval. The application includes a completed form signed by my research instructor, an informed consent and debriefing statement, a copy of all instruments used with the approval of the authors to use them, and a summary of the design and sampling procedures used along with an approval form from Isabella County Adult Protective Services to conduct the research using a sample of clients with open cases of abuse in that agency.

E. Data Analysis

In this section, explain the way you intend to analyze the data. Include the statistical package you intend to use to run your statistics (SPSS for Windows, as an example), the statistics you intend to use, and why you intend to use them. You also need to explain how you intend to analyze open-ended questions and how you will deal with subjective information including information from focus groups. (See Chapter 6 for more details on open-ended questions and Chapters 11 and 12 for information related to statistics.)

The following is an example of how to write this section:

> SPSS for Windows will be used to analyze the data. Measures of central tendency, *chi*-squares, T-Tests, regressions analysis, and the ANOVA test for variance will be used to analyze the data. Open-ended questions will be evaluated using the content analysis techniques described by Glicken (2003).

F. References

References should follow the American Psychological Association (APA) format or the format required by your instructor. Normally, references come at the end of the proposal and before the appendices. They are listed in alphabetical order. Most researcher instructors expect a fair number of references showing breath and depth of the literature review. (See the discussion in Chapter 5 for more detail about the literature review and issues of breath and depth of scholarship.)

G. Appendix

Here you include instrument(s), debriefing and informed consent statements, any questions or scales you have created, and approval letters to conduct the research.

Constructivist Proposals

A constructivist study requires you to include some additional information in the proposal. You need to identify the initial group of people to be included in your study explaining how you will allow new members to join the group and how you will decide when the group has enough members (usually when new information is not being given). You also need to indicate the answers to the following questions:

1. What open-ended questions will be asked to develop major themes of the study?
2. How will the information gathered through open-ended questions be evaluated?
3. How will you report back to the initial group any major themes that evolve from your initial discussion?
4. What process for collecting data will emerge that will maintain the content of the initial round of discussions?
5. How will you report back to the group the procedures used in collecting data?
6. How will you control for the size of your sample, data collection, and conclusions that truly represent what your group has reported?
7. How will you make sure that you have correctly reported the stages of your study so that the reader has an audit trail to follow?

Critical Theory Studies

Because the critical theory paradigm does not have its own unique methodology, you can follow the outline that is most appropriate for your study. However, you must include a discussion of your philosophical and political views and how they relate to the study. You also need to explain how the findings will be used to further, or support, your political and philosophical views. Your literature review should include sources that further articulate your philosophical position and explain how they relate to the study. It's very important in critical theory proposals that you assure the reader of objectivity. One way to do this is to provide an independent review of your procedures, particularly your data collection approach and the analysis of your data. Another way to maintain objectivity in your discussion is to strive not to politicize the reason for doing the study and to use objective language in your proposal. You have an opportunity to use more emotional language when you discuss the implications of the study.

An Evaluation Protocol for Research Proposals

The following is an example of the way I evaluate the quality of a research proposal. I'm sure your instructor has his or her way of doing the same thing, but this may help you recognize the salient points instructors are looking for when evaluating a proposal.

I. Abstract and Title (5 points): The title is clear, relevant, and appropriate. The abstract clearly indicates what you intend to do in the study and is consistent with the material presented in the following sections.

II. Problem Formulation (25 points): A well-done problem formulation makes a strong case about why an existing problem needs to be studied. It presents prior research and data to support the need to study an existing problem. It clearly describes that aspect of the problem the researcher wishes to study and some good reasons why this is so. And finally, it briefly explains how the researcher hopes to approach the problem, methodologically, and describes the paradigm without going into the detail one would expect in the methodology section.

III. Literature Review (40 points): A good literature review has covered some primary issues related to the study. It should include data on the severity of the problem in more detail than the problem formulation. It should present a number of prior studies of the problem and their methodologies and conclusions. There should be a sufficient number of references to let us believe that the issues related to the study have been covered in detail. About twenty-five or more references would be indicative of a well-done literature review at this point. When we finish reading the literature review, we should know a great deal about the problem to be studied.

IV. Methodology (30 points): A good methodology section includes clearly written research questions, hypotheses, or statements of purpose for doing the study that are consistent with the problem formulation. It should tell us about sampling, instrumentation, and the paradigm you intend to use in clear and concise language. The methodology section should suggest any problems you may encounter and how those problems or limitations may affect your study. And finally, it should also indicate the importance of the study and what the data might suggest regarding the social sciences and the social change process.

Summary

This chapter discusses the way to approach a research proposal and includes the format, outline, and areas of content to include in a proposal. Examples are given of the way to approach positivist and post-positivist proposals as well as alternative proposals including critical theory and constructivist proposals.

REVIEW QUESTIONS

1. The idea that a social researcher can be absolutely objective seems very unlikely. How would you be able to control your impulse to see that a study turns out the way you want it to when you are emotionally tied to the results?

2. The null hypothesis seems fine in medical or physical research, but in social research, shouldn't you have a pretty good idea of what the results will be from your literature review?

3. Isn't it a little tedious to suggest that a study must have tight controls and audit trails when the natural inclination of science is to permit great leaps of thought that suggest a less structured approach to inquiry?

4. Consider the problem formulation and how it guides your literature review and your methodology. Isn't it incorrect to think that the problem formulation is static and remains the same when, as you begin collecting and evaluating data, you discover that you've asked the wrong questions for the wrong reasons?

REFERENCES

Becker, H. S. (1998). *Tricks of the trade: How to think about research while you're doing it.* Chicago: University of Chicago Press.

Cook, J. A., & Fonow, M. M. (1990). Knowledge and women's interest: Issues of epistemology and methodology in feminist sociological research. In J. McCarl Nielsen (Ed.), *Feminist research methods* (pp. 69–93). Boulder, CO: Westview.

Duelli-Klein, R. (1983). How to do what we want to do: Thoughts about feminist methodology. In G. Bowles and R. Duelli-Klein (Eds.), *Theories in women's studies,* (pp. 88–104). London: Routledge & Kegan Paul.

Eichler, M. (1988). *Nonsexist research methods.* Boston: Allen & Unwin.

Glicken, M. (2003). *A simple guide to social research.* Boston: Allyn & Bacon.

Gorelick, S. (1991). Contradictions of feminist methodology. *Gender and Society, 5,* 459–477.

Keller, E. F. (1990). Gender and science. In J. McCarl Nielsen (Ed.), *Feminist research methods* (pp. 41–57). Boulder, CO: Westview.

Krathwohl, D. R. (1965). *How to prepare a research proposal.* Syracuse, NY: Syracuse University Press.

Moss, K. E. (1988). Writing research proposals. In J. R. Grinnell, Jr., (Ed.), *Social work research and evaluation* (pp. 429–445). Itasca, IL: Peacock.

Reinharz, S. (1992). *Feminist methods in social research.* New York: Oxford University Press.

Sandelowski, M., Holditch-Davis, D. H., & Harris, B. G. (1989). Artful design: Writing the proposal for research in the naturalistic paradigm. *Research in Nursing and Health, 12,* 77–84.

RECOMMENDED INTERNET SITES

PsycINFO
<http://www.apa.org/psycinfo>

Beginner's Guide to the Research Proposal
<http://www.ucalgary.ca/md/CAH/research/res_prop.htm>

Proposal Writer's Guide, University of Michigan
<http://www.research.umich.edu/research/proposals/proposal_dev/pwg/pwgpage.html>

The Literature Review: A Few Tips on Conducting It
<http://www.utoronto.ca/writing/litrev.html>

Resources for Proposal Writers, University of Wisconsin, Madison
<http://www.wisc.edu/writing/Handbook/handbook.html>

CHAPTER 5

LITERATURE REVIEW AND SECONDARY RESOURCES

Perhaps the image that first comes to mind when one thinks of a scientist is that of a laboratory and a white-coated individual holding a clipboard. Experiments are a key tool for all of the sciences, and the social sciences are no exception. The basic design of the experiment has also served as the inspiration for other research methods. It is thus a logical place to begin our investigation into research methods.

CONTROL

The key to understanding experimental methods is control. In an experiment, the researcher attempts to control all extraneous variables so that only the effects of the relevant variables are important. The experimenter tries to understand the effect that a given stimulus has on a particular phenomenon, and in order to do this all other variables that might have an effect on the phenomenon must be accounted for so that only the stimulus remains as the likely culprit. For example, if one wants to understand the effect of football on an individual's propensity to commit a violent act, a simple experiment could be arranged where subjects are exposed to a video of a football game and their level of interest in violence is measured afterwards. Such a design, however, would fail to control for a series of possible variables. The individual's background could be a significant variable, and so sampling would need to ensure a random selection of subjects. Also, the level of violence on the video would need to remain constant across all subjects so that the results would reflect the effects of the same game. Similarly, the environment in which the game is watched would need to be controlled—some people may become more excitable in the presence of others, regardless of what is on television. In other words, every variable that *might* influence an individual's propensity toward violence must be controlled so that the researcher can be certain that it is the effect of football itself that is being measured.

THE PLAYERS

Experiments have a number of personnel components. The experimenter, obviously, is the researcher. The people on whom the experiment is run are referred to as *subjects*. Subjects are generally sampled from an appropriate population, such as college students or the local community. While the experiment is taking place, the experimenter at times finds it necessary to have coconspirators who are not identified as working with the experimenter but rather in some other capacity. These coconspirators are called *confederates*. For instance, Solomon Asch (1958) conducted experiments in which a subject was placed at a table with a number of confederates posing as fellow subjects. The subject and confederates were shown a series of lines, one shorter than the rest, and asked if the lines were the same length. Each confederate answered "yes"—an obvious error—until the subject was finally asked for her or his opinion. The experiment tested the subjects' willingness to conform to social pressure, and the confederates were part of the experimental stimulus (see later).

In this experiment, Solomon Asch felt it necessary to conceal the true nature of the experiment. If the subjects had known what was being studied, this surely would have biased the results. Many experiments rely on such concealment of their true purposes, but subjects must be informed about the true nature of study at the earliest possible moment. Therefore, many experiments include a *debriefing* immediately after the experiment so that subjects may be informed about the purpose of the study.

CLASSICAL EXPERIMENTAL DESIGN

As discussed in Chapter 1, most research methods incorporate an independent and a dependent variable. In the classical experiment, the researcher attempts to isolate these two variables so that it can be said, "This experiment shows a relationship between watching football and violence," or "This experiment shows no relationship between watching football and violence." In the previous example, "viewing football" is the independent variable because we are interested in studying its influence on one's propensity to commit violence (the dependent variable).

The effect of the independent variable can be ascertained by measuring the dependent variable of each subject before and after the exposure to the independent variable. The measurement of the dependent variable before exposure to the independent variable is called a *pretest*, whereas the measurement that is done afterward is called the *posttest*. In our current example, one may choose to measure one's violence propensity with a questionnaire, physiological tests, or preferably some combination of both. The tests may show the following hypothetical results:

PRETEST	POSTTEST
85	85

This experiment shows no difference between the pretest and the posttest, and we may conclude that the independent variable had no effect on the dependent variable.

In other words, we measured no significant effect on violence propensity by viewing football. However, our experiment may also yield the following results:

PRETEST	POSTTEST
85	100

Here there is a significant difference between the pretest and the posttest. If a higher score indicates a higher propensity to violence, we may conclude that viewing football increases one's propensity to violence. Similarly, if we had a lower posttest score on the same scale, it would indicate a lower propensity to violence as a result of watching football.

In order to have a valid experiment, the subjects are divided into two groups: the control group and the experimental group. A *control group* is a group of subjects who are not exposed to the independent variable, or stimulus, whereas the *experimental group* is exposed to the stimulus. The initial sample obtained for conducting the experiment is divided, at random, between the two groups so that they are similar to each other in every way except for exposure to the stimulus. In the current example, we would want to ensure that, for instance, all football fans are not assigned to the control group and that the experimental group has no football fans. By assigning subjects randomly to the control and experimental groups, we minimize the possibility that the two groups are biased in any particular direction and thus have a more valid study. We then carry out the experiment.

Experimental group: Pretest → Exposure to stimulus → posttest
Control group: Pretest → No exposure to stimulus → posttest

In some cases, especially in medical research, a placebo may be used to simulate exposure to a stimulus but it does not contain the experimental stimulus. For instance, an experiment testing the effects of aspirin on a headache may administer a sugar pill to the control group while the experimental group receives aspirin. In pharmaceutical research, it has been found that some subjects will show a change from pretest to posttest even when given a placebo, the change being attributable to the power of one's mind when subjects *think* they are being given a substance that will work even when there is no chemical reason for it to do so. Although placebos are relatively rare in social research, the placebo effect must still be accounted for in experiments. Similarly, in social research one must be wary of the Hawthorne effect, wherein subjects will show a response simply because of the attention being given by the experimenter.

INTERPRETATION AND ANALYSIS

Experiments are interpreted by examining the results of the pretest and posttest. In a classical experiment, the result may be quite clear:

	PRETEST	POSTTEST
Experimental group	85	100
Control group	85	85

In this example, there is a very clear change in the experimental group but no change in the control group. In our football experiment, we can surmise that watching football has an effect on violence, for the control group (which did not watch football) showed no change in its posttest score. It is possible to use a placebo in this case, such as exposing the control group to a documentary about house cats, in which case the results may look more like this:

	PRETEST	POSTTEST
Experimental group	85	100
Control group	85	80

The control group does show some change as a result of watching a video, but the stimulus is different and so are the results. The changes may be the result of watching a video, any video, or they could be the result of watching a film about cats, but they are not the results of watching football as in the experimental group. Similarly, even with the absence of a placebo, there may still be some change in the posttest caused by the boredom of not watching a video.

VARIATIONS ON EXPERIMENTAL DESIGN

There are many variations on the classical experimental design, too numerous to discuss fully here. One way in which experiments may vary is based on blindness. In a single blind experiment, the researcher knows which individuals are assigned to the experimental and control groups, but the subjects do not. Subjects are rarely, if ever, told to which group they are assigned because this knowledge can bias the results. However, researchers are people too, and the knowledge of who is in what group can also bias the researcher's perception of effects. To guard against this effect, some experiments are double blind: Neither the researchers nor the subjects know to which group a subject is assigned.

Experiments could also vary by including more than one experimental group so that the effect of intervening variables can be tested. In some cases, more than one control group may be used, one with a placebo and one without. In still other cases, certain components of the classical experiment may be excluded. Classical experiments are often best conducted in a laboratory of some kind, but such an environment itself can bias the results for social scientists. To avoid this effect, quasi-experiments can be conducted that, while not controlling for extraneous variables, more precisely mimic real world scenarios. A quasi-experiment may, for instance, include only an experimental group (a one-group experiment) or not include a pretest (a static group experiment). In both cases, some level of validity is sacrificed for the relative ease of finding subjects or more accurately mimicking the real world.

THE READINGS

The following experiments are both variations on classical design but must necessarily work within the limits imposed by their subject matter. The first reading, "Placing Alcohol Warnings before, during, and after TV Beer Ads: Effects on Knowledge and Responses to the Ads and Warnings," by Michael Slater and colleagues (1994), tests a series of independent variables. The second reading, "Experimentally Manipulating Race: Perceptions of Police Brutality in an Arrest," by Jack Levin and Alex Thomas (1997), is an example of an "after-only" design that, because of the nature of the stimulus videotape, cannot include a pretest of the subjects.

■ ■ ■ ■ ■ ▄▄

PLACING ALCOHOL WARNINGS BEFORE, DURING, AND AFTER TV BEER ADS: EFFECTS ON KNOWLEDGE AND RESPONSES TO THE ADS AND THE WARNINGS

Michael D. Slater, Donna Rouner, David Karan, Kevin Murphy, and Frederick Beauvais
Colorado State University

This experiment compared the effects of warnings placed before, during, or after television beer advertisements. Warnings before or after the ads led to higher knowledge scores and fewer negative comments about the warning presentation than did warnings scrolled during the ads; warnings after and during but not before the ads significantly decreased positive comments about the ads. Earlier findings regarding effects of warning topic and quantitative information in the warnings were replicated.

INTRODUCTION

During the past decade, warnings have been mandated on alcohol container labels, and several U.S. senators have proposed legislation to require warnings on alcohol advertising similar to those required on cigarette advertising. However, beer—unlike cigarettes—is heavily advertised on television. If warnings are to be required with televised alcohol advertisements, several practical issues must be confronted, and the resulting policy decisions should be informed by empirical research. One such issue is how warnings are placed with respect to the television advertisement.

A warning in a print advertisement can be boxed and separated from the rest of the ad, and research suggests it can be overlooked in a visual scan of the page.[1] A warning accompanying a television advertisement may be harder to ignore. Presentation of information is typically sequential and controlled by the videotape editor, not by the eye movements of the viewer over a printed graphic image. Given the sequential nature of videotape, one important issue in designing warnings for ads is their sequencing relative to the ad. This study examines the effects of placing an alcohol warning before, during, or after a beer ad; on responses to the warning and responses to the ad; as well as on other outcomes such as recall and knowledge. In addition, this study serves to replicate ealier research which found distinctive interactions between alcohol warning topics and the presence or absence of quantitative information in the warnings.[2]

From *Journalism & Mass Communication Quarterly*, 76, 3 (Autumn 1999): 468–84. Copyright

Implications of the Sequential Placement of a Warning on Responses to and Recall of the Warning. There has been some research on the location of warnings within print cigarette ads.[3] We have located no parallel studies comparing the effects of placing warnings before or after a televised ad. Nonetheless, if warnings are paired with televised ads, there are two plausible placement strategies. For example, when advertisers include a responsible drinking slogan, it normally comes at the end of the ad. On the other hand, a Seagram's ad introduced in 1997 included a six-second warning regarding underage drinking at the beginning of the ad. There are important questions regarding placement of warnings before or after the ad. First, there are questions about how viewers respond to, and recall, the warnings themselves. Second, there are questions about effects of the warnings on responses to the advertisements, and on knowledge and attitudes relative to alcohol use. The second set of questions, unlike the first, can best be gauged in comparison to an advertisement-only, no-warning control condition. The two sets of questions, then, will be addressed separately below.

An alternative to placing the warning before or after an ad is including it during the advertisement. Obviously, many constraints operate on such a placement strategy. Warning text cannot occupy the screen to the exclusion of the ad, nor can a voice read the warning without interfering with the ad soundtrack. However, the use of scrolled text under television programming is now familiar to most viewers, most often in the form of weather advisories.[4] Such scrolled warnings were also used during the Persian Gulf war to indicate newscasts that were subject to Iraqi censorship. Research on the censorship disclaimers indicated that the scrolled messages reduced thought elaboration about the disclaimer, presumably by increasing cognitive load on the viewers.[5] It is likely that the same phenomenon would be found for scrolled warnings. Therefore,

H1: Warnings scrolled under a televised beer ad will result in less thought elaboration about the warnings compared to warnings placed before or after the ad.

The ad and the warning, when presented sequentially rather than simultaneously, can be considered a paired set of stimuli. Therefore, the placement of the warning may also influence processing set, or the tendency to process social information either to remember it or to glean social impressions from it.[6] Because warnings are largely informational, people should process them as such and tend to remember their contents, whereas ads tend to be processed as social information, leading people to form impressions rather than remember details.[7] If the ad is processed with an impression set, then the presence of scrolled warnings would interfere with the viewer's processing goals,[8] which should prove frustrating or annoying to the viewer. Therefore,

H2: Viewers will respond more negatively regarding the presentation of warnings scrolled under a televised beer ad than to the presentation of warnings before or after the ad.

Existing research does not provide clear guidance regarding implications of placement for recall of warning content. However, some inferences can be made. If scrolling a warning under an advertisement splits the viewer's attention and increases cognitive load, then recall of warnings should be less than when the warning is shown before or after the ad—assuming, of course, that recall of warnings is sensitive to such differences in cognitive effort. Also when an ad follows a warning, the ad might establish an impression set that interferes with the ability to remember the content of the warning seen just earlier. Therefore,

H3: Recall for warning content will be lowest when the warning is scrolled under a televised beer advertisement, highest when the warning follows the ad, and be intermediate when the warning precedes the ad.

Treatment/Control Comparisons of Warning Effects. One of the most intriguing aspects of warnings is their possible impact on viewer responses to the televised beer advertisements. Treatment/control comparisons make it possible to assess the impact of warnings on responses to advertisements. For example, in the Newhagen studies discussed above, scrolled disclaimers tended to reduce memory for the televised story.[9] Therefore, we might expect reduced thought elaboration concerning the ads in the warning conditions, as compared to the control condition. In addition, scrolled disclaimers at the beginning of the news story tended to increase thought elaboration about the news story relative to disclaimers at the end of the story. Assuming that placement of warnings before or after the ad will have similar effects to placing a disclaimer at the beginning or end of a news story leads us to expect a similar pattern with respect to warnings. Finally, we might also expect that warnings scrolled during the ad will be directly competitive for cognitive resources with the ad, leading to the greatest reduction in thought elaboration concerning the ad. Therefore:

H4: In the warning conditions, viewers will show the least thought elaboration about televised beer advertisements when the warning is scrolled during the ad, and will show the most thought elaboration when the warning is shown before the advertisement, with warnings after the ad showing intermediate values; the greatest elaboration will be found in the no-warning control condition.

The amount of thought elaboration does not speak to a more important question from the applied perspective: the effect of the warnings on the valence of responses to the ad. As mentioned earlier, warnings and ads can be thought of as paired stimuli. Therefore, the first stimulus processed may serve to prime attitudes that will be activated when the succeeding message is processed.[10] Previous research has found that alcohol warnings presented after the ad result in relatively less positive net responses to beer ads than when no warnings are present,[11] an effect that increased with repeated exposures to the warnings and ads. It would therefore seem plausible to expect that such an effect would be even more pronounced when the warning appeared before the ad, priming negative attitudes regarding alcohol use. Similarly, warnings scrolled dur-

ing the ad should result in relatively negative overall responses to the ad even more than for the before condition, as the negative attitudes are being primed simultaneously with the processing of the ad. Therefore,

H5: Viewers will show (a) the fewest positive and most negative responses to the televised beer advertisements when the warning is scrolled during the ad, followed by when the warning precedes the ad and then by the condition in which warnings are after the ads, with the control condition showing the most positive and fewest negative responses to the ads; (b) this effect will increase with repetition of the ads and warnings.

Most research on alcohol warnings has focused on recall of the container warning label.[12] The one positive effect of alcohol warning exposure typically found is greater knowledge concerning alcohol risks, especially when the information in the warnings has novel elements.[13] Assuming that there is some novel information in the warnings, one should expect some knowledge effect due to warning exposure. However, this may vary by placement condition. As argued above, warnings shown simultaneously with the ads should result in greater difficulty processing the information in the warnings and the ads. Similarly, the ads will interfere least with learning information in warnings shown after the ads. Therefore,

H6: Viewers will score highest in knowledge of information contained in the warnings when the warning is after the beer advertisement, followed by when the warning precedes the ad, and then by the condition in which warnings are scrolled during the ad, with the control condition showing the least knowledge about alcohol risks addressed in the warnings.

Evidence for some attitudinal effects of short-term warning exposure has also been found. Two studies of college students indicated that the container warning, when appended to print advertisements, actually served to increase perceived product benefits and/or reduce perceived risks.[14] Another study of college students, using televised advertisements and more specific, stronger warnings, found no such boomerang effect. The latter study also found evidence that the warnings decreased confidence in beliefs about the riskiness of alcohol among those students who tended to believe alcohol was relatively risk-free.[15] Given the use of warnings that are stronger and more specific than the container warning, we might expect:

> H7: Viewers in the warning conditions who believe beer to be relatively risk-free will show reduced confidence in their risk beliefs relative to controls.

Replication of Findings regarding Warning Topic and Quantitative Information. An earlier study showed that the effects of including quantitative information in warnings was contingent on the topic of the warning.[16] In particular, more positive responses were found to the quantitative versions of an alcohol and cancer warning than the non-quantitative version, with the opposite pattern for warnings about drinking and driving and alcohol/drug interactions. Topic effects were also found for negative responses to the warnings and for perceived risk of alcohol, in which drinking and driving warnings were best received, followed by alcohol/drug and alcohol/cancer warnings in that order.

The present study utilized these same warnings and many of the same dependent measures, permitting replication insofar as the topic and quantitative information variables do not interact with our present treatment conditions (that is, warning placement). Therefore:

> H8: Interactions between alcohol warning topic and the presence or absence of quantitative information in the warnings will be found concerning positive responses to the warnings; and topic effects will be found for (a) negative responses to the warnings, and (b) perceived product risks.

METHODS

This experiment used a 4 (warnings before, warnings during, warnings after, and no warn-

ings) × 3 (drunk-driving, alcohol and cancer, and alcohol/drug interactions warning topics) × 2 (warnings with and without quantitative information) factorial design. The warning placement factor was between subjects. The warning topic and quantitative information factors were within-subjects factors.

Stimuli Production and Presentation. For the before-ad and after-ad warning conditions, the warnings were presented in white reversed out of black background, with a professional announcer reading the warning text. For the during-ad warning, white text scrolled across the bottom of the screen beginning a few seconds after the beginning of the ad and concluding before the ad ended. Details on warning content and the warning development process are provided elsewhere.[17] Seven warnings were produced of each type, six representing the crossed topic by quantitative information factors and the seventh the container warning. Seven television beer ads were selected to accompany the warnings, selected from a random sampling of beer ads. The selection incorporated the restriction that no more than one ad be included from any one advertising campaign. The warnings and ads were counterbalanced using a 7 × 7 Greco-Latin template, which assured that stimulus order and sequence would be counterbalanced. To increase the realism of the viewing experience, the ads and warnings were presented in three "pods" of four ads, with a beer ad at the beginning and end of the pod and two randomly selected non-beer ads serving as filler; a seventh ad-warning pair concluded the presentation. The pods were presented during randomly selected sports programs, as nearly all beer advertisements are shown during sports programming.[18]

Procedure. Alcohol use information (see below) was collected on the telephone during the screener prior to agreement to participate in the on-site data collection session. Participants met in groups of three to seven in which they saw the stimulus tapes and provided open- and closed-end responses (see below) when the tape was stopped after each ad-warning pair. Posttest and demographic data were collected at the end of the videotape presentation.

Participants and Recruiting Procedures. A commercial market research company under the supervision of the investigators recruited participants in the experiment using a random telephone sample for a Western county that closely approximates national averages for many demographic variables. The reason for this procedure was that the policy implications of a study on warnings required the most representative participants that we could reasonably obtain, rather than the convenience samples typical of most experimental research. We offered a $35 incentive for participation in the experiment. We found that 57% of those persons who completed the screener and qualified for participation would in fact come to the university campus to participate in the research, and that 44.3% of the persons contacted would complete the screener. These response rates are quite high for recruitment to central location research, and, combined with the random digit dial recruitment strategy, suggest that the participants were in fact unusually representative by the standards of controlled experimental research.

Qualifying participants were required to be 21 to 65 years old and use alcohol a minimum of once a month. The sample was stratified to ensure equal gender representation. Heavier drinkers (14+ drinks per week) were quota-sampled to be proportionate to the national norm of 9%, based on the quantity/frequency measurement method.[19] Our sample reached within 1% of the quota without oversampling, which increased our confidence in the sample's representativeness. Participants included 181 males and 179 females. Nearly half—46.7%—of participants were between 21 and 34 years old, with the remainder falling between 35–65 years. Participants were 85% Euro-American, 4.2% Native American, 3.9% Latino, 5.3% other, with the remainder being African- or Asian-American. Lighter drinkers were about a quarter of the study population, with 26.7% of participants reporting having fewer than 1 drink per week, 54.2% consuming 1–7 drinks per week, and 19.1% consuming more than 7 drinks per week.

Measured Variables. Cognitive responses are the thoughts that arise in the recipient of a persuasive message in response to that message.

Research indicates that such responses mediate the persuasive impact of messages in general,[20] the impact of alcohol education messages on alcohol-related attitudes,[21] and the impact of alcohol warnings on associated attitudes.[22] Warning coding categories included the following: issue- or content-related comments, style- or presentation-related comments, nonspecific emotional reactions, and non-sequiturs. Responses in each category were also coded as being either positive (consistent with the alcohol warning message), neutral, or negative. The Cohen's kappa for intercoder reliability (using two coders with 10% of the sample) was .83 for polarity and .58 for category. Kappa is a conservative statistic, and kappas greater than .5 are considered adequate for analysis.[23] Responses to the advertisement were coded, for the purposes of this study, simply in terms of polarity, with a kappa of .97. Consistent with our earlier research, polarity was not collapsed into net scores. We have found in the context of warnings that analyzing positive and negative responses to warnings and advertisements independently is more productive than using a computed net polarity score.[24]

Two semantic-differential type items, using a 9-point response scale, were used after each message exposure to measure the perceived hazard and safety of the product (beer) advertised.[25] The risk items were combined into an index (Cronbach's alphas ranged from .63 to .74 across the 7 repetitions of these items in the repeated measures design). Confidence in these ratings was also assessed after each risk item, yielding alphas ranging from .84 to .92.[26]

Recall was measured via an open-ended item: "If you can recall even a part of any of the warnings you have just seen, please write down those warnings or phrases from those warnings." Correctly recalled phrases were summed to create an addictive scale of recall across all warnings. Two coders separately created counts on 10% of the sample, and achieved a Pearson's correlation of .84 on the recall count.

Knowledge of alcohol risks discussed in the warnings was assessed by summing correct responses to 7 true/false items that reflected the content of the alcohol warnings shown. Alcohol use was computed by combining a quantity of drinks per occasion measure and a frequency of drinking measure into a standard quantity/frequency measure indicating average number of drinks per week.[27]

RESULTS

The first three hypotheses concerned effects of warning placement on responses and recall of warnings, in which the control condition was irrelevant. These hypotheses were tested using repeated measures analyses of variance, with placement included as a between-subjects factor.[28] H1 proposed that there would be less thought elaboration in response to warnings scrolled during a beer advertisement relative to warnings shown before or after the ad. Warning placement did not in fact significantly affect the number of thoughts about the warnings. H2 predicted that viewers would respond more negatively to the presentation style of warnings scrolled under ads than to warnings before or after the ads. This hypothesis was supported. Planned contrasts using the scrolled condition as the reference category indicated differences between the scrolled condition and both the before and after conditions were statistically significant. No interactions between warning placement and the warning content variables (i.e., topic and quantitative information) were found. It should be noted, however, that the number of negative comments about warning presentation were highly skewed. While analyses of variance in general are robust against violations of normality due to skewness and skedasticity, highly skewed data can render probability estimates less precise.[29] Therefore, as a check we also tested the presence or absence of negative presentation comments by condition using the chi-square statistic. Over half the viewers of the scrolled warnings made at least one negative comment about presentation, compared to slightly more than a third of those who saw warnings before the ads and under a third of those who saw the warnings after the ad. Such a test is particularly defensible given the lack of effect of other treatment or design factors on this dependent variable. We also examined other data, skewed to a lesser extent, using square root transformations (e.g., H5 analyses). Since these analyses proved essentially the same as the untransformed analyses, we report the untransformed versions here.

H3 predicted that recall for warning content would be lowest for the scrolled warning and highest when the warning follows the ad. There was no support for this hypothesis: recall means were virtually the same for the three treatment conditions.

H4 and H5 concerned the effects of warning placement on responses to the beer advertisements.[30] H4 predicted that viewers would show the least thought elaboration about the ads when warnings were scrolled under the ads, and the most elaboration (except for the control condition) when warnings were shown before the ads. the prediction was partially supported. A planned polynomial contrast for the predicted linear trend was significant. As predicted, thought elaboration about the ads was highest in the control condition and was highest among the treatment conditions when the warning was shown before the ad. However, thought elaboration about the ads tended to be slightly lower when the warning followed the ad than when warnings were scrolled.

H5 predicted that viewers would respond most positively to the beer advertisements in the control condition, followed by the warning after, warning before, and the warning during conditions, in that order. H5 also predicted that the effect would increase with repetition. H5 was partially supported. The treatment main effects were significant, as was the planned polynomial contrast for the predicted linear trend, but the rankings for warnings before and warnings after were reversed. As treatment/control differences were of particular interest here, we also ran contrasts with the control condition for each treatment condition. Positive responses to the ads were significantly lower when warnings were shown during and after the ad, but not when warnings were shown before the ad. Warning effects on the number of negative responses to the ad were not significant, nor was the treatment by time interaction for either positive or negative responses.

The next two hypotheses concerned treatment versus control effects on two cognitive/attitudinal outcomes: knowledge and confidence in beliefs about the riskiness of beer. H6 proposed that viewers would show the greatest posttest knowledge when the warning appeared after the beer advertisement, followed by the condition in which the warning precedes the ad, then by the scrolled condition, and finally by the control condition. This hypothesis was supported. Planned polynomial contrasts indicated that the linear trend was much as predicted. However, there was very little difference between knowledge posttest scores and warnings being shown before or after the ad, with the warning before condition being marginally higher.

Given these knowledge effects, the absence of recall differences between the during and the other warning conditions was surprising. Therefore, we ran a correlation between the recall and knowledge measures to estimate the relationship between these two outcomes. The correlation between the two was statistically significant but small.

H7 predicted that viewers exposed to warnings who believe beer to be relatively risk-free would show reduced confidence relative to comparable viewers in the control condition. This hypothesis was not supported.[31]

Finally, H8 predicted that the interactions between warning topic and the presence or absence of quantitative information found in previous research on positive responses to the warnings[32] would be replicated here. The hypothesis was supported and the predicted interaction was found. The pattern of means suggested that quantitative warnings were preferred for the alcohol and cancer warnings, and that the reverse was true for the other topics—the same pattern found previously. Topic main effects paralleled the earlier study, with drinking and driving warnings receiving the most positive and least negative responses, with the opposite true of alcohol and cancer. As in the earlier study, there was no statistically significant interaction between quantitative information and topic on negative responses. However, there was such an interaction for perceived risk of alcohol, that suggested slightly higher perceived risks for the quantitative versus the non-quantitative version of the drinking and driving warning, and the opposite pattern for the drinking/drug interaction warning.

DISCUSSION
Comparisons of the warning treatment to the no-warning control support existing literature which suggests that alcohol warnings, especially those that contain new information, can be expected to increase knowledge.[33] In addition, previous research found that alcohol warnings paired with ads result in less positive responses to those ads.[34] Similar results were found in the present study.

More important, this study provides new insights into the effects of various alternative ways to place warnings on television ads. For example, warnings before and after the ad generated relatively few negative comments and resulted in relatively higher post-test knowledge scores compared to the scrolled warnings. However, warnings placed before the ads did not significantly reduce positive responses to the ads relative to no-warning controls. In contrast, warnings during and after the ad did reduce positive responses to the ads. Therefore, warnings before ads may prove an acceptable compromise option from both the public health and industry vantage points should warnings eventually be mandated. Warnings scrolled during the ads were the least effective warning variant in terms of knowledge levels at post-test and generated the most negative comments about warning presentation, as well as evidently interfering with the processing of the ads. As a result, scrolled warnings are the most problematic of the three options. However, it should be noted that these scrolled warnings did show a statistically significant difference from controls in post-test knowledge levels. The scrolled warnings, then, appear to be less effective but not ineffective as an informational tool.

It should also be noted that warnings after the ads reduced total thought elaboration about the ads even more than did warnings during the ad. This finding further underscores the relative undesirability of warnings after ads compared to warnings before the ads from the advertiser's perspective. One explanation for this result is that the warnings were more available in memory than the ads when warnings were shown last. The relative availability of the warnings in memory would tend to reduce the thoughts generated about the ads. If this interpretation is correct, it would suggest, per the theoretical issues discussed earlier, that recency and availability effects are more influential than response set influences in the context of ads and warnings. After all, warnings before the ads, which should have been more influential on ad responses from the response set perspective, had less impact on responses to the ad than did warnings shown during and after the ad. It may be that viewers are accustomed to having very different messages juxtaposed within the same pod of commercial messages, and are able to process the ad without prior warning messages greatly influencing their responses via response set or other priming mechanisms. Or, more simply, a six-second warning may not be enough to prime a response set.

As described above, there were differences in knowledge as a function of placement: warnings scrolled during the ads were associated with less knowledge. There were no such differences for the recall measure. These results suggest an interesting difference between recall and knowledge in the context of this study—a difference further attested by the weak correlation between the two measures. The gist of the warnings were relatively familiar. Therefore, it is possible that any warning exposure simply made whatever people already knew more salient in memory. As priming existing knowledge is not processing-intensive, warning placement might make little difference. As a result, no differences in recall would be apparent: the participant could typically reel off several already familiar points made in the warnings because they had been brought back to mind. On the other hand, the knowledge items required successfully having processed specific, and in some cases, new information. Acquisition of new information, assimilating it into existing knowledge structures or schemata, is cognitively demanding. Therefore, knowledge impacts would be less in the scrolled condition, in which cognitive capacity is challenged by having to process the ad and the warning simultaneously. Such knowledge gain apparently was not reflected in open-ended recall: it is easier to correctly recognize complex information based on a brief exposure than to repeat it without cuing in an open-ended response.

This study also largely confirmed earlier findings[35] that responses to quantitative information in warnings were contingent on the warning topic. In addition, the lack of topic or quantitative

vs. non-quantitative content interactions with warning placement indicated that these effects were consistent across all those conditions.

Any controlled, laboratory study suffers from limitations to generalizability. This study is not exempted from that caveat, as participants self-selected in terms of willingness to participate. However, the use of random digit dial recruiting and incentives adequate to encourage participation does mean that this study population is far more diverse and less subject to systematic biases than the typical convenience sample used in experimental research. Certainly the close match between our recruited population and the expected percentage of heavy drinkers from national survey norms is encouraging in this respect.

In summary, these results are consistent with other studies of warnings in underscoring the importance of knowledge as an outcome. If knowledge gain is a principal benefit of warning exposure, then use of varied warnings providing various relevant facts may be preferred to single or generic warnings, and should be recommended to policymakers.[36] These results suggest, too, that measuring recall alone is insufficient to assess knowledge gain in an experimental context.

Most relevant to the intent of this study, these results provide guidance for policymakers regarding placement of warnings with respect to televised alcohol ads. Warnings scrolled during the ad result in lower post-test knowledge levels compared to other warning placements, and generate more negative responses to the warnings as well as fewer positive responses to the ads. As a result, they appear to be the least attractive of the three placement alternatives from either the industry or the public health perspective (unless the public health priority is to undermine the ad, rather than educate the audience). Warnings placed after the ads appear to be effective from the public health standpoint, in terms of minimizing negative comments about warnings and reducing positive responses to beer ads while producing good post-test knowledge levels. Warnings placed before the ads, however, also performed comparably well in terms of audience response and post-test knowledge scores, but did not reduce positive responses to the ads relative to controls at a statistically significant level. Therefore, warnings placed before televised ads may prove a viable compromise strategy should legislators or regulators again pursue inclusion of warnings with alcohol advertising.

NOTES

1. Gaurav Bhalla and John L. Lastovicka, "The Impact of Changing Cigarette Warning Message Content and Format," in *Advances in Consumer Research*, ed. Thomas C. Kinnear (Provo, UT: Association for Consumer Research, 1984), 305–310; Eddie M. Clark and Timothy C. Brock, "Warning Label Location, Advertising, and Cognitive Responding," in *Attention, Attitude, and Affect in Response to Advertising*, ed. Eddie M. Clark, Timothy C. Brock, and David W. Stewart (Hillsdale, NJ: Erlbaum, 1994), 287–99.

2. Michael D. Slater, David Karan, Donna Rouner, Frederick Beauvais, and Kevin Murphy, "Developing and Assessing Alcohol Warning Content: Responses to Quantitative Information and Behavioral Recommendations in Warnings with TV Ads," *Public Policy and Marketing* 17 (spring 1998): 48-60.

3. Clark and Brock, "Warning Label Location, Advertising, and Cognitive Responding."

4. One study did attempt to compare placement of alcohol warnings during versus after the advertisement; see Todd Barlow and Michael S. Wogalter, "Alcoholic Beverage Warnings in Magazine and Television Advertisements," *Journal of Consumer Research* 20 (June 1993): 147–56. In that study, the "during" condition was a warning superimposed on the last frame of the ad, which provided a still backdrop. This, of course, is little different from the after condition as compared to the scrolling approach. Barlow and Wogalter found no difference between their conditions and suggested that the during condition might better have been executed during the sound

5. John E. Newhagen, "Effects of Televised Government Censorship Disclaimers on Memory and Thought Elaboration During the Gulf War," *Journal of Broadcasting & Electronic Media* 38 (summer 1994): 339–51.

6. Robert S. Wyer and Thomas K. Srull, "Human Cognition in its Social Context," *Psychological Review* 93 (July 1986): 322–59.

7. Marion Friestad and Esther Thorson, "Remembering Ads: the Effects of Encoding Strategies, Retrieval Cues, and Emotional Response," *Journal of Consumer Psychology* 2 (1993): 1–23.

8. See, for a more complete discussion, Michael D. Slater, "Persuasion Processes Across Receiver Goals and Message Genres," *Communication Theory* 7 (1997): 125–48.

9. John E. Newhagen, "Effects of Censorship Disclaimers in Persian Gulf War Television News on Negative Thought Elaboration," *Communication Research* 21 (April 1994): 232–48; Newhagen, "Effects of Televised Government Censorship Disclaimers."

10. R. H. Fazio, D. M. Sanbonmatsu, M. C. Powell, and F. R. Kardes, "On the Automatic Activation of Attitudes," *Journal of Personality and Social Psychology* 50 (February 1986): 505–514.

11. Michael D. Slater and Melanie M. Domenech, "Alcohol Warnings in TV Beer Advertisements," *Journal of Studies on Alcohol* 156 (May 1995): 361–67.

12. Janet R. Hankin, Ira J. Firestone, James J. Sloan, Joel W. Ager, Allen C. Goodman, Robert J. Sokol, and Susan S. Martier, "The Impact of the Alcohol Warning Label on Drinking During Pregnancy," *Public Policy and Marketing* 12 (1993): 10–18; Michael E. Hilton, "An Overview of Recent Findings on Alcohol Beverage Labels," *Public Policy and Marketing* 12 (1993): 1–9; Robert N. Mayer, Ken R. Smith, and Debra L. Scammon, "Evaluating the Impact of Alcohol Warning Labels," *Advances in Consumer Research* 18 (1991) 706–714.

13. Andrea M. Fenaughty and David P. MacKinnon, "Immediate Effects of the Arizona

Alcohol Warning Poster," *Journal of Public Policy and Marketing* 12 (spring 1993): 69–77; Michael J. Kalsher, Steven W. Clarke, and Michael S. Wogalter, "Communication of Alcohol Facts and Hazards by a Warning Poster," *Journal of Public Policy and Marketing* 12 (spring 1993): 78–90; David P. MacKinnon, Mary Ann Pentz, and Alan W. Stacy, "The Alcohol Warning Label and Adolescents: The First Year," *American Journal of Public Health* 83 (April 1993): 585–87; Slater et al., "Developing and Assessing Alcohol Warning Content: Responses to Quantitative Information and Behavioral Recommendations in Warnings with TV Ads."

14. Deborah Blood and Leslie B. Snyder, "Why Warnings Boomerang: the Failure of the Surgeon General's Alcohol Warning to Affect Young Adults" (paper presented at the annual meeting of the International Communication Association, Health Communication Division, Washington, D.C., May 1993); Leslie B. Snyder and Deborah J. Blood, "Caution: Alcohol Advertising and the Surgeon General's Warnings May Have Adverse Effects on Young Adults," *Applied Communication Research* 20 (February 1992): 37–53.

15. Slater and Domenech, "Alcohol Warnings in TV Beer Advertisements."

16. Slater et al., "Developing and Assessing Alcohol Warning Content: Responses to Quantitative Information and Behavioral Recommendations in Warnings with TV Ads."

17. Slater et al., "Developing and Assessing Alcohol Warning Content: Responses to Quantitative Information and Behavioral Recommendations in Warnings with TV Ads."

18. Patricia A. Madden and Joel W. Grube, "The Frequency and Nature of Alcohol and Tobacco Advertising in Televised Sports, 1990–1992," *American Journal of Public Health* 84 (February 1994): 297–99.

19. Lorraine T. Midanik, "Comparing Usual Quantity/Frequency and Graduated Frequency Scales to Assess Yearly Alcohol Consumption: Results from the 1990 U.S.

National Alcohol Survey," *Addiction* 89 (April 1994): 407–412.

20. Richard E. Petty and John T. Cacioppo, *Communication and Persuasion: Central and Peripheral Routes to Attitude Change* (New York: Springer-Verlag, 1986).

21. Michael D. Slater and Donna Rouner, "Value Affirmative and Value Protective Processing of Alcohol Education Messages that Include Statistics or Anecdotes," *Communication Research* 23 (April 1996): 210–35.

22. J. Craig Andrews, Richard G. Netemeyer, and Srinivas Durvasala, "The Role of Cognitive Responses as Mediators of Alcohol Warning Label Effects," *Journal of Public Policy and Marketing* 12 (spring 1993): 57–68.

23. J. Richard Landis and Gary G. Koch, "The Measurement of Observer Agreement for Categorical Data," *Biometrics* 33 (March 1977): 159–74.

24. Slater et al., "Developing and Assessing Alcohol Warning Content: Responses to Quantitative Information and Behavioral Recommendations in Warnings with TV Ads."

25. Slater and Domenech, "Alcohol Warnings in TV Beer Advertisements"; Snyder and Blood, "Caution: Alcohol Advertising and the Surgeon General's Warnings May Have Adverse Effects on Young Adults."

26. Slater and Domenech, "Alcohol Warnings in TV Beer Advertisements."

27. Midanik, "Comparing Usual Quantity/Frequency and Graduated Frequency Scales to Assess Yearly Alcohol Consumption: Results from the 1990 U.S. National Alcohol Survey."

28. Multivariate analyses of variance were conducted prior to running the individual analyses of variance reported here; relevant effects were significant in the omnibus models. Total alcohol consumption was used as a covariate in all the analyses of variance reported.

29. Gene V. Glass, P. D. Peckham, and J. R. Sanders, "Consequences of Failure to Meet Assumptions Underlying the Fixed Effects Analysis of Variance and Covariance," *Review of Educational Research* 42 (summer

1972): 237–88.

30. These analyses of variance incorporated the control condition (as the control condition measured responses to advertisements but not of course responses to warnings) and used serial position as the repeated measures factor.

31. It should be noted that the adult population in this study rated beer consumption, on average, as much riskier than did the college students in the Slater and Domenech study; the lack of impact on confidence in risk estimates found here may be due to the adults' relatively more realistic risk assessments.

32. Slater et al., "Developing and Assessing Alcohol Warning Content: Responses to Quantitative Information and Behavioral Recommendations in Warnings with TV Ads."

33. Fenaughty and MacKinnon, "Immediate Effects of the Arizona Alcohol Warning Poster"; Kalsher, Clarke, and Wogalter, "Communication of Alcohol Facts and Hazards by a Warning Poster"; MacKinnon, Pentz, and Stacy, "The Alcohol Warning Label and Adolescents: The First Year"; Slater et al., "Developing and Assessing Alcohol Warning Content: Responses to Quantitative Information and Behavioral Recommendations in Warnings with TV Ads."

34. Slater and Domenech, "Alcohol Warnings in TV Beer Advertisements."

35. Slater et al., "Developing and Assessing Alcohol Warning Content: Responses to Quantitative Information and Behavioral Recommendations in Warnings with TV Ads."

36. Richard F. Beltramini, "Perceived Believability of Warning Label Information Presented in Cigarette Advertising," *Journal of Advertising* 17 (1988): 26–32; Barbara Loken and Beth Howard-Pitney, "Effectiveness of Cigarette Advertisements on Women: An Experimental Study," *Journal of Applied Psychology* 73 (August 1988): 378–82.

EXPERIMENTALLY MANIPULATING RACE: PERCEPTIONS OF POLICE BRUTALITY IN AN ARREST*

Jack Levin and Alexander R. Thomas
Northeastern University

This study was designed to test, in a controlled setting, the effects of racial identity of the police on perceptions of police brutality. We produced three videotapes, each showing a black male suspect being arrested by two police officers whose racial identity was varied. One version of the tape then was viewed by each randomly assigned subject, 28 white and 33 black college students. Subjects' perceptions of violence and illegality were influenced by the officers' racial identity: Both black and white subjects were significantly more likely to see violence and illegality when both arresting officers were white. Implications for social policy and future research were discussed.

Research on civil disturbances suggests that confrontations between white police and local resi-

From *Justice Quarterly*, 14, 3 (September 1997): 573–85. Copyright © 1997 Academy of Criminal Justice Sciences.

*We are grateful to Lt. Zoel A. Roy, Lt. Mark J. Porter, and Det. James V. Casinelli of the Division of Public Safety at Northeastern University for their participation in the experimental treatments; to Keith Motley and Jen Klein of Northeastern University for their valuable assistance; to Michael Markowitz at Widener University for his comments and suggestions; to Leonard Caplan for his technical skills in colorizing the videotapes; and to James A. Fox and Jack McDevitt of Northeastern University and to anonymous reviewers for their suggestions on improving the manuscript. Direct correspondence to the authors at the Department of Sociology & Anthropology, 500 Holmes Hall, Northeastern University, Boston, MA 02115.

dents often serve as a precipitating episode for riots in inner-city neighborhoods (Carter 1986, 1990; Schneider 1992; Smelser 1962; Weller 1985). In an early study, Knopf (1975) identified "police brutality" as a dominant content theme in the rumors circulated among blacks before and during a riot.

According to the report of the National Advisory Commission on Civil Disorders (1968), many of the riots of the 1960s in Harlem, Watts, Detroit, and other major cities were ignited by routine arrests of black citizens by white police officers. Civil disturbances occurring since 1980 have similarly involved charges of police brutality and racism during the arrest of minority residents (Jackson 1989). The most famous recent case was the videotaped beating of black motorist Rodney King on March 3, 1991, by white members of the Los Angeles Police Department. Many black Americans were convinced that the excessive violence and illegal procedures involved in King's arrest resulted specifically from racism—white police beating a black victim because of his race (Murty, Roebuck, and Armstrong 1994).

Perceptions of discrimination by the police and the criminal justice system against black Americans have been documented clearly (Allport 1979; Arnold 1971; Bullock 1961; Foley 1982; Malpass 1974; Miller, Rossi, and Simpson 1986; Nagel & Weitzman 1972; Thornberry 1973). In some cases, these perceptions are held so widely by black Americans that they have assumed the status of urban legends regarding conspiracy by police institutions (Turner 1993).

As in the Rodney King incident, the actual severity of police brutality often plays a role in molding public sentiment and galvanizing collective behavior. Even in the most benign circumstances, however, many black residents still may believe that the police use a double standard of justice when dealing with urban residents: one for blacks and another for whites. Research in social psychology has provided compelling evidence that individuals often "selectively perceive" a social situation to make it consistent with their stereotyped preconceptions (Bardach and Park 1996). In any particular encounter, even the most contradictory evidence may be ig-

nored or interpreted so as to support a sterotyped image of out-group behavior. In addition, simply knowing an individual's group identity (e.g., his or her race, ethnicity, or gender) may be enough to evoke a generalized belief about the group, which then leads the evaluator to regard that individual as guilty or criminal behavior (Bodenhausen 1987). Therefore, given the history of friction between the police and the minority community, the very presence of white arresting officers in a black neighborhood may be enough to generate a charge of police brutality (Hagen & Albonetti 1982).

The purpose of the present study was to examine, in a controlled setting, the effect of police officers' racial identity on perceptions of brutality when a black suspect is under arrest. According to previous research, brutal police behavior during an arrest is measured by the degree of force or violence as well as the illegality of a police response—in particular, by the use of "unnecessary," "excessive," and therefore "unlawful" force in subduing a suspect (Bouza 1990). As a result, we hypothesized that respondents who viewed the arrest of a black suspect would perceive significantly more police violence and illegality (i.e., brutality) when both arresting officers were white than when they were both black or when they were a black-and-white team.

METHOD

In attempting to manipulate police officers' racial identity during an arrest, we initially considered adopting a tactic widely employed in social psychology, namely varying the race of a paper-and-pencil stimulus target (in this case, the police officer) by informing the respondents that he is either black or white. This approach, however, not only is unnecessarily artificial but also lacks the visibility that is critical in assessing police brutality. As in Pearce's (1979) study of racial discrimination by real estate agents, we also considered filming different actors in the roles of black or white officers. Unfortunately this approach fails to control for variation in individual characteristics other than race (such as size, physical stature, personal grooming, and even gestures and expressions) that might account for differing perceptions of brutality.

Therefore, to simulate a realistic arrest, we finally decided to produce three videotaped arrest scenes in which the same actor played the role of a black suspect being arrested by two armed police officers. The police were actually members of a university campus security force who were instructed, for the purpose of staging the scene, to use standard operating procedures in making the "arrest." The "suspect" resisted slightly; thus the officers were obliged to use a moderate amount of force, but always "by the book."

We made the video recording using a household VHS camcorder with the same video quality as the equipment employed to videotape the Rodney King episode. The three arrest scenes were taped during a single evening on the floor of a large lecture hall. The camera was kept at a distance of 25-30 feet so that the actors' "skin color" could be discerned but not their physical features or age.

The three arrest situations were as close to identical as possible, with one exception. We varied the racial identity of the two arresting officers—two whites, one black and one white, or two blacks—by giving each one a full face mask to wear, consisting of either light- or dark-colored panty hose. The officers' other features were covered with police caps, uniforms, and gloves. Therefore respondents could use only the officers' facial features to determine racial identity. In all three conditions, the "black suspect" wore a dark mask. Thus respondents could not compare the artificial masks worn by police with the genuine facial characteristics of a black individual playing the role.

To eliminate any other differences between taped arrests, we removed the audio portion from all showings. In addition, as an indication that the level of violence was consistent across the arrest incidents, versions of all three tapes were colored red, which completely obscured the racial characteristics of the two officers and the suspect. A panel of 12 students, viewing the colorized videotapes in a pretest, detected no significant differences between the three scenes with respect to the degree of violence employed by the police officers (chi-square = .54, df = 2, p > .05).

In another pretest, we measured the realism of the taped arrest scenes by asking a panel of 13 judges (all graduate students) to view one of the three tapes and then to state whether it had been simulated. Only six of the 13 judges believed that the scene they observed had been artificially constructed; the other seven believed they might have viewed an actual arrest.

Sixty-one undergraduate students at Northeastern University—33 blacks and 28 whites, all between ages 18 and 23—volunteered to participate in the study. Each respondent was paid five dollars to view one of the three videotaped arrest scenes, randomly assigned, and then to answer a few qeustions about what they had seen.

The experiment was a 3 × 2 factorial design employing three levels of racial identity of police (two white vs. one white and one black vs. two black) and two levels of respondent's race (black vs. white). Thus all possible combinations of racial identities for both police and respondents were represented. Approximately one-third of all black respondents viewed each of the three racially varied videotapes; about one-third of all white respondents viewed each of these tapes.

The experiment was conducted in a meeting room at the university and was designed to simulate the "Rodney King effect," whereby witnesses viewed an arrest as recorded on videotape. Respondents were told only that they would view an arrest scene and then would be asked to answer a few questions about what they had observed. None were informed beforehand that the arrest was simulated for research. A tape was shown to one respondent at a time; roughly equal numbers of blacks and whites viewed each arrest scene. Then all respondents gave their answers to an "after only" measure of the dependent variables.

We measured both dependent variables by asking respondents to estimate the degree of violence and illegality (i.e., brutality) employed by police in the arrest they had viewed. All respondents answered on five-point, bipolar scales ranging from "violent" to "nonviolent" and from "illegal" to "legal." As a check on the effectiveness of the manipulation, respondents also were asked to indicate the racial identity—black or white—of the two police officers they had seen in the tape. All respondents included in the analysis identified the officers' race correctly. Immediately after their participation, respondents were debriefed individually. None realized the true intent of the study. Most expressed complete surprise when we informed them that the arresting officers' racial identity had been simulated with masks.

FINDINGS

A 3 × 2 analysis of variance for violence uncovered significant main effects for respondent's race and racial identity of the police.

A 3 × 2 analysis of variance for illegality yielded a main effect at a borderline level of significance for respondent's race and a significant main effect for racial identity of the police.

In both analyses, the interaction between racial identity of police and respondent's race was nonsignificant, an indication that the results obtained in main effect B applied to both black and white respondents.[1]

Tukey's multiple comparison of main-effect means revealed a consistent pattern of results for both dependent variable measures. As hypothesized, respondents perceived significantly greater violence and illegality when both police officers were white (violence: $\overline{X} = 3.32$, $n = 22$; illegality: $\overline{X} = 3.36$, $n = 22$) than when both were black (violence: $\overline{X} = 2.50$, $n = 14$; illegality: $\overline{X} = 2.14$, $n = 14$) or when one was black and the other white (violence: $\overline{X} = 2.72$, $n = 25$; illegality: $\overline{X} = 2.32$, $n = 25$). The difference between black/black and white/black officers was nonsignificant.

DISCUSSION

Because many black Americans tend to view the police as a tool of repression, it is not surprising that black respondents in our study were more likely than their white counterparts to perceive violence and illegality on the part of arresting officers. This finding is consistent with national survey evidence suggesting that black Americans are more likely than whites to believe that "police overreaction to crime" is a serious threat to Americans' rights and freedoms (U.S. Department of Justice 1995). National surveys also report that black Americans are much more likely than whites to express little or no confidence in the police and less likely to imagine any situation in which they would approve of a police officer "striking an adult male citizen" (U.S. Department of Justice 1995).

Results obtained in the present study strongly suggest in addition that perceptions of police violence and illegality during the arrest of black suspects are influenced by the racial identity of police on the scene. We found that respondents tended to perceive more brutality when both arresting officers were white than when at least one of the officers was black.

Witnesses may regard exclusively white police as "representatives of the white power structure" who illegitimately harass and batter black residents. If they do so, then the act of police brutality may be regarded as a race-specific crime, stereotypically committed by white rather than black police officers.[2] Our findings showed that the presence of a black officer along with a white partner tends to mitigate the negative perception of racial bias.

Our results applied not only to black but also to white respondents. Thus whites who witness the arrest of a black suspect are influenced in their perception of brutality, like their black counterparts, by the racial identity of the police. As a result, when the arresting officers are white, white residents may be as likely as those in the black community to perceive brutality based on racial bias. This finding may have practical implications for gaining the support of white Americans—those who serve on juries, vote, or hold powerful public offices—for policies and programs to change the role of the police in black communities. Many whites are likely to agree, for example, that a change in the complexion of a local police force might reduce the potential for racial conflict.

In the present study, the suspect's racial identity was held constant: In all three versions of the arrest, he was black. Therefore we can only speculate about the results we might have obtained for a white suspect under the same experimental conditions. Because black Americans are culturally stereotyped as violent, one might argue that the results obtained here would not apply to the case of police arresting a white suspect (Levin & McDevitt 1993). In the present study, however, white respondents associated police brutality with white, but not black, officers. Therefore the presence of a black officer at the scene of an arrest might well reduce the perception of brutality toward any suspect, regardless of race.

Experimental research is uniquely able to rule out spuriousness in establishing a causal relationship between two or more variables. An experimental approach gives investigators the advantage of manipulating an independent variable (in this case, racial identity of police) in order to observe its effects (in this case, on perceptions of brutality), carefully controlling for the impact of other possible variables. For example, there is reason to believe that perceptions of police brutality also may be influenced by factors such as previous experiences with the police and socioeconomic status. Because all respondents were assigned randomly to treatment groups, however, it is safe to assume that these other variables were not responsible for the results we obtained here.

At the same time, findings obtained through experimental research are often flawed by their lack of external validity. In the present study we constructed an artificial arrest situation to which only 61 respondents were exposed. Moreover, in the absence of random sampling, it becomes extremely problematic to generalize beyond the narrow confines of the experiment itself, regardless of how realistic it might have been. We simply do not know, for example, the relative effect of arrest interactions in relation to other potential causal factors such as political climate, perceptions of police conduct, and police professionalism. Future researchers might seek to broaden the external validity of this study by testing its applicability in a survey format under a variety of conditions and in the presence of a number of important variables.

Insofar as they are generalizable, however, our present findings may have important implications for effectively assigning police officers to inner-city neighborhoods, in which tensions run high and civil disturbances are likely to occur. Though only a few officers account for a large proportion of complaints of excessive force, a much larger number of officers are likely to be regarded as perpetrators of acts of brutality. Many complaints of excessive force ultimately are determined by police review to be "not sustained." Granted, some of these unverified complaints may reflect an "us versus them" attitude on the part of police, which supports a code of silence and even lying to protect fellow officers (NAACP and Criminal Justice Institute 1995). Yet on the basis of results obtained in the present study, one might hypothesize that at least some of the invalid complaints about police brutality reflect a stereotyped view of white police officers, who may be operating "by the book" but are not viewed in the black community as doing so.

Thus it might be expected that police-community relations will be strained severely whenever exclusively white police are stationed in such communities. On the other hand, the assignment of officers according to race (e.g., black police to black neighborhoods and white police to white neighborhoods) would create, among other things, a racially segregated police force. Therefore, we tentatively offer a modest proposal. Our results suggest that police-community tensions in black neighborhoods might be reduced without the need for segregated police forces by assigning teams of white and black officers. Fortunately, as a result of affirmative action guidelines, a growing number of agencies across the country have increased their hiring of black officers (Armstrong & Wood 1991). Future research may give such departments an additional incentive to continue their minority recruitment.

NOTES

1. Although not reported here, gender differences were found to be nonsigificant for the interaction effect (violence: $F = .84$, df $= 2/49$, $p > .05$; illegality: $F = .04$, df $= 2/49$, $p > .05$).
2. For a discussion of race-stereotypic crime, see Gordon (1990, 1993); Gordon et al. (1988); Sunnafrank and Fontes (1983).

REFERENCES

ALLPORT, G. W. 1979. *The Nature of Prejudice.* New York: Addison-Wesley.

ARMSTRONG, S. & D. B. WOOD. 1991. "Curbing Brutality Starts at the Top." *Christian Science Monitor,* March 25, p. 1.

ARNOLD, W. R. 1971. "Race and Ethnicity Relative to Other Factors in Juvenile Court Dispositions." *American Journal of Sociology* 77:211–27.

BARDACH, L. & B. PARK. 1996. "The Effect of In-Group/Out-Group Status on Memory for Consistent and Inconsistent Behavior of an Individual." *Personality and Social Psychology Bulletin* 22:169–78.

BODENHAUSEN, G. V. 1987. "Stereotypic Biases in Social Decision Making and Memory: Testing Process Models of Stereotype Use." *Journal of Personality and Social Psychology* 55:726–37.

BOUZA, A. 1990. *The Police Mystique.* New York: Plenum.

BULLOCK, R. 1961. "Significance of the Racial Factor in the Length of Prison Sentences." *Journal of Criminal Law, Criminology, and Police Science* 52:411–15.

CARTER, G. L. 1986. "In the Narrows of the 1960s U.S. Black Rioting." *Journal of Conflict Resolution* 30:115–27.

———. 1990. "Black Attitudes and the 1960s Black Riots: An Aggregate-Level Analysis of the Kerner Comission's '15 Cities' Data." *Sociological Quarterly* 31:269–86.

FOLEY, R. 1982. "The Effect of Race and Personality on Mock Jurors' Decisions." *Journal of Psychology* 112:47–53.

GORDON, R. A. 1990. "Attributions for Blue-Collar and White-Collar Crime: The Effects of Subject and Defendant Race on Simulated Juror Decisions." *Journal of Applied Social Psychology* 20:971–83.

———. 1993. "The Effect of Strong versus Weak Evidence on the Assessment of Race Stereotypic and Race Non-Stereotypic Crimes." *Journal of Applied Social Psychology* 23:734–49.

GORDON, R. A., T. A. BINDRIM, M. L. MCNICHOLAS, T. L. WALDEN. 1988. "Perceptions of Blue-Collar and White-Collar Crime: The Effect of Defendant Race on Simulated Juror Decisions." *Journal of Social Psychology* 28:191–97.

HAGAN, J. & C. ALBONETTI. 1982. "Race, Class, and the Perception of Criminal Injustice in America." *American Journal of Sociology* 88:329–55.

JACKSON, P. I. 1989. *Minority Group Threat, Crime, and Policing.* New York: Praeger.

KNOPF, T. A. 1975. *Rumors, Race, and Riots.* New Brunswick, NJ: Transaction Books.

LEVIN, J. & J. MCDEVITT. 1993. *Hate Crimes: The Rising Tide of Bigotry and Bloodshed.* New York: Plenum.

MALPASS, R. S. 1974. "Racial Bias in Eyewitness Identification." *Personality and Social Psychology Bulletin* 1:42–44.

MILLER, J. L., P. H. ROSSI, & J. E. SIMPSON. 1986. "Perceptions of Justice: Race and Gender Differences in Judgments of Appropriate Prison Sentences." *Law and Society Review* 20:313–34.

MURTY, K. S., J. B. ROEBUCK, and G. R. ARMSTRONG. 1994. "The Black Community's Reaction to the 1992 Los Angeles Riot." *Deviant Behavior* 15:85–104.

NAGEL, S. & L. J. WEITZMAN. 1972. "Double Standard of American Justice." *Society* 9:18–25.

NATIONAL ADVISORY COMMISSION ON CIVIL DISORDERS. 1968. *Report on the National Advisory Commission on Civil Disorders.* Washington, DC: U.S. Government Printing Office.

NATIONAL ASSOCIATION FOR THE ADVANCEMENT OF COLORED PEOPLE AND THE CRIMINAL JUSTICE INSTITUTE. 1995. *Beyond the Rodney King Study: An Investigation of Police Misconduct in Minority Communities.* Boston: Northeastern University Press.

PEARCE, D. M. 1969. "Gatekeepers and Homeseekers: Institutional Patterns in Racial Steering." *Social Problems* 26:325–42.

SCHNEIDER, H. J. 1992. "Criminology of Riots." *International Journal of Offender Therapy and Comparative Criminology* 36:173–86.

SMELSER, N. 1962. *Theory of Collective Behavior.* New York: Free Press.

SUNNAFRANK, M. & N. E. FONTES. 1983. "General Crime Related Racial Stereotypes and Influence on Juridicial Decisions." *Cornell Journal of Social Relations* 17:1–15.

THORNBERRY, T. P. 1973. "Race, Socioeconomic Status, and Sentencing in the Juvenile Court System." *Journal of Criminal Law and Criminology* 64:90–98.

TURNER, P. A. 1993. *I Heard It through the Grapevine.* Berkeley: U. of California Press.

U.S. DEPARTMENT OF JUSTICE. 1995. *Sourcebook of Criminal Justice Statistics—1994.* Washington, DC: Bureau of Justice Statistics.

COMMENTARY ON THE READINGS

In the first reading, Michael Slater and colleagues were testing the effectiveness of alcohol warnings during advertisements on television. To do this, they employed a design utilizing several variations, or factors, within the experiment. They were interested in the placement of the warning within the advertisement, and this included four factors: the warning before the main body of the advertisement, the warning appearing after the main body of the advertisement, the warning being scrolled along the bottom of the screen during the advertisement, and no warning at all. They were also interested in the effectiveness of different warning topics, and this category yielded three factors: warnings about drunk driving, about cancer, and about possible drug interactions. They also tested the effectiveness of advertisements with statistics, a category that included two factors: warnings with or without statistics.

The authors were very concerned with making their experiment more "lifelike." Experiments are good at isolating variables, but that efficiency can also make the experience seem less real for the experimental subject. Thus, much effort has been expended to make the experiment seem more real in order to have a valid experiment. This quest for realism in the laboratory is also found in the article by Jack Levin and Alex Thomas investigating the perceptions of police brutality. The experiment was conducted shortly after a 1991 incident in which members of the Los Angeles police department were videotaped using excessive violence against a black man, Rodney King, during an arrest situation. The incident eventually led to a series of riots in Los Angeles and elsewhere. The authors decided to mimic the effect of watching a videotaped arrest.

Because the experiment relied on using a videotaped scene, a pretest of the subjects could have biased the results by giving clues on what the videotape would be about and what was being tested. Therefore, they relied on an "after-only" design that tested their perceptions to the stimulus itself.

There are two dependent variables: the subject's perception of violence and the subject's perception of illegality on the arresting officers. These are being measured in regard to two independent variables: the racial identity of the arresting officers and the racial identity of the subjects themselves. The stimulus in this case was not the independent variable per se, but a videotape produced to mimic the tape shown in connection with the Rodney King case. To ensure that subjects were responding to the racial identity of the police, each actor played the same role in each production and the racial identity was altered with light or dark colored panty hose. To ensure that the three productions had the same level of violence and illegality, all were colorized and tested on subjects. Similarly, the videotape was also tested for realism before conducting the experiment with subjects.

After the data were collected, researchers in both experiments conducted a series of statistical tests to see if the results were significant. Slater and colleagues found that from the perspective of the alcohol industry it is more desirable to run the warning prior to the commercial than during or after. They learned this by testing the eight hypotheses they introduced during the literature review. Levin and Thomas found that the racial identity of the police officers was significant; that is, both white and black suspects were more likely to perceive violence and illegality when both arresting officers were white than when they were both black or in a black/white team.

CONCLUSION

It is common usage to refer to any piece of scientific research as an experiment. Of course, experiments do include a range of variation. However, experiments are something very specific; they are designed to isolate their variables and test the relationships among them. Although some other methods try to mimic the control found in experiments, these research methods do not emphasize control to the same degree that experiments do.

CHAPTER 6

SAMPLING

One of the characteristics of a profession is autonomy. It is usually defined as "the ability to initiate and conclude action, to control the content, manner and speed with which a task is done" (Spenner, 1983). Meiksins and Watson (1989) wanted to study the consequences for professional engineers who worked in organizational settings in which autonomy was restricted. They decided to draw a sample of 800 engineers from the Rochester, New York, area (near their New York University), and they wanted the sample to be representative of all engineers in the area who worked for commercial firms.

Many cities have a city directory that lists workers and their family members, with occupation and place of employment, among other items. They used the 1986 city directory for the Rochester area to identify all engineers in Rochester who worked in for-profit, commercial organizations. Because they were worried that engineers outside the two very large firms in the area might not be adequately represented in their study, they decided to divide the list of engineers into three separate lists: two lists of engineers in each of the two large firms and a third list of all other engineers. Then they numbered each engineer on each list and randomly selected 800, making sure that the number drawn from each of the three lists was in proportion to the number of engineers on each list. Questionnaires were then mailed to the home address of each of the 800 engineers in the sample. Responses indicated that a number of engineers had retired, moved, or died (and thus were not part of the defined population), so they randomly selected replacement engineers from their lists. Overall, 585 of the 800 engineers responded, making a response rate of 73.1%. Meiksins and Watson discussed their findings as representative of engineers (in for-profit organizations in 1986) in the Rochester area, not just descriptive of the 585 engineers who responded. How can it be legitimate to make statements about all Rochester engineers from the responses of only 585 of them? The reasons for sampling and the answer to this question are the subjects of this chapter.

TERMINOLOGY

Sampling is one of the areas in which topics from a statistics course become most relevant to research methods. In this chapter we do not pursue the details of statistical inference but instead provide an overview of the reasons for sampling and its logic. Before we start, some terms must be defined.

Meiksins and Watson were interested in the responses of individual engineers. Thus, an engineer is the case or unit of analysis for their study. Information on each engineer was gathered. The set of cases (e.g., engineers) they wanted to study was all engineers in for-profit organizations in the Rochester, New York, area at the time of their study in 1986. This is their definition of the **population** they wanted to study. In this case their population was finite (bounded in time and place), not infinite, as it is for some studies. A study's population is all relevant cases, and the investigator has to define what is relevant. Each case in a population (or sample) is called an element of the population (or sample). The list of engineers found in the Rochester city directory is called a **sampling frame.** It is simply an available list of all cases in the population that can be used to draw a sample. Ideally, an available sampling frame lists all cases in the defined target population (and only these cases). In this example, they divided engineers in their sampling frame into three groups depending on where they worked, groups that are called **strata.** The 800 engineers selected from the sampling frame (by a special technique called random sampling) constitute the desired **sample** for their study. However, the **achieved sample** included responses of 585, or 73.1% of the 800 to whom questionnaires were sent. The most desired situation, of course, is one in which the sampling frame exactly matches the defined population and data are available from all elements of the desired sample.

Researchers often use various *statistical descriptions of data from a sample* (called **statistics**) to make estimates of what the values of the same *descriptions would be for the population from which the sample was drawn* (called **parameters**). A statistic may, for example, be a percentage or an average computed from sample data that is used to estimate a corresponding percentage or average for the population. Using sample statistics to make estimates of unknown population parameters involves some expected sampling error. **Sampling error** is the amount of variation in sample statistics that is expected if, instead of only one sample, many samples of the same type and size are drawn from the same population (or sampling frame) and compared. In general, the larger the random sample, the smaller the sampling error. As we shall see, it is important to be able to compute the size of sampling error. Here, we do not present formulas for doing so. There are different formulas for different descriptive statistics and different kinds of samples. You can look up the appropriate formulas in a standard statistics text (e.g., Loether and McTavish, 1993), and most computer statistical programs provide the necessary computations. Here we describe the logic of sampling and sampling error.

WHY SAMPLE?

An ultimate goal of research is to arrive at findings that have general applicability. The more general the applicability of the findings, the more impact they are likely to have on sociological knowledge. When research involves testing hypotheses (as is the case with theory-testing research), those hypotheses are meant to apply to some significant population. In the ideal case, the hypotheses apply to an **infinite**

population (i.e., to a population such as all human groups or human beings who existed in the past, are in existence now, or will exist in the future). However, when sociologists find evidence bearing on their hypotheses, that evidence typically applies to some **finite (limited) population,** such as the current population of the United States.

If the data used to test hypotheses come from a complete **enumeration** of the cases in a population, then analysis of those data provides parameters that are descriptive of the population and presumably are accurate. In brief, a parameter is a number that describes some characteristic of a population (e.g., the average age of the people in the population). When parameters are examined, the hypotheses can be verified or rejected directly. No inference is necessary. Obviously, then, whenever it is possible and practical to do a complete enumeration of a population, that is the course that should be taken. However, it is not always possible and practical to do so. This may be because the population is too large or too complex, an accurate list of all of the elements in the population is unattainable (as in the case of an infinite population), or the cost of carefully collecting data from all of the elements in the population (either in time or in money) is prohibitive. When cases are contaminated or destroyed in the process of testing (e.g., in a time-one test that may oversensitize subjects to later testing, or when testing lightbulbs on a production line in which tested bulbs are destroyed in the process), sampling is obviously required.

The next best thing to a total enumeration of a (small) population is the selection of a representative portion or **sample** of it. If selected properly, the data from a sample may be analyzed and the results of that analysis may be used to make generalizations about the population. In fact, to ensure the quality of data, a carefully drawn sample may be far superior to enumeration as a basis for estimating population parameters.

THE LOGIC OF INFERENCE

Sampling from a population, analyzing sample data, and generalizing the results of that analysis to the population sampled make up the process of **inference.** The third step, generalizing the results, is the one in which the inferences are actually made. **Sampling theory** provides the rationale for optimizing the representativeness of a sample, and **probability theory** provides the rationale for generalizing the results of the data analysis to the population sampled.

A sample is a partial enumeration of the elements constituting a population. For example, all the registered voters in a state would represent a population of registered voters, so one might select a sample of 100 of those voters. As you will find later, the 100-voter sample is not constituted of simply any 100 voters. Rather, the 100 voters must be selected to maximize the chance that they represent the total population.

Analysis of sample data results in the computation of statistics. A statistic is generally a number that describes some characteristic of the elements in the sample.

For example, in the case of a sample of a state's registered voters, one statistic of interest would be the percentage in the sample who said they were going to vote for candidate A. This statistic would be descriptive of the voting intentions of the people (elements) who constituted the sample. Note that the resulting statistic is, in itself, not of interest. Interest in the statistic depends on whether it is possible to generalize from it to a corresponding parameter of the population the sample is meant to represent. The corresponding parameter for this example would be the percentage of *all* of the registered voters in the state who said that they were going to vote for candidate A.

Sampling theory deals with strategies for selecting a sample of the elements (cases) in a population to instill confidence that those elements are representative of the population and that any statistics computed from the sample data are optimal estimates of the corresponding population parameters. This sampling theory is based on probability theory. A **representative sample** of a population that justifies generalization to the population is a **probability sample.** Such a probability sample is called a **random sample.**

In probability terms, *random* means that every element in the population sampled has a known probability of being included in the sample (thus, haphazard selection is not random). In the simplest case, every element in the population would have an equal probability of being included in the sample drawn. Furthermore, every possible sample of a given size would have an equal probability of being the sample drawn. A sample meeting these two criteria is known as a **simple random sample (SRS).** Of course, in addition to the SRS there are other types of random samples. Some of these are described and discussed later in this chapter.

Although a properly drawn random sample can be assumed to be a representative sample of the population, that does not mean that statistics computed from such a sample will have exactly the same values as the (usually unknown) population parameters they are used to estimate. However, statistics based on a random sample are likely to be close to population parameters, so they are very good estimates of a population parameter. Furthermore, it is possible to calculate how much those parameter estimates are likely to be in error. In other words, because random sampling is based on probability theory, the random sampling process allows one to compute estimates of sampling error. This is important because it supports the logic of making inferences from sample statistics to population parameters. When a sample is not drawn randomly, we cannot legitimately argue that estimates based on the sample are most likely to be close to the population values, nor is it legitimately possible to compute sampling error. Thus, it is not possible logically and legitimately to support one's inference about a population parameter from nonrandom sample data. Recall that a key feature of scientific research is that one is able to show, by the methods one uses, how one logically draws conclusions based on data.

It is possible in a given instance that an estimate from a **nonrandom sample** may be more accurate than from a random sample. Strengths of the random sampling technique are that estimates are most likely to be accurate or close to the true population parameter, and that it is possible to calculate how much the estimate is likely to be in error. Larger random samples generally have less sampling error. Of course, if the kind of feedback is available that allows one to eventually determine the actual population parameter, then the accuracy of the estimate from even non-random samples can be gauged. For example, if a quota sample (a type of nonrandom sample in which quotas are filled by any means available) is used to sample registered voters and the percentage of those voters saying that they would vote for candidate A is computed, then that percentage can be compared with the actual percentage vote when the election takes place.

The problem with most research is that there is no definitive feedback such as a final election tally with which to compare a sample estimate. In fact, if the actual population parameter being estimated through the sample data were accessible to the researcher, then there would be no point in doing a sample estimate in the first place.[1]

RANDOM SELECTION

As mentioned earlier, a random sample is one in which every element in the population has a known probability of being included. In the case of an SRS, every element in the population has an equal probability of being included, and each possible sample of a given size has an equal chance of being the sample chosen.

The SRS is the basic sampling technique in statistics and is the model assumed when most statistical formulas were derived. The procedures used to draw an SRS are described first. Later on, variations on the SRS are discussed.

Because every element of a population is supposed to have an equal probability of being included in an SRS, it is necessary to have a list of all of the elements in the population and to assign a number to every element on that list. This is generally done by assigning the number 1 to the first element on the list and continuing, assigning numbers consecutively, until all elements have unique case numbers. Once the list has been obtained and the elements have been numbered, the next step is to select a given number of those elements through some **random selection** procedure. **Sample size** is often abbreviated as *N*, the number of cases.

In earlier days a printed table of **random numbers** was created and used as a basis for random selection. Perhaps the earliest of these tables was constructed by L. H. C. Tippett, an English statistician who collected about 40,000 four-digit numbers from British census reports and shuffled them thoroughly so that the order in which they appeared would approximate random order (Hagood and Price, 1952:274). Since computers have come on the scene, they have been programmed to generate pseudorandom numbers on command. Truly random numbers are

---

[1]Election polls are a special case in that the intent of the poll is to estimate a final vote tally that will become known in the future. In other words, an election poll is a device for predicting a parameter that will be known in the future but is not known when the poll is conducted.

those in which each of the single digits from 0 through 9 has a 10% probability of occurring but whose sequence of occurrence is unpredictable. The pseudorandom numbers produced by computers meet the first criterion, and the sequence of digits behaves much as if the second criterion were true as well. The appendix provides a table of random numbers and shows how one might create random digits using a spreadsheet program such as Excel.

To have a computer select a random sample, a program called a random number generator is used. The computer is commanded to select a given number of cases (or percentage of cases) from a range of numbers representing the numbers assigned to the cases in the population list. The computer program randomly generates the requested number (or percentage) of case numbers from the population and prints those case numbers. Cases bearing those numbers are then included in the random sample. For example, if there were 10,000 cases in a population and you wanted to draw a sample of 500 ($N = 500$), you could assign the cases numbers in the range from 00001 to 10000 then have the random number generator select 500 numbers in that range.

Recall that an SRS is one that meets two criteria: Every case in the population has an equal probability of being included in the sample selected and every sample of a given size has an equal probability of constituting the sample drawn. Use of a random number generator fulfills the first criterion for an SRS, but the fulfillment of the second criterion depends on whether restrictions are placed on the case numbers that are drawn. If the 500 case numbers drawn by the computer must be 500 unique numbers (that is, no case number appears more than once), then the sample is said to be drawn **without replacement.** On the other hand, if there is no requirement that the 500 case numbers all be different, then the sample is said to be drawn **with replacement.**[2] If a sample is drawn without replacement, the number of possible samples of a given size (500, for example) is much smaller than the number possible with replacement because replacement allows for all of the samples in which individual cases are included in the resulting sample more than once.[3]

Some random number generators draw only samples without replacement. Others allow you to decide whether to sample with or without replacement. Strictly speaking, sampling theory calls for sampling *with* replacement; however, in sociology both types of random samples are drawn. Later in this chapter we discuss the ramifications of sampling without and with replacement.

[2]The term *replacement* refers to the time, before computers, when pseudorandom samples were drawn by putting all of the case numbers in a container, thoroughly mixing them in the container, and drawing case numbers from the container by hand. If a case number drawn was not put back in the container after it was selected, it was selected without replacement. If the case number was returned to the container after being drawn, it was selected with replacement. For an explanation of the probability principles involved in sampling with and without replacement, see Loether and McTavish (1993:382).

[3]In the extreme case of sampling with replacement, it would (and should) be possible to draw a sample of size 500 in which a single case occurred 500 times. Of course, the probability of occurrence of such a sample is extremely small.

OTHER SAMPLING CONSIDERATIONS

The SRS is the base model used for the process of inference. Presumably, whenever population parameter estimates are needed, the simple random sampling technique would be the one used. As described earlier, it is necessary to obtain a list of all **population elements.** Even before obtaining the list of population elements, however, it is necessary to specify which population is the appropriate one to sample.

Specifying the Population

If the research is theory testing, then the theory being tested should include a scope statement pointing to the population or populations to which the hypotheses of the theory apply. That population, or at least one of the populations specified by the theory, is the one that must be described.

As an example of how specification of an appropriate population might work, consider the theory of homogamy (Burgess and Wallin, 1943) as it is applied to mate selection. Basically, this theory states that when people select mates, selection of those whose backgrounds, interests, attitudes, and values are similar to their own will result in lasting relationships. Furthermore, the more similar the mates are in these characteristics, the more stable and lasting their relationships will be. To what population or populations should this theory apply? Implied in this particular theory is the assumption that the duration of a relationship is problematic. Therefore, the theory would be expected to apply only to a society in which there is provision (such as divorce) for terminating a relationship. If all relationships established in a given society were permanent (at least until death), then the theory would not apply to that society.

Even in cases in which the research is not theory testing, it is important to identify the population to which the findings are meant to apply and use that population as the sampling base. The population so identified should be an important population in terms of what is being researched rather than just a population that happens to be available. Unfortunately, some research is conducted using samples of populations that are selected not because they are the most relevant ones for the research being conducted, but primarily because they are conveniently available. For example, researchers studied the seeming contradiction between poll reports of regular church attendance (in the 40% range) and other indications that regular church attendance is actually lower. As one of their data sources, the authors conducted a random telephone survey of 602 residents of Ashtabula County, Ohio. With respect to their data collection strategy as it applied to the analysis of Protestant church attendance, the authors say,

> The first step in our research strategy was to compare actual counts of church attendance to self-reported church attendance. We collected three types of data in a circumscribed area: (1) poll-based estimates of religious preferences for residents

of the area; (2) poll-based estimates of church attendance for Protestants; and (3) actual counts of church attendance for all Protestant churches in the area.

We selected Ashtabula County, located in extreme northeastern Ohio, because of its manageable-sized population (100,000 persons) and the location of its population centers. The two largest towns in the county are situated near its center, and there are no large towns near the county line. Thus, the number of persons from Ashtabula County who attend church in other counties should be offset by persons from other counties attending church in Ashtabula. (Hadaway, Marler, and Chaves, 1993:743)

In addition to the telephone survey, the researchers obtained estimates of actual church attendance from the Protestant churches in the area. Because they were not able to get comparable data from Catholic churches, the authors turned to data collected from 18 dioceses scattered throughout the United States to compare with the 53% attendance figure reported by the Catholic respondents to their telephone survey.

The telephone survey of the Protestant churches produced a reported attendance figure of 35.8%, compared with their estimate that the actual attendance was closer to 19.6%.

Their study led the authors to conclude,

We have shown that the church attendance rate is probably one-half what everyone thinks it is. But the practical difficulties involved with this research limited our data collection efforts. Although the evidence is compelling because it is so uniform, the fact remains that our data pertain to fewer than 20 Catholic dioceses and to Protestants in only one Ohio county. To confirm the existence of this "gap" and to determine if it has widened in recent decades, researchers should examine existing time-series data from local churches, denominations, regional polls, and religious censuses—any data that permit a comparison of poll-based and count-based measures of religious activity. (Hadaway et al., 1993:750)

Why did Hadaway et al. choose Ashtabula County, Ohio, as the population for their study? It appears that a major consideration for the choice was that the senior author of the article was based in Cleveland, which is situated very near Ashtabula County. In their conclusions the authors recognize their choice of population to be sampled as a weakness of their study. Nevertheless, they state, "We have shown that the church attendance rate is probably one-half what everyone thinks it is" (1993:750).

The abstract to this article also suggests an interest in generalizing findings to the whole population of the United States, based on a sample of residents of Ashtabula County, Ohio. The abstract to the article says,

Characterizations of religious life in the United States typically reference poll data on church attendance. Consistently high levels of participation reported in these data suggest an exceptionally religious population, little affected by secularizing trends. This picture of vitality, however, contradicts other empirical evidence indicating declining strength among many religious institutions. Using a variety of data sources and data collection procedures, we estimate that church attendance rates for Protestants and Catholics are, in fact, approximately one-half the generally accepted levels. (1993:741)

Such a broad generalization is certainly not warranted. If the authors wanted to study church attendance of the U.S. population, they should have sampled that population.

The article cited here is an example of the common practice of researchers setting out to study and to reach conclusions about one population, then collecting data from another population because the second population is easier to sample. The authors would have been on sounder ground if they had stated, up front, that the population they were studying was the population of Ashtabula County and that any resulting findings could be applied only to that particular population.

Identifying a Sampling Frame

Once the appropriate population to be sampled is specified, it is necessary to obtain a list of the elements of that population. Such a list is known as a sampling frame. A sampling frame is distinguished from the population it is meant to represent because the elements listed in the sampling frame are probably not an exact duplication of a list of the elements in the actual population to be sampled. This is generally the case because the elements in some populations are in an almost constant state of change. New elements are continually being added, and existing population elements are continually being lost. For example, the population of Chicago changes constantly. At any time of the day or night babies are being born, people are dying, and others are moving into or out of the city. Any sampling frame that could be assembled for the city would necessarily include elements that are no longer in the population and exclude elements that were added to the population while the sampling frame was being compiled.

Of course, some populations are more stable than others. The population of a prison, for example, changes at a slower rate than the population of a city. Furthermore, because of the nature of a prison, the authorities have more complete information about who is in the prison than would be the case for an organization in which people are free to come and go. In addition, compared to the population of a city, the population of a prison is small, and it is easier to compile a reasonably accurate list of a small population than of a large one. In the case of the prison, then, one could compile a sampling frame that should vary little from a list of the actual elements of the population.

Another factor that affects the accuracy of sampling frames is the level of the unit of analysis represented by the population elements. When the elements are individual people, the rate of change in the population is greater than when the elements are collectivities. For example, if one were interested in studying 4-year colleges and universities in the United States, it would be possible to compile a fairly accurate sampling frame of that population because collectivities such as colleges and universities do not appear and disappear as often or as quickly as individual people.

Sampling frames may be different from the intended population in many ways. First, the sampling frame may include elements that are not in the targeted population and must be screened out. For example, if a study called for a sample of people aged 65 and older but sampled households, some screening procedure would have to be used to rule out those under age 65 who live in the same household. Second, the sampling frame may not include all of the desired cases (e.g., those with unlisted phone numbers). Available lists tend to better represent non-movers than movers, or fully processed cases rather than cases in process, or populations of some public policy interest rather than populations that are not. Finally, if one is interested in an infinite population, a population limited in time and place would have to be specified so that a sampling frame could be identified. Repeated sampling (in time and place) and development of tested theory help to establish propositions that apply to the infinite population in which the investigator was initially interested.

At any rate, the researcher must endeavor to compile or gain access to the most accurate sampling frame available because it forms the base from which the random sample is selected. Once an acceptable sampling frame has been obtained, the researcher may proceed with the selection of a random sample. However, the researcher must never lose sight of the fact that a sampling frame is not a population; when the results of the study are evaluated, possible flaws in the frame should be taken into consideration.

The Sampling Procedure

The sampling frame from which the actual sample is selected is essentially an approximate list of the elements in the population. The elements or cases listed are numbered consecutively, then a previously determined number of those cases is selected randomly by number for inclusion in the sample. The numbers randomly selected are drawn from a range of eligible numbers between 1 and N, where N is the total number of cases listed in the sampling frame. (Here we use a boldface capital N to symbolize the population or sampling frame size and a lightface capital N for the sample size.) A computer program that generates random numbers or a carefully prepared table of random numbers is used to select the case numbers to be included in the sample; consequently, each case in the sampling frame has an equal chance of being included in the final sample.

Assume that the predetermined sample size will be 500 cases. Then 500 random numbers between 1 and N are selected for inclusion in the sample. Because the SRS is drawn with replacement, the first 500 random numbers selected would constitute the sample. Should one or more of those numbers be selected more than one time within the 500 cases drawn, that case or those cases would be counted more than once in the sample. In an interview study, for example, if a case appeared in the sample twice, then the responses to the interview for that case would be treated as two separate cases in the final analysis of the data. Typically, the interview results would be entered in the database twice and assigned two separate case numbers.

Because random numbers were used to select the sample cases, each case in the sampling frame would have an equal probability of being included in the sample. Furthermore, because the sampling of cases was carried out with replacement, each possible sample of N cases (in this example, $N = 500$) would have an equal probability of constituting the final random sample to be used for the research. Meeting these two criteria of an SRS justifies the estimation of sampling error and allows the researcher to generalize the results of the study from the sample to the population (or sampling frame) within the sampling error computed.

Sampling Without Replacement

Strictly speaking, the usual formulas used to measure sampling error are based on the premise that the random selection of sample cases is carried out with replacement. However, social scientists often select random samples without replacement. That is, they select cases in such a way as to eliminate the possibility that any single case from the sampling frame will occur more than once in the sample. Although the first criterion of the SRS, that every case in the sampling frame has an equal chance of appearing in the sample, is still satisfied when sampling is done without replacement,[4] the second criterion, that every possible sample of a given size has an equal chance of constituting the final sample, is no longer met. Sampling without replacement restricts the possible samples that may constitute the final sample to those in which no single case appears more than once. If the population represented by the sampling frame is small, then sampling without replacement can significantly influence the makeup of the final sample.

For example, assume that a sampling frame consists of 1,000 cases. If a sample of 200 cases is selected from that frame without replacement, the number of different samples of 200 cases will be much smaller than the potential number of different samples that could be selected if sampling is carried out with replacement. Furthermore, because the pool of cases from which the sampling is carried out (the sampling frame list) is smaller, it is more probable that one of the samples with duplicated cases will appear if sampling is done with replacement.

On the other hand, if the sampling frame is very large in proportion to the number of cases to be selected for inclusion in the sample, then the probability that any one case in the frame will be selected more than once in the sample is low. Assume, for example, that a sample of 500 cases is selected from a sampling frame consisting of 50 million cases. Whether sampling is carried out with or without replacement, it is unlikely that any single case will be repeated in the sample drawn. In such cases, therefore, the decision whether to sample with or without replacement is of little consequence.

Sometimes the decision to sample without replacement is made in order to ensure an adequate spread of the cases. For example, if a sample of 20 states is drawn from the 50 U.S. states and the sampling is done with replacement, it is highly likely that one or more states will be drawn at least twice in the sample. For

---

[4]See Loether and McTavish (1993:382) for an explanation of why this is so.

the purposes of the study, it might be considered undesirable to count data from a state more than once in analyzing the database. For instance, California's population constitutes more than 10% of the total population of the United States. If California were drawn twice in the sample, data from California would constitute more than 20% of all of the data in the study. For this reason a researcher might decide that sampling without replacement is warranted. In cases such as this, a correction factor can be applied in computing sampling error (see Loether and McTavish, 1993:445).

Although sampling without replacement may be justified in specific research situations and it may be a moot consideration when drawing small samples from large populations, the practice should not be followed merely because the researcher feels uncomfortable about counting a case twice in the analysis of data. This is so because it is not the *case* that is significant in the analysis of data. Rather, it is the *distribution* on variables of interest for the study that is significant.

Perhaps the easiest way to explain this statement is through an example. A traditional illustration used to explain the sampling procedure deals with red balls and black balls in a container. Assume that there are 100 balls in the container and that 60 of the 100 are red and the others are black. To sample with replacement from the container, one would reach in and draw out a ball. There would be a 60% chance of drawing a red ball and a 40% chance of drawing a black ball. Once the color of the ball drawn from the container was recorded, the ball would be returned to the container and a second ball would be drawn.

Note that the important fact is the color of the ball. When the second ball is drawn, its color is recorded and it is returned to the container. The same procedure is repeated until the desired sample size is obtained (say, 20 balls). Each time a ball is drawn from the container, the only bit of information that is gleaned is the color of the ball. No consideration is given to the fact that it is possible to draw the same ball from the container more than once. Thus, what the sampler is paying attention to is the distribution of red and black balls in the container, not which particular ball is red or black.

This same reasoning applies to random sampling with replacement when the elements being drawn are people or collectivities rather than balls. In the case of people, for example, the researcher might be interested in the distribution of a characteristic of the people in the population such as gender. If 60% of the people in the population are female and 40% male, random sampling with replacement from that population should result in a sample that is representative of the population with respect to gender (within sampling error). Furthermore, the example can be extended to the case in which the researcher is interested in the joint distribution of two or more variables in a population. If gender and level of education are related, for example, the relationship would be reflected in the joint distribution of those two variables, regardless of the specific cases included in the sample. When one looks at the situation from this point of view, it is not really essential that the cases in a sample all be unique. Consequently, random sampling should be executed with replacement unless there are good reasons to do otherwise.

OTHER TYPES OF RANDOM SAMPLES

Because the SRS is the basic sampling procedure underlying statistical inference, it should be the sampling procedure of first choice in doing research involving generalization from a sample to a population. In order to draw an SRS, it is essential that a single accurate sampling frame be available. Unfortunately, it is often not possible to acquire such a sampling frame. This is particularly true when the population that the sampling frame is meant to represent is a large population. The population of the United States is over 280 million. Obviously, no accurate sampling frame available lists all those cases, nor is it possible to compile such a sampling frame. Because the composition of the population is constantly changing, any attempt to gather an accurate sampling frame would be futile. The composition of the population would change faster than the identity of the cases for the sampling frame could be ascertained. Various probability sampling strategies provide alternative ways to achieve a representative sample when there are problems obtaining an overall sampling frame list.

The Random Cluster Sample

Fortunately, it is not necessary to abandon the notion of random sampling in drawing a sample for a large, volatile population. An alternative random sampling strategy is available in place of the SRS. That strategy, called the **random cluster sample,** involves obtaining a series of sampling frames (nested from broader to narrower) from which random samples may be obtained. The random cluster sample is essentially a **multistage random sample,** with each stage corresponding to its own sampling frame or frames.

The procedure involves starting with a first-stage sampling frame that is accessible, sampling elements (**primary sampling units**) from that frame, and then compiling additional stages of sampling frames within the selected broader frames (at levels less general than the original one) and sampling from them until the random sampling procedure culminates in a sample or samples of cases (**ultimate sampling units**) at the level at which the data are to be collected.

Perhaps an example of such a random cluster sample will make it easier to understand the sampling process. Assume that we want to draw a random cluster sample of all the high school seniors in the United States as of May 1 of this year. It would not be practical and probably not possible to compile a single sampling frame that suitably identified all high school seniors in the United States as of the designated date.

However, it would be possible to compile a list of all of the states plus the District of Columbia (DC). This list would constitute the primary sampling frame and would accurately replicate a list of the population of states and DC. The states and DC could be listed, numbered from 1 to 51, then randomly sampled. States and DC would be the primary sampling units. Perhaps 20 of the 51 would be selected through the use of random numbers (see Appendix 1).

Once the 20 states (or states and DC) were selected from the original sampling frame, each of these 20 units could be used to generate a sampling frame consisting of a list of the counties in each. California is divided into 58 counties; therefore, if California were one of the 20 states selected, these 58 counties could be listed in a second-stage sampling frame and these could be sampled randomly. The other 19 units selected in the first stage of sampling would be treated similarly. For each, the counties would be listed and then a random sample of those units would be drawn. When the counties sampled from the 20 states had been determined, they would constitute the sampling units for the second round of random cluster sampling (i.e., secondary sampling units).

The third stage of sampling frames would consist of lists of all of the high schools in each of the counties that had survived the second round of sampling (third-stage sampling units). For each of these lists (third-stage sampling frames), a certain number of high schools could be randomly sampled.

For each high school selected at this third level of random sampling, we might sample high school seniors (the ultimate sampling unit), or we might decide to collect data from all seniors in each of those schools. The high school seniors from whom data were ultimately collected could be considered a random sample of all seniors in the United States because they were selected randomly for inclusion in the study.

In an actual cluster sampling procedure, the number of units sampled at each stage would be carefully worked out to fit the needs of the study and to arrive at a final sample of the appropriate size. In the preceding example it was suggested that 20 states (or 19 states and DC) might be sampled from the first sampling frame. This number was selected arbitrarily in order to describe a possible cluster sampling technique. The number of units drawn from the primary sampling frame for an actual study would be considered carefully and would be decided upon in terms of such factors as the desired spread of states, the cost of collecting data from different states, and the heterogeneity of the cases in the different states. Often at this stage of a complex sampling project, a specialist in sampling statistics would be consulted.

It should be noted that the heterogeneity of the cases in a sampling frame is often an important consideration in deciding how many of those cases to sample because the more heterogeneous the sampling frame is, the larger the number of cases from that frame must be drawn to ensure a given level of sampling error. In order to increase the homogeneity of cases to be sampled, some primary sampling frames are divided into a number of separate frames and samples are selected from each of those. For example, the states in the United States might be arranged into nine regions (the South, New England, the Midwest, etc.), then random samples of states would be selected from each of those regions. This strategy is based on the notion that states within a given region are more homogeneous than states from different regions.

This and some of the other considerations (e.g., geographic spread) mentioned earlier would enter into the determination of how many counties would be sampled as secondary sampling units from each of the 20 states sampled as the primary sampling units. As a matter of fact, sampling proportions would be very carefully determined at each sampling level so that the final sample arrived at would be optimally representative of the population to which we wanted to generalize our findings.

The random cluster sample derives its name from the fact that the cases from which the data are finally collected are (usually geographically) clustered. For example, in the case of the cluster sample of high school seniors, the seniors from whom the data would be collected would be clustered in a given number of high schools. Numerous cases would be located at each high school that ended up in the cluster sample, thus making it less expensive to collect data than if cases were spread all over the United States. In this sense the random cluster sample is more economical than an SRS for collecting data.

As a matter of fact, the cluster sample enjoys at least two advantages over the SRS: It is feasible to do when the SRS may not be, and the cases from which data are to be collected are conveniently geographically clustered (if clusters are geographic units), often saving travel costs.

On the other hand, the SRS enjoys the advantage of having a smaller sampling error for a given sample size. Because the cluster sample involves the selection of a series of random samples from the various sampling frames, sampling error is risked each time another random sample of units is selected. Thus, the sampling error is generally compounded.

The consolation to be gained from the random cluster sample despite its generally larger sampling error is that it is feasible when an SRS may not be. Consequently, random samples of large populations are usually cluster samples or some variation thereof. Furthermore, although the formula used to estimate sampling error for an SRS does not apply to a random cluster sample, the procedure for determining the proper formula for estimating sampling error has been worked out (Kish, 1965).

The Stratified Random Sample

Another variation on the SRS is the **stratified random sample.** This type of sample was used in the study described at the beginning of the chapter. The motivation for using a stratified random sample rather than an SRS is quite different from that for the random cluster sample. Furthermore, whereas the random cluster sample requires less detailed information about the population to be sampled than the SRS, the stratified random sample requires more.

In order to use a stratified random sample, it is not only necessary to have a single primary sampling frame, but it must also be possible to divide that sampling frame accurately into separate strata based on some characteristic or characteristics of the cases in the population. For example, suppose we wished to draw a random sample of all institutions of higher education in the United States. There are approximately 3,000 of these. Because it would be possible to get a fairly accurate primary sampling frame of all of these, it would be possible to draw an SRS. However, institutions of higher education fall into a number of different categories. There are 2-year community colleges, 4-year colleges limited to undergraduate education, colleges and universities that offer graduate degrees but not doctorates, and universities that offer a full range of degrees from the baccalaureate to the doctoral degree. If an SRS of all institutions of higher education were drawn from a single sampling frame, some of the possible SRS sample outcomes might include only a few or none of the less common types of institutions. Although this is less likely than getting a proper proportion of each type of institution, a researcher may not want to risk drawing a sample with too few of the more uncommon types of institutions because comparisons may need to be made between types of institutions.

Because of the nature of the study being conducted, it might be very important not only that the full range of institutions be included, but that they be included in the sample *in the same proportions* as they are represented in the population. In order to ensure that the resulting random sample meets these criteria, a stratified random sample could be drawn instead of an SRS. To draw such a sample, the primary sampling frame would be divided into a number of subframes (called strata), each of which would consist only of institutions falling into a single category. Thus, one stratum could consist of all of the 2-year community colleges in the country, another of all of the 4-year undergraduate institutions, a third of all of the colleges and universities offering graduate degrees but not the doctorate, and a final stratum of all of the universities offering the doctorate.

If the study being planned required a sample of 300 institutions of higher education in the United States (approximately 10% in this instance, called the sampling fraction), once the separate strata were compiled the same proportion of cases (here about 10%) from each stratum would be randomly drawn. Because the numbers of institutions falling into each stratum would differ, using the same sampling fraction (here 10%) in drawing a random sample from each stratum would result in an overall random sample that would match the population in terms of proportions of institutions of higher education of each type.

Suppose that it was desirable to divide the institutions not only into the four types mentioned earlier but also in terms of whether they were public or private. The primary sampling frame would be divided into eight strata representing the four types of institutions, public and private. Again, a random sample of the same proportion of the cases (here, 10%) would be drawn from each of the strata; however, in this case there would be eight strata rather than four.

The stratified random samples described thus far are called **proportionate stratified random samples** because the sample strata use the same sampling fraction (have the same proportions of cases) as the population strata from which the cases are sampled. This proportionate sampling is important in generalizing sample results back to the population sampled because it ensures that no stratum in the combined sample has undue influence on the overall results of the study.

Disproportionate Sampling.   If one purpose of a study is to make comparisons between strata on a variable such as religious affiliation, in which strata sizes vary greatly in the population, the small strata may deliberately be oversampled so that the sizes of the sample strata being compared are equal. When this is done the resulting sample is called a **disproportionate stratified random sample.** This type of sample is drawn in order to ensure that there will be enough cases in the smaller sample strata that the comparisons of interest can be performed.

The minimum number of cases needed in any stratum in a sample, of course, depends on the nature of the analysis. Suppose that the study being conducted dealt with attitudes toward capital punishment. If the effect of religious affiliation on attitudes toward capital punishment were of interest, in order to compare Protestants, Catholics, and Jews (a breakdown of religion used in the U.S. Census), a sufficient number of Jewish respondents would need to be sampled. Because most people in the United States identify themselves as either Protestant or Catholic, a proportionate stratified sample drawn from a population of Americans would be most heavily weighted with cases from these two categories. Because Jews constitute the smallest population for these three particular religious denominations, the needed size of the sample for Jews could be the determinant of how many cases were needed for the overall sample. For example, if the Jews constituted 10% of the religious population and 500 cases were needed for the analysis of their attitudes toward capital punishment (a need determined by such things as distinguishing gender or income in the analysis of each religious group), an overall sample of 5,000 would have to be drawn by proportionate random sampling. The analysis may not need such a high number of Protestants and Catholics (i.e., 4,500), and funding may not permit such a large overall sample. In this instance a disproportionate stratified random sample could be used to provide for analysis needs and still minimize the overall sample size. For example, a sample of 500 could be drawn from each stratum for an overall sample size of 1,500 rather than 5,000 cases (500 each from Jews, Catholics, and Protestants).

Weighting Responses. An important caution is necessary with regard to generalizing results from a disproportionate stratified random sample. Because disproportionate sampling leads to overrepresentation of some strata, in generalizing results from the overall sample to the population sampled it is necessary to **weight** the responses of subjects from the various strata. Thus, greater weight should be given to the responses of the respondents in the larger population strata and less weight to those of respondents from smaller population strata. If such an adjustment is not made, generalizations will be misleading. For example, assume that an overwhelming proportion of the Jewish respondents are not in favor of capital punishment. Because a third of the cases in the overall sample are Jews, the impression might be given that a third or more of all those in the population, regardless of religious affiliation, are not in favor of capital punishment. Reweighting responses as shown in Box 5.1 accurately represents the overall percentage opposed to capital punishment by properly balancing the views of all strata.

Optimum Allocation Sampling. A third type of stratified random sample technique, called **optimum allocation sampling,** combines features of both the proportionate and disproportionate techniques. This technique takes into account

■ ■ ■ ■ ■ ▬▬▬▬▬▬▬▬

BOX 5.1

REWEIGHTING DATA FROM A DISPROPORTIONATE STRATIFIED RANDOM SAMPLE

If a sample has used disproportionate stratified random sampling and the results from all strata are to be combined for an overall description of results, then the cases in each stratum must be reweighted so that the overall results accurately represent the population. If each stratum is analyzed separately and an overall description of the total sample is not needed, then reweighting is not needed.

To reweight a sample, the following procedure is used:

1. *Determine the sampling fraction used in each stratum.* That is, the proportion of available cases in the sampling frame for that stratum that were drawn into the sample for that stratum. For example,

	Number of cases in the		
Stratum	*Sampling Frame*	*Final Sample*	*Sampling Fraction*
Protestants	100,000	500	.00500
Catholics	50,000	500	.01000
Jews	15,000	500	.03333
	165,000	1,500	**.00909**

If 15,000 Jewish people were in the sampling frame for that stratum and 500 were drawn in the sample, then the sampling fraction would be 500/15,000 = .033. Notice that the sampling fractions differ by stratum with disproportionate stratified random sampling. Overall, Jews are overrepresented in the $N = 1,500$ sample. Catholics are overrepresented as well.

2. *Reweight each case in each stratum by the reciprocal of its sampling fraction times the overall sampling fraction.* For Protestants, the reciprocal of the sampling fraction is $1/.005 = 200$. This is multiplied by the overall sampling fraction, which is $1,500/165,000 = .00909$: $200 \times .00909 = 1.818$. Each Protestant case would be multiplied by 1.818, so 500 cases would be reweighted to 909 ($1.818 \times 500 = 909$). As shown in the following table, the weighting factor for each other group is computed in a similar way:

Weight for Protestants = $(1/.005) \times .00909 = 1.818$
Weight for Catholics = $(1/.01) \times .00909 = .909$
Weight for Jews = $(1/.03333) \times .00909 = .2727$

In doing statistical summaries of the overall sample, data for any variable would be weighted for each case, using the weight for the appropriate group. This would preserve the overall sample size $[(1.818 \times 500 = 909) + (.909 \times 500 = 455) + (.2727 \times 500 = 136) = 1,500]$.

both the sizes of the strata being sampled and the homogeneity of the cases in the strata on one or more important variables. Consequently, a larger stratum that is homogeneous in the characteristics of the elements in that stratum would result in the selection of fewer cases than a smaller stratum or a stratum that is more heterogeneous. For example, assume that a study of attitudes toward abortion is being conducted in which a comparison is being made between Protestants and Catholics. It is decided that the desired sample size would be achieved with a sampling fraction of 5% of the population of interest. Assume further that the stratum of Protestants is one-third larger than the stratum of Catholics, but the stratum of Catholics is more homogeneous on attitudes toward abortion than the stratum of Protestants. Given these conditions, it would not be necessary to sample the same proportion of Catholics (5%) as of Protestants. Because Catholic attitudes are more homogeneous, the proportion of cases sampled from the Catholic stratum might be smaller than 5%, and the proportion sampled from the Protestant stratum might be somewhat larger than 5% despite the fact that the stratum of Protestants is larger.[5]

Advantages and Disadvantages of Stratified Random Samples. Under certain conditions stratified random samples may be preferable to SRSs because smaller sampling error may be achieved. The conditions that would make stratified random sampling preferable include the following:

■ **Enough accurate information about the population of interest is available to divide the sampling frame into strata based on variables that are relevant to the study being conducted.** That is, it must be possible to identify variables that are relevant to the study, and the representation of those variables in the population must be known so that appropriate sampling frames may be constructed. For example, if religious affiliation is a relevant variable for studying attitudes toward abortion, then the religious affiliation of cases in the population must be known so that the overall sampling frame can be divided into subframes based on religious affiliation. If gender is a second variable relevant to the study, then the distribution of cases in the population by gender must also be known so that the subframes on religious affiliation can be divided further into subframes for males and females. If religious affiliation is divided into Protestant, Catholic, and Jews, and males and females are distinguished, six subframes must be identified.

■ **The resulting subframes from which to select the sample will be more homogeneous on variables relevant to the study than is the overall population sampling frame.** If the resulting subframes are not more homogeneous, then the sampling error of the stratified random sample will not be any smaller than the sampling error would be for an SRS and all the effort put into stratification would be futile.

---

[5]See Kish (1965) for a comprehensive discussion of optimum allocation sampling.

■ **No variables relevant to the study being conducted would be overlooked in the stratification process.** If the researcher is unaware of some variables that are relevant to the study being conducted and, for that reason, fails to take them into consideration in the stratification process, a stratified random sample might be inferior to an SRS. An important virtue of an SRS is that it generally accounts for relevant variables of a study, whether they are anticipated or not, and results in a sample in which those variables are represented proportionately.

If these conditions are met, a stratified random sample has an advantage. A stratified random sample equal in size to an SRS will have smaller sampling error than the SRS because of the greater homogeneity of the sampling frames of the strata constructed for the sample as compared to the sampling frame of the SRS. This fact makes it possible for the researcher to choose between drawing a stratified random sample equal in size to an SRS, but with a smaller sampling error, or a stratified random sample smaller than an SRS, but with a sampling error equal to that of the larger SRS.

A major disadvantage of the stratified random sample is that it requires more information about the elements of a population being sampled than an SRS. It is necessary not only to be able to access an overall sampling frame, but also to have enough accurate information available to divide that sampling frame into subframes based on information on relevant variables in the population. Furthermore, it is necessary to have enough information about the variables involved in the study being undertaken to be able to identify all that are relevant to the study so that they can be used as a basis for stratification. If the wrong variables are selected as a basis for stratification or a stratifying variable is inaccurate, then the process of stratifying can be a waste of time and money. Furthermore, if variables that are relevant to the study are overlooked in the stratification process, then the process of stratification can likewise be futile.

Although the optimum allocation stratified random sample is the most efficient stratification design (resulting in the smallest sampling error), it is even more difficult to accomplish than the stratified random sample because, in addition to having all the information necessary for the stratified random sample, one must also be able to estimate the degree of homogeneity present in each of the population strata to be sampled.

NONRANDOM SAMPLES

Given a choice, the random sample is always to be preferred over a nonrandom sample. For various reasons, however, nonrandom sampling techniques are used. Sometimes researchers resort to nonrandom samples because they cannot draw random samples. In other cases nonrandom samples are used because they are cheaper or more convenient, or because of ignorance of sampling principles. In any case, several nonrandom sampling designs appear in the literature. Some of these nonrandom designs are described here, and problems of using them are discussed.

Systematic Samples

A sampling frame usually takes the form of an organized list of cases alphabetized by name, arranged chronologically, or arranged by some other characteristic (such as age). If for some reason the list cannot be sampled randomly, a **systematic sample** may be drawn by selecting some interval (such as every twentieth case) from which to draw sample cases. The interval selected determines what proportion of the cases in the population will appear in the sample. Thus, every twentieth case will provide a sample of 5% of the cases in the population.

For the sake of illustration, assume that the file folders of all 2,000 clients of a social service agency are arranged alphabetically in a set of file cabinets. If it were decided that a sample of size 100 of the 2,000 clients was to be drawn in order to provide interviewees for a study, then the **sampling interval** would be computed as 2,000/100 = 20. Thus, every 20th file folder in the drawers would be selected (the 20th, 40th, 60th, etc.). Note that the resulting sample would *not* be a random sample because the particular cases drawn for the sample would depend on the system used to arrange the file folders in the drawers, the interval used to sample them, and the starting point used for determining which file folders were in the proper interval. File folders that did not happen to fall on the interval selected would have *no chance whatsoever* of being included in the sample, and those on the interval would be *certain* to be included. Therefore, there would be no legitimate basis for estimating sampling error.

A variation of the systematic sampling technique introduces an element of probability into the selection of cases for the sample. This variation is called a **systematic sample with a random start.** For example, if the decision is made to select every twentieth file in the list, the starting point for the interval might be determined randomly. Thus, a number between 1 and 20 might be selected randomly as a starting point for drawing sample cases, and the remaining cases might be set at the interval of 20 following the location of the first case. If the random number drawn happened to be 13, for example, then that would be the first case in the sample and the other cases would be arrived at by adding 20 each time to the number of the last case. The second case, therefore, would be the thirty-third, the next would be the fifty-third, and so on.

This random start procedure has the effect of dividing the cases in the population into a number of sets, each with an equal probability of constituting the sample. If the interval being used is 20, then there are 20 sets of cases or 20 different samples that might be drawn. Which set is drawn for the sample depends on the first number drawn randomly and the size of the interval to be sampled. In this example, the set consists of case 13 and every case in the population separated by an interval of 20, starting with that thirteenth case. The 20 sets (or potential samples) would be those beginning with the first case, the second case, and so on through the set beginning with the twentieth case. Each of these 20 sets of cases would have 1 chance out of 20 of being the sample set; therefore, each individual case in the population would have 1 chance out of 20 of being included in the sample drawn.

Although the random start provides a basis for assigning a probability of selection to the cases in the sampling frame, it does not solve some of the basic problems involved in systematic sampling. For example, the arrangement of the cases in the list might be a biasing factor that would produce a sample that was unrepresentative of the population. If the list was arranged alphabetically by name, there could be a bias in the nationalities of the subjects because the first letters of the surnames of some nationalities tend to be concentrated in just a few letters of the alphabet, whereas those of other nationalities are widely spread across the alphabet. If both spouses in a couple should have a chance of being drawn in the sample, an alphabetical list might present problems because spouses tend to share the same surname, so their names would be likely to be near each other or even adjacent to each other in the list. A list arranged chronologically might also present problems of bias. Depending on how the cases in the list were spread across time, cases falling on the sampling interval might overrepresent certain times of the month or the year and underrepresent others. For example, this would happen in sampling a chronological list of elections in which all presidential elections could be included or omitted, depending on the starting date and the sampling interval (4 years).

Obviously a researcher must look critically at a list to be used for a systematic sample to try to determine whether the arrangement of the cases in the list presents problems. If the cases in the list are randomly arranged, then a systematic sample of that list is the equivalent of a random sample. Unfortunately, it is seldom the case that the list to be sampled is randomly arranged.

Quota Samples

A second type of nonrandom sample is the **quota sample**. To execute a quota sample it is necessary to determine how variables relevant to the study being conducted are distributed in the population. This can often be determined by consulting census data or other research conducted earlier on the same population. Once the distributions of relevant variables are determined and the sample size is decided upon, specifications for sampling are prepared and distributed to interviewers. Thus, a given interviewer might be told to find 10 married women between the ages of 40 and 45 to interview. Finding respondents who fit these criteria is left to the initiative or convenience of the interviewer.

Perhaps an example of a quota sample design will clarify what is involved in the technique. Assume that a researcher is to conduct a study of the inhabitants of a city to determine their attitudes toward the police force. It is decided that the respondents of the survey should match the population with respect to gender, ethnic group, and age distributions. By consulting the latest census data, the researcher might find that 53% of the inhabitants are female; 15% are Black, 20% are Hispanic, and 65% are White; 30% are young, 50% are middle-aged, and 20%

are old. Given this information and having decided that the sample should include 500 respondents, the researcher could draw up a list of specifications for interviewers that would guide them in finding respondents. Thus, an interviewer who is to interview 25 respondents might be directed to find 25 who are middle-aged White women. These specifications would be assigned to the interviewers so that when all of the interviews are completed the sample will match the population proportions on age, ethnic group, and gender.

A properly drawn quota sample may give accurate estimates of the parameters of interest in the population sampled. The problem is that because the technique is nonrandom, it is not possible to estimate sampling error legitimately. Unless there is final feedback, as in an election poll, it is not possible to judge the accuracy of estimates the sample statistics provide.

Furthermore, the efficiency of the quota sample depends on astute selection of the variables used to provide specification criteria for the interviewers. If the variables used are not relevant to the study or if equally or more important variables are overlooked, the sample may turn out to be a distorted representation of the population sampled.

A particularly risky aspect of the quota sample design is allowing interviewers to find the subjects of the study on their own. There is no assurance that the interviewers will make any attempt to find respondents who are representative of the population. Rather, they may seek out those who are most accessible, those who are concentrated in a small geographical area (e.g., a mall or section of a city), or those who are most willing to cooperate in answering questions.

Snowball Sampling

In some situations it is not possible to acquire a sampling frame to represent a population. This is often the case when the population of interest engages in some sort of deviant behavior. For example, if one were interested in studying swingers (couples who exchange sex partners with other couples), it would be difficult to find an extensive sampling frame. One might be able to contact a swingers' club and seek to collect data from the club's members, but the club might have a very small membership and there might be a suspicion that the members of that particular club are not very representative of the larger population of swingers.

An alternative would be to execute a **snowball sample** of swingers. A snowball sample is accomplished by finding one case from the population of interest, collecting data from that case, and then having the respondent (or respondents) from that case refer the researcher to one or more other cases. Once the second case is contacted and interviewed, the respondent from that case is asked to refer the researcher to additional cases. Thus, the researcher goes from one case to another, being referred each time to additional cases that belong to the population of interest. Once the researcher exhausts the cases available or decides that he or she has enough interviews to proceed with the data analysis, the sampling is discontinued. This technique makes it possible to obtain data from subjects who would otherwise not be accessible to the researcher. However, it should be remembered that a snowball sample is not equivalent to a random sample. Hence, there is no assurance that the subjects from whom the data are collected are representative of the population of interest. Consequently, a snowball sample should not be used if it is possible to obtain a random sample.

Other Nonrandom Sampling Techniques

In addition to the three nonrandom sampling techniques just mentioned, other types are found in the literature. One type of nonrandom sample is an **analytic sample,** which may be a case or a small set of cases that are selected because they fit some analytic specifications. They may be a classic example of some phenomenon or a current instance of a rare phenomenon (e.g., a prototypical small town or a tornado disaster). Case studies often select a case or a few contrasting cases because of their theoretical relevance. An in-depth analysis of the cases may provide useful description, an example of the operation of some principle, or a basis for elaborating hypotheses for future testing.

Another type of nonrandom sample is what might be called the **convenience sample.** This technique uses cases that are available without regard to the question of their representativeness. When interviewers in a shopping mall stop passersby and ask them to participate in a survey (perhaps of their breakfast cereal preferences), chances are that the agency sponsoring the interviews is a market research company compiling a convenience sample. This type of research is aimed at collecting data that can be used to satisfy the terms of a contract with some company and provide the company with information about the popularity of its product. Often there is little concern about whether the data are representative of the population of current or potential purchasers of the company's product.

In fairness it should be noted that companies that put interviewers in shopping malls sometimes give them guidelines as to whom they are supposed to interview. Thus, interviewers may be given specifications with respect to the personal characteristics of the people they are supposed to interview. This results in a sample that has many of the characteristics of a quota sample, with the difference that the interviewers are assigned to specific locations from which they must find their subjects.

Shere Hite used another version of the nonrandom sample to collect data on the sexual behavior of American women (Hite, 1976). She describes the distribution of her questionnaire as follows:

> Great effort was put into mailing and distribution of the questionnaires in an attempt to reach as many different kinds of women, with as many different points of view, as possible. Early distribution was done through national mailings to women's groups, including chapters of the National Organization for Women, abortion rights groups, university women's centers, and women's newsletters. Soon after, notices in *The Village Voice, Mademoiselle, Brides,* and *Ms.* magazines informed readers that they could write in for the questionnaires, and later there were also notices placed in dozens of church newsletters. In addition, *Oui* magazine

ran the questionnaire in its entirety, and 253 replies were received from its women readers. Finally, the paperback *Sexual Honesty by Women for Women,* which contains forty-five complete early replies, has asked readers to send in their own replies since its publication in 1974. All in all, one hundred thousand questionnaires were distributed, and slightly over three thousand returned (more or less the standard rate of return for this kind of questionnaire distribution). (1976:xxi)

Even though Hite received completed questionnaires from 3,019 women (a sizable sample), one might legitimately ask whether women who belong to the organizations to which she sent questionnaires or who read the magazines, newsletters, and the book from which she solicited respondents are representative of American women and whether the 3,019 women who filled out the questionnaires are even representative of those to whom the questionnaires were distributed. In a follow-up of the original study, Hite also distributed questionnaires to organizations (Hite, 1987). As she explains,

Clubs and organizations through which questionnaires were distributed included church groups in thirty-four states, women's voting and political groups in nine states, women's rights organizations in thirty-nine states, professional women's groups in twenty-two states, counseling and walk-in centers for women or families in forty-three states, and a wide range of other organizations, such as senior citizens' homes and disabled people's organizations, in various states.

In addition, individual women did write for copies of the questionnaire using both the address given in my previous works and an address given by interview programs on television and in the press. . . . All in all, one hundred thousand questionnaires were distributed, and four thousand five hundred were returned. (1987:777)

She touted her 4.5% rate of return as "almost twice as high as the standard rate of return for this kind of questionnaire distribution" (1987:777). She states, "A probability method of sampling might have yielded a higher rate of return, but then an essay questionnaire would not have been possible" (1987:777). This statement is followed shortly by another curious statement: "But an even more important reason for not using random sampling methods for this study is that a random sample cannot be anonymous; the individuals chosen clearly understand that their names and addresses are on file" (1987:778).

It appears that Hite goes to great trouble to justify a nonrandom sampling technique so that the reader will be left with the impression that her findings have much wider generality than they deserve.

Evaluation of Nonrandom Samples

Nonrandom samples such as the ones just described are common. There are times when it is not possible to draw a random sample; in such cases a nonrandom sample might be preferred to no sample (and no data) at all.

Because there are no legitimate techniques for estimating sampling error from nonrandom samples, there is no basis for inference to larger populations. Generalizability is sacrificed as a trade-off. It should be kept in mind that the principal reason for sampling is to use the sample data to make inferences about a population. Therefore, whenever feasible, random samples should be drawn. Unfortunately, however, nonrandom samples are often used in lieu of random samples because they are cheaper or easier to execute. These are not valid reasons for using nonrandom sampling techniques.

When random sampling is not feasible, if the study is still pursued using nonrandom sampling, the results of data analysis are limited in application to the subjects who contributed the data. Of course, it is legitimate to describe the subjects of the study in terms of personal characteristics, but this does not ensure that they are even representative of other people who share those same characteristics.

SAMPLE SIZE

A question often asked is, "How large does a sample need to be in order to be representative of the population?" The obvious answer seems to be "The bigger, the better." However, it must be remembered that one purpose of sampling is to get representative data at a reasonable cost. Each additional case sampled adds to the cost of the overall sample. In fact, there is a point of diminishing returns in sampling whereby each additional case beyond a certain point adds smaller and smaller increments to the accuracy with which the sample data estimate the population data. Consequently, it does not pay to increase sample size indiscriminately.

Typical national opinion polls are based on approximately 1,500 cases. When such polls are used to predict national election results, for example, the sample size used can be seen to be a very small segment of the total electorate. Nevertheless, sampling error for such polls is often as small as plus or minus 3 percentage points. This is so because the size of the sampling error does not depend on the proportion of the total population included in the sample.[6] Rather, the sheer number of cases in the sample affects the size of the sampling error (Loether and McTavish, 1993:388, 416–17). Therefore, it is generally the case that the larger the sample is, the smaller the sampling error will be. Because the efficiency in sampling and inference comes from making satisfactory estimates from samples that are small segments of the populations sampled, it is in the interest of the researcher to draw a sample large enough to suit the purposes of the study, but not any larger than needed.

Three important considerations in determining needed sample size are the degree of sampling error tolerable in making inferences from the sample to the population, the number of cases needed in order to carry out the data analysis nec-

[6]An exception to this rule occurs when the sample is nearly an enumeration of the whole finite population, in which case sampling error becomes less. This can be taken into account by a finite population correction factor described in many statistics books.

essary to test the hypotheses of the study, and the response rate or percentage of those sampled who end up providing data.

The tolerance level in sampling error depends on what is being studied. For example, if the purpose of the research is to predict an election result, a 3% sampling error is tolerable in a campaign in which the two candidates are widely separated in popularity, but it might be considered too large in a closely contested campaign. If one candidate were leading the other in a poll by 10%, even with a 3% error it would be fairly clear that the leading candidate had a comfortable margin. On the other hand, if the poll results gave 51% of the vote to one candidate and 49% to the other, a 3% error would be too large to enable the pollster to predict who really had more support.

Thus, the researcher must decide what a tolerable level of sampling error is for the particular study being undertaken. Once a decision is made on how much sampling error can be tolerated it may be possible to compute the necessary sample size. In order to do this, it is necessary to be able to gauge the degree of homogeneity of the population being sampled. If it is possible to estimate how homogeneous the cases in the population are, then this information can be entered into an estimation formula, along with the maximum tolerable sampling error, to solve for sample size (Loether and McTavish, 1993:496–99).

Table 5.1 shows the effect of sample size on sampling error for percentages, assuming that an SRS has been used. Notice that the sampling error gets smaller when the population percentage in question is further from a 50%–50% split. Sampling error is also larger for smaller samples. If we expected a 51% to 49% split in voting for two candidates, for example, we would need a sample of size 10,000 to reduce the sampling error down to .5%, which might be needed to predict a very close election outcome.

With respect to the second consideration mentioned—the planned analysis of data—the more elaborate the data analysis, the more sample cases are required to do the analysis. If a simple univariate or bivariate level of analysis is planned, then a small sample may be adequate. However, if the researcher intends to do a multivariate analysis, then more cases will be required because the data must be spread

**TABLE 5.1   Random Sampling Error as a Function of
Selected Population Percentages and Sample Sizes**

SAMPLE SIZE	ANTICIPATED POPULATION PERCENTAGE				
	90%	70%	50%	30%	10%
10	9.5%	14.5%	15.8%	14.5%	9.5%
50	4.2	6.5	7.1	6.5	4.2
100	3.0	4.6	5.0	4.6	3.0
1000	0.9	1.4	1.6	1.4	0.9
10000	0.3	0.46	0.5	0.46	0.3

over more score categories of the variables being analyzed. As mentioned earlier in this chapter, a study of attitudes toward capital punishment that compared the responses of subjects classified by their religion, gender, and age would require a sample large enough to distribute the cases over all of the cells in the tables used for the analysis. Given two response categories on capital punishment, two for gender, three religious categories (Protestants, Catholics, and Jews), and three age categories (young, middle-aged, and old), there would need to be enough cases in the sample to distribute over 36 different combinations of scores, or 36 cells in the tables used for analysis of the data (the number of cells is the product of the number of categories of the variables, here, $2 \times 2 \times 3 \times 3 = 36$). If all variables in the study were evenly distributed, it would take a minimum of 720 cases to get 20 cases in each of the 36 cells. Given that variables are not generally evenly distributed, a considerably larger sample size would need to be used.

Response rates from samples vary by the way in which data gathering is approached. In well-done surveys, a response rate of 70% to 80% is achievable, but poorly done studies or studies of difficult topics and populations may result in considerably lower response rates. As we shall see in later chapters, nonresponse is generally not a random behavior on the part of subjects. Thus, samples with high nonresponse are likely to reflect biases in addition to reducing the desired sample size. Researchers take account of expected nonresponse and boost the sample size so that the achieved sample size is sufficient for their analysis.

It should be obvious that the decision about the size of sample needed for a study is not simple. It requires careful consideration and much advanced planning of all stages of the research project, including data analysis, to determine an adequate sample size. Computer programs called expert systems are available to help an investigator think through factors that affect sample size in the process of determining how many cases to draw (Brent, Scott, and Spencer, 1988).

SUMMARY

When population data are available for study, it is possible to reach conclusions about the population directly. The purpose of a sample is to collect data from a representative portion of the population of interest and use those data to make inferences about that population. Random selection of the cases in a sample provides a basis for measuring sampling error and using that information for making inferences about population characteristics that are not directly observable.

The basic random sampling technique is the simple random sample (SRS), in which every case in the population has an equal probability of being sampled and every sample of a given size has an equal probability of being the sample selected for study. SRSs are drawn with replacement. Random samples drawn without replacement are also used and, if the population being sampled is very large in comparison to the size of the sample drawn, then there is little difference between the random sample drawn without replacement and that drawn with. However, random sampling with replacement is generally preferred unless specific reasons necessitate sampling without replacement.

Because an SRS requires a single sampling frame, it is sometimes not possible to draw an SRS. In lieu of an SRS, a random cluster sample may be drawn because it is feasible when the SRS is not. The random cluster sample is essentially a multi-stage random sample, drawn through a series of accessible sampling frames.

Another alternative is the stratified random sample. Although stratified random samples often have smaller sampling errors than SRSs, they are usually harder to accomplish because the technique requires more information about the population than the SRS. The primary stratified random sampling technique involves sampling proportionate to the presence of sampled characteristics in the population. Variations on this primary technique include the disproportionate stratified random sample and the optimum allocation stratified random sample.

Alternatives to random samples include such nonrandom sampling techniques as systematic samples (with or without a random start), quota samples, snowball samples, and convenience samples. These techniques all share the shortcoming of lacking a basis for estimating sampling error; therefore, they do not support generalization to a population. Nonrandom samples are generally frowned on as sampling techniques except in cases in which random sampling of any kind is not a viable alternative and a more limited description of sample data is acceptable.

Determining the optimum sample size for a study is a somewhat complicated procedure that depends on how large a sampling error can be tolerated and how elaborate the data analysis contemplated will be. The goal is to select a sample large enough to suit the requirements of the study being undertaken but not so large as to waste research resources.

Random sampling and inference are two closely related processes, and one should not be undertaken without the other. Studies in which nonrandom samples are used as a basis for inference should be looked on with suspicion.

Even when a random sample is used as a basis for inference, it is necessary to ask whether the population sampled is the appropriate one for the study being conducted. A crucial consideration in any research is whether the target population studied, either directly or inferentially, is the one to which the researcher wants to apply the findings.

TERMS TO KNOW

Achieved sample
Analytic sample
Convenience sample
Disproportionate stratified random
   sample
Enumeration
Finite (limited) population

Inference
Infinite population
Multistage random sample
Nonrandom sample
Optimum allocation sampling
Parameter
Population

Population elements
Primary sampling unit
Probability sample
Probability theory
Proportionate stratified random sample
Quota sample
Random cluster sample
Random numbers
Random sample
Random selection
Representative sample
Response rate
Sample
Sample size
Sampling error

Sampling frame
Sampling interval
Sampling theory
Simple random sample (SRS)
Snowball sample
Statistic
Strata
Stratified random sample
Systematic sample
Systematic sample with a random start
Ultimate sampling unit
Weighting
Without replacement
With replacement

ISSUES AND COMPARISONS

Strengths of random sampling
Logic of inference about populations on the basis of samples
How to draw a simple random sample from a finite population
Problems in creating an accurate sampling frame
Advantages and disadvantages of different kinds of samples

EXERCISES

1. Discuss the pros and cons of using a telephone directory as the sampling frame for a study of city residents' attitudes about their community's public services (e.g., fire, police, parks, streets, and other public programs).

2. Design a sampling procedure that would enable one to compare the number of hours worked per week for minority and majority men and women in your college's freshman class. What are its strengths and limitations?

REFERENCES

Brent, Edward E., Jr., James K. Scott, and John C. Spencer, *EX-SAMPLE, An Expert System to Assist in Designing Sampling Plans,* Idea Works, Columbia, MO, 1988.

Burgess, E. W., and P. Wallin, "Homogamy in Social Characteristics," *American Journal of Sociology* 1943;49:109–24.

Hadaway, Kirk, Penny Long Marler, and Mark Chaves, "What the Polls Don't Show: A Closer Look at U.S. Church Attendance," *American Sociological Review* December 1993;58(6):741–52.

Hagood, Margaret Jarman, and Daniel O. Price, *Statistics for Sociologists,* revised ed., Holt, New York, 1952.

Hite, Shere, *The Hite Report,* Macmillan, New York, 1976.

Hite, Shere, *Women and Love: A Cultural Revolution in Progress*, Knopf, New York, 1987.

Kish, Leslie, *Survey Sampling*, Wiley, New York, 1965.

Loether, Herman J., and Donald G. McTavish, *Descriptive and Inferential Statistics: An Introduction*, 4th ed., Allyn & Bacon, Boston, 1993.

Meiksins, Peter F., and James M. Watson, "Professional Autonomy and Organizational Constraint: The Case of Engineers," *Sociological Quarterly* 1989;30(4):561–85.

Spenner, Kenneth, "Deciphering Prometheus: Temporal Change in the Skill Level of Work," *American Sociological Review* December 1983;48:824–37.

CHAPTER 7

SURVEY RESEARCH

Surveys are a common method of data collection in the United States today. There are many polling organizations, which act as independent businesses or as units within newspapers, government agencies, and universities. By now the U.S. public knows what to expect of polls and surveys. For example, one university-based survey organization conducts an annual survey of households in the state in which it is located to find out about a variety of topics of interest to academic researchers and various other agencies that submit questions for the survey. Topics such as gambling, quality of life, public issues, community, the media, and awareness of different organizations are included, in addition to background and demographic questions such as age, marital status, gender, residential area, social class, and work status.

Survey organizations such as this university-based one typically invest considerable effort in creating a schedule of questions to be asked and conduct a number of trial interviews to test the procedure and question wording. Then the survey is started. This particular survey targets a random sample of households throughout the state and conducts telephone interviews using a staff of trained interviewers in a central university location. A sample of phone numbers to call is purchased from a company that specializes in supplying updated lists of this sort. Interviewers call each number, identify a randomly selected member of the household who is 18 years of age or older (those in institutions such as college dorms, nursing homes, or prisons are excluded from this survey), and then complete an interview schedule. There is a routine for calling back (up to six times) those who do not answer the phone the first time. Interviewing takes several weeks.

In a recent Minnesota household survey, about 2,300 phone numbers were called, of which 1,228 were potential or actual interviews (some refused and some numbers were still active on the callback list by the interviewing deadline). Of the original 2,300 phone numbers used, nearly half (40%) were not households, were not working telephone numbers, or were disconnected. A few were omitted because of language problems or because there was no response after six attempted calls. Overall, 65% of the potential interviews were completed (response rates of 70% to 85% or more are desired and generally achievable with careful follow-up).

In this case, each interviewer sat in front of a computer that automatically presented questions in the proper order and allowed the interviewer to enter answers directly into a computer file (the system is called **computer-assisted telephone interviewing**, or **CATI**). This step is done using a printed schedule filled in by hand when a CATI system is not available. Then the actual interview schedules are assigned a case identification number and edited for completeness, and responses are coded, usually numerically; then data are entered into a computer file for statistical analysis.

From an analysis of these data they are able to say, for example, that 39% of the households were two-person households, 62% would like to work at home at least part of the time, and 52% agree that one of their greatest fears is being financially dependent on their family in old age (Armson, 1997). Within margins of sampling error, the results presumably describe views characteristic of Minnesota households at the time the survey was conducted.

This study is illustrative of the kinds of survey research designs, techniques, and issues involved in surveys that are discussed in this chapter. We start with a discussion of four important principles that underlie the choice of survey research designs.

PRINCIPLES

Like other research strategies, surveys have distinctive features that focus much of the investigator's attention and effort. In survey research, four principles tend to be at the center of planning efforts: representativeness, time, competing explanations,

"*A recent survey showed that ninety-five per cent of the nation's high-school students had never heard of Costa Rica, but they all knew about yours truly!*"

and the distinctive data-gathering social encounters of survey research. These are considered in turn.

Representativeness

Surveys generally strive to represent a defined population, such as all households in Minnesota in 1996 or all adults in the United States in 1990 or all manufacturing firms in New York in 1997. To do this, a sample is drawn from a defined population of cases of interest. The sample is usually a random sample or one that approximates a random sample, giving each unit in the population a known (often equal) chance of being included in the sample. Sample outcomes are usually described statistically, using procedures of inferential statistics, and findings from the sample are generalized to stand as a description of the entire target population. Chapter 5 describes how this is possible, and statistics books also describe the inferential logic behind random sampling. Box 7.1 reviews the argument.

Survey research designs represent a different research trade-off than the experimental research designs discussed in Chapter 6. Surveys are very good at generalizing a description of characteristics that are measured on a carefully drawn sample of cases. Emphasis is placed on attaining results that are representative of a larger, defined population of cases. Recall from Chapter 6 that representativeness (external validity) is one of the weaknesses of typical experimental designs. Thus, survey designs are a welcome addition to the investigator's toolkit. Surveys, like other methods, have their own strengths and weaknesses.

As described in Chapter 5, surveys stress defining the case (i.e., unit of analysis) and the population to which results are to be generalized, identifying a sampling frame that accurately lists members of the population, and then drawing a suitably sized sample by random sampling (or other probability sampling) procedures. Problems in drawing a sample generally revolve around finding an

■ ■ ■ ■ ■ ▬▬

BOX 7.1

ON THE INFERENTIAL ARGUMENT

An investigator's educated guess from very little data may be correct. Conclusions based on a carefully drawn random sample also may be incorrect. The problem is that an investigator needs to show how the conclusion is reached: *How* does one know what one claims to know? The value of a random sample (or one derived from another probability sampling procedure) from a population is that it provides criteria for making generalizations and helps an investigator assess the risks of making false generalizations. This line of reasoning has proved useful in reaching conclusions that others can replicate. Educated guesses generally do not provide a basis for replication by others and are thus less desirable as a way to support generalizations about a broader population.

accurate and up-to-date **sampling frame** from which to draw a sample and engaging respondents sufficiently so that the **nonresponse rate** is very small in order to minimize the chance of ending up with a biased sample. There are other ways of sampling (e.g., cluster samples, multistage samples, stratified samples) that help implement the process of drawing a representative sample with a sufficiently small sampling error (see Chapter 5). Questionnaire design, interviewer training, and follow-up procedures that we discuss in this chapter help minimize nonresponse.

Time

Survey research generally is conducted at one point in time and thus is called a **cross-sectional design** (surveys may take weeks to complete, but respondents are generally asked questions at only one point in time). In the symbols used in Chapter 6, a survey design would be expressed as

$$x \quad O$$

Only one observation or measurement occasion is used. In this case, any x (treatment or causes, known or unknown) will have had its impact before the survey is conducted and, in any event, is generally not under the control of the investigator. Surveys thus must ask about the state of independent variables (the x) at the same time that the dependent variables are measured because it is generally not known ahead of time what prior experiences or treatments cases have had. Some information that may help establish time order can be gathered by using retrospective questions, asking the respondent about some event in the past (such as "Was your mother working outside the home when you were sixteen?"), although current circumstances may color reporting of past events.

Sometimes the survey design can track changes over time by including repeated surveys of the same respondents; this design is called a **panel study**. Alternatively, a series of samples might be used, sampling different cases that are nevertheless drawn from a similarly defined sampling frame at one or more later points in time (a **trend study**). Thus, in the United States one can identify trends in attitudes toward the police, for example, by examining successive national surveys that measure this variable. Yet each survey is a time-slice, like a frame in a motion picture. Surveys provide a good description of the state of some variable at some point in time but generally give a poorer picture of the details of an ongoing social process. Time order is especially important in studies that attempt to explain outcomes by identifying factors that may influence or produce certain outcomes under certain conditions, or studies of social processes.

Can surveys be experiments? It is sometimes possible to use a true experimental design in survey research. This would happen when the stimulus is given to a random subset of those surveyed. For example, studies of question order or question wording might involve randomly using different forms of a questionnaire. In this case, the researcher has control of the time order (e.g., question ordering, then the subject's response) and over whom is given the experimental stimulus (e.g., respondents getting questions in one order versus another), a central requirement for experimental designs.

Competing Explanations

Although survey designs are excellent for descriptive generalizations at one point in time, they are problematic for explanatory research. If investigators expect that family type (coming from a divorced home rather than an intact family) has some impact on juvenile delinquency, they could ask in a survey what type of home the respondent came from, and they could ask about participation in delinquency. Then the researcher could determine whether the association of home type and delinquency is statistically significant (see Chapter 6 for a definition of this term). Even assuming that these variables are accurately measured, it would be difficult to claim that type of home causes delinquency. Why?

You will recall that a causal claim needs three kinds of evidence. First, there must be a correlation between the cause and its effect (which may be shown in survey research data); second, the cause must occur *before* the effect in that time order; third, there can be no other competing (alternative) explanations that account for the findings. Survey research has problems providing data for the latter two requirements (time order or causal order, and competing explanations).

First, surveys typically measure all variables at the same time. Thus, it is difficult to determine whether the measured cause occurred before its outcome. In some cases this problem can be handled by looking at what is plausible. For example, if one asked whether the subject's parents were divorced when the respondent was 16 (a retrospective question), one might expect these data to represent accurately the true state of affairs at a point in the past. This would be reasonable even though the question was answered at a later time. But memory could be a problem, and there may be other reasons for giving a false answer to the question. Retrospective questioning works well for such things as "How old were you when you graduated from high school?" and less well when you ask "How did you feel about your parents' marriage before you knew they were divorcing?" Therefore, retrospective questioning poses problems that must be considered.

As Davis (1985) points out, there may be other logical bases for establishing a probable time order of variables. For example, graduation from college comes after graduation from high school, a respondent's parents' first jobs probably came before the respondent's first job, gender socialization usually comes before current views on how best to get a job, religious background might come before one's current attitude toward the death penalty, and being married may or may not come before having a child. But what about work status and job skills ("Do you have a journalism job?" and "Are you good at spelling?"). Notice that the time order is sometimes tenuous when it is based only on reasoning rather than direct measurements. Experimental designs that control when a treatment is introduced and then measure the outcome at a later time make the time order of cause and effect much clearer.

The second problem for survey research, handling alternative explanations of findings, is even more serious. Typically, in experiments both the time order and alternative explanations problems are eliminated by the way the research is designed. The investigator controls when the causal variable (treatment) is introduced and when outcomes are measured, and eliminates alternative explanations by random assignment of cases to experimental and control groups (see Chapter 6). In survey research, such controls are typically not possible. Whatever has caused a measured response by a subject has already occurred, along with many other things. The investigator does not know which of these possible events led to the measured outcomes. In order to rule out alternative explanations, the investigator must develop a strategy to control for these other possible effects. In survey research, this is attempted by using **statistical controls.**

For example, if an investigator finds that boys' self-esteem continues to rise throughout high school but girls' self-esteem does not rise as steadily, the investigator would want to control statistically for other things that might have produced different growth rates of self-esteem. Did the girls come from larger families than the boys? To check this, one could divide the sample into those who came from large families and those who came from small families and see whether the difference in self-esteem development between boys and girls is still evident, controlling for family size. Would intact versus broken families account for differences in self-esteem of boys and girls? Maybe the difference can be explained by the different types of school systems through which the boys and girls traveled. The number of alternative explanations of the findings may be quite large. To do this kind of dividing up into subgroups that are similar on some potential causal variable, the survey must ask questions about each of these potential explanatory variables so they can be statistically controlled. Surveys tend to be longer if there is an explanatory interest because the investigator must ask about all possible alternative explanations. This process is limited, of course, to factors that the investigator can think of or are suggested by relevant literature on the topic. In any event, resources and the length of the questionnaire usually limit the number of potential explanatory variables that can be included. This means that surveys can never be definitive about whether a particular "cause" is really the cause of some outcome. By contrast, experimental research, by random assignment of cases to control and experimental groups, provides greater assurance about whether a particular variable is a potential cause of some outcome (at least for the cases in the experiment).

A strength of survey research is that it can begin to address questions for which experimental manipulation of cases is not possible. One could not randomly assign people to different genders, and even if it were possible, one probably would not randomly assign people to different careers. Practical considerations and ethical norms prevent experimental research on many important research problems. The survey research approach, by statistically accounting for at least the potential alternative explanations that theory or creative insight suggest, permits serious explanatory research on many of the important research questions that social scientists investigate.

The Social Context of the Data-Gathering Encounter

Data are always gathered in some type of social encounter. Social encounters generally involve expectations, certain skills, and various social pressures that may affect the data. This is as true of survey research as of every other type of social science research (and probably all research). What type of social encounter is generally involved in survey research, and what are its consequences?

Survey research usually involves asking questions rather than observing as a way of measuring concepts. Questions are formed, ideally in an understandable and standard way, and posed for the respondent. The encounter is generally a one-time, fairly brief affair between strangers. A minimal level of confidence and trust must be established, and the respondent must feel that it is sufficiently worthwhile to participate in the question-and-answer episode and provide accurate information. Three general data-gathering encounters are typical of survey research: personal interviews, phone interviews, and mailed questionnaires (with a range of other variations).

Personal Interviews.   The **personal interview** is an encounter in which an interviewer (someone who is acceptable to the respondent, often a middle-aged woman who is similar in background to the respondent) asks questions and records answers. This encounter usually takes place in the respondent's own location (e.g., at home, work, in school, or on the street). Interviewers often try to find situations that are calm, when the respondent is alone and distractions are minimized. The interviewer has been trained in personal interviewing and is experienced in asking questions and recording answers. The list of questions is called an **interview schedule,** and it often contains various notes and reminders to the interviewer that make asking questions and recording responses easy and accurate. An advantage of personal interviews is that the interviewer can clarify questions that the respondent does not readily understand and can observe the respondent during the interview.

Phone Interviews.   In the case of the phone interview, the interviewer may be located anywhere as long as a phone connection can be made with the respondent. Respondents are near phones when they are at home or at work, and this affects the time of the call. Getting a desired person on the phone may involve going through some gatekeeper who screens calls. In fact, many phones are unlisted, many people share the same telephone (some have more than one phone), and some people do not have a telephone. These facts are related to possible contaminating factors such as social class and life stage. In a more remote (but less costly) way, the interviewer must establish rapport and complete the interview. Phone etiquette may keep the respondent from abruptly hanging up. Phones also allow the interviewer (with permission) to make a good recording of an open-ended response. Again, the interviewer is equipped with an interview schedule, which often includes aids to the interviewer who makes the call and fills in responses. Phone interviews are more efficient and less expensive than personal interviews.

Mailed Questionnaires. Although questionnaires are used in many different settings, the more common one is the mailed questionnaire, which the respondent receives in the mail, reads and completes, and returns by mail. Here the encounter occurs entirely through what is said in a **cover letter** and in the questionnaire itself, as well as its general appearance. The measuring instrument is called a **questionnaire** (rather than an interview schedule) because the respondents themselves fill in the answers. The questionnaire must be clear and easy to answer. In most industrialized countries the questionnaire has become so familiar that most respondents know what to expect and how it is handled. In some communities, norms and skills for this type of data-gathering encounter have not been developed, which can pose a problem with this type of research.

Other Data-Gathering Social Encounters. A number of other settings involve surveys in one way or another. For example, as part of some other transaction, the subject may be asked questions and is expected to record answers. Other situations might be surveys sent by e-mail or asked as a part of an application form, or made available in a restaurant or business to get customer satisfaction feedback. There are many others, as well as combinations of those mentioned.

In his total design method, Dillman (1978) suggests that it is useful to think of the respondent going through a cost–benefit analysis: What are the costs of becoming involved in the survey, and is there a sufficient perceived benefit that offsets the costs? Furthermore, the respondent must have a sense of trust that the encounter is what it seems to be. Costs can include many things, such as the time it takes to respond to the survey, the inconvenience of answering at the point the respondent happens to be contacted, the survey's interest or importance to the respondent, the ease of providing responses, the extent to which offensive or intrusive questions are raised, and the annoyance of deciding whether it is really a survey or another disguised sales pitch. According to Dillman, reducing costs might involve reducing the effort of the task, eliminating embarrassment or any sense of subordination, and making the task appear brief.

Benefits are equally subtle and varied. A respondent may be particularly interested in the topic and in voicing his or her opinion about that topic. Answering survey questions may be a nice break in whatever the respondent had been doing. The respondent may simply want to help the investigator complete his or her task. It may even appear to be a very important topic to investigate. An investigator can show positive regard for the respondent, use a consulting approach, and make the survey instrument interesting, according to Dillman. Sometimes an investigator attempts to provide low-cost extra benefits such as offering to send a summary report of the results, or giving a coin, pencil, or coupon of some sort in advance for the respondent's cooperation. A professional-looking questionnaire suggests that the investigator is careful and thoughtful and considers the topic important and cares about the respondent's ease in doing the task. Statements about the investigator's intention to treat the data as confidential or anonymous, an easy-to-answer, well-thought-out instrument, friendliness, and a return envelope with postage affixed are among the many items sometimes used to address the cost–benefit equation (Dillman, 1978). Trust is developed through research sponsors who are known and felt to be legitimate and neutral. Thinking back on the questionnaires you have answered, you can probably recall what led you to decide that it was worth responding.

Investigators and their subjects can be thought of in role terms, interacting according to perceptions of the situation and norms they can draw upon. Often the subject's role changes within the same encounter from one of a subject who is providing personal information to one of an expert informant who is providing factual information about someone or something else with which he or she is familiar (e.g., from "What is your gender?" to "What are your parents' occupations?").

The point is that a survey encounter, like other approaches to research, must be carefully examined as a social event and the implications for research taken into account. The type of encounter has a strong impact on how measuring instruments are created, what types of information and research questions can be addressed through surveys, and the kinds of bias and error that are likely to occur.

Ethical Issues in Survey Research

Typical survey research on adults usually raises few ethical issues. It is usually clear that a potential subject may ignore the questionnaire or refuse to be interviewed. Subjects are generally in their own territory and thus may feel a greater sense of control than in an experimental laboratory, for example. Sensitive questions may be skipped.

There are ethical considerations in the use of subject responses, and generally assurances of **anonymity** or at least **confidentiality** are given. With surveys, particularly those by mail, anonymity can be achieved. Often the identities of organizations and individuals are avoided in reporting specific survey findings.

Survey research on minors or vulnerable adults requires greater care. For example, certain sensitive topics are generally avoided unless prior approval is obtained from responsible caretakers. Harassment during survey research is generally avoided.

Finally, the ethical responsibility to those who use study findings demands the highest standards of care and accuracy in conducting the study and fully reporting findings.

TECHNIQUES OF SURVEY RESEARCH

Survey research typically involves four steps. Beyond the usual conceptualization and problem definition and basic design steps, survey research involves

- Finding a sampling frame for the desired population and selecting a sample
- Creating suitable measurement instruments
- Gathering the desired data
- Analyzing the data and writing up the results

In many respects surveys share these steps with other forms of research. Although many types of research involve identifying a sample of cases, the contexts of survey research give rise to special problems and opportunities. Random digit dialing (RDD) and computer-assisted telephone interviewing (CATI) are two examples discussed here.

Measurement also involves many issues and concerns that are common to all research. Survey research differs in the ability to ask questions and expect good answers. For example, considerable time is devoted to planning question order and keeping the subject's task clear and simple, considering how questions are posed, how they engage the respondent, and how easy they are to answer. Special ways of gathering data may or may not be possible in survey research and, because a large number of cases are typically gathered, analyzing survey data often involves statistical analysis. At each of these steps, survey research design influences the options that are available and the typical choices researchers make. We describe each of these steps in turn.

Establishing a Sampling Frame and Selecting a Sample

Conceptualization of a problem that calls for survey research generally implies that a target population has been identified. It is to this population that sample results are intended to be generalized. Some examples of populations that have been used include adults (or households) in various-sized political units such as cities, counties, states, or the coterminous United States (i.e., the lower 48 states, excluding Alaska and Hawaii). Sometimes definitions of a population are more detailed, such as "owners of Utah firms that employed more than 50 full-time employees in 1997," "people over age 65 whose household income is under the defined poverty level," "customers of various types of services from a specific bank," "upper-income baby-boom generation women who have retired from a career," "blocks in an urban area that are ethnically mixed," or "single-parent families with school-aged children." In addition, an explicit or implicit time frame and geographic location usually define the population of interest (e.g., "firms in Utah in 1997"), which makes it a finite population. Whatever the specifics of the definition, the target population must be clearly identified. Chapter 5 deals with these topics in more detail.

Once the population is clearly defined, a sampling frame (a list that comes as close as possible to identifying all cases in the specified population) must be identified. This is where investigators need to be resourceful. There is no current list of large or specialized populations, so some strategy must be developed that will give each member of the population some known chance of being drawn in the sample.

Usually the sampling frame has some inadequacies that must be corrected. For example, one might think that the current phone directory would be an appropriate sampling frame for households in the area. Unfortunately, phone books go out of date at rates as high as a third of the entries each year. Thus, a phone book does not cover families who have recently moved in or out of the area. Furthermore, some phones are intentionally unlisted, some families do not have private phones in their names, and some families have several phone lines. Some have one or more cellular phones and may not have a listed home phone apart from these. Others have special access codes known only to acquaintances. In the United States as a whole, approximately 92% of families have a phone, but this varies by family characteristics. It is also possible for local numbers to be forwarded to nonlocal households. Finally, several special populations are not covered by phone book entries, such as people who live in group quarters or institutions (e.g., nursing homes, college dorms, prisons, shelters). Thus, phone lists are problematic and likely to be biased toward more settled, conventional, economically secure households.

So how do investigators get their sampling frames? One source is commercial organizations that keep more up-to-date lists from censuses and other public records. These organizations have staff who can collate and organize lists and make them available to researchers. Another way is to sample from a more general list but ask **screening questions,** which allow the researcher to discard those not of the type that the conceptual population calls for. Sometimes this is done in studies of older people; the researcher calls homes and asks whether anyone in the household is, say, 65 years old or older and then asks to talk with that person (or randomly samples from two or more older people in the household). Many popular surveys screen to include only adults aged 18 or older. For studies focusing on formal organizations such as the government, a church, or a firm, there are often good lists of members or customers. Some retail firms ask each customer for his or her name and phone number for their computer database. Lacking a customer or membership list, many other innovative techniques provide an approximate sampling frame. For example, a store might survey car licenses in its parking lot over time and use public records to identify car-owner names and addresses in order to contact a sample of customers.

Multistage sampling procedures are often useful in solving sampling frame problems. For example, because there are usually good lists of geographic areas but not of entire populations of individuals or households, a first stage in sampling might be to select a sample of geographic areas randomly (such as cities or counties), followed by a second stage that establishes a sampling frame of desired cases from the selected geographic areas. This makes the creation of a sampling frame more manageable even if one needs to do a field trip to identify households in the selected geographic areas for purposes of drawing a sample. If a list of households is not available in some target community, one might randomly identify city blocks and assign interviewers in the field to start at a specific point (e.g., the house on the northeast corner of a block) and proceed in a defined direction, selecting households for interviews (according to a predetermined sampling plan). This gets around the need to identify households (e.g., where an up-to-date list is not available) until the interviewer is in the field.

Another technique that telephone interviewing permits is called **random digit dialing (RDD).** A computer randomly generates telephone numbers and thus provides a random sample of those with telephones at the time of the survey. Because many numbers are not assigned or are business numbers, researchers can use lists of telephone prefixes (the first three or four digits in a telephone number) where these have been screened by a commercial list provider to eliminate unassigned numbers. The computer then randomly generates the last digits to complete the phone number. Sometimes, if a list of complete telephone numbers is available, the last digit is increased by one for the purpose of potentially including unlisted numbers and to help ensure the subject's anonymity (i.e., the interviewer would not know the identity of the respondent).

The sampling frame must be examined to ensure accuracy and determine any biases that prevent it from adequately covering the intended population. Checks include comparing survey results with preexisting data from a sampling frame list or known characteristics of the target population (e.g., using census records to compare on relevant, available characteristics such as gender, age, work status, and residential area).

Developing a Survey Instrument

As noted in Chapter 3, measurement involves conceptual clarity about the phenomenon one wants to measure and operational definitions that reliably and validly measure that concept. Different research settings dictate a somewhat different selection among possible ways of measuring any given concept.

Unlike experimental research, the typical data-gathering social encounter in survey research (i.e., telephone or face-to-face interview or a mailed survey) generally takes place in the subject's own home or work context and is a brief, one-time encounter. In most survey research situations, the investigator and the subject are strangers so the investigator must gain acceptance from the subject and establish trust sufficient for getting complete, valid, and reliable answers. Thus, the questionnaire or interview schedule must be designed to help the interviewer establish rapport with respondents. Dillman's (1978) advice on reducing perceived costs and increasing perceived benefits is an important guide to creating a survey instrument. The investigator has several tools to accomplish this goal.

Introducing the Study. Often a brief explanatory introduction is given to the subject that explains what the investigator wants (stated briefly and in a way that doesn't bias future responses), why the subject was selected, for what the data will be used, and who is sponsoring the study. A good introduction also provides cues as to how the questioning will proceed. Sometimes an introductory letter is used, sent before the researcher mails the questionnaire, makes the phone call, or arrives for the personal interview. In the case of mailed surveys, a cover letter is generally included with the questionnaire to give needed explanations.

The purpose of an introductory letter is to alert a respondent to future contacts, help establish the legitimacy of the study (e.g., by the letterhead or signature on the letter), explain the importance of the study and its consequences, explain the tasks to be done, and begin to establish rapport. An introductory letter often is a signal of respect and importance, and it often decreases the nonresponse rate.

The survey instrument is usually in the form of a questionnaire or schedule of questions to be asked, with provision for recording answers. It differs in form depending on the method of data collection (a mailed questionnaire, a personal interview schedule, or a phone interview schedule). Whatever the form, the survey instrument includes measures of the study's dependent variables, the independent variables, and any other variables that may be an alternative explanation or may help in controlling or identifying important conditions affecting the relationship of independent and dependent variables. This list of variables is limited only by the purposes of the research, suggestions found in the literature, and the investigator's ideas.

Asking Good Questions. The survey instrument reflects the hypotheses and topics an investigator is pursuing. The temptation is to include things one is curious about even if they don't relate to the key purpose of the study. Good survey instruments are limited to the concepts that must be measured. To accomplish this, Labaw (1980) suggests that the investigator write down the reasoning and use of each potential question (i.e., questions and rationales side by side in two columns on a page) during the instrument development phase. The reasoning column is not included in the questionnaire, of course. If each question has a purpose, the overall questionnaire is likely to be efficient and effective.

Osgood (1957) identifies a number of ways questions can be asked that involve somewhat different tasks for the respondent and provide somewhat different kinds of information. Chapter 3 shows some of the alternatives Osgood identifies. One could ask respondents to

Rank a small set of items in terms of some criterion

Accept or reject (yes or no) an item in terms of his or her own opinions or internal standards

Indicate (on a scale) the degree to which he or she judges an item to approach some standard

Choose one or more items from a list, expressing his or her judgment of appropriateness for some purpose

Provide his or her own characterization of something posed by the researcher, as in writing down a word or paragraph or giving a verbal response in an open-ended way

Match one or more items in terms of some standard

Questions can be asked about attitudes, beliefs, events, behavior, and characteristics, as illustrated here.

ATTITUDES
1. How much of the time do you think you can trust the government in Washington to do what is right: just about always, most of the time, only some of the time, or almost never?
   1. Just about always
   2. Most of the time
   3. Only some of the time
   4. Almost never

2. Please tell me how much you agree or disagree with the following statement:
   "The success of my organization depends a lot on how well I do my job."
   1. Strongly agree
   2. Agree
   3. Disagree
   4. Strongly disagree

BELIEFS

3. Do you feel that the quality of life is better in America than in most other
   advanced industrial countries or about the same, or do you feel that people
   are better off in most other advanced industrial countries than they are in the
   United States?
   1. Better in America
   2. About the same
   3. Better in other advanced industrial countries
   4. Don't know
   5. No answer
   6. Not applicable

4. Do you believe that there is life elsewhere in the universe beyond the earth?
   1. Yes
   2. No
   3. Don't know

5. In your opinion, who should be most responsible for paying the cost of an
   aged parent's medical care, including mental health care and treatment?
   1. The person him/herself
   2. His/her family
   3. Government
   4. Insurance
   5. Private charity
   6. Don't know
   7. No answer
   8. Not applicable

EVENTS

6. Did you have a paying job last week?
   1. Yes
   2. No

7. The following questions are about your sister. If you have more than one
   adult sister, please think about the sister you have most contact with. How
   often did you see or visit with your sister in the past 12 months?
   _____ number of times in last 12 months

8. Sometimes at work people find themselves the object of sexual advances,
   propositions, or unwanted sexual discussions from coworkers or supervi-

sors. The advances sometimes involve physical contact and sometimes just involve sexual conversations. Has this ever happened to you?

1. Yes
2. No
3. Never have worked

BEHAVIOR

9. Listed on this card [in the personal interview, a card was shown to the subject] are examples of the many different areas in which people do volunteer activity. By volunteer activity I mean *not* just belonging to a service organization, but actually working in some way to help others for no monetary pay. In which, if any, of the areas listed on this card have you done some volunteer work in the past 12 months?

☐ health
☐ education
☐ religious organizations
☐ human services
☐ environment
☐ public/society benefit
☐ recreation: adults

☐ arts, culture, and humanities
☐ work-related organizations
☐ political organizations or campaigns
☐ youth development
☐ private and community foundations
☐ international/foreign
☐ informal/alone/not-for-pay
☐ other (specify)

CHARACTERISTICS

10. In what year were you born? _____ year (to compute age, subtract from survey year)

11. How many brothers or sisters did you have? Please count those born alive but no longer living as well as those alive now. Also include stepbrothers, stepsisters, and children adopted by your parents.
    _____ number of brothers and sisters

12. Are you currently married, widowed, divorced, or separated, or have you never been married?
    1. Married
    2. Widowed
    3. Divorced
    4. Separated
    5. Never married

13. What is the highest level of school you have completed?
    1. Less than high school
    2. Some high school
    3. High school graduate
    4. Some technical school
    5. Technical school graduate
    6. Some college

7. College graduate
8. Postgraduate or professional degree

14. What kind of work do you (did you normally) do? That is, what (is/was) your job called? _____

Once the list of concepts to be measured has been developed, specific questions must be developed to measure each concept. Measures may be single indicators of a concept or multiple indicators that are combined in some way (see Chapter 3 on scaling) to form a measure of a concept. Notice that response categories for closed-ended or **structured questions** are mutually exclusive (categories don't overlap each other) and exhaustive (categories cover all substantive possibilities). Researchers prefer to use existing measures that have been checked and published and for which there is information about the measure's reliability and validity for the intended population. Lacking these, investigators must develop questions on their own. There are several good guides to developing questions, such as Payne (1951), Labaw (1980), Converse and Presser (1986), Fowler (1995), and Schuman and Presser (1996). We summarize some considerations they discuss at greater length.

Question Wording. A very large proportion of the words people use come from a fairly short list. Ninety percent of what is said or written comes from a vocabulary of about 5,000 words. These are the words that are known and used by most people and are preferred in phrasing questions for the general population. To communicate effectively with the broadest audience, one needs to phrase questions in simple, direct, and unambiguous language. Asking questions in the investigator's technical jargon rarely works well.

Word choice can have a large impact on responses one gets. For example, the words *could, might,* and *should* denote different things. Payne (1951) gives the example, "Do you think anything [might, could, should] be done to make it easier for people to pay doctor or hospital bills?" When the questions were asked in an early poll, 63% said something "might" be done, 77% said something "could" be done, and 82% said something "should" be done. How these words are used is known to make a substantial difference in outcomes!

Questions can be structured in an open-ended or closed-ended fashion. An **open-ended question** is one in which the respondent provides the answer without benefit of listed response categories. Examples such as age or number of sisters ask for a brief response. Other questions might require a word (e.g., occupation title) or a more extensive description (e.g., "What is the most important problem facing our nation today?"). An advantage of open-ended questions is that they do less prompting and thus reduce the potential bias in suggestive response categories. Open-ended questions may also save space when the number of potential response categories is large (e.g., zip codes, state, occupation). It is also a necessary approach when the investigator does not know what the response categories are (e.g., most important problem facing the nation). Disadvantages of open-ended questions are the coding efforts that are required to go through all the responses to develop categories and then apply those categories to the responses. An investigator may want only certain kinds of information, and providing the categories may help clarify precisely what is wanted. Sometimes a question combines both structured and unstructured responses, as in questions that provide a list of most common responses with an "other, please specify" category.

There are many lists of suggestions for making good survey questions, and the reader is urged to consult with some of the references mentioned earlier. Dillman (1978:96), for example, provides a few rules for desirable features of good questions:

Use simple words	Do not talk down to respondents
Do not be vague	Avoid bias
Keep it short	Avoid objectionable questions
Be specific but not too specific	Avoid hypothetical questions

How these work out in any given question is a matter of experience and pretesting. Ideally, a question will mean the same thing to different respondents. Some examples from Dillman (1978), shown in Figure 7.1, will help illustrate some of these points.

Question wording also depends on how questions are going to be presented. Questions presented in a self-administered questionnaire must stand alone without the possibility of explanations by an interviewer. An appropriate question on a

FIGURE 7.1   Illustration of Questions

POOR	BETTER REVISION
What percentage of your monthly income is spent on rent (or house payments)?	How much is your monthly rent (or house payment)? _____ dollars
	How much is your average monthly income? _____ dollars
Should the city manager not be directly responsible to the mayor? Yes No	To whom should the city manager be directly responsible: the mayor or the city council? 1. mayor 2. city council
When you go out to restaurants, which kind of restaurants do you most often go to? Those that serve foreign-style foods Those that serve American-style foods	If you were planning to eat out in a restaurant soon, do you think you would probably go to a restaurant that serves Foreign-style foods American-style foods

questionnaire may seem too formalistic and elaborate if spoken over the phone or in person. Phone interview questions must include response categories in the phrasing of the question itself because subjects cannot see the potential responses. On the other hand, personal interviews can present somewhat more complicated response tasks, such as sorting a small stack of cards, each having a response alternative, into some specified order or answering a series of questions with response categories that have been printed on a card given to the respondent for reference. Both telephone surveys and in-person interviews can do much more elaborate branching and skipping to follow-up questions that are relevant to an earlier response by the subject. An example of a question tailored to the different data-gathering encounters is as follows:

MAILED QUESTIONNAIRE
What do you think is the single most important problem facing people in Minnesota today?

_____

_____

TELEPHONE INTERVIEW
The first questions are about quality of life.
What do you think is the single most important problem facing people in Minnesota today?
 (IF "TAXES," PROBE: Is that income taxes, property taxes, or sales tax?)

_____

(PROBE "DON'T KNOW" RESPONSES)

IN-PERSON INTERVIEW
What do you think is the single most important problem facing people in Minnesota today?
 (IF "TAXES," PROBE: Is that income taxes, property taxes, or sales tax?)

_____

(PROBE "DON'T KNOW" RESPONSES)

Translating Questions into Other Languages. When a survey instrument used in one language is to be used with respondents who speak a different language, the investigator must translate the questions. It is often difficult for a literal translation of a question to capture the same meaning in another language. To accomplish the translation of a survey instrument, a process called **back translation** is used (Marsh, 1967: Chapter 8). This typically involves having a bilingual person who is a native in the other culture carefully translate the questions. This translation (not the original language version) is then given to another bilingual person to translate back into the first language. The back-translated version is compared to the original version to see whether the meaning remained the same.

Question Order and Formatting. The order of questions makes a difference in several respects. First, the flow of the entire survey instrument must help establish rapport and trust. Second, answers to preceding questions may affect answers to later questions. Third, grouping questions on similar topics together avoids the appearance of a confusing and chaotic instrument that has not been well thought out. Finally, some questions logically depend on answers to a prior question in a branching fashion.

The order of questions is one of the main ways in which an investigator can contribute to a respondent's developing interest in responding, build rapport, and engender trust. Usually the flow of questions moves from easier (but topically relevant and important) questions, to more difficult or detailed substantive questions, to background or demographic types of questions. For example, a first question might ask for an opinion on the topic at hand in a way that permits an easy entry into the subject of the survey (e.g., "The first questions are about quality of life. What do you think is the single most important problem facing people in the United States today?"). Selection of the first question is of special significance. Background characteristics (questions such as age, gender, marital and work status, education, and income) are best left to the end of the instrument. One reason for this is that the cover letter probably attempts to make the topic of the survey interesting and important, so starting with basic background information breaks the expectation that the researcher is interested in getting the respondent's ideas on the announced topic of the survey. Questions on similar topics should be kept together, and this may necessitate a statement to smooth the transition (e.g., "Now I'd like to ask you some questions about yourself.").

Similar questions are often grouped together for ease of response and efficiency. For example, a series of questions that have the same response categories may be presented in a **matrix format,** with the response categories listed across the top of a matrix-like form and the questions listed down the rows. Response categories for each question could then be lined up in columns under the proper headings, as in the following example.

Should it be possible for a pregnant woman to obtain a legal abortion under each of the following conditions? Please circle a number to indicate the extent to which you agree or disagree.

	STRONGLY DISAGREE	DISAGREE	AGREE	STRONGLY AGREE
a. If there is a strong chance of serious defect in the baby	1	2	3	4
b. If she is married and does not want any more children	1	2	3	4
c. If the woman's health is seriously endangered by the pregnancy	1	2	3	4
d. If the family has a very low income and cannot afford any more children	1	2	3	4
e. If she became pregnant as a result of rape	1	2	3	4

f. If she is not married and does not want to marry the man	1	2	3	4
g. If the woman wants it for any reason	1	2	3	4

A drawback of this type of format is that respondents may circle the same category by way of convenience (a **response set bias**) rather than considering response alternatives carefully after reading each question.

Some questions apply only to certain respondents. For example, questions on hours of work are relevant only for those who work. Some topics require further **probes,** necessitating follow-up questions relevant to certain respondents. The solution to these situations is to have **branching questions,** in which a respondent is directed to go to other questions depending on his or her answers to earlier ones. The branching structure may be quite extensive and, in the case of a questionnaire, a respondent may be directed to questions several pages later if the intervening ones are not relevant. Simple branching can be used in mailed questionnaires; boxes and arrows or special instructions direct the respondent to the question he or she should answer next. The problem is somewhat easier in the case of telephone or personal interviews because the interviewer (perhaps with the aid of a CATI program) is trained to skip over irrelevant questions easily and present only the relevant ones. The respondent is unaware that questions have been skipped. An example of a simple branching question follows.

Was your total household income in 1997 above or below $35,000? (circle the number that applies)
1. Above (if above, go to question **a,** below)
2. Below (if below, go to question **b,** below)
   a. (IF ABOVE) I am going to mention a number of income categories. When I come to the category that describes your total household income *before* taxes in 1997, please stop me.
      □ $35,000 to $40,000
      □ $40,000 to $50,000
      □ $50,000 to $60,000
      □ $60,000 to $70,000
      □ $70,000 to $80,000
      □ $80,000 or more

   b. (IF BELOW) I am going to mention a number of income categories. When I come to the category that describes your total household income before taxes in 1997, please stop me.
      □ Under $5,000
      □ $5,000 to $10,000
      □ $10,000 to $15,000
      □ $15,000 to $20,000
      □ $20,000 to $25,000
      □ $25,000 to $30,000
      □ $30,000 to $35,000

There are a number of studies of features of questions, including question order and their consequences (Schuman and Presser, 1996; Schwarz et al., 1991). The sequence of questions may have an effect and must be examined carefully—for example, knowledge questions preceded by the information the next question requires or attitude questions preceded by questions that suggest a particular issue or context might alter responses. In phone interviews it is becoming standard practice to order randomly the sequence of questions within a topic area (e.g., a series of Likert scale items on a topic) so that any order effect is balanced out for the sample as a whole. This is possible when CATI programs are used but not practical (except through multiple forms of a questionnaire) for mailed questionnaires.

Length of Questionnaire or Interview.   Well-crafted survey instruments may be very brief, such as one or two questions, or very lengthy. There have been successful questionnaires with several hundred questions. The key is the way in which the instrument is put together and how well it engages the interest of targeted respondents. Nevertheless, the general rule is to keep questionnaires as brief as possible and, by the format and number of questions on a page, to help the respondent feel a sense of progress through the questions. However, instrument length is generally not among the main reasons for nonresponse.

Pretesting the Instrument.   The most important step in constructing a survey instrument is **pretesting.** The purpose of pretesting is to see whether respondents understand questions and give responses that can be interpreted by the investigator. In the case of interview schedules, a pretest also helps determine whether interviewers can use the instrument effectively. Pretesting involves giving the instrument to a small sample that includes as much of the variety of potential subjects as possible. Often respondents are observed as they answer a questionnaire or are asked afterward about their understanding, confusion, and frustration in answering the instrument. Dillman (1978) recommends that the investigator's professional colleagues and any users of the survey information also be recruited to review the instrument. All of this information leads to a revision of the problematic items and further pretesting until a satisfactory instrument has been developed. This step is perhaps the most important in creating a measurement instrument that works well in the planned data-gathering encounter.

Deciding on the Data-Gathering Approach

We have seen that the type of data-gathering encounter presents opportunities and constraints on the way questions are formed and put together in a measurement instrument. Here we summarize some of the strengths and weaknesses of each of these typical survey research procedures.

Phone Interviews.   The telephone interview is a quick and efficient method of data collection. It is useful for rapidly unfolding events such as election campaigns or shifts in public opinion. Having a live interviewer helps in establishing rapport in a diverse sample of respondents and explaining questions as needed. Having an interviewer also aids in screening and in sampling among potential respondents within a family or small group, for example. Most people can be accessed by telephone, at least in more affluent societies. Computer aids to telephone interviewing can help handle problems of the sequence of presentation of items, complex branching, and direct data entry for more rapid analysis. Computer assistance also helps in randomly selecting numbers to call and in managing repeated callbacks at different times. In fact, telephone interviewing is quite helpful in tape recording open-ended responses because the respondent is comfortably close to a microphone (the telephone) and a tape recorder can be connected to the telephone line (with permission) for higher-quality recording that can be transcribed. The telephone interview helps bring reality to promises of anonymity because the interviewer need not know the identity of the respondent. Telephone interviews tend to have higher response rates than mailed questionnaires.

But telephone interviews also have drawbacks. Most phone lists such as the telephone directory are out-of-date and thus lead to underrepresentation of more mobile people. An increasing number of people cannot be accessed by phone, either because they cannot afford the service or they use various blocks to prevent others from knowing their number. Residents in group quarters may not be contacted directly by phone and institutional gatekeepers pose a problem for accessing the desired party. The telephone interview is a somewhat more remote encounter than the personal interview, requiring somewhat different efforts in establishing rapport. Because it is entirely auditory, the interviewer cannot observe body language, which might be useful in detecting problems with questions. In fact, the interviewer has little control over the respondent's social setting during the interview, which may be a problem when the survey is about sensitive issues. Only a low level of complexity can be readily handled in a telephone interview. No visual cues can be used, long response category lists are difficult to convey, and some forms of questions such as ranking or rating on a graphic scale are not readily adapted to this type of encounter. Phone interviews are more costly than questionnaires because they require the time of interviewers to make calls and, potentially, long-distance telephone charges. Finally, the telephone interview requires a coordination of interviewing time between interviewer and subject. Subjects working odd hours may have little chance of being interviewed, and lengthy interruption of respondents busy at other things may lead to more refusals.

Mailed Questionnaires. Mailed questionnaires are very cost-effective in a society with a good public postal service. Because most people are familiar with questionnaires and can read, most questions can be asked effectively. More-elaborate response formats (e.g., matrix-formatted questions, semantic differential scales) can be used when the mode is paper and pencil. A respondent is able to refer back to prior answers and that may help reduce inconsistencies. Mailed questionnaires can also preserve subject anonymity (the investigator generally does not know who is identified with a particular questionnaire) and confidentiality (a detached matching list of identities can be used to mask the identity of questionnaires when respondents are known). Potential interviewer effects are avoided in mailed surveys. A mailed survey, unlike the personal interview, can take a short time to conduct, depending on mail delays.

Mailed questionnaires also have drawbacks. The response rate is generally lower than for telephone or in-person interviews, but follow-up strategies are effective in increasing response rates. Editing and data entry tasks generally increase the time to compile the final data file ready for analysis. More-complex kinds of data, such as life histories or topics that require extensive probing, are less easily handled by mailed survey. Essentially, the questionnaire must be complete and self-contained.

Personal Interviews.   Among the advantages of a personal interview is that the interviewer can do some observing as well as listening. Body language, the setting of the data-gathering encounter, and personal attributes of the subject are all within view and can be noted. Interviewers are more in control of the interview setting and can be sure that the subject is alone and not distracted. Establishing rapport and trust may also be more direct and easier. Interviewers are able to introduce and move through complex topics, probe as needed, and introduce more complex tasks such as having the subject sort cards (e.g., Q-sorts), become involved in data-gathering games and simulations, or give responses to pictures. The ability to follow up and probe unclear responses is especially helpful. Field interviewers may also be able to handle difficult sampling problems, such as randomly selecting an adult from a household or determining how to sample a block of houses when data about the block are not otherwise available. Personal interviews receive high marks for accuracy of information, completeness, ability to handle sensitive material, and overall reliability and validity. The response rate for personal interviews is generally highest among the three survey modes discussed here, generally five percentage points higher than phone interviews.

Drawbacks of personal interviews include the high cost of travel and interviewing time. It is a time-consuming activity that requires skilled interviewers. Unlike the CATI possibility for telephone interviews, personal interview schedules must be edited, coded, and entered in a computer file for analysis. It is harder to make good on promises of confidentiality (and impossible to assure anonymity) because the interviewer knows the location of the respondent and could recognize the person in other settings. Like telephone interviews, in-person interviews require coordinating schedules.

Reducing Nonresponse Bias

The greater the nonresponse in surveys, the greater the likelihood that the resulting sample will be biased in some respect. Nonresponse is unlikely to be random. Thus, it is important to reduce nonresponse as much as possible in order to limit the possibility for bias. Many techniques have been proposed for reducing nonresponse, including using hand-affixed rather than metered postage and using personalized cover letters (Parton, 1950; Dillman, 1978). Managing the cost–benefit problem from the respondent's point of view helps reduce nonresponse. Given an otherwise adequate survey instrument, following up on nonrespondents is the most effective strategy. In personal and phone interviews, repeated callbacks would be used. In mailed surveys it is common practice to send reminder postcards a week or so after the initial mailing and send repeated requests, including new questionnaires, to those who have not responded. Finally, phone calls may be used to identify reasons for nonresponse and to seek more responses. In order to preserve anonymity, an investigator may include a separate response postcard for the subject to return, indicating that he or she has completed the questionnaire. The postcard, not the questionnaire, would have the respondent's identity. Then follow-up efforts could be limited to those who had not mailed in the separate response card. Good introductions, affiliation with trustworthy sponsors, assurances of confidentiality or anonymity, and professionally produced survey instruments all contribute to higher response rates.

Finally, as noted earlier, it is helpful to know the nature of any sampling bias so that this can be taken into account in interpreting the findings. Comparison of the achieved sample with other data taken from census records or prior research helps in this task.

Preparation for Statistical Analysis

Once the survey has been completed, several steps are needed before the data are ready for analysis. Typically, questionnaires or interview schedules are scanned and edited to be sure that they are clear for coders. Coding involves establishing variables and categories, usually including nonresponse categories such as don't know (DK), no response (NR), not applicable (NA), and refused. A codebook that lists variables and instructions for coding them is essential. This is used by trained coders to code the data in preparation for data entry into a computer file. Data entry is followed by preliminary computer runs to identify coding and transcription errors (see Chapter 10 on data analysis).

Open-ended responses generally require more-extensive reading and coding and thus take more time. Computer-assisted content analysis may be helpful when verbatim text responses are used. When coding is done by hand, random recoding is useful to detect errors and measure coder reliability.

A hallmark of good research is thorough checking, both minor and major, that occurs before the analysis begins. This step applies to all research, but survey research often involves some special checks. For example, because surveys strive for good representation of a population, checks are usually used to see whether the sample corresponds to the desired population. Sometimes this is not possible because little is known about a population. In other cases some checks can be made. For example, for a sample that is to represent the general adult population, a comparison might be made of the age distribution in the sample with an age distribution from a recent census, making sure to compare only relevant categories meeting the sampling criterion (adult).

Archives of Survey Data

Increasingly, an investigator may be fortunate enough to find that the relevant data have already been gathered by someone else, perhaps the U.S. Census or an academic or commercial polling agency. The General Social Survey is a nearly annual survey of noninstitutionalized adults in the continental United States, using a questionnaire that includes many of the variables important to social scientists. There are also longitudinal data sets on individual development (see Chapter 9 on secondary data). Cases include individuals as well as organizations of various types. Archives of carefully checked, documented, and maintained machine-readable research data are available from a number of sources, including the Inter-University Consortium for Political and Social Research (ICPSR) at the University of Michigan (Web site: http://www.icpsr.umich.edu). Miller (1991:189–213) provides a useful list of some of these archives.

An investigator who uses **archival data** needs complete information about the context in which the data were gathered and the processes of coding and checking that lie behind the data set.

ISSUES IN SURVEY RESEARCH

Problem of Nonexperimental Design and Trade-offs

The survey strategy generally trades off clarity about cause for representation of a larger, defined population. The consequence is that those interested in causal linkages must go beyond showing a relationship between dependent and independent variables and directly address the two other requirements for documenting causal influences. First, survey researchers must deal with the question of time order (did the cause come before the effect?) and then with the question of other potential causes of a relationship between independent and dependent variables. This leads to the need to measure those other factors and the possibility of missing some, plus the general need for larger volumes of data to analyze more-complex relationships adequately. Depending on the stage of progress on a research question, establishing a probable causal relationship may be less critical than establishing that a relationship is probably a characteristic of the larger population. Descriptive research (such as a public opinion poll) is particularly interested in population descriptions, so the survey trade-off strategy is suitable. Finally, the survey strategy may be the only available strategy if the independent variables cannot or should not be manipulated. Randomly assigning marital status, for example, is probably not possible, so an experimental design may not be possible for studies of the effects of marital status.

Problem of Sampling Frame Availability

Another problem for survey research is finding an adequate sampling frame for the population of interest. Most sampling frames (e.g., the phone book) are quickly dated and exclude important segments of the population. Sampling strategies can often help achieve the goals of representative sampling in the absence of some lists (e.g., multistage samples), but the overall problem remains and inspires creativity among survey researchers.

Problem of Data-Gathering Social Encounters and Sources of Bias

Data-gathering encounters always have an impact on the data that are generated. The objective of survey research, as with other forms of research, is to minimize these influences. Thus, in some situations mailed questionnaires are better than telephone or face-to-face interviews. Data-gathering encounters should be designed to reduce subjects' tendencies to give more socially desirable answers, withhold criticism or sensitive information, and exaggerate or conceal private information.

In this regard, in the case of face-to-face interviewing, it is important to give consideration to possible effects of interviewer characteristics. For some studies female interviewers may be more effective than males. For other studies the ways the interviewers are dressed may be more important than their gender. It may even be necessary to do a pilot study involving some preliminary interviewing to determine what interviewer characteristics are relevant for a particular study.

Confidentiality and Anonymity

Anonymity means that it is impossible (or that no attempt will be made) to determine the identity of a case (i.e., a person or organization). *Confidentiality* means that an investigator knows the identity of the case but will not reveal it. There are no laws in the United States that protect research confidentiality or anonymity. Identity lists can be legally obtained by subpoena. Thus, to make an assurance of confidentiality real, an investigator must take steps to make it real. For example, questionnaires or interview schedules generally request that the respondent not provide his or her name or identity, but each instrument is assigned a sequential identification number. This permits researchers to correct errors in a computer data file by referring to the correct survey instrument (with the same ID number) without using personal identifiers such as the respondent's name. When there is a genuine research need to recontact the respondent, a **matching list** that contains the assigned ID number and the respondent's identity is kept in a safe place. This might be necessary for checking on interviewer performance early in a study, filling in missing information during the instrument editing and coding phase, matching the survey data with variables from other sources, or reinterviewing the same respondents in a panel study. Under threat of disclosure, an investigator would have to decide whether to destroy the matching list in order to protect the assurance of confidentiality. The main point here is that ethical investigators must conduct their research in such a way that assurances given to a subject are carried out.

Myths about Survey Research

The following are claims that are heard about survey research.

- "Only short questionnaires will be answered."

According to Dillman (1978:55), questionnaires up to 12 pages or about 125 items appear to pose no response-rate problem. Unless the mail questionnaire is especially well designed, introduced, and followed up, some drop in response rate may occur for longer questionnaires. Face-to-face or personal interviews do not appear to have the same limitations, although a clear focus on the study's intent is always important. Phone interviews can also be long, although the cost of a separate phone interview may not be very different from the cost of adding additional items to a single interview.

- "It's an easy, quick process that anyone can do well enough."

Any inquiry that hopes to generate findings that will stand critical examination requires a great deal of planning, clarity, and skill. For example, insight into the consequences of a particular type of data-generating social encounter is needed. Knowing steps to ensure high response rates and to carry out sampling so that inference can be made to a population is both a technical specialty and an art. Surveys by uninformed people rarely achieve more than a 50% response rate, but the norm for professionally designed and executed surveys is 70% or higher. Knowing how to select needed measures or convert measures so that they work well in different survey contexts also requires considerable skill and pretesting.

- "It's the method of choice in the social sciences."

Although it is true that many research reports in journals are based on surveys, this design is often not the best option. Surveys are strong when the problem is one of generalizability of findings to a defined, larger population. They are weak in eliminating alternative explanations of an outcome and addressing historic or through-time process issues. Reasons for the survey popularity may have more to do with short turnaround times for reporting findings, the socialization of people who are able to answer short, structured questions, and research funding limitations, rather than requirements of a research question. As a method, it is probably more popular than it should be.

- "Results can't be trusted because people lie."

When properly asked, most questions appear to receive honest answers. One problem is phrasing a question that a respondent is in a position to answer and creating a situation of trust that is as neutral as possible. Some survey approaches raise special problems. For example, face-to-face interviews introduce greater opportunities for a respondent to feel under pressure to give a socially desirable answer. This pressure is diminished by the telephone interview and the mailed questionnaire. Voting polls are very accurate if they are well done. Exit polls often predict the outcome of elections within very, very narrow margins, for example.

- "Some data are better than no data."

Confronted with a low response rate, questions that are ambiguous or misunderstood, or a survey that doesn't include critically needed variables, an investigator may nevertheless be tempted to analyze the findings and report them under the assumption that some data are better than none. But poor data lead to poor conclusions. Defective data should be set aside and not used. Sometimes it is possible to compare the sample with expected population characteristics, and sometimes this comparison may suggest that nonresponse bias is low. In such situations, indicators of data quality (such as a low response rate) may turn out not to indicate response bias problems. Defective data are worse than no data at all.

SUMMARY

In this chapter we have presented a variety of ways in which surveys are designed and conducted. One of the main strengths of a survey trade-off is that of external validity: the generalizability of findings from a sample to a population. The cost of this trade-off is in the need to ask about potential explanatory variables so that statistical controls can be used. There are ethical issues in survey research. Although these are generally less problematic than in other forms of research discussed here, they are important.

Three types of data-generating encounters are usually associated with survey research: mailed questionnaires, phone interviews, and personal interviews. The first requires an instrument that the subject can read and understand. Questionnaires may contain precoding of structured questions and may also include unstructured questions. Design of this instrument so that it provides a proxy dialog between the investigator and the subject requires attention to introductions (sponsorship and instructions), question wording, question order, and the overall professional appearance of the instrument.

Phoned and personal interviews permit the interviewer to probe and explain questions further than is possible in mailed questionnaires. The instrument used in phoned or personal interviews is called an interview schedule. It generally contains considerable information of use to the interviewer, such as suggested probes, space to record responses, and items that the interviewer may fill out but not ask directly of the respondent (observations about the setting, notes on how well the interview went, recording obvious things that can be observed, etc.).

TERMS TO KNOW

Alternative (competing) explanations
Anonymity
Archival data
Back translation
Branching questions
Causal order
Computer-assisted telephone
    interviewing (CATI)
Confidentiality
Cover letter
Cross-sectional design
Interview schedule
Matching list
Matrix format

Nonresponse rate
Open-ended questions
Panel studies
Personal interviews
Pretesting
Probes
Questionnaire
Random digit dialing (RDD)
Response set bias
Sampling frame
Screening questions
Statistical control
Structured questions
Trend studies

ISSUES AND COMPARISONS

Confidentiality versus anonymity
Respondent as subject versus expert informant
Trade-offs of survey versus experimental design
Methods of handling competing explanations of findings in survey research
Source of sampling frames
Types of samples
Data-gathering social encounters in surveys
Ethical concerns in survey research
Dillman's total design method
Myths of survey research
Costs and benefits for respondents in surveys
Different tasks in questions to a respondent
Advantages and disadvantages of structured versus unstructured questions
Qualities of good questions
Issues of question ordering and format

EXERCISES

1. Find two examples of survey instruments. Perhaps one could be a commercial survey and one could be from an academic survey organization. Critique the strengths and weaknesses of these using the criteria in this chapter.

2. Identify a concept you might be interested in measuring (not a standard one such as age, sex, or income). Then develop an item to measure that concept in a questionnaire and then in an interview schedule. What differences are there between these two questioning formats?

3. If you are to do your own research project in this course, draft the instrument in the Labaw format of question (in one column) and corresponding rationale or use (in a parallel column).

4. Use a questionnaire or interview schedule you have developed for your project (or a questionnaire you have available from some other source) to conduct one or two pretests. What have you learned about the questions from using them? What changes would you make and why?

REFERENCES

Armson, Rossana, *The 1996 Minnesota State Survey: Results and Technical Report*, Minnesota Center for Survey Research, University of Minnesota, Minneapolis, 1997.

Converse, Jean M., and Stanley Presser, *Survey Questions: Handcrafting the Standardized Questionnaire*, Sage, Newbury Park, CA, 1986.

Davis, James A., *The Logic of Causal Order* (Sage University Paper 55), Sage, Newbury Park, CA, 1985.

Dillman, Don A., *Mail and Telephone Surveys: The Total Design Method*, New York, Wiley, 1978.

Fowler, Floyd J., Jr., *Improving Survey Questions: Design and Evaluation*, Sage, Newbury Park, CA, 1995.

Labaw, Patricia, *Advanced Questionnaire Design*, Abt Books, Cambridge, MA, 1980.

Marsh, Robert M., *Comparative Sociology: A Codification of Cross-Societal Analysis*, New York, Harcourt, Brace, 1967.

Miller, Delbert C., *Handbook of Research Design and Social Measurement*, 5th ed., Sage, Newbury Park, CA, 1991.

Osgood, Charles E., George J. Suci, and Percy H. Tannenbaum, *The Measurement of Meaning*, Urbana, University of Illinois Press, 1957.

Parton, Mildred, *Surveys, Polls, and Samples: Practical Procedures*, New York, Harper, 1950.

Payne, Stanley L., *The Art of Asking Questions*, Princeton University Press, Princeton, NJ, 1951.

Schuman, Howard, and Stanley Presser, *Questions and Answers in Attitude Surveys: Experiments on Question Form, Wording and Context*, Sage, Newbury Park, CA, 1996.

Schwarz, N., B. Knauper, H. J. Hippler, E. Noelle-Neumann, and L. Clark, "Rating Scales: Numeric Values May Change the Meaning of Scale Labels," *Public Opinion Quarterly* 1991;55:570–82.

CHAPTER 8

INSTRUMENTS

Introduction

To help you see the options available in using an existing instrument or in creating your own, I provide four instruments here for you to consider.

Instrument 1: A Vague Likert Scale

The first instrument on spirituality shows the vagueness of certain types of measurements found when using a Likert Scale format. On this type of scale, it's up to the respondent to determine what the answers on the Likert Scale mean. The probability is that the scores will cluster around the mean. Vague Likert Scales generally show the emergence of social desirability. People want to say they *have* spiritual feelings but that they aren't necessarily *strong* feelings. Your findings on these scales will very likely be meaningless, because the instrument is vague and responses are too open to socially desirable answers.

> ### *The Dakota Measure of Spirituality*
> **Directions:** This is a measure of the importance of spirituality in your life. There are three parts to the questionnaire. All three parts should be answered as honestly as possible. **Please do not skip any of the questions.**
>
> *Part One: Socio-Demographic Questions*
>
> 1. Age _____
> 2. Years of Education _____
> 3. Marital Status _____
> 4. Occupation (the work you do) _____
> 6. Race/Ethnicity _____
> 5. Number of Children in Your Family _____

Part Two: Spirituality Questions

Spirituality is defined as the degree to which thoughts of a higher being or of a higher meaning in life define the way you approach life issues, your value base, and the way in which you cope with life decisions.

Directions: From the following scale, please place the number that best represents your level of spirituality after each question asked: 1 = Very Low/Very Seldom; 2 = Low/Seldom; 3 = Neither Low Nor High Nor Seldom Nor Often; 4 = Somewhat High/Somewhat Often; 5 = Very High/Very Often.

1. What is the degree to which a higher being plays a role in your life?
2. How often do you attend spirituality meetings?
3. Do you feel there is carryover from your involvement in spirituality to your personal life?
4. Do you pray?
5. Do you read about spiritual subjects?
6. Do you attend study sessions on spiritual subjects?
7. Do you financially support spirituality organizations or provide services as a volunteer?
8. Do you have a joyous feeling inside when you think about your spirituality?
9. Do your friends and family support your spiritual beliefs?
10. Do you have objects in your home of a spiritual nature (paintings, poems on the wall, spiritual messages, as examples)?
11. How often do you find yourself thinking about spiritual issues?
12. Are your personal spiritual beliefs related to an organized spiritual doctrine?
13. Does your notion of spirituality come from an organized religious doctrine or affiliation?
14. Would you celebrate major events in your life (marriage, birth, death) in a religious institution?

Part Three: Questions Concerning Your Physical and Emotional Health

Please use the following scale in responding to these questions: 1 = Almost Never; 2 = Perhaps Once a Month; 3 = Twice a Month; 4 = Once a Week; 5 = Almost Everyday.

1. I generally feel discouraged about my life.
2. I feel great, physically.
3. I have moments of intense panic.
4. I see the doctor _____.

5. I feel the need for a drink _____.
6. My anxiety attacks occur _____.
7. I exercise _____.
8. I feel the love of others_____.
9. I see a therapist for emotional problems _____.
10. I feel very low self-esteem _____.

Discussion

You can readily see that this instrument is full of vagueness. The definition of spirituality is much too broad. I'm sure a better definition is available, since this one might be called an "Aunt Fanny" definition: it fits everyone in the world including our Aunt Fanny. The questions are also vague. Is this about religion or spirituality? These are, of course, two different concepts. I fail to see the tie to anything substantive in many of the questions. Consider question 8. It asks, "Do you have a joyous feeling inside when you think about your spirituality?" I mean, really! What does a "joyous feeling" mean, and how often do most of us have one? Those feelings could be confused with happy feelings or feelings of contentment. Joyous feelings are serious and connote a sense of euphoria. Would you define "joyous" that way? Perhaps not, but you can see the problem of trying to understand unclear language. This Likert Scale is much too vague. What do the words "Very Low" and "Very High" mean? What may be high for one person is very likely to be low for another person. And finally, what is this about, anyway? Is it about believing in God? Is it about believing in a moral view of life? Is it about being religious? I'm not sure, and I created the scale.

The physical and mental health questions aren't bad and having a Likert Scale tied to measurable behaviors is a good idea. After answering the questions about spirituality, however, the respondent may see the link made between high levels of spirituality and good physical and mental health. If so, knowing that the researcher is suggesting that spiritual people are also healthy people insures that the answers suggest that respondents have good emotional and physical health. It might be interesting to see if there really is a tie between spirituality and good physical and emotional health, but I'm not sure this scale can accomplish that function. Additionally, in this type of measurement, we only have the subject's word regarding their level of spirituality and their physical and emotional health. A better measure of spirituality and health would be a standardized instrument to measure spirituality, a doctor's evaluation of physical health, and a mental health worker's evaluation of emotional health. Now *that* could make for a very interesting study, because an entire movement in the health field believes that high levels of spirituality correlate with better ability to cope with physical and emotional difficulties in life. Anyone want to give it a try?

Instrument 2: A Behaviorally-Oriented Likert Scale

The second instrument is one in the public domain called the CES-D (Radloff, 1977), a measure of depression. It is very behaviorally oriented and gives the respondent a definite idea of how to answer questions. Questions are based on a one-week time frame and the number of times certain behaviors related to depression are experienced. You'll need to be the judge of which instrument is the most appealing to you and how it relates to the intent of your study.

The CES-D: A Measure of Depression

Directions: I am going to read you some statements about the ways people act and feel. On how many of the last 7 days did the following statements apply to you?

	None	1 or 2 Days	3 or 4 Days	5 or more Days
1. I was bothered by things that usually don't bother me.	0	1	2	3
2. I did not feel like eating. My appetite was poor.	0	1	2	3
3. I felt that I could not shake off the blues even with help from friends and family.	0	1	2	3
4. I felt I was just not as good as others.	0	1	2	3
5. I had trouble keeping my mind on what I was doing.	0	1	2	3
6. I felt depressed.	0	1	2	3
7. I felt that everything I did was an effort.	0	1	2	3
8. I felt hopeful about the future.	0	1	2	3
9. I thought my life was a failure.	0	1	2	3
10. I felt fearful.	0	1	2	3
11. My sleep was restless.	0	1	2	3
12. I was happy.	0	1	2	3
13. I talked less than usual.	0	1	2	3

14. I felt lonely.	0	1	2	3
15. People were unfriendly.	0	1	2	3
16. I enjoyed life.	0	1	2	3
17. I had crying spells.	0	1	2	3
18. I felt sad.	0	1	2	3
19. I felt people disliked me.	0	1	2	3
20. I could not get going.	0	1	2	3

Discussion

The CES-D is one of the simplest depression inventories available. The choices are easy to make, the language is simple, the instrument appears culturally neutral, and it is very short. In other words, it's quite a good measure of depression. But are there problems with the instrument? Yes, there are. One problem is that a person may have been depressed last week but feel hunky-dory this week. A week of depression is a very short period of time. Even the *Diagnostic and Statistical Manual,* the DSM-IV (American Psychiatric Association 1994) says that one needs to have been depressed for at least a month before the term *depression* can be used clinically or diagnostically. If you reflect back on the questions, some of them seem just a little too vague. Question 20 is an example: "I just could not get going." I can imagine some confused clients, or those unfamiliar with English, wondering where they were supposed to get going to? Also, some of the questions might confuse medical problems with depression. Question seven is a good example. It says: "I felt that everything I did was an effort." People with the flu often feel that way. Consider question 15: "People were unfriendly." People often *are* unfriendly, particularly in large cities. That doesn't mean that the respondent is depressed, does it? And so on. I like the behavioral aspect of the questions, and many of them really do look at depression. But in the light of the issues I've raised here, you should look for the small and large flaws in all instruments. Flaws usually occur because the instrument hasn't been pre-tested to the extent that it should have been. If enough qualified people read an instrument, trust me, they'll come up with problems in the instrument pretty quickly.

Instrument 3: The Use of Vignettes

The third instrument uses vignettes combined with open-ended questions. Answers are difficult to manufacture. It is an instrument with the least possible likelihood of socially desirable answers.

The San Bernardino Crisis Scale
Directions: A series of short vignettes describing the crisis situ-

ations in people's lives will be presented. Please write down the first thought that comes to you since this is almost certain to be the most relevant answer. We will appreciate your cooperation in writing about 150 words on each question, because we would like to know not only what you would do, but why you would do it. Don't worry about whether the answer is right or wrong. We are only interested in knowing what you might do in each stressful situation. This scale is meant to measure how people deal with crisis situations.

1. You are driving along in your car when suddenly the driver in front of you swerves off the road. You watch the car flip over several times and come to a halt. Smoke is coming from the car, and your fear is that the car might explode. What would you do next?

2. You have just been informed by a doctor that preliminary tests show that you have a serious form of cancer that could end your life in less than a year. What is the first thing you would do?

3. The person you love the most in life has just informed you that they no longer love you, and that they have found someone else to be with. What is the first thing you would do?

4. The person next to you in class is cheating on examinations. You see that she has a crib sheet with her every time she takes an examination. The course is graded on a curve and even though you're doing well in the course, that person's grade is throwing the curve off. Instead of getting the A you deserve, you're getting a B−. What would you do?

5. You go to your place of worship and are asked to help pass the donation plate around and then count the money. You're stone-broke and haven't had a meal in two days. You begin counting the money and see that the donations are higher than usual. You could probably take $10 from the donation plate without anyone missing the money. You are so hungry that your judgment is poor. What would you do?

6. Your parents throw a party for your older brother (or sister) and his girlfriend (or boyfriend). You happen to be in your bedroom getting dressed when the girlfriend/boyfriend comes into your room and tells you that he or she really isn't in love with your sibling. The person needs to be honest about it, because it's making him/her very unhappy. What would you do next?

7. Your best friend at work is using liquor on the job. He's very careful about it, but you've seen him drink on the job a number of times. His work has been going downhill lately and it's affecting your salary and opportunities for advancement because both are dependent on how well your department does. What would you do?

8. You've just been "reamed out" by your boss who used gender-specific terms with you like bitch, dyke, queer, and so on. Your boss and his boss are best friends. There really isn't anyone else on the job to whom you can complain about what's happening without it affecting your job. What would you do?

9. You know for a fact that your father is having an affair, because he's shared that information with you on the promise that it remains confidential. Your mother calls you up to talk about the problems in their marriage: She tells you that Dad just doesn't seem interested in her anymore whereas before, he was very interested in her. She's become very depressed, almost suicidal because of the change in their relationship. What would you do?

10. Your best friend, not one of the greatest students in the world but a really wonderful friend who has done lots of favors for you, asks you to take her place in a national examination. If she gets a high enough score, she'll be certain to be admitted to the school and the profession she has dreamed of for years. You know your friend would make a wonderful professional in her chosen field and she *is* your best friend. What would you do?

Discussion

This scale is an open-ended scale that is pretty difficult to fake, although not impossible. There are certainly socially desirable answers that some people might be able to think up. For the most part, however, it would be difficult to fake responses on every question, because there isn't necessarily a correct or socially desirable response. The problem with this instrument is, what is it measuring? The directions say that it's measuring the way people might act in a crisis, but the underlying theme is the respondent's value system. Could you see someone giving you this instrument at your job? I can, because within the questions are choices that not only suggest someone's ability to handle stress, but they also suggest the person's value base. This type of instrument might be used to determine whether you would cheat or steal at work. It's an instrument that appears to be about one thing but it certainly could be about something else. And yet, it's not a bad instrument, and it does demonstrate the use of short vignettes to elicit open-ended answers that would probably contain minimal levels of social desirability.

One thing to consider when using this type of instrument is the amount of time it could take a respondent to complete the instrument. Very often, people with poor writing skills just give up or they make answers so brief that they can be meaningless. Let's take Question 10. It asks if you would cheat on a test for a really good friend. The briefest answer would be "No, because it's dishonest." What you're hoping for, though, is a more detailed response, perhaps something on the order of: "I wouldn't cheat for my friend because I might get caught. I would help him study for the test and I'd probably encourage him a great deal. I'd certainly have negative things to say about cheating and I'd also point out that asking me to cheat goes way beyond what friends ask other friends to do. I'm wondering if I don't cheat for him, if it will affect our relationship." The trick in this type of open-ended instrument is to give the subject encouragement to provide more complete and informative answers. One way to do this is to provide a sample question with a possible answer. You may affect the way the subject responds to the remaining questions by doing this, but it *is* a possible way of getting respondents to give more self-disclosing answers. You might also ask the respondent to provide written answers and then, in a second part of each question, to explain the answers more fully.

Instrument 4: An Open-Ended Instrument

The fourth instrument is an open-ended instrument developed by a former student of mine in an MSW program. It tries to determine the reasons Hispanic HIV Positive/AIDS victims fail to inform their families about their health problems. The instrument also tries to note the coping mechanisms used by this population in dealing with a socially stigmatizing terminal illness.

This instrument was given verbally in Spanish, although the respondents could refer to the written questions in both English and Spanish. All of the subjects chose to speak in Spanish. The questionnaire was done verbally because many of the subjects had poor writing skills and some were too weak from AIDS to write. The researcher also felt that doing the questionnaire verbally would encourage the subjects to speak at length about each question. This did happen but it made recording the interview difficult. After several interviews, the researcher asked the respondents if he could tape the conversation. All consented, although he asked each of them to sign a release form giving him the right to record the interviews and promising to destroy the tapes after they had been analyzed for content.

Hispanic Men and the Disclosure of Their HIV\AIDS Status to Family Members

Socio-Demographic and Self-Disclosure Questions

1. What is your age?
2. Where were you born?
3. How many years have you lived in the United States?
4. What church do you attend?
5. What is the actual date of your diagnosis of HIV positive?
6. What is your HIV positive status? Asymptomatic or symptomatic?
7. Describe the type of relationship you currently have with your family.
8. How often do you see your family?
9. What does your family know medically about HIV/AIDS?
10. How would you describe your parent's view of life?
11. Describe your family's attitude toward gay men.
12. If your family knew that you were HIV positive, how do you think they would react?
13. Explain why you haven't disclosed your HIV/AIDS status to your family.
14. If you had an opportunity to disclose your HIV/AIDS status to a family member, who would that be? Why would you choose that person?
15. In explaining how you are dealing emotionally and physically with your HIV/AIDS status, what *dicho* (a proverb or wise saying commonly used in Hispanic culture to convey metaphorical meaning) best describes it?
16. In dealing with your family regarding your HIV/AIDS status, what dicho best describes it?
17. In dealing with your sexual orientation, what dicho best describes it?
18. In your heart, what has it done to you not to tell your family about your illness?

Questions Related to the Culture Subjects Identify With (An Acculturation Scale)

The following scale was added to the prior instrument because the instrument developers thought it might be important to know the extent to which traditional Hispanic values were related to the answers the respondent's gave.

One way to determine the level of a person's identification with his or her country of origin is to give what is called an *accultura-*

tion measurement. That simply means that an instrument will be used to help determine the extent to which the values, beliefs, and experiences of someone's country of origin still affect their lives today. A high score on the five following questions suggests that the respondent is primarily identifying himself as a traditional, Hispanic male and that American culture plays a limited role in his self-identity. This is relevant to the study since acculturation may affect whether men in this sample disclose their HIV/AIDS status to their families. The more strongly the level of acculturation to North American culture, the more it might be possible for men to disclose their illness to their family. At least that was the theory held by the developers of the instrument.

An Acculturation Scale
Directions: Please use one of the five answers provided to let us know about the way you view your ties to your country of origin.

1 = Not at all
2 = Very little or not very often
3 = Moderately
4 = Very often
5 = Almost always

1. I like to identify myself as _____.(country of origin)
   1 2 3 4 5
2. I speak Spanish.   1 2 3 4 5
3. My thinking is done in the Spanish language. 1 2 3 4 5
4. I write in Spanish. 1 2 3 4 5
5. I listen to Spanish language radio/television. 1 2 3 4 5

Discussion

This instrument deals with heartbreaking issues: AIDS, homophobia, family denial and rejection, and issues of the subject's own feelings about his sexual orientation and AIDS. These are not easy subjects, and one could predict that the respondents would have a difficult time answering truthfully. That certainly was the case in this study. Many of the answers given by the men in the sample were very socially desirable even though, in the end, it became painfully clear that Hispanic men in the sample did not disclose their illness because of the shame they thought it would bring to their families and the family rejection they might experience as gay men with AIDS. These are painful issues and no instrument will get it exactly right. I like the acculturation scale and many of the questions seem right on the mark. There is an opportunity in this instrument for some very revealing answers. This, as we discovered, was the case. The thrust of the responses received indicated that Hispanic men in this sample, dying of AIDS, would prefer the anonymity of dying alone rather than the rejection of their families. And while the respondents often told mothers and sisters about their AIDS, they almost never told fathers or brothers. The thought of living with this sort of deception in the midst of the absolute misery of dying from AIDS troubled us a great deal. That's why we added questions about dichos or proverbs. We wanted to know what coping philosophies the subjects used, and we thought that asking them questions about their philosophy of life would result in very revealing responses.

What we received were a number of proverbs suggesting that the subjects were as homophobic as their families. Many of them said that they were living doomed, unnatural lives and that they would eventually pay for it. They were able to deal with AIDS because they saw it as a form of "punishment" for having chosen an "unnatural and unhealthy" lifestyle (in the subject's words). These are tragic thoughts about their lives, made at a time of supposed enlightenment toward gender issues. You can see, however, that the instrument tries to study socially upsetting issues in a gentle and unobtrusive way, if that is ever completely possible.

Making Sense out of Open-Ended Answers

Okay. We have an interesting open-ended instrument. What do we do with the material we've collected? First, we read through the answers and sort them by categories (discrete groups) of answers until we have six or seven (more or less) categories. Then, for computing purposes, we assign each subject's response a number related to the category the answer most closely resembles. Clear? Maybe not.

To help explain how we create categories from open-ended responses, let's take question number 10 in the preceding measure of client disclosure of their AIDS status to their families. That question asks, "How would you describe your parent's view of life?" Let's say respondent number one answers, "Very traditional." We create a category we call "Very Traditional" and assign it the number 1. The next respondent says, "Very Catholic." We then create a new category and assign that category, "Very Catholic," the number 2. The third respondent says, "Very traditional." We already have a category for "very traditional" so that response gets a number 1. Respondent four says, "A small town view of life." We now have another category to which we assign the number 3. (In reality, the responses usually include roughly 5 to 7 categories.) Instead of having 20 or 30 statements, we now have 5 to 7 categories. Each response is given the number corresponding to the category it most closely resembles. In effect, we have created a Likert Scale from the open-ended responses on the instrument. We can now enter open-ended answers into the computer as numbers and conduct a statistical analysis from our open-ended responses.

You might be thinking that it would be easier to create a Likert Scale to begin with and that doing so would have saved us a lot of work. Well, yes, that's probably true. But how would we know the categories for our Likert Scale without first having asked open-ended questions? Furthermore, open-ended answers sometimes provide elegant answers that can be quoted in our report and tend to add more meaning to the study. If we are using a standardized instrument, one that is valid and reliable and has been created to measure a certain kind of behavior like depression or self-esteem, our open-ended responses can sometimes completely negate the findings on the standardized instrument. The reason for this is that the answers to the closed-ended questions may be socially desirable while the answers to the open-ended questions may be painfully honest. Even the most instrument-oriented researcher knows that when dissonance (disagreement) exists between a closed-ended and an open-ended response, you should give more meaning to the open-ended response.

As an example, I did a very large job satisfaction survey of MSW Social Workers in the western part of the United States (Glicken, 1977). The instrument I used was called the Job Descriptive Index or, as it is known in its abbreviated version, the JDI (Bowling Green State University, 1997). It defines and attempts to measure job satisfaction in five primary categories: satisfaction with pay, promotional opportunities, co-workers, the work itself, and the supervision. All five categories of satisfaction, after the study was completed, showed very high levels of satisfaction with the exception of satisfaction with co-workers, which was fairly low (odd that social workers can't get along with one another, don't you think?). On the face of it, the sample looked pretty job satisfied except in the area of co-worker satisfaction. Satisfied, that is, until I read the open-ended answers to three questions asking respondents: 1) what they didn't like about their jobs; 2) their future work plans; and 3) anything they would change on the job, if they could. The responses to these three open-ended questions were so negative, and there were so many of them (80% of the 400 returned questionnaires had written responses to the open-ended questions), that I concluded the sample was very job dissatisfied even though the standardized measure (the JDI) said they were quite satisfied. Respondents provided highly negative statements such as, "I love my clients, but the agency is so punitive and so brutalizes clients that I can no longer continue working here." Another respondent wrote, "My clients are wonderful, but when I listen to colleagues calling them bums and other insulting things, I just can't see myself continuing on in social work."

I had so many negative responses and so many of them were very well written, that I created an entire section in the appendix of the final report with verbatim responses to each of the three open-ended questions. It was, according to the readers of the study, the best part of the report. Had I not included an open-ended section of the survey, you can bet that my conclusion would have been that social workers in my sample were fairly satisfied with their work. My experience, and that of many other social researchers, makes a strong argument for having enough open-ended questions in any study to check the validity of a standardized instrument. While the instrument I chose to use had validity and reliability data that were compelling, the fact is that my sample demonstrated that the instrument was not a valid measure of job satisfaction with a social work population.

But how could that be? Social workers were included in the original data norming the instrument. I wouldn't have used the instrument had I not been able to compare my data against that of the normative data on social workers found by the instrument developers. Several reasons come to mind. First of all, I think job satisfaction is a subject influenced by social desirability. It just isn't okay for most of us to tell strangers about our job unhappiness. Social workers who work in organizations that can be very meddlesome and autocratic (large public agencies, for the most part) may worry about the impact their statements have on their professional identity. Social workers, like many people in the helping professions, hate to admit that they're in life situations that cause them pain. I can imagine the respondents saying to themselves as they filled out the survey that social workers should be in control of their emotional lives. Being unhappy at work suggests poor control and, therefore, that something is wrong with the social worker. Secondly, the open-ended questions were about issues external to the social worker. I can also imagine the social workers who filled out the open-ended questions saying to themselves, "I'm a hard-working, honorable, and responsible person but that darn agency or those darn co-workers of mine—if only they'd shape up." In other words, the JDI was a measure of their satisfaction with *their* performance on the job while the open-ended questions were a measure of other people's performance on the job. Finally, it's possible that my sample of social workers differed from the sample on which the JDI was normed. I find that difficult to believe but, none-the-less, it's possible.

Isn't research interesting? Who would have thought that I would get such unusual data? This is the sort of puzzling thing that happens a good deal of the time in social research. If you like trying to solve mysteries, you'll love doing social research.

Cover Letters Used with Instruments

If you are planning on using an instrument that is mailed, or one that you might pass out at an agency or some other public setting, it's a very good idea to include a cover letter. A cover letter is probably most effective if you use the letterhead of some official organization. In the case of students, perhaps you could use the letterhead of your university department with your instructor co-signing the letter. Good cover letters explain the reason the research is being conducted. They also give a strong emotional argument about why the respondent should complete the questionnaire and return it as quickly as possible. Good cover letters can substantially increase the response rate.

In a cover letter, you need to give vital information that includes: who you are, what the study is about, why it's important for the respondent to complete the questionnaire, how the research will be disseminated, and how it might positively affect the life of the respondent, or of others. You also need to include an informed consent and debriefing statement. More on that in Chapter 13. The letter should be short, direct, and to the point. Let's give it a try.

Example of a Cover Letter

Dear Sir or Madam:

Please, please, please complete the enclosed questionnaire and mail it back to me today. If you don't, I'll fail research, my parents will go into a depression, I'll never graduate, and I will spend the rest of my life breaking rocks in the local rock quarry. That will lead to alcoholism, depression, and homelessness. Please don't let this happen to me.

Signed,

Desperate

Well, maybe not. Too emotional. Let's give it another try.

Dear Sir or Madam: January 1, 2003

The questionnaire I've enclosed is very brief. It should take no more than 10 minutes to complete. The questionnaire asks you to rate your work satisfaction. All responses are confidential. None of the questionnaires are coded and I can assure you of complete anonymity.

This national survey of teachers is an attempt to find out what is good and bad about life at work for primary and secondary teachers in America. The results will be published in most local papers and will be presented on the CBS, ABC, and NBC nightly news. You will also be sent, free of charge, a brief synopsis of the findings.

People often feel that there is nothing they can do to change how they feel at work. This is your opportunity to respond to a national survey on the work satisfaction of teachers. Your responses can have a direct and immediate impact on your workplace and your job happiness.

Please take the few minutes it will require you to complete the survey and send it in the enclosed, stamped, self-addressed envelope by January 21, 2003.

Thank you for your assistance.

(Your name and title)

Sending out the Results to Participants

If possible, send the results to everyone in the survey. A one or two page report makes people feel good about taking part in the study. The following is a short report (in Spanish) sent to a group of professionals in Chiapas, Mexico where several of my students did a depression study on the impact of the civil war in Chiapas, Mexico on women near the war zone. I wrote the report in English and it was presented at a symposium on international research at California State University, San Bernardino (Glicken & Alamsha, April 1998).

> *The Brief Report: Depression among Women in Chiapas, Mexico*
> Seventy women in rural and urban areas of Chiapas, Mexico were given a depression scale (the CES-D), translated into Spanish by the Mexican Institute of Psychiatry, to determine if the political unrest in Chiapas was having a detrimental affect on the mental health of women living in, or near, the most violent areas of unrest. Additionally, the seventy women were interviewed at length about support systems that kept them well, emotionally. Finally, eighteen professional mental health workers in Chiapas were interviewed regarding their impressions of the level of depression among Chiapas women with particular concern for the helping networks these women had developed to cope with the stressors of living in an area beset by political unrest.
>
> The research was conducted by two graduate social work students at California State University, San Bernardino under the direction of a social work faculty member and with assistance from several faculty members at a university setting in Chiapas. The Mexican Institute of Psychiatry gave additional assistance. The research was done during the last two weeks of December 1997 when forty-five dead bodies were discovered in a community not far from where the research was being conducted.

Preliminary findings of the study are as follows:

1. The women interviewed had levels of depression lower than the average of other women living in Mexico as normed by the Mexican Institute of Psychiatry.

2. Support systems for the women interviewed included extended family and church affiliation although, for the most part, church affiliation was non-Catholic and was what we in the United States would probably consider Evangelical or Fundamentalist Christian. Many of the women, however, also attended traditional Catholic mass and saw no particular inconsistency in their involvement in two dissimilar Christian denominations.

3. There was considerable distance between what the professional mental health workers thought about the way this population coped with political unrest and the way the women themselves reported their coping. One example is that professionals believed that most women in the sample used folk healers to treat depression, yet every woman interviewed (n=70) denied the use of folk healers, informing the interviewers that folk healers were primitive and unhelpful. However, the interviewers spoke to four folk healers in the geographic area of the study who estimated that their average client load was about 150 clients per day, many seeking help for problems with depression.

4. While the women in the study had very low scores on the depression instrument (the CES-D), suggesting that they were not depressed, they did admit to hiding feelings of depression. The literature refers to this as *masking* depression, and there is some anecdotal evidence collected by the interviewers that the women may have been more depressed than noted by the depression instrument. It's possible, of course, that social desirability played a strong role in lowering depression scores on the instrument.

5. The researchers used a technique that compares pictures of people who are depressed to the facial expressions of actual clients. The National Institute of Mental Health in the United States developed this technique. Using this method of testing, more than one half of the women in the sample looked depressed. This subjective approach was tested against the clinical impression of the two researchers, one of whom is originally from Chiapas. Both researchers felt that almost 90 percent of the sample, through verbal and non-verbal communications, indicated levels of depression that would sug-

gest the need for treatment (counseling or medication). The differences in these three measures suggest that scores on the CES-D depression instrument were influenced by social desirability.

6. The women were far more sophisticated about depression than the researchers expected. Many had heard of anti-depressant drugs familiar in the United States (such as Prozac), and most knew something about counseling and psychotherapy. However, most of the subjects denied that they had ever been in therapy or that they had ever used anti-depressants. Many of the rural women interviewed admitted that they used alcohol in excess, but explained that it was almost always used in conjunction with social events, holidays, and celebrations where heavy drinking was socially condoned.

7. While the women interviewed were quite aware of the political situation in Chiapas and the personal risks involved in being critical of the government, the researchers found them to be surprisingly open in their opinions about the various problems facing the people in Chiapas and the role played by the opposing political factions in contributing to or resolving these problems.

8. There were very few women who refused to be interviewed, but the interviewers felt that the women, while honest in their responses, were also very guarded. This may have been a function of the fact that none of the women in the study had ever been interviewed by a researcher. It may also have been possible that the subjects were uncomfortable with what they felt was an obtrusive process (homes were chosen at random and the interview protocol, even though it was pre-tested at length before the study began, turned out to take over an hour to complete). Politeness is an important aspect of Mexican behavior and the women, rather than being guarded, may have felt some degree of hostility.

Summary

In this chapter, we considered four common types of instruments. Each instrument was evaluated for its potential use as a way of collecting data. The chapter considered ways of writing cover letters and the brief report that might be sent to the respondents in a study as a way of informing them about the findings in the study and thanking them for their help with the study.

REVIEW QUESTIONS

1. When would a Likert Scale be most useful to the researcher?

2. When might open-ended questions be most useful in a research study?

3. Why should you abide by the 10-minute rule in instrument construction?

4. Questions that are interesting but not really relevant are called "fishing expedition" questions. What are the pluses and minuses of these sorts of questions?

5. When might it be appropriate to create and use our own instrument?

REFERENCES

American Psychiatric Association. (1994). *DSM-IV questions and answers*. [Online]. Retrieved January 2, 2002 from the World Wide Web: <http://www.psych.org/clin_res/q_a.cfm>

Bowling Green State University. (1997). *Job descriptive index*. [Online]. Retrieved January 2, 2002 from the World Wide Web: http://www.bgsu.edu/departments/psych/JDI/

Camilli, G., & Shepard, L. A. (1994). *Methods for identifying biased test items*. Thousand Oaks, CA: Sage.

Dean, J. P., & Whyte, W. F. (1969). How do you know if the informant is telling the truth? In G. McCall and J. L. Simmons (Eds.), *Issues in participant observation* (pp. 105–115). Reading, MA: Addison-Wesley.

Fink, A., & Kosecoff, J. (1985). *How to conduct surveys*. Thousand Oaks, CA: Sage.

Geer, J. G. (1988). What do open-ended questions measure? *Public Opinion Quarterly, 552*, 365–371.

Glicken, M. (1977). *The job satisfaction of social workers in the southwest*. Unpublished doctoral dissertation, University of Utah.

Glicken, M., & Alamsha, K. (1998, April). Levels of depression in women of Chiapas, Mexico. *Symposium of International Scholarship*, California State University, San Bernadino.

Herzog, R. A., & Bachman, J. G. (1981). Effects of questionnaire length on response quality. *Public Opinion Quarterly, 45*, 549–559.

Mooney, L., & Gramling, R. B. (1991). Asking threatening questions and situational framing: The effects of decomposing survey items. *Sociological Quarterly, 32*, 227–288.

Ostrom, T. M., & Gannon, K. M. (1996). Exemplar generation: Assessing how respondents give meaning to rating scales. In N. Schwarz and S. Sudman (Eds.), *Answering questions* (pp. 293–318). San Francisco: Jossey-Bass.

Pearson, M. R., & Dawes, R. M. (1992). Personal recall and the limits of retrospective questions in surveys. In J. Turner (Ed.), *Questions about questions: Inquiries into the cognitive bases of surveys* (pp. 65–94). New York: Russell Sage Foundation.

Radloff, L. S. (1977). The CES-D scale: A self-report depression scale for research in the general population. *Applied Psychological Measurements, 1*, 385–407.

Schaefer, D., & Dillman, D. A. (1998). Development of a standard email methodology. *Public Opinion Quarterly, 62*, 378–397.

Schumann, H., & Presser, S. (1979). The open and closed question. *American Sociological Review, 44*, 692–712.

Schumann, H., & Presser, S. (1981). *Questions and answers in attitude surveys: Experiments on question form, wording and content*. New York: Academic Press.

Schwarz, N., Knauper, B., Hippler, H. J., Noelle-Neumann, E., & Clark, L. (1991). Rating scales: Numeric values may change the meaning of scale labels. *Public Opinion Quarterly, 55*, 570–582.

Schwarz, N., & Hippler, H. J. (1995). Subsequent questions may influence answers to preceding questions in mail surveys. *Public Opinion Quarterly, 59,* 93–97.

Smith, T. W. (1995). Trends in non-response rates. *International Journal of Public Opinion Research, 7,* 156–171.

Wiens, A. N., & Matarazzo, J. D. (1983). Diagnostic interviewing. In M. Hersen, A. E. Kazdin, & A. S. Bellack (Eds.), *The clinical psychology handbook* (pp. 309–328). New York: Pergamon.

Zook, A., Jr., & Sipps, G. J. (1985). Cross-validation of a short form of the Marlowe-Crowne social desirability scale. *Journal of Clinical Psychology, 41,* 236–238.

RECOMMENDED INTERNET SITES

APA Testing Information Clearinghouse
<http://www.apa.org/science/testclearinghs.html>
Code of Fair Testing in Education
<http://www.apa.org/science/fairtestcode.html>
Statement on the Disclosure of Test Data
<http://www.apa.org/science/disclosu.html>
Statement on the Use of Secure Psychological Tests in the Education of Graduate and Undergraduate Psychology Students
<http://www.apa.org/science/securetests.html>
Rights and Responsibilities of Test Takers
<http://www.apa.org/science/ttrr.html>

CHAPTER 9

CASE STUDY

Experiments and surveys, the research strategies discussed in Chapters 6 and 7, typically involve many cases, and data on the cases are usually pooled or averaged in some way. Social scientists also conduct **systematic research** using only a single case or a few contrasting cases. Social scientists have conducted **case studies** of slum neighborhoods, various immigrant communities, social movements, drug gangs, neighborhood organizations, small rural communities, religious groups, small friendship groups, and large corporations. Whyte and Gans provide examples of field observation case study research.

A classic line of research on urban slum communities was conducted in the north end of Boston by William F. Whyte, Jr., and reported in his book, *Street Corner Society* (1955). Later, Herbert Gans conducted a similar study of second-generation Italians in the adjacent west end of Boston, reporting it in his book *Urban Villagers* (1962). Both researchers spent considerable time living and working in the communities, participating in events, observing everyday life, asking questions, and keeping copious notes. Gans and his wife lived in this "slum" neighborhood as he carried out his research. His observations identified the kinds of social networks in which the west-enders, young and old, were embedded, which he calls the peer group society. His analysis identified a basic paradox. Although the peer group provided people with a setting to express their individuality, these groups rarely worked together on problems and issues, such as an impending urban renewal project slated for their area.

Data for Gans's study came from observations he made while using the stores and facilities in that neighborhood, attending meetings and public gatherings, visiting with neighbors and friends, interviewing community representatives (formally and informally), talking with **informants,** and generally observing what was going on around him. Overall, he estimates that he actually talked with 100 to 150 of the 3,000 west-enders, intensely with 20 who were most involved in the peer group he joined at the invitation of a neighbor. Because peer groups were generally segregated by gender, Gans's wife provided information about women's groups she attended. Gans wrote his observations and reflections about them in a research journal. Later these voluminous notes served as the data to be coded or organized by the themes and topics in which he became interested (Gans, 1962).

The process of doing case study research by field observation techniques raised a number of problems about gaining access, building trust and rapport, finding a comfortable role that permitted asking questions and recording answers, deciding how much of his research objectives to reveal, and determining whether his observations adequately captured what was going on in Boston's west end. These issues and the techniques used in case study research are discussed in this chapter.

Case study research may lead to new perspectives on old theoretical issues, the discovery of new phenomena, and the development of new concepts and theoretical perspectives. Some of this work provides a detailed description of a setting, illustrates important concepts, fills in the dynamic details of how things influence each other, uncovers reasons and meanings behind behaviors or attitudes, and challenges existing theories and stereotypes.

In this chapter we lay out some of the principles and techniques, key issues, strengths, and weaknesses of case study research as a strategy for systematic social science research. Case study research may use many different types of data (e.g., interviews, secondary data, as discussed in Chapter 9, and surveys or historic records), but in this chapter we emphasize field observation, a data-gathering procedure not emphasized in other chapters.

PRINCIPLES

The Rationale for Case Study Research

Case studies are used in social science research for several reasons. For example, a case study is appropriate when there is only one or a very few cases available to study, perhaps because a phenomenon occurs very rarely (e.g., the study of the impact of a particular program, the development of a social movement, the effects of an earthquake, or why a specific riot occurred the way it did). Case study research might be especially desirable as a way to investigate complex social phenomena such as street gang activity or to find out how things are related in some depth, such as how the social dynamics of bar-hopping friendship groups affects how much people drink, or how lifetime conscientious objectors can maintain their beliefs. Case studies help provide insight into meanings people give to the reality around them. It is also common for social scientists embarking on a new line of inquiry to examine a few cases in detail in order to become oriented to the phenomenon and how it can be studied.

Yin (1994) suggests that case study research is most useful when an investigator is interested in how and why events are interconnected, when the phenomenon under consideration is contemporary (not historical), and when an investigator does not have sufficient control to consider, for example, an experimental design. By studying one or a few contrasting cases, the investigator can often describe something in greater depth than would otherwise be possible.

Case study research often involves considerable personal involvement by the investigator in the day-to-day events of some social setting. This kind of study is often described as **field observation** research or **participant observation** research, even though observation is only one of the data-gathering techniques that might be used. Case studies use data from many relevant sources, including various census and other data archives, published records, diaries, personal interviews, and even surveys. In this chapter we highlight the field observation aspect of case study research. In Chapter 9 we discuss the use of archived data in social science research.

Typical Design Choices for Case Study Research

What distinguishes case study research is the overall pattern of choices across Riley's research design decisions (see Figure 4.1). For example, case study research generally involves work in the settings in which social behavior takes place, with implications for loss of control over what happens. This contrasts with experimental research, in which the researcher is typically in control of a special observational setting and phenomena to be observed are induced. In case study research the investigator needs patience and skill to deal with this lack of control in order to take advantage of opportunities and avoid pitfalls in the process of the research.

Cases are often some kind of collectivity or set of role relationships (e.g., a street corner gang or nursing home), and often the boundaries of a case and its context are blurred or the context is especially important to the understanding of the case itself. By choice or because of the required effort and cost of a large-scale case-by-case approach, case study research involves a single case (e.g., a particular immigrant neighborhood or a single firm) or very few cases. Cases are picked for their analytical value rather than in some random sampling fashion to represent accurately the distribution of some phenomenon in a specified population. This focus on a few handpicked critical cases may be helpful in research addressing some theoretical point, or when the researcher needs to know more about the phenomenon before creating more-formal measurement instruments, or because little is known and exploration is the first order of business in a line of research.

Usually a small number of key **organizing concepts** are at the forefront of case study research, but many phenomena are observed in rich detail. Data are usually original observations made by the investigator rather than secondary data from observations made by others, but existing reports and archives may also be used (e.g., newspaper stories, diaries, second-hand accounts of events). Case study research also tends to involve a longer data-gathering period than the typical experiment or survey. An investigator in the field is able to conduct interviews and observe how things are put together and how they change during the course of the observation. Case study research would be considered cross-sectional to the extent that a complex setting is described as it exists at one point in time regardless of the fact that it may take an investigator some time and repeated visits to a field site to complete the observations or other data-gathering work. On the other hand, case studies often involve some attention to changes through time or dynamic social processes. A case study would be considered longitudinal to the extent that repeated visits to the field site result in an analyzed record of changes through time. Still, the sociotemporal context is primarily contemporary: a specific geographic location and time period that are contemporaneous with the investigator's work.

Finally, analysis of the rich, often voluminous observational record (and any other data) is generally handled in a more summative way by the investigator, weighing the evidence and providing a **thick description** of the findings. That is, key aspects of the case are pulled together in an analytic way, with considerable attention to illustrative detail. Although some systematic tallying may occur, the overall conclusions are often more like an in-depth story or conceptual critique rather than a systematic discussion of tabulated data or statistical findings. As in other forms of research, attention is given to ensuring the **validity** and **reliability** of data and reasoning through **alternative explanations** of the phenomenon, mustering evidence for and against them.

The following are illustrative of the wide range of areas in which case study research has been used:

- Jaber Gubrium (1975) spent several months at a nursing home he called Murray Manor (a pseudonym), taking on several roles as participant–observer from work as a staff gerontologist's aide. His purpose was to examine how care in a nursing home is accomplished by the people who participate in its everyday life.

- Lawrence Wieder (1974) studied a halfway house for ex-convicts in East Los Angeles and became interested in the convict code, the subculture language used by ex-convicts. His job was to conduct an exploratory study to see why ex-convicts going through the program did not improve. He had an office in the halfway house, tried to avoid being thought of as a staff member, and used informants and observation in his work.

- Phyllis Baker (1996) used participant observation and interviewing with 16 White women in a shelter for battered women. The experiences of the women with services they received allowed Baker to trace out how they attempted to control their situations in the face of the professional perspectives of the shelter staff.

- Festinger, Riecken, and Schachter (1956) conducted a largely covert study of how a group that predicted the destruction of the world at a specific time prepared for the end and coped with the fact that the world did not end.

- William Thompson and Jackie Harred (1992) studied how topless dancers manage stigma by interviewing dancers and observing their relationships with managers, waiters, and bartenders in seven topless bars in a southwestern city.

- Hans Mauksch (1966) studied nursing practice in the context of a hospital.

- Loree Guthrie (1996), for her PhD dissertation, conducted a case study of teen parents in a school district by intensively studying four teen parents.

- Maxim Kiselev (1996) conducted a case study of children involved in the Chernobyl radiation disaster in Russia.

- Lumane Claude (1996) did a dissertation in which four rural Pennsylvania communities were compared on various aspects of community activity and well-being.

The focus of case studies is quite diverse, including studies of individuals, types of status or role relationship, an historic event, an occupational category, a community or neighborhood, various organizational settings, a certain category of behavior, or a category of norm or belief. Systematic study of cases, particularly field observation of cases, is a widely used approach to many lines of inquiry in the social sciences. As in other forms of inquiry, there are both strengths and characteristic weaknesses that must be considered. (See Box 8.1.)

Humans Observing Humans: Problems of Observation

As Madge (1965) and others point out, special research problems arise with human observation, particularly when humans observe humans. An initial problem is that of longevity. Given a professional researcher's career of, say, 30 years and current average lifetime of around 80 years, a trained human observer can never observe a

■ ■ ■ ■ ■ ────────────────────────────────────

BOX 8.1

ETHNOMETHODOLOGY

Inspired by the works of Schutz (1962, 1964, 1966), Harold Garfinkel (1967) developed a phenomenological approach to the study of the social world that he called ethnomethodology. This approach is mentioned here because it lends itself particularly to the case study approach described in this chapter. Garfinkel rejects the notion that a researcher should study a situation armed with preconceived sociological concepts because people, in their everyday lives, construct their social reality as they participate in social situations. As Turner says, "ethnomethodology is concerned with the common methods people employ—whether scientists, homemakers, insurance salespersons, or laborers—to create a sense of order about the situations in which they interact. I think that the best clue to this conceptual emphasis can be found in the word *ethnomethodology* itself—*ology*, 'study of'; *method*, 'the methods [used by]'; and *ethno*, 'folk or people' " (1991:476). Maleness, for example, is not a status that is assigned to a person and once assigned is a known and taken-for-granted characteristic of that person. Rather, the male through his actions in social situations is in a constant process of establishing and validating his maleness. It is the job of the ethnomethodologist, then, to observe the behavior of the "male" in a social situation in order to identify the actions he uses to establish for himself and others that he is, in fact, a male. Furthermore, the ethnomethodologist is not as interested in the substance of the concept of maleness as he or she is in the method the person uses to establish that the concept exists in the social order. As a result of their perspective, ethnomethodologists generally reject the research strategies of conventional sociologists because they consider it counterproductive to impose preconceived notions about the social world on their observations. They approach a case to be studied with a research question in mind, but they allow the data to evolve out of their observations, then try to make sense of what they are observing.

complete, typical human life course. Thus, of necessity, what a person can observe first-hand is time-limited.

The psychological and physiological characteristics of sight also affect observational findings. We sift through things we see, retaining some as important and discarding others as inconsequential or irrelevant. What humans see is conditioned by who they are and what they have learned. Often this is systematically structured by the researcher's position in the social class structure of his or her society (affected by other status characteristics such as age, ethnicity, and gender; see Bailey, 1996, for a discussion of status effects). For example, certain gestures and nods mean something that we have learned ourselves. Experience in a different society quickly underscores the great potential for error in some of these assumptions.

Furthermore, many social concepts are not readily observable. Concepts such as "peer group," "social class," or "leader" are often based on putting together details that are not all in one place at one time. Looking for relevant patterns takes special training and experience. Good observers of social phenomena are rare.

Human researchers cannot be everywhere all the time. They are caught up in some position in the social setting and can only observe some things from that position at a given time and place. There is an inherent need for triangulation, or looking at the same phenomenon repeatedly from different points of view, but humans can't do this instantaneously. Being a student in a class provides insights but also limits what one can observe about how the class is conducted, a problem shared by teachers and principals, who have different opportunities and limitations on what they can observe.

In the end, not all social phenomena are accessible for observation. Researchers may be barred from observing private behaviors, illegal events, or high-security areas. Researchers may not want to be around when some social behaviors happen, regardless of how important the behaviors are (e.g., an observer would not want to witness a murder or burglary because he or she may be considered an accomplice or be put in great danger).

The act of observing humans affects their social behavior to some extent (Sykes, 1978). If an observer joins a family at dinner to observe family dinnertime behavior, the act of joining itself influences what happens (i.e., a guest is at dinner and family members will be on their best behavior).

Although observations may be readily made, remembering what happened until it can be recorded is a problem. Memory functions to highlight certain things and discard others. Some social settings readily permit the researcher to make a systematic, on-the-spot recording of much of what happened (i.e., taking immediate notes or making video or audio recordings). In other settings, techniques must be developed to aid memory until details can be written down.

Finally, there are difficulties when researchers are attached emotionally or in some other way to the people they are observing, and this will affect the observations that are made as well as their interpretation.

The point is that good observation of social phenomena by human observers is a demanding task that requires specialized training, knowledge, experience, careful placement of the observer, good informants, repeated observations, calm reflection on the consequences of one's observational behavior, a healthy skepticism about one's abilities and conclusions, and a good dose of luck. The techniques of field observation research, as of survey and experimental research, are designed to help investigators avoid pitfalls and improve their chances of collecting useful, accurate data. Some of these techniques are briefly introduced here.

TECHNIQUES

Good field observation involves a keen awareness of the social setting and the role of the investigator in it. It involves social skills on the part of the investigator that are not used in the same way in other styles of research. Patience, empathy, and careful listening are key.

There are several books in addition to Yin's (1994) that provide unusually helpful discussions of field observation research. Habenstein (1970) provides a collection of researchers' explanations of their case study research experience, from gaining access to analyzing results. Lofland and Lofland (1984) describe what to look for and how to proceed in analyzing social settings. In this section we summarize the main steps in case study research, which many of these researchers describe in greater detail.

Preparing for the Field

Although case studies often are exploratory, this does not mean that the investigator can start without a research problem in mind and initial ideas about what to examine and what to look for. To study a specific setting, the Loflands (1984) suggested that the investigator needs to use his or her own interests, background, and experiences as a starting point. Then the possible study sites must be evaluated for appropriateness for the research problem and for accessibility. Prior knowledge of a setting is very valuable, so case studies are often focused around places in which investigators are employed or places in which they have been involved that provoke their intellectual curiosity. It is also important that the investigator have the skills needed to operate in the environment. For example, knowing the language or argot of the site and having necessary social skills or the ability to participate may be important. The Loflands (1984) point out that field observation research may put special demands on an investigator to handle feeling lonely or rejected, being marginal in a group, becoming involved in events that are morally repugnant or dangerous, or feeling anxiety about being in a social setting that is uncertain and not under their control. Not all researchers are well suited for field observation work.

Prior research on the topic of interest and any theory that has been proposed in the literature will be helpful in establishing a background for case study research. This background will help determine which research settings are likely to provide relevant information so that one or more cases can be chosen for analytic purposes. Rarely is there sufficient background information for case study research. In fact, one of the strong motivations for case study research is to gain first-hand, in-depth information that can be used as background for further study.

Many case study investigators use some variant of the Glaser and Strauss (1967) grounded theory approach (Strauss and Corbin, 1997). It is an inquiry process that develops inductively from detailed familiarity with first-hand observational data. But case study research may also begin with alternative hypotheses about what is going on, and these hypotheses can be examined with data from a case study.

Case studies may involve selected, contrasting cases that help eliminate alternative explanations of the phenomenon of interest. Contrasts are almost always helpful in interpreting data. Nevertheless, cases are treated individually rather than averaged, as would be appropriate when estimates of characteristics of some defined population are sought, based on a representative sample of cases.

Gaining Access

Once the investigator has clarified the research problem and selected one or more research sites, the next problem is to gain **access**. The researcher may be able to choose whether to gain access without disclosing the fact that he or she is conducting research (e.g., observing people at a ball game or in a bar, getting hired by a firm, or volunteering at a homeless care center) or by disclosing his or her intent and the nature of the research.

Not disclosing the researcher's agenda may pose minimal ethical problems in public settings, but ethical issues are of more concern when access to private settings is gained by misrepresenting one's intent. An example would be research on a closed group such as the one Festinger et al. (1956) describe. Their team became covert members of a group in order to observe the consequences of beliefs that did not come true.

If the choice is to disclose the nature of the research, then the investigator needs a brief and readily understood account or explanation of what he or she is doing. Often this is not detailed, in part because the investigator may feel that full disclosure might affect the quality of data being gathered. More often it is because the details of one's research are not understandable or of interest to gatekeepers or other participants in the research. Although the story remains the same, how it is phrased may vary depending on the audience. Some investigators choose to account for their work simply by saying that they are writing a book about the setting, for example.

How one moves into a research setting has important consequences for what data can be gathered. For example, when there are traditional tensions between employers and employees, coming in under the auspices of management may make it very difficult to get in-depth information from employees (and vice versa). Often the investigator does not have sufficient information ahead of time to understand the tensions in the setting. Prior familiarity with the site pays off, but the investigator needs the social skill to understand potential problems quickly so they can be avoided.

Gatekeepers guard access to most social settings. Nursing home administrators and families may control access to older residents. School staff and parents guard access to research involving school classes. Prison staff quite literally are gatekeepers for research on prisoners. Higher-level organizational staff control research access to most firms. Research on virtually any group must take account of those who have a strong stake in controlling access. Even research in communities may run amok if appropriate stakeholders are not consulted first. Thus, it is not uncommon for researchers doing research in a community to notify city officials, including the police. A concern is whether to enter a setting from the top down or the bottom up or in some other way. Each has potential consequences for the research process.

Gatekeepers (and others in the research setting) will want to assess the trustworthiness of the researcher and the potential threat of the research. The researcher's genuine interest in the setting and professional commitment to inquiry help. Spending time in the setting is important for establishing trust. The researcher's auspices and connections may also help. University research, for example, usually suggests importance, neutrality, objectivity, and skill. William F. Whyte's study of the streetcorner gang in Boston illustrates the importance of the gatekeeper to the success of a study (Whyte, 1955). Whyte sought and received the endorsement of Doc, the leader of the gang, before embarking on his study. Furthermore, his behavior in his role as an observer legitimized his presence.

Sometimes preliminary correspondence is written on official letterhead to convey sponsorship and affiliation. Introductions by appropriate people known to those in the setting also help establish the researcher's credibility and trustworthiness. Assurance of confidentiality helps, but the researcher's behavior is paramount. Specific ways to develop a sense of trust and neutrality include not disclosing to others in the setting things informants from different factions have shared in confidence and inventing pseudonyms for the organizations and informants discussed in a research write-up.

Concern for potential sources of harm and ethical considerations are important for case study research, as they are for all research, although the specific issues vary. Courtesy, respect, open-mindedness, and friendliness help in field research, as they do in most social encounters.

Habenstein (1970) notes that a researcher may "get in," but the real question is, "How far in?" Simply gaining physical access is not sufficient for most case study research; one needs cooperation in getting accurate and full information. Again, "how far in" depends a good deal on how trusted the researcher becomes and how important the researcher's interest seems to be.

What Role to Play

Researchers in a field setting will have one or more roles. These provide opportunities to find out about certain things, and they also limit the extent to which some things can be seen or known. The role also affects research data in distinctive ways. Selecting appropriate and useful roles is important for case study research that uses field observation. Whether the researcher is a participant or a nonparticipant in the social activities of the research setting is a common distinction. If one is a participant, that often improves the sense of trust and openness and it may get the researcher into settings that would otherwise be hard to observe. On the other hand, being a participant often limits observation or possibilities for accurately recording data. One could also decide to be known as an observer or researcher. There often is value in being known explicitly as an observer because questions can be asked that would not be possible if one were only a participant. Field study researchers often underscore the desirability of not appearing to know too much (so one can be "educated"), but not knowing too little (being so uninformed as to not understand what is going on and not being credible). Usually field observers choose to be some combination of observer and participant. The student role is often useful because of the balance it provides between interest, knowledge, and willingness to be taught.

The researcher is unlikely to have only a single role in a setting. For example, in parts of the study or with certain groups or events, an investigator may be a participant–observer, participating in a perfunctory way in unfolding events but being known as an observer too. In other situations the researcher may be simply a nonparticipant–observer, sitting back and observing what is happening. One could be a participant in a community but only an observer of a specific event. Needless to say, an investigator needs considerable social skill to recognize what is going on and behave appropriately to accomplish research objectives. Awareness of the consequences of one's behavior and ability to listen with a trained social scientist's understanding makes the field observer's role difficult.

The experienced researcher in a field setting monitors his or her own emotional reactions and involvement in the setting. It is not difficult to become so engrossed in a setting and the people that one loses some perspective and ability to question events. **Going native** means becoming so much a part of a setting that researchers think of themselves as members, uncritically adopt the perspectives and beliefs, and interpret events like other members of the group. Careful preparation for fieldwork may include a colleague or adviser outside the setting who can help a field worker maintain an analytic perspective and monitor his or her own behavior as a researcher.

Gathering and Recording Data

Case study research may involve data from a variety of different sources, gathered in many of the ways discussed in earlier chapters. Field research often involves data from interviews with key participants. A brief interview schedule or list of question topics may be developed so that the investigator covers the needed topics. Interviews might be conducted with people selected because of the role they play in the setting (e.g., mayor, banker, police officer, leader, "typical" participant), asking about their activities, beliefs, norms, and connections as well as their view of the setting and other actors. Case studies may also involve information from **key informants** who are in a position to know some aspects of the case and are willing to share their information. Selection of qualified informants greatly expands the range of information a researcher can obtain. A range of informants in different positions is one triangulation technique used to check the validity of one's observations.

Both words and behavior are usually included as data. Often it is helpful to have a series of questions in mind to guide observation (e.g., what the setting is like, who is there, what their roles are, why they are there, what time of day it is, how long something takes, what actually happened, what meanings it has for participants, and who communicates with whom). Lofland and Lofland (1984) suggest questions such as, "Who is he? What does he do? What do you think she meant by that? What are they supposed to do? Why did she do that? Why is that done? What happens after ___? What would happen if ___? What do you think about ___? Who is responsible if ___?" Becker (1970) suggests asking "how" questions rather than "why" questions to avoid getting only rationalizations of action.

Data from field observations, information from informants, and interviews must be recorded as close to the time of observation as possible to avoid problems with memory and factual distortion. It is said that if it doesn't exist in one's notes, it didn't happen. Full and careful notes are key. Sometimes note keeping can be aided by tape recordings (video or audio), which are later transcribed and reviewed. Although some investigators worry about the distortion recording equipment might cause in the events being recorded, they often find that with explanation and after a short period of time, subjects ignore or forget about the recording device.

Field notes are usually kept as a journal, chronologically, with care in recording what actually happened and, *separately,* what the researcher thinks it means. As in all research, it is important to identify the time and place of observations. A system is needed to identify actors so that observations relating to a given actor can be pulled together later in the analysis. Although detailed notes are recorded as soon as possible, field researchers usually devote considerable time at the end of each day to go over their notes, write out cryptic abbreviations, fill in gaps that are remembered later (with an indication that it is a later addition), add interpretations and reflections (again, with a clear indication that it is an interpretation), and generally put their notes in order for later use (e.g., adding key words, numbering paragraphs).

If an investigator chooses not to disclose the fact that he or she is doing research, then recording data at the time of observation is more difficult. It would be suspicious to have someone in a group making notes when he or she should be participating in what is going on. When the research role is not disclosed, investigators have a number of ways to do the recording, using mnemonic schemes to aid memory and recall of events until they can be recorded or strategies for going to a private place (e.g., a bathroom) to record notes.

Some rather elaborate techniques have been developed to capture what is going on. One example is research by Richard Sykes and Brent (1980), who developed a computer keypad on a clipboard that could be used to enter codes rapidly for unfolding interaction between police and citizens. This provided a time-marked sequence of codes that were used later to examine how sequences of behavior led to certain outcomes (Brent and Sykes, 1979, 1980; Sykes and Brent, 1980). In this case, field observers had to be trained in an **observational language,** which was used in the recording process.

In a study of the effect of drinking-group interaction on amount of drinking, Sykes and his colleagues used a multichannel tape recorder disguised in a gym bag to pick up the conversation of each member of a drinking group (Sykes et al., 1980, 1993). Groups were recruited and members wore small microphones while they were in the bar. The field observer sat at a different table with the gym bag of recording equipment and kept observational notes. One of the skills that observers had to learn in that study was to judge the amount of alcohol consumed. In preparation for this, Sykes conducted a series of studies of local bar glassware (to determine how much different kinds of glasses typically held, allowing for the style of ice cubes used and the kind of drink). In fact, one of the graduate students who was a key part of the research team was sent to bartending school to attain the skill base needed to identify the kind of drink being served.

Field notes and textual data can be kept in a handwritten journal, but increasingly investigators are entering their data and observations directly into computer files. This saves later transcription so that the investigator can enter field notes into one of the computer programs available for organizing, coding, and retrieving segments of field notes for analysis.

Leaving the Field

Getting out of a field setting with feelings of having ended things in an appropriate way is sometimes difficult. Personal friendships have been established and a participating researcher will have built up expectations and obligations. Should one maintain contact with friends? What if they have come to depend on the investigator as a participant in some planned event? How does one bring a role relationship to an end? The case study researcher may want to return to the community to fill in gaps or see how things have changed. Once the research has been written up (in final or draft form), the researcher may want to have selected informants review the conclusions in order to catch obvious misinterpretations or to add their own reflections on the research. The investigator would have to guard assurances of confidentiality and avoid emphasizing a narrower view based on a single perspective.

Analyzing Findings

Case study research, especially if it involves extensive field observations, generally results in a voluminous file of notes and recordings, identified and time-dated, ready for analysis. Usually the researcher continuously analyzes the data as they are collected so that the research journal or other record contains a growing set of reflections on what is going on (kept separate and labeled as such). It is usually suggested that field observation continue until the researcher has a sense that nothing new is being uncovered. To reach that sense, analysis in some form must occur as the field work unfolds. In the end, once the data are available, the researcher reviews all the material, does any comparison that is needed, and verifies that positive and negative evidence for conclusions has been adequately considered. Illustrative incidents and quotes are often identified for use in the final write-up of the research. How do investigators do this?

There are several discussions of the analysis process, often under the label of **qualitative analysis.** Of course, case study research involves both quantitative and qualitative information, but the process of analysis is often more descriptive and interpretive rather than primarily statistical. For example, the analyst goes over all the data, sorting segments into categories by topics, actors, or important concepts that the investigator has identified. Interpretive memos and comments are added, and the process of organizing and interpreting takes many iterations before the evidence, conclusions, and illustrations are all together. Good discussions of qualitative analysis can be found in texts devoted to the purpose, such as Bailey (1996), Lofland and Lofland (1984), Yin (1994), Cresswell (1994), Coffey and Atkinson (1996), Denzin (1994), and Emerson (1983).

Lofland and Lofland (1984) suggest that in analyzing field notes an investigator should consider 11 "thinking units": meanings, practices, episodes, encounters, roles, relationships, groups, organizations, settlements, worlds, and lifestyles. In each case, they suggest raising seven questions: What type is it? What is its structure? How frequent is it? What are its causes? What are its processes? What are its consequences? and What are people's strategies?

Computer aids to the analysis of field notes and other case study data are increasingly available. Weitzman and Miles (1995), Fielding and Lee (1993), and Richards and Richards (1994), for example, describe many of these programs in detail. With the widespread use of computers, many new procedures are being developed. Chapter 9 describes some content analysis procedures that are useful in analyzing and organizing field notes and verbatim transcripts of conversations. Here we mention two programs that have gained some broader usage in the social sciences.

One is called Ethnograph (Seidel et al., 1995). It is a microcomputer-based program that uses a computerized file of field notes and other textual data as its input. The program permits the researcher to mark off segments of text and assign a code. For example, one could mark instances of prisoners talking about guards. Multiple codes can be assigned to the same text segment (e.g., date of observation, characteristics of the person being observed, topical codes for what is being discussed). Text segments can be retrieved and printed so all data relevant to a particular point can be examined and compared. Ethnograph is particularly useful for organizing and analyzing field observation notes.

NUD*IST (Non-numerical, Unstructured Data Indexing, Searching and Theorizing) is another program that is useful in handling voluminous field notes and transcribed text (Weitzman and Miles, 1995). It is similar in many ways to Ethnograph but it permits a different style of analysis. Codes can be organized hierarchically and viewed in useful graphic tree displays. Memos can easily be embedded in the original text, and the memos themselves can be coded and organized.

More-complex logical combinations of codes can be searched and retrieved so that a researcher can go into considerable detail in examining various special conditions within the data.

Once the data are summarized and the report written with illustrations of events and quotations, the write-up is sometimes shown to other colleagues and sometimes to selected key informants who may have been privy to the purposes of the research in the field setting. Reactions and suggestions help improve and correct the interpretation the investigator has reached. Outside perspectives are often helpful when an investigator becomes highly involved in the research and may take many things for granted.

ISSUES IN CASE STUDY RESEARCH

Three main issues are usually raised about case study research. First is the issue of **generalization.** To what extent can findings from a well-conducted case study be generalized to a larger class of cases? One perspective is that a sample of one case is very unreliable and likely to be biased by any number of selection factors. Cases are generally selected for their analytic value, convenience, or availability and thus are not intended to address the issue of representativeness. The extent to which the case is representative of a larger group of cases is unknown. When generalization to a larger, defined population is important, other research strategies such as a survey would be more appropriate if it could be achieved. It should be noted that many theoretical problems do not have an existing population from which a random sample could be drawn, even ignoring the problem of availability of sampling lists. Most theories refer to a broad class of cases that may exist in an infinite number of times and places. A large random sample of contemporary cases in the United States, as well as a single contemporary case, are only time- and place-bounded instances that may be relevant to a theory. What is needed, of course, is a continuing program of replicated studies in different times and places in order to test theories adequately and establish stable theoretical principles. Case studies often reveal and illustrate general principles, although the question of how broadly these principles may apply requires further inquiry.

A second issue concerning case studies has to do with the **level of rigor** with which they are conducted. Examining only evidence that supports preconceived ideas is not rigorous research. Both confirming and disconfirming evidence must be entertained (see Becker, 1958). It is often difficult for another researcher to examine reports and confirm that alternative explanations were considered unless the case study researchers provide **detailed documentation** of their examination of potential alternatives and how they handle potential biases and alternative explanations (see Liebow's description of his field observations in studying low-income males in Washington, DC, 1970). If a field setting permits an investigator to use repeatable and systematic procedures to observe and record data, greater rigor is gained (e.g., using a standardized measurement process to measure some concept). Systematic research procedures are often difficult to implement in field observation studies, and this may raise concerns about rigor. Validity and reliability of observations, in the case of field observation research, come from a researcher's discipline of checking out interpretations or descriptions of what happened by triangulation, always having more than one source of confirmation. This applies as much to reports by informants as to the observations by the investigators themselves. Finally, most research questions, explicitly or implicitly, involve comparison that give meaning to descriptions and explanations (e.g., whether the observed actions are usual for all groups or unusual for the group being observed). Case study research often involves carefully selected contrasting cases or contrasting expectations. Contrasts may be made with prior descriptions or theoretical expectations found in the literature. Greater rigor stems from relevant comparison.

Third is the issue of **how case study research is implemented.** This includes concerns about unbiased availability of information or access to situations that must be understood. There are practical matters such as the time required, especially for field observation case studies, and the skills the investigator needs to operate effectively as a researcher in a field setting. The discipline and ability needed to record germane and useful field notes accurately and to analyze them systematically raise many practical problems. Finally, there are issues of actually implementing solutions to ethical concerns in field observation studies. Most issues relevant to case studies and field observation are also relevant to other research strategies, although the possibilities for handling them differ.

Strengths of Case Studies

Case study research has a number of important advantages for systematic social science research. The payoff of a case study is that it provides greater detail about one or more instances of some social phenomenon. Case studies can lead to a more holistic, contextualized characterization of a case than is often possible with other research strategies. It is a research design that is particularly well suited to studying contemporary phenomena that call for an in-depth examination or detailing some process of change over time. It is one of the few options for studying rare or inaccessible cases. Case study research is helpful when research questions call for in-depth study of why and how something happened. Study of a single case or a few selected contrasting cases may be especially useful when detailed theoretical contrasts are called for. Case studies are also very useful in exploratory stages of research, when the distinction between a case and its context is contingent and not clear-cut, or when large-scale phenomena are being studied, such as a social movement in a community or society. Case study research permits investigators to follow more-dynamic processes and the detailed interplay between a case and its context. Finally, case studies can be less expensive than surveys and experiments.

Case studies use a number of different sources of data, including field observation, detailed interviews, key informants, surveys, and historic records. In this chapter we have focused on field observation as a somewhat distinctive approach to data gathering often used in case study research. Field observation has some distinctive strengths as well.

Field observation is a flexible inquiry procedure that permits the observation of nonverbal behavior, the shuttle of social interaction, and the relationships and activities of individuals or groups. It is useful in situations in which the researcher does not have control over what is happening. Seeing social phenomena in their natural environment leads to better understanding of the conditions and settings under which they occur. Probes and follow-up questions can be easily modified and adapted in new situations to better understand what is going on. When justified, **covert field observation** permits the study of situations that would be distorted or misreported in other modes of data gathering. It is often less reactive than other forms of data gathering. Field observation and interviewing are often better suited to getting at meanings and emotions. Being closer to the things being observed helps researchers avoid being misled about the meaning of events because further observations (triangulation) can help them decide between alternative interpretations. Establishing **rapport** with an informant permits the investigator to use that relationship to gain understanding.

Field observation reports are often used in other studies as a way of illustrating concepts and helping understand some phenomenon. Good field observation in the social sciences is akin to good observational work in astronomy. A data point is well established and can be used by others. Almost all lines of research include field observations somewhere in their development.

Weaknesses of Case Studies

Case study research cannot support generalization of findings to a broader, defined population. It is generally not possible to use statistical tools for descriptive or explanatory analysis in a case study because of the limit on the number of independent observations. However, in some situations, when a case is composed of a number of subunits, these subunits can be statistically examined. For example, in studying a community, distributions of individual characteristics such as age or income may be statistically handled and used to characterize the community as a whole. Nevertheless, case studies can be used to develop and clarify theory, develop useful concepts, and provide a good basis for generating testable hypotheses about broader populations, which can be used in research based on representative samples.

When field observation is the primary mode of data collection, there are a number of other weaknesses to consider. One is the lack of control over what happens in a field setting. This may make it impossible to achieve the observations one wants. It hampers systematic data recording, and it may make it hard to rule out alternative interpretations of what is happening. The sheer effort and skill of doing superior field observations may rule it out as a viable strategy for some problems and researchers. It may be difficult to measure some variables such as alienation, using standard scale instruments that are not available in a version based on observation. This, coupled with less control, may result in measurements that are less standardized than might be desired. Problems of gaining entry may bias what one can and cannot observe, as can the social skills of investigators and their personal relationships with participants. When anonymity is important (e.g., in studies of deviance), field researchers cannot promise confidentiality beyond what the law permits.

As in all research, the investigator must pick the research approach that maximizes strengths and minimizes problems.

SUMMARY

In this chapter we have described research that uses one case or a few contrasting cases. It is best suited to contemporary cases and settings over which an investigator has little control. Although many forms of data gathering may be a part of case study research, field observation was emphasized in this chapter as a distinctive procedure of many case studies in the social sciences. First-hand observation of instances of some phenomenon is basic to scientific inquiry in many fields. Observation presents some distinctive opportunities and advantages as well as distinctive issues for human observers.

Case study research is widely used in the social sciences even though issues of generalizability, rigor, and implementation have been raised. Case studies are used for descriptive as well as explanatory research, especially when an in-depth examination of more-complex social processes occurring in their natural setting is important.

Field observation involves skill in clarifying one's research interests and identifying one's skills and opportunities. The process of gaining access, developing an **account of researcher intent,** and choosing an appropriate role or roles has very important consequences for the quality of observational data. Field researchers need to decide whether to reveal their research role and whether and to what extent to be a participant in the setting. Case study research generally gathers in-depth information on a wide range of topics. What to observe and how to record it in a timely fashion are special concerns of fieldwork. A chronological research journal of field notes and (separately identified) reflections on their meaning is usually a part of the process. Once the researcher leaves the field (and this also calls for planning), the field notes and other data are analyzed. Often this involves tagging, sorting by topics, finding illustrations that illustrate concepts, and writing a thick description of findings. Computer programs are available to help in organizing and analyzing field notes, although most of these also require considerable time in coding and comparing alternative explanations.

Case study strengths include assembling a more holistic and in-depth description of a case, developing new theoretical and conceptual insights, handling more-complex social situations, and following the details of some social process over time. In field settings, case study research may be less reactive and provide greater opportunities for probing meanings and comparing different perspectives on the same event. Weaknesses of case study research in generalizability of findings have been noted. Field observation has its own problems with gaining access to desired information, achieving systematic data, and assessing alternative explanations. Chapter 9 describes the use of archives and secondary data for research.

TERMS TO KNOW

Access

Account of researcher intent

Case study

Covert research

Detailed documentation

Field notes

Field observation

Going native

Informant

Key informants

Observational language

Organizing concepts

Participant observation

Qualitative analysis

Rapport

Reliability

Systematic research

Thick description

Validity

ISSUES AND COMPARISONS

Participant observation or nonparticipation

Disclosure versus covert research

Computer aids to analyzing field notes

Confidentiality versus anonymity

Alternative explanations of case study findings

Ethics of case study research

Reasons for conducting case studies

Strengths and weaknesses of case study research

Cross-sectional versus longitudinal study

Constraints on the observer role

Mnemonic aids

Analyzing field data

When to stop and how to leave a field setting

Level of rigor, generalization, implementation of case study research

---

EXERCISES

1. Identify some social phenomenon in which you are keenly interested and a site, convenient to you, in which it can be observed for some time. For example, you might be interested in the way aides in a nursing home interact with each other, or etiquette in white-collar and blue-collar restaurants, or child care behaviors in a daycare setting. Be sure to identify clearly the phenomena you are interested in observing and characteristics of the site you have selected. To what extent and in what ways might this starting point lead to better knowledge about the phenomenon, or to biased or misleading findings about the phenomenon you propose to study.

2. Set up a realistic way to gain meaningful access to the site chosen in exercise 1 and set up a way to record observations you plan to make in that setting.

3. Pretest the procedures you developed in exercise 2. Spend several hours in the setting, recording observations you have made. What role did you play in the field setting? What consequences do you see about how your role affected the observations you were able to make? How comfortable was your chosen role? What would you change about your behavior in the field setting? When you are out of the field, discuss how well the procedures worked and the extent to which you may be recording a biased or selective set of materials.

4. After revising your procedures, spend several more hours in the field setting gathering careful data on the phenomenon you are studying. Briefly summarize your findings, identify and define any new insights or concepts you discovered, and reflect back on the methodological adequacy of this mini–research project.

5. Find an interesting research report that uses field observation. Carefully examine it and lay out the research procedure in terms of the ideas and relevant concepts discussed in this chapter. What can be said to be known, based on the research procedures?

REFERENCES

Bailey, Carol A., *A Guide to Field Research*, Pine Forge Press, Thousand Oaks, CA, 1996.

Baker, Phyllis L., "Doin' What It Takes to Survive: Battered Women and the Consequences of Compliance to a Cultural Script," *Studies in Symbolic Interaction* 1996;20:73–90.

Becker, Howard S., "Problems of Inference and Proof in Participant Observation," in George J. McCall and J. L. Simmons, *Issues in Participant Observation*, Addison-Wesley, Reading, MA, 1958.

Becker, Howard S., "Practitioner of Vice and Crime," Chapter 2 in Robert W. Habenstein, ed., *Pathways to Data: Field Methods for Studying Ongoing Social Organizations*, Aldine, Chicago, 1970.

Brent, Edward E., Jr., and Richard E. Sykes, "A Mathematical Model of Symbolic Interaction Between Police and Suspects," *Behavioral Science* November 1979;24(6):388–402.

Brent, Edward E., Jr., and Richard E. Sykes, "The Interactive Bases of Police-Suspect Confrontation: An Empirically Based Simulation of a Markov Process," *Simulation and Games* September 1980;11(3):347–63.

Claude, Lumane Pluviose, *Community Activeness, Success and Well-Being: A Comparative Case Study of Four Pennsylvania Rural Communities*, Ph.D. dissertation, University Park, Pennsylvania State University, 1996.

Coffey, Amanda, and Paul Atkinson, *Making Sense of Qualitative Data*, Sage, Newbury Park, CA, 1996.

Cresswell, John W., *Research Design: Qualitative and Quantitative Approaches*, Sage, Newbury Park, CA, 1994.

Denzin, Norman K., ed., *Handbook of Qualitative Research*, Sage, Newbury Park, CA, 1994.

Emerson, Robert M., *Contemporary Field Research: A Collection of Readings*, Little, Brown, Boston, 1983.

Festinger, Leon, Henry W. Riecken, and Stanley Schachter, *When Prophecy Fails*, Harper & Row, New York, 1956.

Fielding, Nigel G., and Raymond M. Lee, eds., *Using Computers in Qualitative Research*, Sage, Newbury Park, CA, 1993.

Gans, Herbert, *Urban Villagers*, Free Press, New York, 1962.

Garfinkel, Harold, *Studies in Ethnomethodology*, Prentice Hall, Englewood Cliffs, NJ, 1967.

Glaser, B., and A. L. Strauss, *The Discovery of Grounded Theory: Strategies for Qualitative Research*, Aldine, Chicago, 1967.

Gubrium, Jaber F., *Living and Dying at Murray Manor*, St. Martin's Press, New York, 1975.

Guthrie, Loree Price, *Teen Parents of Millcreek School District: A Qualitative Case Study of Four Teen Parents*, Ph.D. dissertation, Temple University, Philadelphia, 1996.

Habenstein, Robert W., ed., *Pathways to Data: Field Methods for Studying Ongoing Social Organizations*, Aldine, Chicago, 1970.

Kiselev, Maxim Y., *Living with Radiation: A Case Study of the Chernobyl Children*, Ph.D. dissertation, Yale University, New Haven, CT, 1996.

Liebow, Elliot, "A Field Experience in Retrospect," Chapter 12 in Glenn Jacobs, ed., *The Participant Observer: Encounters with Social Reality*, George Braziller, New York, 1970.

Lofland, John, and Lyn H. Lofland, *Analyzing Social Settings*, 2nd ed., Wadsworth, Belmont, CA, 1984.

Madge, John, *The Tools of Social Science: An Analytical Description of Social Science Techniques*, Doubleday, Garden City, NY, 1965.

Mauksch, Hans O., "The Organizational Context of Nursing Practice," in Fred Davis, ed., *The Nursing Profession*, Wiley, New York, 1966.

Richards, T., and L. Richards, "Using Computers in Qualitative Analysis," Chapter 28 in N. Denzin and Y. Lincoln, eds., *Handbook of Qualitative Research*, Sage, Newbury Park, CA, 1994.

Schutz, Alfred, *Collected Papers I: The Problem of Social Reality*, Martinus Nijhoff, The Hague, 1962.

Schutz, Alfred, *Collected Papers II: Studies in Social Theory*, Martinus Nijhoff, The Hague, 1964.

Schutz, Alfred, *Collected Papers III: Studies in Phenomenological Philosophy*, Martinus Nijhoff, The Hague, 1966.

Seidel, John, Susanne Friese, and D. Christopher Leonard, *The Ethnograph v4.0: A Users Guide*, Qualis Research Associates, Amherst, MA, 1995.

Strauss, Anselem, and Juliet Corbin, *Grounded Theory in Practice*, Sage, Newbury Park, CA, 1997.

Sykes, Richard E., "Toward a Theory of Observer Effects in Systematic Field Research," *Human Organization* Summer 1978;37(2):148–56.

Sykes, Richard E., and Edward E. Brent, "The Regulation of Interaction by Police: A Systems View of Taking Charge," *Criminology* August 1980;18(2):182–97.

Sykes, Richard E., Richard D. Rowley, and James M. Schaefer, "Effects of Group Participation on Drinking Behaviors in Public Bars: An Observational Survey," *Journal of Social Behavior and Personality* 1980;5(4):385–402.

Sykes, Richard E., Richard D. Rowley, James M. Schaefer, "The Influence of Time, Gender and Group Size on Heavy Drinking in Public Bars," *Journal of Studies on Alcohol* March 1993;54(2):133–38.

Thompson, William E., and Jackie L. Harred, "Topless Dancers: Managing Stigma in a Deviant Occupation," *Deviant Behavior* 1992;13(3):291–311.

Turner, Jonathan, *The Structure of Sociological Theory*, Wadsworth, Belmont, CA, 1991.

Weitzman, Eben A., and Matthew B. Miles, *Computer Programs for Qualitative Data Analysis: A Software Sourcebook*, Sage, Newbury Park, CA, 1995.

Whyte, William F., Jr., *Street Corner Society*, 2nd ed., University of Chicago Press, Chicago, 1955.

Wieder, D. Lawrence, *Language and Social Reality: The Case of Telling the Convict Code*, Mouton & Company, The Hague, 1974.

Yin, Robert K., *Case Study Research: Design and Methods*, 2nd ed., Applied Social Research Methods Series #5, Sage, Newbury Park, CA, 1994.

FIELD RESEARCH

193

INTRODUCTION

This chapter and the two that follow represent a major shift away from the quantitative style of the past several chapters to the qualitative research style. You may recall that the qualitative and the quantitative styles can differ a great deal, and that nonpositivist social science supports the qualitative research style. This chapter describes field research, also called *ethnography* or *participant-observation research*. It is a qualitative style in which a researcher directly observes and participates in small-scale social settings in the present time and in the researcher's home culture.

Many students are excited by field research because it involves hanging out with some exotic group of people. There are no cold mathematics or complicated statistics, no abstract deductive hypotheses. Instead, there is direct, face-to-face social interaction with "real people" in a natural setting.

In field research, the individual researcher directly talks with and observes the people being studied. Through interaction over months or years, the researcher learns about them, their life histories, their hobbies and interests, and their habits, hopes, fears, and dreams. Meeting new people, developing friendships, and discovering new social worlds can be fun. It is also time consuming, emotionally draining, and sometimes physically dangerous.

Research Questions Appropriate for Field Research

Field research is appropriate when the research question involves learning about, understanding, or describing a group of interacting people. It is usually best when the question is: How do people do Y in the social world? or What is the social world of X like? It can be used when other methods (e.g., survey, experiments) are not practical, as in studying street gangs.

Field researchers study people in a location or setting. It has been used to study entire communities. Beginning field researchers should start with a relatively small group (30 or fewer) who interact with each other on a regular basis in a relatively fixed setting (e.g., a street corner, church, barroom, beauty parlor, baseball field, etc.).

In order to use consistent terminology, we can call the people who are studied in a field setting *members*. They are insiders or natives in the field and belong to a group, subculture, or social setting that the "outsider" field researcher wants to penetrate and learn about.

Field researchers have explored a wide variety of social settings, subcultures, and aspects of social life[1] (see Figure 11.1). Places my students have conducted successful short-term, small scale field research studies include a beauty parlor, day-care center, bakery, bingo parlor, bowling alley, church, coffee shop, laundromat, police dispatch office, nursing home, tattoo parlor, and weight room.

Ethnography and Ethnomethodology. Two modern extensions of field research, ethnography and ethnomethodology, build on the social constructionist perspective. Each is redefining how field research is conducted. They are not yet the core of field research, so they are discussed only briefly here.

Ethnography comes from cultural anthropology.[2] *Ethno* means people or folk, and *graphy* refers to describing something. Thus *ethnography* means describing a culture and understanding another way of life from the native point of view. Ethnography assumes that people make inferences—that is, go beyond what is explicitly seen or said to what is meant or implied. People display their culture (what people think, ponder, or believe) through behavior (e.g., speech and actions) in specific social contexts. Displays of behavior do not give meaning; rather, meaning is inferred, or someone figures out meaning. Moving from what is heard or observed to what is actually meant is at the center of ethnography. For example, when a student is invited to a "kegger," the student infers that it is an informal party with other student-aged people at which beer will be served, based on his or her cultural

FIGURE 11.1 Examples of Field Research Sites/Topics

Small-Scale Settings

Passengers in an airplane
Bars or taverns
Battered women's shelters
Camera clubs
Laundromats
Social movement organizations
Social welfare offices
Television stations
Waiting rooms

Community Settings

Retirement communities
Small towns
Urban ethnic communities
Working-class neighborhoods

Children's Activities

Children's playgrounds
Little League baseball
Youth in schools
Junior high girl groups

Occupations

Airline attendants
Artists
Cocktail waitresses
Dog catchers

Door-to-door salespersons
Factory workers
Gamblers
Medical students
Female strippers
Police officers
Restaurant chefs
Social workers
Taxi drivers

Deviance and Criminal Activity

Body/genital piercing and branding
Cults
Drug dealers and addicts
Hippies
Nude beaches
Occult groups
Prostitutes
Street gangs, motorcycle gangs
Street people, homeless shelters

Medical Settings and Medical Events

Death
Emergency rooms
Intensive care units
Pregnancy and abortion
Support groups for Alzheimer's caregivers

---

knowledge. Cultural knowledge includes symbols, songs, sayings, facts, ways of behaving, and objects (e.g., telephones, newspapers, etc.). We learn the culture by watching television, listening to parents, observing others, and the like.

Cultural knowledge includes both explicit knowledge, what we know and talk about, and tacit knowledge, what we rarely acknowledge. For example, *explicit knowledge* includes the social event (e.g., a "kegger"). Most people can easily describe what happens at one. *Tacit knowledge* includes the unspoken cultural norm for the proper distance to stand from others.

People are generally unaware that they use this norm. They feel unease or discomfort when the norm is violated, but it is difficult to pinpoint the source of discomfort. Ethnographers describe the explicit and tacit cultural knowledge that members use. Their detailed descriptions and careful analysis take what is described apart and put it back together.

Ethnomethodology is a distinct approach developed in the 1960s, with its own unique terminology. It combines theory, philosophy, and method. Some do not consider it a part of sociology.

A simple definition of *ethnomethodology* is the study of commonsense knowledge. Ethnomethodologists study common sense by observing its creation and use in ongoing social interaction in natural settings. Ethnomethodology is a radical or extreme form of field research, based on phenomenological philosophy and a social constructionist approach. It involves the specialized, highly detailed analysis of micro-situations (e.g., transcripts of short conversations or videotapes of social interactions). Compared to other field research, it is more concerned about method and argues that research findings result as much from the method used as from the social life studied.

Ethnomethodology assumes that social meaning is fragile and fluid, not fixed, stable, or solid. Meaning is constantly being created and re-created in an ongoing process. For this reason, ethnomethodologists analyze language, including pauses and the context of speech. They assume that people "accomplish" commonsense understanding by using tacit social-cultural rules, and social interaction is a process of reality construction. People interpret everyday events by using cultural knowledge and clues from the social context. Ethnomethodologists examine how ordinary people in everyday settings apply tacit rules to make sense of social life (e.g., to know whether or not someone is joking).

Ethnomethodologists examine ordinary social interaction in great detail to identify the rules for constructing social reality and common sense, how these rules are applied, and how new rules are created. For example, they argue that standardized tests or survey interviews measure a person's ability to pick up implicit clues and apply common sense more than measuring objective facts.

THE LOGIC OF FIELD RESEARCH

What Is Field Research?

It is difficult to pin down a specific definition of *field research* because it is more of an orientation toward research than a fixed set of techniques to apply.[3] A field researcher uses various methods to obtain information. A *field researcher* is a resourceful, talented individual who has ingenuity, and an ability to think on her feet while in the field.

Field research is based on naturalism, which is also used to study other phenomena (e.g., oceans, animals, plants, etc.). *Naturalism* involves observing ordinary events in natural settings, not in contrived, invented, or researcher-created settings. Research occurs in the field and outside the safe settings of an office, laboratory, or classroom.

A field researcher examines social meanings and grasps multiple perspectives in natural social settings. He or she gets inside the meaning system of members and then goes back to an outside or research viewpoint. The researcher switches perspectives and sees the setting from multiple points of view simultaneously.

Let us look at what practicing field researchers do (see Box 11.1). Research is usually conducted by a single individual, although small teams have been effective. A researcher is directly involved in and part of the social world studied, so his or her personal characteristics are relevant in research.

The researcher's direct involvement in the field often has an emotional impact. Field research can be fun and exciting, but it can also disrupt one's personal life, physical security, or mental well-being. More than other types of social research, it reshapes friendships, family life, self-identity, or personal values.

Steps in a Field Research Project

Naturalism and direct involvement mean that field research is more flexible or less structured than quantitative research. This makes it essential for a researcher to be well organized and prepared for the field. It also means that the steps of a project are not entirely predetermined but serve as an approximate guide or road map (see Figure 11.2).

Flexibility. Field researchers rarely follow fixed steps. In fact, flexibility is a key advantage of field

BOX 11.1 What Do Field Researchers Do?

A field researcher does the following:

1. Observes ordinary events and everyday activities as they happen in natural settings, in addition to any unusual occurrences

2. Becomes directly involved with the people being studied and personally experiences the process of daily social life in the field setting

3. Acquires an insider's point of view while maintaining the analytic perspective or distance of an outsider

4. Uses a variety of techniques and social skills in a flexible manner as the situation demands

5. Produces data in the form of extensive written notes, as well as diagrams, maps, or pictures to provide very detailed descriptions

6. Sees events holistically (e.g., as a whole unit, not in pieces) and individually in their social context

7. Understands and develops empathy for members in a field setting, and does not just record "cold" objective facts

8. Notices both explicit (recognized, conscious, spoken) and tacit (less recognized, implicit, unspoken) aspects of culture

9. Observes ongoing social processes without upsetting, disrupting, or imposing an outside point of view

10. Copes with high levels of personal stress, uncertainty, ethical dilemmas, and ambiguity

FIGURE 11.2 Steps in Field Research
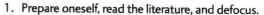

1. Prepare oneself, read the literature, and defocus.
2. Select a field site and gain access to it.
3. Enter the field and establish social relations with members.
4. Adopt a social role, learn the ropes, and get along with members.
5. Watch, listen, and collect quality data.
6. Begin to analyze data and to generate and evaluate working hypotheses.
7. Focus on specific aspects of the setting and use theoretical sampling.
8. Conduct field interviews with member informants.
9. Disengage and physically leave the setting.
10. Complete the analyses and write the research report.

Note: There is no fixed percentage of time needed for each step. For a rough approximation, Junker (1960:12) suggested that, once in the field, the researcher should expect to spend approximately one-sixth of his or her time observing, one-third recording data, one-third of the time analyzing data, and one-sixth reporting results. Also see Denzin (1989:176) for eight steps of field research.

research, which lets a researcher shift direction and follow leads. Good field researchers recognize and seize opportunities, "play it by ear," and rapidly adjust to fluid social situations.

A field researcher does not begin with a set of methods to apply or explicit hypotheses to test. Rather, he or she chooses techniques on the basis of their value for providing information. In the beginning, the researcher expects little control over data and little focus. Once socialized to the setting, however, he or she focuses the inquiry and asserts control over the data.

Getting Organized in the Beginning. Human and personal factors can play a role in any research project, but they are crucial in field research. Field projects often begin with chance occurrences or a personal interest. Field researchers can begin with their own experiences, such as working at a job, having a hobby, or being a patient or an activist.

Field researchers use the skills of careful looking and listening, short-term memory, and regular writing. Before entering the field, a new researcher practices observing the ordinary details of situations and writing them down. Attention to details and short-term memory can improve with practice. Likewise, keeping a daily diary or personal journal is good practice for writing field notes.

As with all social research, reading the scholarly literature helps the researcher learn concepts, potential pitfalls, data collection methods, and techniques for resolving conflicts. In addition, a field researcher finds diaries, novels, journalistic accounts, and autobiographies useful for gaining familiarity and preparing emotionally for the field.

Field research begins with a general topic, not specific hypotheses. A researcher does not get locked into any initial misconceptions. He or she needs to be well informed but open to discovering new ideas. Finding the right questions to ask about the field takes time.

A researcher first empties his or her mind of preconceptions. The researcher should move outside his or her comfortable social niche to experience as much as possible in the field without betraying a primary commitment to being a researcher.

Another preparation for field research is self-knowledge. A field researcher needs to know himself or herself and reflect on personal experiences. He or she can expect anxiety, self-doubt, frustration, and uncertainty in the field. Especially in the beginning, the researcher may feel that he or she is collecting the wrong data and may suffer emotional turmoil, isolation, and confusion. He or she often feels doubly marginal: an outsider in the field setting and also distant from friends, family, and other researchers.[4] The relevance of a researcher's emotional make-up, personal biography, and cultural experiences makes it important to be aware of his or her personal commitments and inner conflicts (see the later section on stress; see also Box 11.2).

BOX 11.2   Field Research at a Country and Western Bar

Eliasoph (1998) conducted field research on several groups in a California community to understand how Americans avoid political expression. One was a social club. Eliasoph describes herself as an "urban, bicoastal, bespectacled, Jewish, Ph.D. candidate from a long line of communists, atheists, liberals. bookreaders, ideologues, and arguers" (p. 270). The social club's world was very foreign to her. The social club, the Buffalos, centered on country and western music at a bar, the Silverado Club. She describes it:

> The Silverado huddled on a vast, rutted parking lot on what was once wetlands and now was a truck stop, a mile and a half from Amargo's [town name] nuclear battleship station. Occasional gulleys of salt water cattails poked through the wide flat miles of paved malls and gas stations. Giant four-wheeled-drive vehicles filled the parking lot, making my miniature Honda look like a toy. . . . Inside the windowless Silverado, initial blinding darkness gave way to a huge Confederate flag pinned up behind the bandstand, the standard collection of

neon beer signs and beer mirrors, men in cowboys hats, cowboys shirts and jeans, women in curly perms and tiered flounces of lace or denim skirts, or jeans, and belts with their names embroidered in glitter on the back. (1998:92)

Eliasoph introduced herself as a student. During her two years of research, she endured smoke-filled rooms as well as expensive beer and bottled-water prices; attended a wedding and many dance lessons; and participated in countless conversations and heard many abusive sexist/racist jokes. She listened, asked questions, observed, and took notes in the bathroom. When she returned home after hours with club members, it was to a university crowd who had little understanding of the world she was studying. For them, witty conversation was central and being bored was to be avoided. The club members used more nonverbal than verbal communication and being bored, or sitting and doing nothing, was just fine. The research forced Eliasoph to reexamine her own views and tastes, which she had taken for granted.

Fieldwork can have a strong impact on a researcher's identity and outlook. Researchers may be personally transformed by the field experience. Some adopt new values, interests, and moral commitments, or change their religion or political ideology.[5]

CHOOSING A SITE AND GAINING ACCESS

Although a field research project does not proceed by fixed steps, some common concerns arise in the early stages. These include selecting a site, gaining access to the site, entering the field, and developing rapport with members in the field.

Selecting a Site

Where to Observe. Field researchers talk about doing research on a setting, or *field site,* but this term is misleading. A site is the context in which events or activities occur, a socially defined territory with shifting boundaries. A social group may interact across several physical sites. For example, a college football team may interact on the playing field, in the locker room, in a dormitory, at a training camp, or at a local hangout. The team's field site includes all five locations.

The field site and research question are bound up together, but choosing a site is not the same as focusing on a *case* for study. A case is a social relationship or activity; it can extend beyond the boundaries of the site and have links to other social settings. A researcher selects a site, then identifies cases to examine within it—for example, how football team members relate to authority figures.

Selecting a field site is an important decision, and researchers take notes on the site selection processes. Three factors are relevant when choosing a field research site: richness of data, unfamiliarity, and suitability.[6] Some sites are more likely than others to provide rich data. Sites that present a web of social relations, a variety of

activities, and diverse events over time provide richer, more interesting data. Beginning field researchers should choose an unfamiliar setting. It is easier to see cultural events and social relations in a new site. When "casing" possible field sites, one must consider such practical issues as the researcher's time and skills, serious conflicts among people in the site, the researcher's personal characteristics and feelings, and access to parts of a site.

A researcher's ascriptive characteristics (eg., age, gender, race) can limit access. Physical access to a site can be an issue. Sites are on a continuum, with open and public areas (e.g., public restaurants, airport waiting areas, etc.) at one end and closed and private settings (e.g., private firms, clubs, activities in a person's home, etc.) at the other. A researcher may find that he or she is not welcome or not allowed on the site, or there are legal and political barriers to access. Laws and regulations in institutions (e.g., public schools, hospitals, prisons, etc.) restrict access. In addition, institutional review boards may limit field research on ethical grounds.

Level of Involvement. Field roles can be arranged on a continuum by the degree of detachment or involvement a researcher has with members. At one extreme is a detached outsider; at the other extreme is an intimately involved insider.

The field researcher's level of involvement depends on negotiations with members, specifics of the field setting, the researcher's personal comfort, and the particular role adopted in the field. Many move from outsider to insider levels with more time in the field. Each level has its advantages and disadvantages. Different field researchers advocate different levels of involvement.

Roles at the outsider end of the continuum reduce the time needed for acceptance, make overrapport less an issue, and can sometimes help members open up. They facilitate detachment and protect the researcher's self-identity. A researcher feels marginal. Although there is less risk of "going native," he or she is also less likely to know an insider's experience and misinterpretation is more likely. To really understand social meaning for those being studied, the field researcher must participate in the setting, as others do.

By contrast, roles at the insider end of the continuum facilitate empathy and sharing of a member's experience. The goal of fully experiencing the intimate social world of a member is achieved. Nevertheless, a lack of distance from, too much sympathy for, or overinvolvement with members is likely. A researcher's reports may be questioned, data gathering is difficult, there can be a dramatic impact on the researcher's self, and the distance needed for analysis may be hard to attain.

Gatekeepers. A *gatekeeper* is someone with the formal or informal authority to control access to a site.[7] It can be the thug on the corner, an administrator of a hospital, or the owner of a business. Informal public areas (e.g., sidewalks, public waiting rooms, etc.) rarely have gatekeepers; formal organizations have authorities from whom permission must be obtained.

Field researchers expect to negotiate with gatekeepers and bargain for access. The gatekeepers may not appreciate the need for conceptual distance or ethical balance. The researcher must set nonnegotiable limits to protect research integrity. If there are many restrictions initially, a researcher can often reopen negotiations later, and gatekeepers may forget their initial demands as trust develops. It is ethically and politically astute to call on gatekeepers. Researchers do not expect them to listen to research concerns or care about the findings, except insofar as these findings might provide evidence for someone to criticize them.

Dealing with gatekeepers is a recurrent issue as a researcher enters new levels or areas. In addition, a gatekeeper can shape the direction of research. In some sites, gatekeeper approval creates a stigma that inhibits the cooperation of members. For example, prisoners may not be cooperative if they know that the prison warden gave approval to the researcher.

Strategy for Entering

Entering a field site requires having a flexible strategy or plan of action, negotiating access and relations with members, and deciding how much to disclose about the research to field members or gatekeepers.

Planning. Entering and gaining access to a field site is a process that depends on commonsense judgment and social skills. Field sites usually have different levels or areas, and entry is an issue for each. Entry is more analogous to peeling the layers of an onion than to opening a door. Moreover, bargains and promises of entry may not remain stable over time. A researcher needs fallback plans or may have to return later for renegotiation. Because the specific focus of research may not emerge until later in the research process or may change, it is best to avoid being locked into specifics by gatekeepers.

Negotiation. Social relations are negotiated and formed throughout the process of fieldwork.[8] Negotiation occurs with each new member until a stable relationship develops to gain access, develop trust, obtain information, and reduce hostile reactions. The researcher expects to negotiate and explain what he or she is doing over and over in the field (see the discussion of normalizing social research, to follow).

Deviant groups and elites often require special negotiations for gaining access. To gain access to deviant subcultures, field researchers have used contacts from the researcher's private life, gone to social welfare or law-enforcement agencies where the deviants are processed, advertised for volunteers, offered a service (e.g., counseling) in exchange for access, or gone to a location where deviants hang out and joined a group.

Disclosure. A researcher must decide how much to reveal about himself or herself and the research project. Disclosing one's personal life, hobbies, interests, and background can build trust and close relationships, but the researcher will also lose privacy, and he or she needs to ensure that the focus remains on events in the field.

A researcher also decides how much to disclose about the research project. Disclosure ranges on a continuum from fully covert research, in which no one in the field is aware that research is taking place, to the opposite end, where everyone knows the specifics of the research project. The degree and timing of disclosure depends on a researcher's judgment and particulars in the setting. Disclosure may unfold over time as the researcher feels more secure.

Researchers disclose the project to gatekeepers and others unless there is a good reason for not doing so, such as the presence of gatekeepers who would seriously limit or inhibit research for illegitimate reasons (e.g., to hide graft or corruption). Even in these cases, a researcher may disclose his or her identity as a researcher, but may pose as one who seems submissive, harmless, and interested in nonthreatening issues.

Entering the Field

After a field site is selected and access obtained, researchers must learn the ropes, develop rapport with members, adopt a role in the setting, and maintain social relations. Before confronting such issues, the researcher should ask: How will I present myself? What does it mean for me to be a "measurement instrument"? How can I assume an "attitude of strangeness"?

Presentation of Self. People explicitly and implicitly present themselves to others. We display who we are—the type of person we are or would like to be—through our physical appearance, what we say, and how we act. The presentation of self sends a symbolic message. It may be, "I'm a serious, hard-working student," "I'm a warm and caring person," "I'm a cool jock," or "I'm a rebel and party animal." Many selves are possible, and presentations of selves can differ depending on the occasion.

A field researcher is conscious of the presentation of self in the field. For example, how should he or she dress in the field? The best guide is to respect both oneself and those being studied. Do not overdress so as to offend or stand out, but copying the dress of those being studied is not always necessary. A professor who studies street people does not have to dress or act like one; dressing and acting informally is sufficient. Likewise, more formal dress and professional demeanor are required when studying corporate executives or top officials.

A researcher must be aware that self-presentation will influence field relations to some degree. It is difficult to present a highly deceptive front or to present oneself in a way that deviates sharply from the person one is ordinarily.

Researcher as Instrument. The researcher is the instrument for measuring field data. This has two implications. First, it puts pressure on the researcher to be alert and sensitive to what happens in the field and to be disciplined about recording data. Second, it has personal consequences. Fieldwork involves social relationships and personal feelings. Field researchers are flexible about what to include as data and admit their own subjective insights and feelings. Personal, subjective experiences are part of field data. They are valuable both in themselves and for interpreting events in the field. Instead of trying to be objective and eliminate personal reactions, field researchers treat their feelings toward field events as data.

Field research can heighten a researcher's awareness of personal feelings. For example, a researcher may not be fully aware of personal feelings about nudity until he or she is in a nudist colony, or about personal possessions until he or she is in a setting where others "borrow" many items. The researcher's own surprise, indignation, or questioning then may become an opportunity for reflection and insight.

An Attitude of Strangeness. It is hard to recognize what we are very close to. The everyday world we inhabit is filled with thousands of details. If we paid attention to everything all the time, we would suffer from severe information overload. We manage by ignoring much of what is around us and by engaging in habitual thinking. Unfortunately, we fail to see the familiar as distinctive, and assume that others experience reality just as we do. We tend to treat our own way of living as natural or normal.

Field research in familiar surroundings is difficult because of a tendency to be blinded by the familiar. By studying other cultures, researchers encounter dramatically different assumptions about what is important and how things are done. This confrontation of cultures, or culture shock, has two benefits: It makes it easier to see cultural elements and it facilitates self-discovery. Researchers adopt the attitude of strangeness to gain these benefits. The *attitude of strangeness* means questioning and noticing ordinary details or looking at the ordinary through the eyes of a stranger. Strangeness helps a researcher overcome the boredom of observing ordinary details. It helps him or her see the ordinary in a new way, one that reveals aspects of the setting of which members are not consciously aware.

People rarely recognize customs they take for granted. For example, when someone gives us a gift, we say thank you and praise the gift. By contrast, gift-giving customs in many cultures include complaining that the gift is inadequate. The attitude of strangeness helps make the tacit culture visible—for example, that gift givers expect to hear "thank you" and "the gift is nice," and become upset otherwise. A field researcher adopts both a stranger's and an insider's point of view.

Strangeness also encourages a researcher to reconsider his or her own social world. Immersion in a different setting breaks old habits of thought and action. He or she finds reflection and introspection easier and more intense when encountering the unfamiliar, whether it is a different culture or a familiar culture seen through a stranger's eyes.

Building Rapport

A field researcher builds rapport by getting along with members in the field. He or she forges a friendly relationship, shares the same language, and laughs and cries with members. This is a step toward obtaining an understanding of members and moving beyond understanding to empathy—that is, seeing and feeling events from another's perspective.

It is not always easy to build rapport. The social world is not all in harmony, with warm, friendly people. A setting may contain fear, tension, and conflict. Members may be unpleasant, untrustworthy, or untruthful; they may do things that disturb or disgust a researcher. An experienced researcher is prepared for a range of events and relationships. He or she may find, however, that it is impossible to penetrate a setting or get really close to members. Settings where cooperation, sympathy, and collaboration are impossible require different techniques.[9]

Charm and Trust. A field researcher needs social skills and personal charm to build rapport. Trust, friendly feelings, and being well liked facilitate communication and help him or her to understand the inner feelings of others. There is no magical way to do this. Showing a genuine concern for and interest in others, being honest, and sharing feelings are good strategies, but they are not foolproof. It depends on the specific setting and members.

Many factors affect trust and rapport—how a researcher presents himself or herself; the role he or she chooses for the field; and the events that encourage, limit, or make it impossible to achieve trust. Trust is not gained once and for all. It is a developmental process built up over time through many social nuances (e.g., sharing of personal experiences, story telling, gestures, hints, facial expressions). It is constantly recreated and seems easier to lose once it has been built up than to gain in the first place.

Establishing trust is important, but it does not ensure that all information will be revealed.

It may be limited to specific areas. For example, trust can be built up regarding financial matters but not to disclose intimate dating behavior. Trust may have to be created anew in each area of inquiry; it requires constant reaffirmation.

Understanding. Rapport helps field researchers understand members, but understanding is a precondition for greater depth, not an end in itself. It slowly develops in the field as the researcher overcomes an initial bewilderment with a new or unusual language and system of social meaning. Once he or she attains an understanding of the member's point of view, the next step is to learn how to think and act within a member's perspective. This is *empathy,* or adopting another's perspective. Empathy does not necessarily mean sympathy, agreement, or approval; it means feeling things as another does. Rapport helps create understanding and ultimately empathy, and the development of empathy facilitates greater rapport.

RELATIONS IN THE FIELD

You play many social roles in daily life—daughter/son, student, customer, sports fan—and maintain social relations with others. You choose some roles and others are structured for you. Few have a choice but to play the role of son or daughter. Some roles are formal (e.g., bank teller, police chief, etc.), others are informal (flirt, elder states person, buddy, etc.). You can switch roles, play multiple roles, and play a role in a particular way. Field researchers play roles in the field. In addition, they learn the ropes and maintain relations with members.

Roles in the Field

Preexisting versus Created Roles. At times, a researcher adopts an existing role. Some existing roles provide access to all areas of the site, the ability to observe and interact with all members, the freedom to move around, and a way to balance the requirements of researcher and member. At other times, a researcher creates a new role or modifies an existing one. For example, Fine (1987) created a role of the "adult friend" and performed it with little adult authority when studying preadolescent boys. He was able to observe parts of their culture and behavior that were otherwise inaccessible to adults. The adoption of a field role takes time, and a researcher may adopt several different field roles over time.

Limits on the Role Chosen. The field roles open to a researcher are affected by ascriptive factors and physical appearance. He or she can change some aspects of appearance, such as dress or hairstyle, but not ascriptive features such as age, race, gender, and attractiveness. Nevertheless, such factors can be important in gaining access and can restrict the available roles. For example, Gurney (1985) reported that being a female in a male-dominated setting required extra negotiations and "hassles." Nevertheless, her gender provided insights and created situations that would have been absent with a male researcher.

Since many roles are sex-typed, gender is an important consideration. Female researchers often have more difficulty when the setting is perceived as dangerous or seamy and where males are in control (e.g., police work, fire fighting, etc.). They may be shunned or pushed into limiting gender stereotypes (e.g., "sweet kid," "mascot," "loud mouth," etc.).

Learning the Ropes

As a researcher learns the ropes on the field site, he or she learns how to cope with personal stress and how to normalize the social research. New researchers face embarrassment, experience discomfort, and are overwhelmed by the details in the field. For example, in her study of U.S. relocation camps for Japanese Americans during World War II, respected field researcher Rosalie Wax (1971) reported that she endured the discomfort of 120-degree Fahrenheit temperatures, filthy and dilapidated living conditions, dysentery, and mosquitoes. She felt isolated, she cried a lot, and she gained 30 pounds from compulsive eating. After months in the field, she thought she was a total failure; she was distrusted by members and got into fights with the camp administration.

Maintaining a "marginal" status is stressful; it is difficult to be an outsider who is not fully involved, especially when studying settings full of intense feelings (e.g., political campaigns, religious conversions, etc.). The loneliness and isolation of fieldwork may combine with the desire to develop rapport and empathy to cause overinvolvement. A researcher may "go native" and drop the professional researcher's role to become a full member of the group being studied. Or the researcher may feel guilt about learning intimate details as members drop their guard, and may come to overidentify with members.

Normalizing Social Research. A field researcher not only observes and investigates members in the field but is observed and investigated by members as well. In overt field research, members are usually initially uncomfortable with the presence of a researcher. Most are unfamiliar with field research and fail to distinguish between sociologists, psychologists, counselors, and social workers. They may see the researcher as an outside critic or spy, or as a savior or all-knowing expert.

An overt field researcher must *normalize social research*—that is, help members redefine social research from something unknown and threatening to something normal and predictable. He or she can help members manage research by presenting his or her own biography, explaining field research a little at a time, appearing nonthreatening, or accepting minor deviance in the setting (e.g., minor violations of official rules).

Maintaining Relations

Social Relations. With time, a field researcher develops and modifies social relationships. Members who are cool at first may warm up later. Or they may put on a front of initial friendliness, and their fears and suspicions surface only later. A researcher is in a delicate position. Early in a project, when not yet fully aware of everything about a field site, the researcher does not form close relationships because circumstances may change. Yet, if he or she does develop close friends, they can become allies who will defend the researcher's presence and help him or her gain access.

A field researcher monitors how his or her actions or appearance affects members. For example, a physically attractive researcher who interacts with members of the opposite sex may encounter crushes, flirting, and jealousy. He or she develops an awareness of these field relations and learns to manage them.

In addition to developing social relationships, a field researcher must be able to break or withdraw from relationships as well. Ties with one member may have to be broken in order to forge ties with others or to explore other aspects of the setting. As with the end of any friendly relationship, the emotional pain of social withdrawal can affect both the researcher and the member. The researcher must balance social sensitivity and the research goals.

Small Favors. *Exchange relationships* develop in the field, in which small tokens or favors, including deference and respect, are exchanged. A researcher may gain acceptance by helping out in small ways. Exchange helps when access to sensitive issues is limited. A researcher may offer small favors but not burden members by asking for return favors. As the researcher and members share experiences and see each other again, members recall the favors and reciprocate by allowing access.

Conflicts in the Field. Fights, conflict, and disagreements can erupt in the field, or a researcher may study groups with opposing positions. In such situations, the researcher will feel pressure to take sides and will be tested to see if he or she can be trusted. In such occasions, a researcher usually stays on the neutral sidelines and walks a tightrope between opposing sides. This is because once he or she becomes aligned with one side, the researcher will cut off access to the other side. In addition, he or she will see the situation from only one point of view.

Appearing Interested. Field researchers maintain an *appearance of interest* in the field. An experienced researcher appears to be interested in and involved with field events by statements and behaviors (e.g., facial expression, going for coffee, organizing a party, etc.) even if he or she is not truly interested. This is because field relations may be disrupted if the researcher appears to be bored or distracted. Putting up such a temporary front of involvement is a common small deception in daily life and is part of being polite.

Of course, selective inattention (i.e., not staring or appearing not to notice) is also part of acting polite. If a person makes a social mistake (e.g., accidentally uses an incorrect word, passes gas, etc.), the polite thing to do is to ignore it. Selective inattention is used in fieldwork, as well. It gives an alert researcher an opportunity to learn by casually eavesdropping on conversations or observing events not meant to be public.

OBSERVING AND COLLECTING DATA

This section looks at how to get good qualitative field data. Field data are what the researcher experiences and remembers, and what are recorded in field notes and become available for systematic analysis.

Watching and Listening

Observing. A great deal of what researchers do in the field is to pay attention, watch, and listen carefully. They use all the senses, noticing what is seen, heard, smelled, tasted, or touched. The researcher becomes an instrument that absorbs all sources of information.

A field researcher carefully scrutinizes the physical setting to capture its atmosphere. He or she asks: What is the color of the floor, walls, ceiling? How large is a room? Where are the windows and doors? How is the furniture arranged, and what is its condition (e.g., new or old and worn, dirty or clean)? What type of lighting is there? Are there signs, paintings, plants? What are the sounds or smells?

Why bother with such details? You may have noticed that stores and restaurants often plan lighting, colors, and piped-in music to create a certain atmosphere. Maybe you know that used-car sales people spray a new-car scent into cars or that shops in shopping malls intentionally send out the odor of freshly made cookies. These subtle, unconscious signals influence human behavior.

Observing in field research is often detailed, tedious work. Instead of the quick flash, motivation arises out of a deep curiosity about the details. Good field researchers are intrigued about details that reveal "what's going on here" through careful listening and watching. Field researchers believe that the core of social life is communicated through the mundane, trival, everyday minutia. This is what people often overlook, but field researchers need to learn how to notice.

In addition to physical surroundings, a field researcher observes people and their actions, noting each person's observable physical characteristics: age, sex, race, and stature. People socially interact differently depending on whether another person is 18, 40, or 70 years old; male or female; White or non-White; short and frail or tall, heavyset, and muscular. When noting such characteristics, the researcher is included. For example, an attitude of strangeness heightens sensitivity to a group's racial composition. A researcher who ignores the racial composition of a group of Whites in a multiracial society because he or she too is White is being racially insensitive.

The researcher records such details because something of significance *might* be revealed. It is better to err by including everything than to ignore potentially significant details. For example, "the tall, White muscular 19-year-old male sprinted into the brightly lit room just as the short, overweight black woman in her sixties eased into a battered chair" says much more than "one person entered, another sat down."

A field researcher notes aspects of physical appearance such as neatness, dress, and hairstyle because they express messages that can affect social interactions. People spend a great deal of time and money selecting clothes, styling and combing hair, grooming with make-up, shaving, ironing clothes, and using deodorant or perfumes. These are part of their presentation of self. Even people who do not groom, shave, or wear deodorant present themselves and send a symbolic message by their appearance. No one dresses or looks "normal." Such a statement suggests that a researcher is not seeing the social world through the eyes of a stranger or is insensitive to social signals.

What people do is also significant. A field researcher notices where people sit or stand, the pace at which they walk, and their nonverbal communication. People express social information, feelings, and attitudes through nonverbal communication, including gestures, facial expressions, and how one stands or sits (standing stiffly, sitting in a slouched position, etc.). People express relationships by how they position themselves in a group and through eye contact. A researcher may read the social communication of people by noting that they are standing close together, looking relaxed, and making eye contact.

A field researcher also notices the context in which events occur: Who was present? Who just arrived or left the scene? Was the room hot and stuffy? Such details may help the researcher assign meaning and understand why an event occurred. If they are not noticed, the details are lost, as is a full understanding of the event.

Serendipity is important in field research. Many times, a field researcher does not know the relevance of what he or she is observing until later. This has two implications. First is the im-

portance of keen observation and excellent notes at all times, even when "nothing seems to be happening." Second is the importance of looking back over time and learning to appreciate wait time. Most field researchers say that they spend a lot of time "waiting." Novice field researchers get frustrated with the amount of time they seem to "waste," either waiting for other people or waiting for events to occur. What novices need to learn is that wait time is a necessary part of fieldwork, and it can be valuable.

A field researcher needs to learn the rhythms of the setting, to operate on other people's schedules, and to observe how events occur within their own flow of time. Also, wait time is not always wasted time. Wait time is time for reflection, for observing details, for developing social relations, for building rapport, and for becoming a familiar sight to people in the field setting. Wait time also displays that a researcher is committed and serious; perseverance is a significant trait field researchers need to cultivate. The researcher may be impatient to get in, get the research over, and get on with his or her "real life" but for the people in the field site, this *is* real life. The researcher should subordinate his or her personal wants to the demands of the field site.

Listening. A field researcher listens carefully to phrases, accents, and incorrect grammar, listening both to *what* is said and *how* it is said or what was implied. For example, people often use phrases such as "you know" or "of course" or "et cetera." A field researcher knows the meaning behind such phrases. He or she can try to hear everything, but listening is difficult when many conversations occur at once or when eavesdropping. Luckily, significant events and themes usually recur.

Taking Notes

Most field research data are in the form of field notes. Full field notes can contain maps, diagrams, photographs, interviews, tape recordings, videotapes, memos, objects from the field, notes jotted in the field, and detailed notes written away from the field. A field researcher expects to fill many notebooks, or the equivalent in computer memory. He or she may spend more time writing notes than being in the field. Some researchers produce 40 single-spaced pages of notes for three hours of observation. With practice, even a new field researcher can produce several pages of notes for each hour in the field.

Writing notes is often boring, tedious work that requires self-discipline. The notes contain extensive descriptive detail drawn from memory. A researcher makes it a daily habit or compulsion to write notes immediately after leaving the field. The notes must be neat and organized because the researcher will return to them over and over again. Once written, the notes are private and valuable. A researcher treats them with care and protects confidentiality. Field notes may be of interest to hostile parties, blackmailers, or legal officials, so some researchers write field notes in code.

A researcher's state of mind, level of attention, and conditions in the field affect note taking. He or she will usually begin with relatively short one- to three-hour periods in the field before writing notes.

Types of Field Notes. Field researchers take notes in many ways.[10] The recommendations here (also see Box 11.3) are suggestions. Full field notes have several types or levels. Five levels will be described. It is usually best to keep all the notes for an observation period together and to distinguish types of notes by separate pages. Some researchers include inferences with direct observations if they are set off by a visible device such as brackets or colored ink. The quantity of notes varies across types. For example, six hours in the field might result in 1 page of jotted notes, 40 pages of direct observation, 5 pages of researcher inference, and 2 pages total for methodological, theoretical, and personal notes.

Jotted Notes. It is nearly impossible to take good notes in the field. Even a known observer in a public setting looks strange when furiously writing. More important, when looking down and writing, the researcher cannot see and hear what is happening. The attention given to note writing is taken from field observation where it belongs. The specific setting determines whether any notes in the field can be taken. The researcher may be able to write, and members may expect it, or he or she may have to be secretive (e.g., go to the restroom).

Jotted notes are written in the field. They are short, temporary memory triggers such as words, phrases, or drawings taken inconspicuously, often scribbled on any convenient item (e.g., napkin, matchbook). They are incorporated into direct observation notes but are never substituted for them.

Direct Observation Notes. The basic source of field data are notes a researcher writes immediately after leaving the field, which he or she can add to later. The notes should be ordered chronologically with the date, time, and place on each entry. They serve as a detailed description of what the researcher heard and saw in concrete, specific terms. To the extent possible, they are an exact recording of the particular words, phrases, or actions.

A researcher's memory improves with practice. A new researcher can soon remember exact phrases from the field. Verbatim statements should be written with double quote marks to distinguish them from paraphrases. Dialogue accessories (nonverbal communication, props, tone, speed, volume, gestures) should be recorded as well. A researcher records what was actually said and does not clean it up; notes include ungrammatical speech, slang, and misstatements (e.g., write, "Uh, I'm goin' home, Sal," not "I am going home, Sally").

A researcher puts concrete details in notes, not summaries. For example, instead of, "We talked about sports," he or she writes, "Anthony argued with Sam and Jason. He said that the Cubs would win next week because they traded for a new shortstop, Chiappetta. He also said that

1. Record notes as soon as possible after each period in the field, and do not talk with others until observations are recorded.

2. Begin the record of each field visit with a new page, with the date and time noted.

3. Use jotted notes only as a temporary memory aid, with key words or terms, or the first and last things said.

4. Use wide margins to make it easy to add to notes at any time. Go back and add to the notes if you remember something later.

5. Plan to type notes and keep each level of notes separate so it will be easy to go back to them later.

6. Record events in the order in which they occurred, and note how long they last (e.g., a 15-minute wait, a one-hour ride).

7. Make notes as concrete, complete, and comprehensible as possible.

8. Use frequent paragraphs and quotation marks. Exact recall of phrases is best, with double quotes; use single quotes for paraphrasing.

9. Record small talk or routines that do not appear to be significant at the time; they may become important later.

10. "Let your feelings flow" and write quickly without worrying about spelling or "wild ideas." Assume that no one else will see the notes, but use pseudonyms.

11. Never substitute tape recordings completely for field notes.

12. Include diagrams or maps of the setting, and outline your own movements and those of others during the period of observation.

13. Include the researcher's own words and behavior in the notes. Also record emotional feelings and private thoughts in a separate section.

14. Avoid evaluative summarizing words. Instead of "The sink looked disgusting," say, "The sink was rust-stained and looked as if it had not been cleaned in a long time. Pieces of food and dirty dishes looked as if they had been piled in it for several days."

15. Reread notes periodically and record ideas generated by the rereading.

16. Always make one or more backup copies, keep them in a locked location, and store the copies in different places in case of fire.

---

the team was better than the Mets, who he thought had inferior infielders. He cited last week's game where the Cubs won against Boston by 8 to 3." A researcher notes who was present, what happened, where it occurred, when, and under what circumstances. New researchers may not take notes because "nothing important happened." An experienced researcher knows that events when "nothing happened" can reveal a lot. For example, members may express feelings and organize experience into folk categories even in trivial conversations.

Researcher Inference Notes. A field researcher listens to members in order to "climb into their skin" or "walk in their shoes." This involves a three-step process. The researcher listens without applying analytical categories; he or she compares what is heard to what was heard at other times and to what others say; then the researcher applies his or her own interpretation to infer or figure out what it means. In ordinary interaction, we do all three steps simultaneously and jump quickly to our own inferences. A field researcher learns to look and listen without inferring or imposing an interpretation. His or her observations without inferences go into *direct observation notes.*

A researcher records inferences in a separate section that is keyed to direct observations.

People never see social relationships, emotions, or meaning. They see specific physical actions and hear words, then use background cultural knowledge, clues from the context, and what is done or said to assign social meaning. For example, one does not see *love* or *anger;* one sees and hears specific actions (red face, loud voice, wild gestures, obscenities) and draw inferences from them (the person is angry).

People constantly infer social meaning on the basis of what they see and hear, but not always correctly. For example, my niece visited me and accompanied me to a store to buy a kite. The clerk at the cash register smiled and asked her whether she and her "Daddy" (looking at me) were going to fly the kite that day. The clerk observed our interaction, then inferred a father/daughter, not an uncle/niece relationship. She saw and heard a male adult and a female child, but she inferred the social meaning incorrectly.

A researcher keeps inferred meaning separate from direct observation because the meaning of actions is not always self-evident. Sometimes, people try to deceive others. For example, an unrelated couple register at a motel as Mr. and Mrs. Smith. More frequently, social behavior is ambiguous or multiple meanings are possible. For example, I see a White male and female, both in their late twenties, get out of a car and enter a restaurant together. They sit at a table, order a meal, and talk with serious expressions in hushed tones, sometimes leaning forward to hear each other. As they get up to leave, the woman, who has a sad facial expression and appears ready to cry, is briefly hugged by the male. They then leave together. Did I witness a couple breaking up, two friends discussing a third, two people trying to decide what to do because they have discovered that their spouses are having an affair with each other, or a brother and sister whose father just died?

Analytic Notes. Researchers make many decisions about how to proceed while in the field. Some acts are planned (e.g., to conduct an interview, to observe a particular activity, etc.) and others seem to occur almost out of thin air. Field researchers keep methodological ideas in analytic notes to record their plans, tactics, ethical and procedural decisions, and self-critiques of tactics.

Theory emerges in field research during data collection and is clarified when a researcher reviews field notes. Analytic notes have a running account of a researcher's attempts to give meaning to field events. He or she thinks out loud in the notes by suggesting links between ideas, creating hypotheses, proposing conjectures, and developing new concepts.

Analytic memos are part of the theoretical notes. They are systematic digressions into theory, where a researcher elaborates on ideas in depth, expands on ideas while still in the field, and modifies or develops more complex theory by rereading and thinking about the memos.

Personal Notes. As discussed earlier, personal feelings and emotional reactions become part of the data and color what a researcher sees or hears in the field. A researcher keeps a section of notes that is like a personal diary. He or she records personal life events and feelings in it ("I'm tense today, I wonder if it's because of the fight I had yesterday with . . . "; "I've got a headache on this gloomy, overcast day").

Personal notes serve three functions: They provide an outlet for a researcher and a way to cope with stress; they are a source of data about personal reactions; they give him or her a way to evaluate direct observation or inference notes when the notes are later reread. For example, if the researcher was in a good mood during observations, it might color what he or she observed (see Figure 11.3).

Maps and Diagrams. Field researchers often make maps and draw diagrams or pictures of the features of a field site. This serves two purposes: It helps a researcher organize events in the field and it helps convey a field site to others. For example, a researcher observing a bar with 15 stools may draw and number 15 circles to sim-

FIGURE 11.3 Types of Field Notes

Direct Observation	Inference	Analytic	Personal Journal
Sunday, October 4. Kay's Kafe 3:00 pm. Large White male in mid-40s, overweight, enters. He wears worn brown suit. He is alone; sits at booth #2. Kay comes by, asks, "What'll it be?" Man says, "Coffee, black for now." She leaves and he lights cigarette and reads menu. 3:15 pm. Kay turns on radio.	Kay seems friendly today, humming. She becomes solemn and watchful. I think she puts on the radio when nervous.	Women are afraid of men who come in alone since the robbery.	It is raining. I am feeling comfortable with Kay but am bored today.

plify recording (e.g., "Yosuke came in and sat on stool 12; Phoebe was already on stool 10"). Field researchers find three types of maps helpful: spatial, social, and temporal. The first helps orient the data; the latter two are preliminary forms of data analysis. A *spatial map* locates people, equipment, and the like in terms of geographical physical space to show where activities occur (Figure 11.4A). A *social map* shows the number or variety of people and the arrangements among them of power, influence, friendship, division of labor, and so on (Figure 11.4B). A *temporal map* shows the ebb and flow of people, goods, services, and communications, or schedules (Figure 11.4C).

Machine Recordings to Supplement Memory. Tape recorders and videotapes can be helpful supplements in field research. They never substitute for field notes or a researcher's presence in the field. They cannot be introduced into all field sites, and can be used only after a researcher develops rapport. Recorders and videotapes provide a close approximation to what occurred and a permanent record that others can review. They help a researcher recall events and observe what does not happen, or nonresponses, which are easy to miss. Nevertheless, these items create disruption and an increased awareness of surveillance. Researchers who rely on them must address associated problems (e.g., ensure that batteries are fresh and there are enough blank tapes). Also, relistening to or viewing tapes can be time consuming. For example, it may take over 100 hours to listen to 50 hours recorded in the field. Transcriptions of tape are expensive and not always accurate; they do not always convey subtle contextual meanings or mumbled words.

Interview Notes. If a researcher conducts field interviews (to be discussed), he or she keeps the interview notes separate.

Data Quality

Reliability in Field Research. The reliability of field data addresses the question: Are researcher observations about a member or field event internally and externally consistent? *Internal consistency* refers to whether the data are plausible given all that is known about a person or event, eliminating common forms of human deception. In other words, do the pieces fit together

FIGURE 11.4 Types of Maps Used in Field Research

A Spatial Map

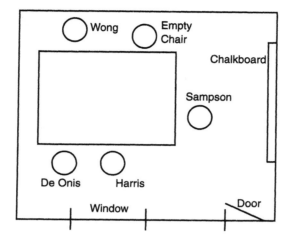

B Social Map

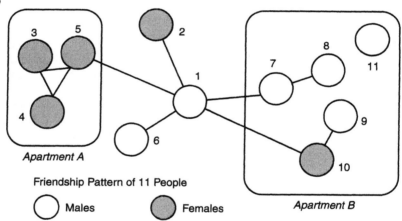

Apartment A

Friendship Pattern of 11 People

○ Males   ● Females

Apartment B

C Temporal Map

Day of Week, Buzz's Bar

	Mon	Tue	Wed	Thr	Fri	Sat
Open 10:00	Old Drunks	Old Drunks	Old Drunks	Old Drunks	Skip Work or Leave Early	Going to Fish
5:00						
	Football Watchers	Neighbors and Bridge Players	Softball Team (All-Male Night)	Young Crowd	Loud Music, Mixed Crowd	Loners and No Dates
Close 1:00						

into a coherent picture? For example, are a member's actions consistent over time and in different social contexts?

External consistency is achieved by verifying or cross-checking observations with other, divergent sources of data. In other words, does it all fit into the overall context? For example, can others verify what a researcher observed about a person? Does other evidence confirm the researcher's observations?

Reliability in field research also includes what is not said or done, but is expected or anticipated. Such omissions or null data can be significant but are difficult to detect. For example, when observing a cashier end her shift, a researcher notices that the money in a drawer is not counted. He or she may notice the omission only if other cashiers always count money at the end of the shift.

Reliability in field research depends on a researcher's insight, awareness, suspicions, and questions. He or she looks at members and events from different angles (legal, economic, political, personal) and mentally asks questions: Where does the money come from for that? What do those people do all day?

Field researchers depend on what members tell them. This makes the credibility of members and their statements part of reliability. To check member credibility, a researcher asks: Does the person have a reason to lie? Is she in a position to know that? What are the person's values and how might that shape what she says? Is he just saying that to please me? Is there anything that might limit his spontaneity?

Field researchers take subjectivity and context into account as they evaluate credibility. They know that a person's statements or actions are affected by subjective perceptions. Statements are made from a particular point of view and colored by an individual's experiences. Instead of evaluating each statement to see if it is true, a field researcher finds statements useful in themselves. Even inaccurate statements and actions can be revealing from a researcher's perspective.

As mentioned before, actions and statements are shaped by the context in which they appear. What is said in one setting may differ in other contexts. For example, when asked "Do you dance?" a member may say no in a public setting full of excellent dancers, but yes in a semiprivate setting with few good dancers and different music. It is not that the member is lying but that the answer is shaped by the context.

Other obstacles to reliability include behaviors that can mislead a researcher: misinformation, evasions, lies, and fronts.[11]

Validity in Field Research. Validity in field research is the confidence placed in a researcher's analysis and data as accurately representing the social world in the field. Replicability is not a criterion because field research is virtually impossible to replicate. Essential aspects of the field change: The social events and context change, the members are different, the individual researcher differs, and so on. There are four kinds of validity or tests of research accuracy: ecological validity, natural history, member validation, and competent insider performance.

Ecological validity is the degree to which the social world described by a researcher matches the world of members. It asks: Is the natural setting described relatively undisturbed by the researcher's presence or procedures? A project has ecological validity if events would have occurred without a researcher's presence.

Member validation occurs when a researcher takes field results back to members, who judge their adequacy. A project is member valid if members recognize and understand the researcher's description as reflecting their intimate social world. Member validation has limitations because conflicting perspectives in a setting produce disagreement with researcher's observations, and members may object when results do not portray their group in a favorable light. In addition, members may not recognize the description because it is not from their perspective or does not fit with their purposes.[12]

Focusing and Sampling

Focusing. The field researcher first gets a general picture, then focuses on a few specific problems or issues (see Figure 11.5). A researcher decides on specific research questions and develops hypotheses only after being in the field and experiencing it firsthand. At first, everything seems relevant; later, however, selective attention focuses on specific questions and themes.

Sampling. Field research sampling differs from survey research sampling, although sometimes both use snowball sampling. A field researcher samples by taking a smaller, selective set of observations from all possible observations. Field researchers sample times, situations, types of events, locations, types of people, or contexts of interest.

For example, a researcher samples time by observing a setting at different times. He or she observes at all times of the day, on every day of the week, and in all seasons to get a full sense of how the field site stays the same or changes. It is often best to overlap when sampling (e.g., to have sampling times from 7:00 A.M. to 9:00 A.M., from 8:00 A.M. to 10:00 A.M., from 9:00 A.M. to 11:00 A.M., etc.).

A researcher samples locations because one location may give depth, but a narrow perspective. Sitting or standing in different locations helps the researcher get a sense of the whole site. For example, the peer-to-peer behavior of school teachers usually occurs in a faculty lounge, but it also occurs at a local bar when teachers gather or in a classroom temporarily used for a teacher meeting. In addition, researchers trace the paths of members to various field locations.

Field researchers sample people by focusing their attention or interaction on different kinds of people (old-timers and newcomers, old and young, males and females, leaders and followers). As a researcher identifies types of people, or people with opposing outlooks, he or she tries to interact with and learn about all types.

For example, a researcher samples three kinds of field events: routine, special, and unanticipated. Routine events (e.g., opening up a store for business) happen every day and should not be considered unimportant simply because they are routine. Special events (e.g., annual office party) are announced and planned in advance. They focus member attention and reveal aspects of social life not otherwise visible. Unanticipated events are those that just happen to occur while a researcher is present (e.g., unsupervised workers when the manager gets sick and cannot oversee workers at a store for a day). In this case, the researcher sees something unusual, unplanned, or rare by chance.

THE FIELD RESEARCH INTERVIEW

So far, you have learned how field researchers observe and take notes. They also interview members, but field interviews differ from survey research interviews. This section introduces the field interview.

The Field Interview

Field researchers use unstructured, nondirective, in-depth interviews, which differ from formal survey research interviews in many ways (see Table 11.1). The field interview involves asking questions, listening, expressing interest, and recording what was said.

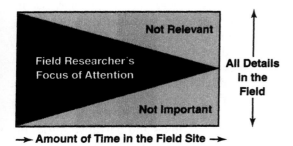

FIGURE 11.5 Focusing in Field Research

TABLE 11.1 Survey Interviews versus Field Research Interviews

Typical Survey Interview	Typical Field Interview
1. It has a clear beginning and end.	1. The beginning and end are not clear. The interview can be picked up later.
2. The same standard questions are asked of all respondents in the same sequence.	2. The questions and the order in which they are asked are tailored to specific people and situations.
3. The interviewer appears neutral at all times.	3. The interviewer shows interest in responses, encourages elaboration.
4. The interviewer asks questions, and the respondent answers.	4. It is like a friendly conversational exchange, but with more interviewer questions.
5. It is almost always with one respondent alone.	5. It can occur in group setting or with others in area, but varies.
6. It has a professional tone and businesslike focus; diversions are ignored.	6. It is interspersed with jokes, asides, stories, diversions, and anecdotes, which are recorded.
7. Closed-ended questions are common, with rare probes.	7. Open-ended questions are common, and probes are frequent.
8. The interviewer alone controls the pace and direction of interview.	8. The interviewer and member jointly control the pace and direction of the interview.
9. The social context in which the interview occurs is ignored and assumed to make little difference.	9. The social context of the interview is noted and seen as important for interpreting the meaning of responses.
10. The interviewer attempts to mold the communication pattern into a standard framework.	10. The interviewer adjusts to the member's norms and language usage.

Source: Adapted from Briggs (1986), Denzin (1989), Douglas (1985), Misher (1986), Spradley (1979a).

The field interview is a joint production of a researcher and a member. Members are active participants whose insights, feelings, and cooperation are essential parts of a discussion process that reveals subjective meanings.

Field research interviews go by many names: unstructured, depth, ethnographic, open ended, informal, and long. Generally, they involve one or more people being present, occur in the field, and are informal and nondirective (i.e., the respondent may take the interview in various directions).

A field interview involves a mutual sharing of experiences. A researcher might share his or her background to build trust and encourage the informant to open up, but does not force answers or use leading questions. She or he encourages and guides a process of mutual discovery.

In field interviews, members express themselves in the forms in which they normally speak, think, and organize reality. A researcher retains members' jokes and narrative stories in their natural form and does not repackage them into a standardized format. The focus is on the member's perspective and experiences. In order to stay close to the member's experience, the researcher asks questions in terms of concrete examples or situations—for example, "Could you tell me things that led up to your quitting in June?" instead of "Why did you quit your job?"

Field interviews occur in a series over time. A researcher begins by building rapport and steering conversation away from evaluative or highly sensitive topics. He or she avoids probing inner feelings until intimacy is established, and even then, the researcher expects apprehension. After several meetings, he or she may be able to probe more deeply into sensitive issues and seek clarification of less sensitive issues. In later interviews, he or she may return to topics and check past answers by restating them in a nonjudgmental tone and asking for verification—for example, "The last time we talked, you said that you started taking things from the store after they reduced your pay. Is that right?"

The field interview is a "speech event," closer to a friendly conversation than the stimulus/response model found in a survey research interview. You are familiar with a friendly conversation, which has its own informal rules and the following elements: (1) a greeting ("Hi, it's good to see you again"); (2) the absence of an explicit goal or purpose (we don't say, "Let's now discuss what we did last weekend"); (3) avoidance of repetition (we don't say, "Could you clarify what you said about . . ."); (4) question asking ("Did you see the race yesterday?"); (5) expressions of interest ("Really? I wish I could have been there!"); (6) expressions of ignorance ("No, I missed it. What happened?"); (7) turn taking, so the encounter is balanced (one person does not always ask questions and the other only answer); (8) abbreviations ("I missed the Derby, but I'm going to the Indy," not "I missed the Kentucky Derby horse race but I will go to the Indianapolis 500 automotive race"); (9) a pause or brief si-

lence when neither person talks is acceptable; (10) a closing (we don't say, "Let's end this conversation"; instead, we give a verbal indicator before physically leaving—"I've got to get back to work now. See ya tomorrow.").

The field interview differs from a friendly conversation. It has an explicit purpose—to learn about the informant and setting. A researcher includes explanations or requests that diverge from friendly conversations. For example, he or she may say, "I'd like to ask you about . . . ," or "Could you look at this and see if I've written it down right?" The field interview is less balanced. A higher proportion of questions come from the researcher, who expresses more ignorance and interest. Also, it includes repetition, and a researcher asks the member to elaborate on unclear abbreviations.

Types of Questions in Field Interviews

Field researchers ask three types of questions in a field interview: descriptive, structural, and contrast questions. All are asked concurrently, but each type is more frequent at a different stage in the research process (see Figure 11.6). During the early stage, a researcher primarily asks descriptive questions. He or she gradually adds structural questions until, in the middle

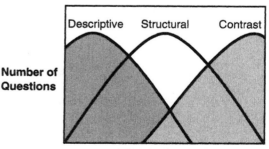

FIGURE 11.6 Types of Questions in Field Research Interviews

stage after analysis has begun, they make up a majority of the questions. Contrast questions appear in the middle of a field research study and increase until, by the end, they are asked more than any other type.[13]

A researcher asks a *descriptive question* to explore the setting and learn about members. Descriptive questions can be about time and space—for example, "Where is the bathroom?" "When does the delivery truck arrive?" "What happened Monday night?" They can also be about people and activities: "Who is sitting by the window?" "What is your uncle like?" "What happens during the initiation ceremony?" They can be about objects: "When do you use a saber saw?" "Which tools do you carry with you on an emergency water leak job?" Questions asking for examples or experiences are descriptive questions—for example, "Could you give me an example of a great date?" "What were your experiences as a postal clerk?" Descriptive questions may ask about hypothetical situations: "If a student opened her book during the exam, how would you deal with it?" Another type of descriptive question asks members about the argot of the setting: "What do you call a deputy sheriff?" (The answer is a "county Mountie.")

A researcher uses a *structural question* after spending time in the field and starting to analyze data, especially with a domain analysis. It begins after a researcher organizes specific field events, situations, and conversations into conceptual categories. For example, a researcher's observations of a highway truck-stop restaurant revealed that the employees informally classify customers who patronize the truck stop. In a preliminary analysis, he or she creates a conceptual category of kinds of customers and has members verify the categories with structural questions.

One way to pose a structural question is to ask the members whether a category includes elements in addition to those already identified by a researcher—for example, "Are there any types of customers other than regulars, greasers, pit

stoppers, and long haulers?" In addition, a researcher asks for confirmation: "Is a greaser a type of customer that you serve?" "Would you call a customer who . . . a greaser?" "Would a pit stopper ever eat a three-course dinner?"

The *contrast question* builds on the analysis that has been verified by structural questions. Questions focus on similarities or differences between elements in categories or between categories as the researcher asks members to verify similarities and differences: "You seem to have a number of different kinds of customers come in here. I've heard you call some customers 'regulars' and others 'pit stoppers.' How are a regular and a pit stopper alike?" or "Is the difference between a long hauler and a greaser that the greaser doesn't tip?" or "Two types of customers just stop to use the restroom—entire families and a lone male. Do you call both pit stoppers?"

Informants

An informant or key actor in field research is a member with whom a field researcher develops a relationship and who tells about, or informs on, the field.[14] Who makes a good informant? The ideal informant has four characteristics:

1. The informant is totally familiar with the culture and is in position to witness significant events makes a good informant. He or she lives and breathes the culture and engages in routines in the setting without thinking about them.
2. The individual is currently involved in the field. Ex-members who have reflected on the field may provide useful insights, but the longer they have been away from direct involvement, the more likely it is that they have reconstructed their recollections.
3. The person can spend time with the researcher. Interviewing may take many hours, and some members are simply not available for extensive interviewing.

4. Nonanalytic individuals make better informants. A nonanalytic informant is familiar with and uses native folk theory or pragmatic common sense. This is in contrast to the analytic member, who preanalyzes the setting, using categories from the media or education.

A field researcher may interview several types of informants. Contrasting types of informants who provide useful perspectives include rookies and old-timers, people in the center of events and those on the fringes of activity, people who recently changed status (e.g., through promotion) and those who are static, frustrated or needy people and happy or secure people, the leader in charge and the subordinate who follows. A field researcher expects mixed messages when he or she interviews a range of informants.

Interview Context

Field researchers recognize that a conversation in a private office may not occur in a crowded lunchroom. Often, interviews take place in the member's home environment so that he or she is comfortable. This is not always best. If a member is preoccupied or there is no privacy, a researcher will move to another setting (e.g., restaurant or university office).

The interview's meaning is shaped by its Gestalt or whole interaction of a researcher and a member in a specific context. For example, a researcher notes nonverbal forms of communication that add meaning, such as a shrug, a gesture, and so on.

LEAVING THE FIELD

Work in the field can last for a few weeks to a dozen years. In either case, at some point work in the field ends. Some researchers (e.g., Schatzman and Strauss, 1973) suggest that the end comes naturally when theory building ceases or reaches a closure; others feel that fieldwork could go on

without end and that a firm decision to cut off relations is needed.

Experienced field researchers anticipate a process of disengaging and exiting the field. Depending on the intensity of involvement and the length of time in the field, the process can be disruptive or emotionally painful for both the researcher and the members. A researcher may experience the emotional pain of breaking intimate friendships when leaving the field. He or she may feel guilty and depressed immediately before and after leaving. He or she may find it difficult to let go because of personal and emotional entanglements. If the involvement in the field was intense and long, and the field site differed from his or her native culture, the researcher may need months of adjustment before feeling at home with his or her original cultural surroundings.

Once a researcher decides to leave—because the project reaches a natural end and little new is being learned, or because external factors force it to end (e.g., end of a job, gatekeepers order the researcher out, etc.)—he or she chooses a method of exiting. The researcher can leave by a quick exit (simply not return one day) or slowly withdraw, reducing his or her involvement over weeks. He or she also needs to decide how to tell members and how much advance warning to give.

The exit process depends on the specific field setting and the relationships developed. In general, a researcher lets members know a short period ahead of time. He or she fulfills any bargains or commitments that were built up and leaves with a clean slate. Sometimes, a ritual or ceremony, such as a going-away party or shaking hands with everyone, helps signal the break for members. Maintaining friendships with members is also possible and is preferred by feminist researchers.

A field researcher is aware that leaving affects members. Some members may feel hurt or rejected because a close social relationship is ending. They may react by trying to pull a researcher back into the field and make him or her more of a member, or they may become angry and resentful. They may grow cool and distant because of an awareness that the researcher is really an outsider. In any case, fieldwork is not finished until the process of disengagement and exiting is complete.

FOCUS GROUPS

The *focus group* is a special qualitative research technique in which people are informally "interviewed" in a group-discussion setting.[15] Focus group research has rapidly grown in the past 20 years. The procedure is that a researcher gathers together 6 to 12 people in a room with a moderator to discuss a few issues. Most focus groups last about 90 minutes. The moderator is trained to be nondirective and to facilitate free, open discussion by all group members (i.e., not let one person dominate the discussion). Group members should be homogenous, but not include close friends or relatives. In a typical study, a researcher uses four to six separate groups. Focus group topics might include public attitudes (e.g., race relations, workplace equality), personal behaviors (e.g., dealing with AIDS), a new product (e.g., breakfast cereal), or a political candidate. Researchers often combine focus groups with quantitative research, and the procedure has its own specific strengths and weaknesses (see Box 11.4).

Several years ago, I conducted an applied study on why parents and students chose to attend a private high school. In addition to collecting quantitative survey data, I formed six focus groups, each with 8 to 10 students from the high school. A trained college-student moderator asked questions, elicited comments from group members, and prevented one person from dominating discussions. The six groups were co-ed and contained members of either one grade level or two adjacent grades (e.g., freshmen and sophomores). students discussed their reasons for attending the high school and whether specific factors were important. I tape-recorded the discussions, which lasted about 45 minutes, then analyzed the tapes to understand what the students saw as important to their decisions. In addition, the data helped when interpreting the survey data.

BOX 11.4 Advantages and Limitations of Focus Groups

Advantages

- The natural setting allows people to express opinions/ideas freely.
- Open expression among members of marginalized social groups is encouraged.
- People tend to feel empowered, especially in action-oriented research projects.
- Survey researchers are provided a window into how people talk about survey topics.
- The interpretation of quantitative survey results is facilitated.
- Participants may query one another and explain their answers to each others.

Limitations

- A "polarization effect" exists (attitudes become more extreme after group discussion).
- Only one or a few topics can be discussed in a focus group session.
- A moderator may unknowingly limit open, free expression of group members.
- Focus group participants produce fewer ideas than in individual interviews.
- Focus group studies rarely report all the details of study design/procedure.
- Researchers cannot reconcile the differences that arise between individual-only and focus group-context responses.

ETHICAL DILEMMAS OF FIELD RESEARCH

The direct personal involvement of a field researcher in the social lives of other people raises many ethical dilemmas. The dilemmas arise when a researcher is alone in the field and has little time to make a moral decision. Although he or she may be aware of general ethical issues before entering the field, they arise unexpectedly in the course of observing and interacting in the field. We will look at four ethical issues in field research: deception, confidentiality, involvement with deviants, and publishing reports.[16]

Deception

Deception arises in several ways in field research: The research may be covert; or may assume a false role, name, or identity; or may mislead members in some way. The most hotly debated of the ethical issues arising from deception is that of covert versus overt field research. Some support it and see it as necessary for entering into and gaining a full knowledge of many areas of social life. Others oppose it and argue that it undermines a trust between researchers and society. Although its moral status is questionable, there are some field sites or activities that can only be studied covertly. Covert research is never preferable and never easier than overt research because of the difficulties of maintaining a front and the constant fear of getting caught.

Confidentiality

A researcher learns intimate knowledge that is given in confidence. He or she has a moral obligation to uphold the confidentiality of data. This includes keeping information confidential from others in the field and disguising members' names in field notes. Sometimes a field researcher cannot directly quote a person. One strategy is instead of reporting the source as an informant, the researcher can find documentary evidence that says the same thing and use the document (e.g., an old memo, a newspaper article, etc.) as if it were the source of the information.

Involvement with Deviants

Researchers who conduct field research on deviants who engage in illegal behavior face additional dilemmas. They know of and are sometimes involved in illegal activity. Fetterman

(1989) called this *guilty knowledge.* Such knowledge is of interest not only to law enforcement officials but also to other deviants. The researcher faces a dilemma of building trust and rapport with the deviants, yet not becoming so involved as to violate his or her basic personal moral standards. Usually, the researcher makes an explicit arrangement with the deviant members.

Publishing Field Reports

The intimate knowledge that a researcher obtains and reports creates a dilemma between the right of privacy and the right to know. A researcher does not publicize member secrets, violate privacy, or harm reputations. Yet, if he or she cannot publish anything that might offend or harm someone, some of what the researcher learned will remain hidden, and it may be difficult for others to believe the report if critical details are omitted.

Some researchers suggest asking members to look at a report to verify its accuracy and to approve of their portrayal in print. For marginal groups (e.g., addicts, prostitutes, crack users), this may not be possible, but researchers must always respect member privacy. On the other hand, censorship or self-censorship can be a danger. A compromise position is that truthful but unflattering material may be published only if it is essential to the researchers' arguments.

CONCLUSION

In this chapter, you learned about field research and the field research process (choosing a site and gaining access, relations in the field, observing and collecting data, and the field interview). Field researchers begin data analysis and theorizing during the data collection phase.

You can now appreciate implications of saying that in field research, the researcher is directly involved with those being studied and is immersed in a natural setting. Doing field research usually has a greater impact on the researcher's emotions, personal life, and sense of self than doing other types of research. Field research is difficult to conduct, but it is a way to study parts of the social world that otherwise could not be studied.

Good field research requires a combination of skills. In addition to a strong sense of self, the best field researchers possess an incredible ability to listen and absorb details, tremendous patience, sensitivity and empathy for others, superb social skills, a talent to think very quickly "on one's feet," the ability see subtle interconnections among people/events, and a superior ability to express oneself in writing.

Field research is strongest when a researcher studies a small group of people interacting in the present. It is valuable for micro-level or small-group face-to-face interaction. It is less effective when the concern is macro-level processes and social structures. It is nearly useless for events that occurred in the distant past or processes that stretch across decades. Historical-comparative research, discussed in the next chapter, is better suited to investigating these types of concerns.

Key Terms

analytic memos
appearance of interest
attitude of strangeness
contrast question
descriptive question
direct observation notes
ecological validity
ethnography
ethnomethodology
external consistency
field site
focus group
gatekeeper
go native
guilty knowledge
internal consistency
jotted notes
member validation

naturalism
normalize social research
structural question

Endnotes

1. For studies of these sites or topics, see Neuman (2002, 2003). On studies of children or schools, see Corsaro (1994), Corsaro and Molinari (2000), Eder (1995), Eder and Kinney (1995), Kelle (2000), and Merten (1999). On studies of homeless people, see Lankenau (1999), and on studies of female strippers, see Wood (2000).
2. Ethnography is described in Agar (1986), Franke (1983), Hammersley and Atkinson (1983), Sanday (1983), and Spradley (1979a:3–12; 1979b:3–16).
3. For a general discussion of field research and naturalism, see Adler and Adler (1994), Georges and Jones (1980), Holy (1984), and Pearsall (1970). For discussions of contrasting types of field research, see Clammer (1984), Gonor (1977), Holstein and Gubrium (1994), Morse (1994), Schwandt (1994), and Strauss and Corbin (1994).
4. See Lofland (1976:13–23) and Shaffir and colleagues (1980:18–20) on feeling marginal.
5. See Adler and Adler (1987:67–78).
6. See Hammersley and Atkinson (1983:42–45) and Lofland and Lofland (1995:16–30).
7. For more on gatekeepers and access, see Beck (1970:11–29), Bogdan and Taylor (1975:30–32), and Wax (1971:367).
8. Negotiation in the field is discussed in Gans (1982), Johnson (1975:58–59, 76–77), and Schatzman and Strauss (1973:22–23).
9. See Douglas (1976), Emerson (1981:367–368), and Johnson (1975:124–129) on the question of whether the researcher should always be patient, polite, and considerate.
10. For more on ways to record and organize field data, see Bogdan and Taylor (1975:60–73), Hammersley and Atkinson (1983:144–173), and Kirk and Miller (1986: 49–59).
11. Adapted from Douglas (1976:56–104).
12. For more on validity in field research, see Briggs (1986:24), Bogdan and Taylor (1975), Douglas (1976), Emerson (1981:361–363), and Sanjek (1990).

13. The types of questions are adapted from Spradley (1979a, 1979b).

14. Field research informants are discussed in Dean and associates (1969), Kemp and Ellen (1984), Schatzman and Strauss (1973), Spradley (1979a: 46–54), and Whyte (1982).

15. For a discussion of focus groups, see Bischoping and Dykema (1999), Churchill (1983:179–184), Krueger (1988), Labaw (1980:54–58), and Morgan (1996).

16. See Lofland and Lofland (1995:26, 63, 75, 168–177), Miles and Huberman (1994:288–297), and Punch (1986).

DATA ANALYSIS

INTRODUCTION

If you read a research report or article based on quantitative data, you will probably find charts, graphs, and tables full of numbers. Do not be intimidated by them. A researcher provides the charts, graphs, and tables to give you, the reader, a condensed picture of the data. The charts and tables allow you to see the evidence collected. When you collect your own quantitative data, you will have to use similar techniques to help you to see what is inside the data. You will need to organize and manipulate the data to get them to reveal things of interest. In this chapter, you will learn the fundamentals of organizing and analyzing quantitative data. The analysis of quantitative data is a complex field of knowledge. This chapter covers only the basic statistical concepts and data-handling techniques necessary to understand social research.

Data collected using the techniques in the past chapters are in the form of numbers. The numbers represent values of variables, which measure characteristics of subjects, respondents, or other cases. The numbers are in a raw form, on questionnaires, note pads, recording sheets, or paper. Researchers reorganize them into a form suitable for computers, present charts or graphs to summarize their features, and interpret or give theoretical meaning to the results.

DEALING WITH DATA

Coding Data

Before a researcher examines quantitative data to test hypotheses, he or she needs to put them in a different form. You encountered the idea of coding data in the last chapter. Here, data *coding* means systematically reorganizing raw data into a format that is machine readable (i.e., easy to analyze using computers). As with coding in content analysis, researchers create and consistently apply rules for transferring information from one form to another.

Coding can be a simple clerical task when the data are recorded as numbers on well-organized recording sheets, but it is difficult when, for example, a researcher wants to code answers to open-ended survey questions into numbers in a process similar to latent content analysis.

Researchers use a set of rules stating that certain numbers are assigned to variable attributes. For example, a researcher codes males as 1 and females as 2. Each category of a variable and missing information needs a code. A *codebook* is a document (i.e., one or more pages) describing the coding procedure and the location of data for variables in a format that computers can use.

When you code data, it is important to create a well-organized, detailed codebook and make multiple copies of it. If you do not write down the details of the coding procedure, or if you misplace the codebook, you have lost the key to the data and may have to recode the data again.

Researchers begin thinking about a coding procedure and codebook before they collect data. For example, a survey researcher precodes a questionnaire before collecting data. *Precoding* means placing the code categories (e.g., 1 for male, 2 for female) on the questionnaire.[1] Sometimes, to reduce dependence on a codebook, researchers also place the location in the computer format on the questionnaire.

If a researcher does not precode, his or her first step after collecting data is to create a codebook. He or she also gives each case an identification number to keep track of the cases. Next, the researcher transfers the information from each questionnaire into a format that computers can read.

Entering Data

Most computer programs designed for data analysis need the data in a grid format. In the grid, each row represents a respondent, subject, or case. Each is the record of data for a single case. A column or a set of columns represents specific variables. It is possible to go from a column and row location (e.g., row 7, column 5) back to the original source of data (e.g., a questionnaire item on marital status for respondent 8).

For example, a researcher codes survey data for three respondents in a format for computers like that presented in Figure 10.1. People cannot easily read it, and without the codebook, it is worthless. It condenses answers to 50 survey questions for three respondents into three lines or rows. The raw data for many research projects looks like this, except that there may be over 1,000 rows, and the lines may be over 100 columns long. For example, a 15-minute telephone survey of 250 students produces a grid of data that is 250 rows by 240 columns.

The codebook in Figure 10.1 says that the first two numbers are identification numbers. Thus, the example data are for the first (01), second (02), and third (03) respondents. Notice that researchers use zeros as place holders to reduce confusion between 1 and 01. The 1s are always in column 2; the 10s are in column 1. The codebook says that column 5 contains the variable "sex": Cases 1 and 2 are male and Case 3 is female. Column 4 tells us that Carlos interviewed Cases 1 and 2, and Sophia Case 3.

There are four ways to get raw quantitative data into a computer:

1. *Code sheet.* Gather the information, then transfer it from the original source onto a grid format (code sheet). Next, type what is on the code sheet into a computer, line by line.
2. *Direct-entry method, including CATI.* As information is being collected, sit at a computer keyboard (or similar recording device) while listening to/observing the information and enter the information, or have a respondent/subject enter the information himself or herself. The computer must preprogrammed to accept the information.
3. *Optical scan.* Gather the information, then enter it onto optical scan sheets (or have a respondent/subject enter the information) by filling in the correct "dots." Next, use an optical scanner or reader to transfer the information into a computer.
4. *Bar code.* Gather the information and covert it into different widths of bars that are associated with specific numerical values, then use a bar-code reader to transfer the information into a computer.

Cleaning Data

Accuracy is extremely important when coding data. Errors made when coding or entering data into a computer threaten the validity of measures and cause misleading results. A researcher who has a perfect sample, perfect measures, and no errors in gathering data, but who makes errors in the coding process or in entering data into a computer, can ruin a whole research project.

After very careful coding, the researcher checks the accuracy of coding, or "cleans" the data. He or she may code a 10 to 15 percent random sample of the data a second time. If no coding errors appear, the researcher proceeds; if he or she finds errors, the researcher rechecks all coding.

Researchers verify coding after the data are in a computer in two ways. *Possible code cleaning* (or *wild code checking*) involves checking the categories of all variables for impossible codes. For example, respondent sex is coded 1 = Male, 2 = Female. Finding a 4 for a case in the field for the sex variable indicates a coding error. A second method, *contingency cleaning* (or *consistency checking*), involves cross-classifying two variables and looking for logically impossible combinations. For example, education is cross-classified by occupation. If a respondent is recorded as never having passed the eighth grade and also is recorded as being a legitimate medical doctor, the researcher checks for a coding error.

A researcher can modify data after they are in a computer. He or she may not use more refined categories than were used when collecting the original data, but may combine or group information. For example, the researcher may group ratio-level income data into five ordinal

FIGURE 10.1 Coded Data for Three Cases and Codebook

Exerpt from Survey Questionnaire

Respondent ID _____   Interviewer Name _____

Note the Respondent's Sex: ____ Male   ____ Female

1. The first question is about the president of the United States. Do you Strongly Agree, Agree, Disagree, Strongly Disagree, or Have No Opinion about the following statement:
   The President of the United States is doing a great job.

   ____ Strong Agree   ____ Agree   ____ Disagree   ____ Strong Disagree   ____ No Opinion

2. How old are you? _____

Excerpt of Coded Data

```
                        Column
00000000001111111111222222222223333333333444 ... etc. (tens)
123456789012345678901234567890123456789012 ... etc. (ones)
01 212736302 182738274 10239 18.82 3947461 ... etc.
02 213334821 124988154 21242 18.21 3984123 ... etc.
03 420123982 113727263 12345 17.36 1487645 ... etc.
etc.
```
Raw data for first three cases, columns 1 through 42.

Excerpt from Codebook

Column	Variable Name	Description
1–2	ID	Respondent identification number
3	BLANK	
4	Interviewer	Interviewer who collected the data: 1 = Susan 2 = Carlos 3 = Juan 4 = Sophia 5 = Clarence
5	Sex	Interviewer report of respondent's sex 1 = Male, 2 = Female
6	PresJob	The president of the United States is doing a great job. 1 = Strongly Agree 2 = Agree 3 = No Opinion 4 = Disagree 5 = Strongly Disagree Blank = missing information

categories. Also, he or she can combine information from several indicators to create a new variable or add the responses to several questionnaire items into an index score.

RESULTS WITH ONE VARIABLE

Frequency Distributions

The word *statistics* can mean a set of collected numbers (e.g., numbers telling how many people live in a city) as well as a branch of applied mathematics used to manipulate and summarize the features of numbers. Social researchers use both types of statistics. Here, we focus on the second type—ways to manipulate and summarize numbers that represent data from a research project.

Descriptive statistics describe numerical data. They can be categorized by the number of variables involved: univariate, bivariate, or multivariate (for one, two, and three or more variables). *Univariate statistics* describe one variable (*uni-* refers to one; *-variate* refers to variable). The easiest way to describe the numerical data of one variable is with a *frequency distribution*. It can be used with nominal-, ordinal-, interval-, or ratio-level data and takes many forms. For example, I have data for 400 respondents. I can summarize the information on the gender of respondents at a glance with a raw count or a percentage frequency distribution (see Figure 10.2). I can present the same information in graphic form. Some common types of graphic representations are the *histogram, bar chart,* and *pie chart.* Bar charts or graphs are used for discrete variables. They can have a vertical or horizontal orientation with a small space between the bars. The terminology is not exact, but histograms are usually upright bar graphs for interval or ratio data.

For interval- or ratio-level data, a researcher often groups the information into categories. The grouped categories should be mutually exclusive. Interval- or ratio-level data are often plotted in a *frequency polygon.* In it the number of cases or frequency is along the vertical axis, and the values of the variable or scores are along the horizontal axis. A polygon appears when the dots are connected.

Measures of Central Tendency

Researchers often want to summarize the information about one variable into a single number. They use three measures of central tendency, or measures of the center of the frequency distribution: mean, median, and mode, which are often called *averages* (a less precise and less clear way of saying the same thing).

The *mode* is the easiest to use and can be used with nominal, ordinal, interval, or ratio data. It is simply the most common or frequently occurring number. For example, the mode of the following list is 5: 6 5 7 10 9 5 3 5. A distribution can have more than one mode. For example, the mode of this list is both 5 and 7: 5 6 1 2 5 7 4 7. If the list gets long, it is easy to spot the mode in a frequency distribution—just look for the most frequent score. There will always be at least one case with a score that is equal to the mode.

The *median* is the middle point. It is also the 50th percentile, or the point at which half the cases are above it and half below it. It can be used with ordinal-, interval- or ratio-level data (but not nominal level). You can "eyeball" the mode, but computing a median requires a little more work. The easiest way is first to organize the scores from highest to lowest, then count to the middle. If there is an odd number of scores, it is simple. Seven people are waiting for a bus; their ages are: 12 17 20 27 30 55 80. The median age is 27. Note that the median does not change easily. If the 55-year-old and the 80-year-old both got on one bus, and the remaining people were joined by two 31-year-olds, the median remains unchanged. If there is an even number of scores, things are a bit more complicated. For example, six people at a bus stop have the following ages: 17 20 26 30 50 70. The median is somewhere between 26 and 30. Compute the

FIGURE 10.2 Examples of Univariate Statistics

Raw Count Frequency Distribution		Percentage Frequency Distribution	
Gender	Frequency	Gender	Percentage
Male	100	Male	25%
Female	300	Female	75%
Total	400	Total	100%

Bar Chart of Same Information

Males

Females

Example of Grouped Data Frequency Distribution

First Job Annual Income	N
Under $5,000	25
$5,000 to $9,999	50
$10,000 to $15,999	100
$16,000 to $19,999	150
$20,000 to $29,999	50
$30,000 and over	25
Total	400

Example of Frequency Polygon

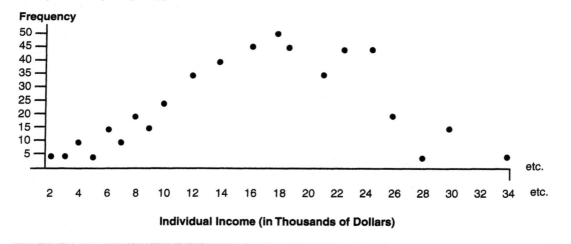

median by adding the two middle scores together and dividing by 2, or 26 + 30 = 56/2 = 28. The median age is 28, even though no person is 28 years old. Note that there is no mode in the list of six ages because each person has a different age.

The *mean,* also called the arithmetic average, is the most widely used measure of central tendency. It can be used *only* with interval- or ratio-level data.[2] Compute the mean by adding up all scores, then divide by the number of scores. For example, the mean age in the previous example is $17 + 20 + 26 + 30 + 50 + 70 = 213$; $213/6 = 35.5$. No one in the list is 35.5 years old, and the mean does not equal the median.

The mean is strongly affected by changes in extreme values (very large or very small). For example, the 50- and 70-year-old left and were replaced with two 31-year-olds. The distribution now looks like this: 17 20 26 30 31 31. The median is unchanged 28. The mean is $17 + 20 + 26 + 30 + 31 + 31 = 155$; $155/6 = 25.8$. Thus, the mean dropped a great deal when a few extreme values were removed.

If the frequency distribution forms a "normal" or bell-shaped curve, the three measures of central tendency equal each other. If the distribution is a *skewed distribution* (i.e., more cases are in the upper or lower scores), then the three will not be equal. If most cases have lower scores with

a few extreme high scores, the mean will be the highest, the median in the middle, and the mode the lowest. If most cases have higher scores with a few extreme low scores, the mean will be the lowest, the median in the middle, and the mode the highest. In general, the median is best for skewed distributions, although the mean is used in most other statistics (see Figure 10.3).

Measures of Variation

Measures of central tendency are a one-number summary of a distribution; however, they give only its *center*. Another characteristic of a distribution is its spread, dispersion, or variability around the center. Two distributions can have identical measures of central tendency but differ in their spread about the center. For example, seven people are at a bus stop in front of a bar. Their ages are 25 26 27 30 33 34 35. Both the median and the mean are 30. At a bus stop in front of an ice cream store, seven people have the identical

FIGURE 10.3 Measures of Central Tendency

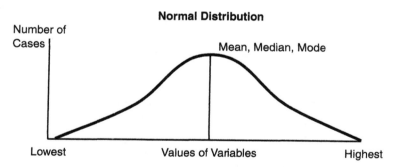

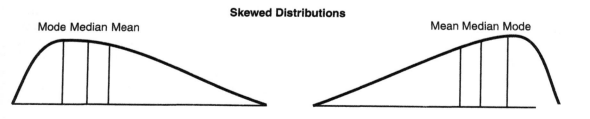

median and mean, but their ages are 5 10 20 30 40 50 55. The ages of the group in front of the ice cream store are spread more from the center, or the distribution has more variability.

Variability has important social implications. For example, in city X, the median and mean family income is $35,600 per year, and it has zero variation. *Zero variation* means that every family has an income of exactly $35,600. City Y has the same median and mean family income, but 95 percent of its families have incomes of $12,000 per year and 5 percent have incomes of $300,000 per year. City X has perfect income equality, whereas there is great inequality in city Y. A researcher who does not know the variability of income in the two cities misses very important information.

Researchers measure variation in three ways: range, percentile, and standard deviation. *Range* is the simplest. It consists of the largest and smallest scores. For example, the range for the bus stop in front of the bar is from 25 to 35, or $35 - 25 = 10$ years. If the 35-year-old got onto a bus and was replaced by a 60-year-old, the range would change to $60 - 25 = 45$ years. Range has limitations. For example, here are two groups of six with a range of 35 years: 30 30 30 30 30 65 and 20 45 46 48 50 55.

Percentiles tell the score at a specific place within the distribution. One percentile you already learned is the median, the 50th percentile. Sometimes the 25th and 75th percentiles or the 10th and 90th percentiles are used to describe a distribution. For example, the 25th percentile is the score at which 25 percent of the distribution have either that score or a lower one. The computation of a percentile follows the same logic as the median. If I have 100 people and want to find the 25th percentile. I rank the scores and count up from the bottom until I reach number 25. If the total is not 100, I simply adjust the distribution to a percentage basis.

Standard deviation is the most difficult to compute measure of dispersion; it is also the most comprehensive and widely used. The range and percentile are for ordinal-, interval-, and

ratio-level data, but the standard deviation requires an interval or ratio level of measurement. It is based on the mean and gives an "average distance" between all scores and the mean. People rarely compute the standard deviation by hand for more than a handful of cases because computers and calculators can do it in seconds.

Look at the calculation of the standard deviation in Figure 10.4. If you add up the absolute difference between each score and the mean (i.e., subtract each score from the mean), you get zero. This is because the mean is equally distant from all scores. Also notice that the scores that differ the most from the mean have the largest effect on the sum of squares and on the standard deviation.

The standard deviation is used for comparison purposes. For example, the standard deviation for the schooling of parents of children in class A is 3.317 years; for class B, it is 0.812; and for class C, it is 6.239. The standard deviation tells a researcher that the parents of children in class B are very similar, whereas those for class C are very different. In fact, in class B, the schooling of an "average" parent is less than a year above or below than the mean for all parents, so the parents are very homogeneous. In class C, however, the "average" parent is more than six years above or below the mean, so the parents are very heterogeneous.

The standard deviation and the mean are used to create z-scores. *Z-scores* let a researcher compare two or more distributions or groups. The z-score, also called a *standardized score*, expresses points or scores on a frequency distribution in terms of a number of standard deviations from the mean. Scores are in terms of their relative position within a distribution, not as absolute values.

For example, Katy, a sales manager in firm A, earns $50,000 per year, whereas Mike in firm B earns $38,000 per year. Despite the absolute income differences between them, the managers are paid equally relative to others in the same firm. Katy is paid more than two-thirds of other employees in her firm, and Mike is also paid more than two-thirds of the employees in his firm.

Here is another example of how to use z-scores. Hans and Heidi are twin brother and sis-

FIGURE 10.4 The Standard Deviation

Steps in Computing the Standard Deviation
1. Compute the mean.
2. Subtract the mean from each score.
3. Square the resulting difference for each score.
4. Total up the squared differences to get the sum of squares.
5. Divide the sum of squares by the number of cases to get the variance.
6. Take the square root of the variance, which is the standard deviation.

Example of Computing the Standard Deviation
[8 respondents, variable = years of schooling]

Score	Score – Mean	Squared (Score – Mean)
15	15 – 12.5 = 2.5	6.25
12	12 – 12.5 = –0.5	.25
12	12 – 12.5 = –0.5	.25
10	10 – 12.5 = –2.5	6.25
16	16 – 12.5 = 3.5	12.25
18	18 – 12.5 = 5.5	30.25
8	8 – 12.5 = 4.5	20.25
9	9 – 12.5 = –3.5	12.25

Mean = 15 + 12 + 12 + 10 + 16 + 18 + 8 + 9 = 100, 100/8 = 12.5
Sum of squares = 6.25 + .25 + .25 + 6.25 + 12.25 + 30.25 + 20.25 + 12.25 = 88
Variance = Sum of squares/Number of cases = 88/8 = 11
Standard deviation = Square root of variance = !11 = 3.317 years.
Here is the standard deviation in the form of a formula with symbols.

Symbols:
X = SCORE of case Σ = Sigma (Greek letter) for sum, add together
$\bar{X}$ = MEAN N = Number of cases

Formula:[a]

$$\text{Standard deviation} = \sqrt{\frac{\Sigma (X - \bar{X})^2}{N}}$$

[a] There is a slight difference in the formula depending on whether one is using data for the population or a sample to estimate the population parameter.

ter, but Hans is shorter than Heidi. Compared to other girls her age, Heidi is at the mean height; she has a z-score of zero. Likewise, Hans is at the mean height among boys his age. Thus, within each comparison group, the twins are at the same z-score, so they have the same relative height.

Z-scores are easy to calculate from the mean and standard deviation (see Box 10.1). For example, an employer interviews students from Kings College and Queens College. She learns that the colleges are similar and that both grade on a 4.0 scale. Yet, the mean grade-point average at Kings College is 2.62 with a standard deviation of .50,

Calculating Z-Scores

Personally, I do not like the formula for z-scores, which is:

Z-score = (Score – Mean)/Standard Deviation,

or in symbols:

$$z = \frac{X - \bar{X}}{\delta}$$

where: X = score, $\bar{X}$ = mean, δ = standard deviation

I usually rely on a simple conceptual diagram that does the same thing and that shows what z-scores really do. Consider data on the ages of schoolchildren with a mean of 7 years and a standard deviation of 2 years. How do I compute the z-score of 5-year-old Miguel, or what if I know that Yashohda's z-score is a +2 and I need to know her age in years? First, I draw a little chart from –3 to +3 with zero in the middle. I will put the mean value at zero, because a z-score of zero is the mean and z-scores measure distance above or below it. I stop at 3 because virtually all cases fall within 3 standard

deviations of the mean in most situations. The chart looks like this:

```
|___|___|___|___|___|___|___|
-3  -2  -1   0  +1  +2  +3
```

Now, I label the values of the mean and add or subtract standard deviations from it. One standard deviation above the mean (+1) when the mean is 7 and standard deviation is 2 years is just 7 + 2, or 9 years. For a –2 z-score, I put 3 years. This is because it is 2 standard deviations, of 2 years each (or 4 years), lower than the Mean of 7. My diagram now looks like this:

```
1   3   5   7   9   11   13   age in years
|___|___|___|___|___|___|___|
-3  -2 -1  0  +1  +2   +3
```

It is easy to see that Miguel, who is 5 years old, has a z-score of –1, whereas Yashohda's z-score of +2 corresponds to 11 years old. I can read from z-score to age, or age to z-score. For fractions, such as a z-score of –1.5, I just apply the same fraction to age to get 4 years. Likewise, an age of 12 is a z-score of +2.5.

whereas the mean grade-point average at Queens College is 3.24 with a standard deviation of .40. The employer suspects that grades at Queens College are inflated. Suzette from Kings College has a grade-point average of 3.62, while Jorge from Queens College has a grade-point average of 3.64. Both students took the same courses. The employer wants to adjust the grades for the grading practices of the two colleges (i.e., create standardized scores). She calculates z-scores by subtracting each student's score from the mean, then dividing by the standard deviation. For example, Suzette's z-score is 3.62 – 2.62 = 1.00/.50 = 2, whereas Jorge's z-score is 3.64 – 3.24. = .40/.40 = 1. Thus, the employer learns that Suzette is two standard deviations above the

mean in her college, whereas Jorge is only one standard deviation above the mean for his college. Although Suzette's absolute grade-point average is lower than Jorge's, relative to the students in each of their colleges Suzette's grades are much higher than Jorge's.

RESULTS WITH TWO VARIABLES

A Bivariate Relationship

Univariate statistics describe a single variable in isolation. *Bivariate statistics* are much more valuable. They let a researcher consider two variables together and describe the relationship between variables. Even simple hypotheses require two variables. Bivariate statistical analysis shows a *relationship* between variables—that is, things that appear together.

Statistical relationships are based on two ideas: covariation and independence. *Covariation* means that things go together or are associated. To covary means to vary together; cases with certain values on one variable are likely to have certain values on the other one. For example, people with higher values on the income variable are likely to have higher values on the life expectancy variable. Likewise, those with lower incomes have lower life expectancy. This is usually stated in a shorthand way by saying that income and life expectancy are related to each other, or covary. We could also say that knowing one's income tells us one's probable life expectancy, or that life expectancy depends on income.

Independence is the opposite of covariation. It means there is no association or no relationship between variables. If two variables are independent, cases with certain values on one variable do not have any particular value on the other variable. For example, Rita wants to know whether number of siblings is related to life expectancy. If the variables are independent, then people with many brothers and sisters have the same life expectancy as those who are only children. In other words, knowing how many brothers or sisters someone has tells Rita nothing about the person's life expectancy.

Most researchers state hypotheses in terms of a causal relationship or expected covariation; if they use the null hypothesis, the hypothesis is that there is independence. It is used in formal hypothesis testing and is frequently found in inferential statistics (to be discussed).

Three techniques help researchers decide whether a relationship exists between two variables: (1) a scattergram, or a graph or plot of the relationship; (2) cross-tabulation, or a percentaged table; and (3) measures of association, or statistical measures that express the amount of covariation by a single number (e.g., correlation coefficient).

Seeing the Relationship: The Scattergram

What Is a Scattergram (or Scatterplot)? A *scattergram* is a graph on which a researcher plots each case or observation, where each axis represents the value of one variable. It is used for variables measured at the interval or ratio level, rarely for ordinal variables, and never if either variable is nominal. There is no fixed rule for which variable (independent or dependent) to place on the horizontal or vertical axis, but usually the independent variable (symbolized by the letter X) goes on the horizontal axis and the dependent variable (symbolized by Y) on the vertical axis. The lowest value for each should be the lower left corner and the highest value should be at the top or to the right.

How to Construct a Scattergram. Begin with the range of the two variables. Draw an axis with the values of each variable marked and write numbers on each axis (graph paper is helpful). Next, label each axis with the variable name and put a title at the top.

You are now ready for the data. For each case, find the value of each variable and mark the graph at a place corresponding to the two values. For example, a researcher makes a scattergram of years of schooling by number of children. He or she looks at the first case to see years of schooling (e.g., 12) and at the number of children (e.g., 3). Then he or she goes to the place on the graph where 12 for the "schooling" variable and 3 for the "number of children" variable intersect and puts a dot for the case.

The scattergram in Figure 10.5 is a plot of data for 33 women. It shows a *negative relationship* between the years of education the woman completed and the number of children she gave birth to.

What Can You Learn from the Scattergram? A researcher can see three aspects of a bivariate relationship in a scattergram: form, direction, and precision.

FIGURE 10.5 Example of a Scattergram: Years of Education by Number of Natural Children for 33 Women

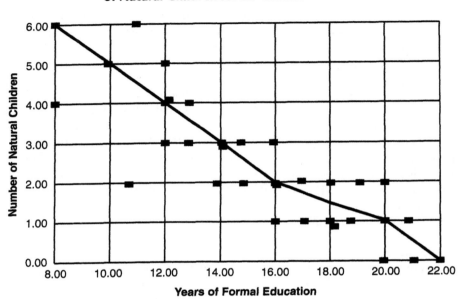

Form. Relationships can take three forms: independence, linear, and curvilinear. *Independence* or no relationship is the easiest to see. It looks like a random scatter with no pattern, or a straight line that is exactly parallel to the horizontal or vertical axis. A *linear relationship* means that a straight line can be visualized in the middle of a maze of cases running from one corner to another. A *curvilinear relationship* means that the center of a maze of cases would form a U curve, right side up or upside down, or an S curve.

Direction. Linear relationships can have a positive or negative direction. The plot of a *positive* relationship looks like a diagonal line from the lower left to the upper right. Higher values on X tend to go with higher values on Y, and vice versa. The income and life expectancy example described a positive linear relationship.

A *negative* relationship looks like a line from the upper left to the lower right. It means that higher values on one variable go with lower val-

ues on the other. For example, people with more education are less likely to have been arrested. If we look at a scattergram of data on a group of males where years of schooling (X axis) are plotted by number of arrests (Y axis), we see that most cases (or men) with many arrests are in the lower right, because most of them completed few years of school. Most cases with few arrests are in the upper left because most have had more schooling. The imaginary line for the relationship can have a shallow or a steep slope. More advanced statistics provide precise numerical measures of the line's slope.

Precision. Bivariate relationships differ in their degree of precision. *Precision* is the amount of spread in the points on the graph. A high level of precision occurs when the points hug the line that summarizes the relationship. A low level occurs when the points are widely spread around the line. Researchers can "eyeball" a highly precise relationship. They can also use advanced statistics to measure the precision of a relationship in a way that is analogous to the standard deviation for univariate statistics.

Bivariate Tables

What Is a Bivariate Table? The bivariate contingency table is widely used. It presents the same information as a scattergram in a more condensed form. The data can be measured at any level of measurement, although interval and ratio data must be grouped if there are many different values. The table is based on *cross-tabulation;* that is, the cases are organized in the table on the basis of two variables at the same time.

A *contingency table* is formed by cross-tabulating two or more variables. It is contingent because the cases in each category of a variable get distributed into each category of a second (or additional) variable. The table distributes cases into the categories of multiple variables at the same time and shows how the cases, by category of one variable, are "contingent upon" the categories of other variables.

Figure 10.6 is a raw count or frequency table. Its cells contain a count of the cases. It is easy to make, but interpreting a raw count table is difficult because the rows or columns can have different totals, and what is of real interest is the relative size of cells compared to others.

FIGURE 10.6 **Age Group by Attitude about Changing the Drinking Age, Raw Count Table (a)**

	Age Group (b)				
Attitude (b)	*Under 30*	*30–45*	*46–60*	*61 and Older*	**Total (c)**
Agree	20	10	4	3	37
No opinion	3 (d)	10	10	2	25
Disagree	3	5	21	10	39
Total (c)	26	25	35	15	101

Missing cases (f) = 8.   (e)

The Parts of a Table
(a) Give each table a *title*, which names variables and provides background information.
(b) Label the row and column variable and give a name to each of the variable categories.
(c) Include the totals of the columns and rows. These are called the *marginals*. They equal the univariate frequency distribution for the variable.
(d) Each number or place that corresponds to the intersection of a category for each variable is a *cell of a table*.
(e) The numbers with the labeled variable categories and the totals are called the *body of a table*.
(f) If there is missing information (cases in which a respondent refused to answer, ended interview, said "don't know," etc.), report the number of missing cases near the table to account for all original cases.

Researchers convert raw count tables into percentaged tables to see bivariate relationships. There are three ways to percentage a table: by row, by column, and for the total. The first two are often used and show relationships.

Is it best to percentage by row or column? Either can be appropriate. Let us first review the mechanics of percentaging a table. When calculating column percentages, compute the percentage each cell is of the column total. This includes the total column or marginal for the column variable. For example, the first column total is 26 (there are 26 people under age 30), and the first cell of that column is 20 (there are 20 people under age 30 who agree). The percentage is 20/26 = 0.769 or 76.9 percent. Or, for the first number in the marginal, 37/101 = 0.366 = 36.6 percent (see Table 10.1). Except for rounding, the total should equal 100 percent.

Computing row percentages is similar. Compute the percentage of each cell as a percentage of the row total. For example, using the same cell with 20 in it, we now want to know what percentage it is of the row total of 37, or 20/37 = 0.541 = 54.1 percent. Percentaging by row or column gives different percentages for a cell unless the marginals are the same.

TABLE 10.1   Age Group by Attitude about Changing the Drinking Age, Percentaged Tables

Column-Percentaged Table

| Attitude | Age Group | | | | Total |
	Under 30	30–45	46–60	61 and Older	
Agree	76.9%	40%	11.4%	20%	36.6%
No opinion	11.5	40	28.6	13.3	24.8
Disagree	11.5	20	60	66.7	38.6
Total	99.9	100	100	100	100
(N)	(26)*	(25)*	(35)*	(15)*	(101)*

Missing cases = 8

Row-Percentaged Table

| Attitude | Age Group | | | | Total | (N) |
	Under 30	30–45	46–60	61 and Older		
Agree	54.1%	27%	10.8%	8.1%	100%	(37)*
No opinion	12	40	40	8	100	(25)*
Disagree	7.7	12.8	53.8	25.6	99.9	(39)*
Total	25.7	24.8	34.7	14.9	100.1	(101)*

Missing cases = 8

*For percentaged tables, provide the number of cases or N on which percentages are computed in parentheses near the total of 100%. This makes it possible to go back and forth from a percentaged table to a raw count table and vice versa.

The row and column percentages let a researcher address different questions. The row percentage table answers the question. Among those who hold an attitude, what percentage come from each age group? It says of respondents who agree, 54.1 percent are in the under-30 age group. The column percentage table addresses the question: Among those in each age group, what percentage hold different attitudes? It says that among those who are under 30, 76.9 percent agree. From the row percentages, a researcher learns that a little over half of those who agree are under 30 years old, whereas from column percentages, the researcher learns that among the under-30 people, over three-quarters agree. One way of percentaging tells about people who have specific attitudes; the other tells about people in specific age groups.

A researcher's hypothesis may imply looking at row percentages or the column percentages. When beginning, calculate percentages each way and practice interpreting, or figuring out, what each says. For example, my hypothesis is that age affects attitude, so column percentages are most helpful. However, if my interest was in describing the age make-up of groups of people with different attitudes, then row percentages are appropriate.

Unfortunately, there is no "industry standard" for putting independent and dependent variables in a percentage table as row or column, or for percentage by row and column. A majority of researchers place the independent variable as the column and percentage by column, but a large minority put the independent variable as the row and percentage by row.

Reading a Percentaged Table. Once you understand how a table is made, reading it and figuring out what it says are much easier. To read a table, first look at the title, the variable labels, and any background information. Next, look at the direction in which percentages have been computed—in rows or columns. Notice that the percentaged tables in Table 10.1 have the same title. This is because the same variables are used. It

would have helped to note how the data were percentaged in the title, but this is rarely done. Sometimes, researchers present abbreviated tables and omit the 100 percent total or the marginals, which adds to the confusion. It is best to include all the parts of a table and clear labels.

Researchers read percentaged tables to make comparisons. Comparisons are made in the opposite direction from that in which percentages are computed. A rule of thumb is to compare across rows if the table is percentaged down (i.e., by column) and to compare up and down in columns if the table is percentaged across (i.e., by row).

For example, in row-percentaged Table 10.1, compare columns or age groups. Most of those who agree are in the youngest group, with the proportion declining as age increases. Most no-opinion people are in the middle-age groups, whereas those who disagree are older, especially in the 46-to-60 group. When reading column-percentaged Table 10.1, compare across rows. For example, a majority of the youngest group agree, and they are the only group in which most people agree. Only 11.5 percent disagree, compared to a majority in the two oldest groups.

It takes practice to see a relationship in a percentaged table. If there is no relationship in a table, the cell percentages look approximately equal across rows or columns. A linear relationship looks like larger percentages in the diagonal cells. If there is a curvilinear relationship, the largest percentages form a pattern across cells. For example, the largest cells might be the upper right, the bottom middle, and the upper left. It is easiest to see a relationship in a moderate-sized table (9 to 16 cells) where most cells have some cases (at least five cases are recommended) and the relationship is strong and precise.

Principles of reading a scattergram can help you see a relationship in a percentaged table. Imagine a scattergram that has been divided into 12 equal-sized sections. The cases in each section correspond to the number of cases in the cells of a table that is superimposed onto the scattergram. The table is a condensed form of the scattergram. The bivariate relationship line in a scattergram corresponds to the diagonal cells in a percentaged table. Thus, a simple way to see strong relationships is to circle the largest percentage in each row (for row-percentaged tables) or column (for column-percentaged tables) and see if a line appears.

The circle-the-largest-cell rule works—with one important caveat. The categories in the percentages table *must* be ordinal or interval and in the same order as in a scattergram. In scattergrams the lowest variable categories begin at the bottom left. If the categories in a table are not ordered the same way, the rule does not work.

For example, Table 10.2a looks like a positive relationship and Table 10.2b like a negative relationship. Both use the same data and are percentaged by row. The actual relationship is negative. Look closely—Table 10.2b has age categories ordered as in a scattergram. When in doubt, return to the basic difference between

positive and negative relationships. A positive relationship means that as one variable increases, so does the other. A negative relationship means that as one variable increases, the other decreases.

Bivariate Tables without Percentages. Researchers condense information in another kind of bivariate table with a measure of central tendency (usually the mean) instead of percentages. It is used when one variable is nominal or ordinal and another is measured at the interval or ratio level. The mean (or a similar measure) of the interval or ratio variable is presented for each category of the nominal or ordinal variable. All cases are divided into the ordinal or nominal variable categories; then the mean is calculated for the cases in each variable category from the raw data.

Table 10.3 shows the mean age of people in each of the attitude categories. The results suggest that the mean age of those who disagree is much higher than for those who agree or have no opinion.

Measures of Association

A measure of association is a single number that expresses the strength, and often the direction, of a relationship. It condenses information about a bivariate relationship into a single number.

There are many measures of association. The correct one depends on the level of measurement. Many measures are called by letters of

TABLE 10.2a Age by Schooling

| Age | Years of Schooling | | | | |
	0–11	*12*	*13–14*	*16+*	Total
Under 30	5%	25	30	40	100
30–45	15	25	40	20	100
46–60	35	45	12	8	100
61 +	45	35	15	5	100

TABLE 10.2b Age by Schooling

| Age | Years of Schooling | | | | |
	0–11	*12*	*13–14*	*16+*	Total
61 +	45%	35	15	5	100
46–60	35	45	12	8	100
30–45	15	25	40	20	100
Under 30	5	25	30	40	100

TABLE 10.3 Attitude about Changing the Drinking Age by Mean Age of Respondent

Drinking Age Attitude	Mean Age	(N)
Agree	26.2	(37)
No opinion	44.5	(25)
Disagree	61.9	(39)

Missing cases = 8

the Greek alphabet. Lambda, gamma, tau, chi (squared), and rho are commonly used measures. The emphasis here is on interpreting the measures, not on their calculation. In order to understand each measure, you will need to complete a beginning statistics course.

If there is a strong association or relationship, then few errors are made predicting a second variable on the basis of knowledge of the first, or the proportion of errors reduced is large. A large number of correct guesses suggests that the measure of association is a nonzero number if an association exists between the variables. Figure 10.7 describes five commonly used bivariate measures of association. Notice that most range from −1 to +1, with negative numbers

---

FIGURE 10.7 Five Measures of Association

Lambda is used for nominal-level data. It is based on a reduction in errors based on the mode and ranges between 0 (independence) and 1.0 (perfect prediction or the strongest possible relationship).

Gamma is used for ordinal-level data. It is based on comparing pairs of variable categories and seeing whether a case has the same rank on each. Gamma ranges from −1.0 to +1.0, with 0 meaning no association.

Tau is also used for ordinal-level data. It is based on a different approach than gamma and takes care of a few problems that can occur with gamma. Actually, there are several statistics named tau (it is a popular Greek letter), and the one here is Kendall's tau. Kendall's tau ranges from −1.0 to +1.0, with 0 meaning no association.

Rho is also called Pearson's product moment correlation coefficient (named after the famous statistician Karl Pearson and based on a product moment statistical procedure). It is the most commonly used measure of correlation, the correlation statistic people mean if they use the term *correlation* without

identifying it further. It can be used only for data measured at the interval or ratio level. Rho is used for the mean and standard deviation of the variables and tells how far cases are from a relationship (or regression) line in a scatterplot. Rho ranges from −1.0 to +1.0, with 0 meaning no association. If the value of rho is squared, sometimes called R-squared, it has a unique proportion reduction in error meaning. R-squared tells how the percentage in one variable (e.g., the dependent) is accounted for, or explained by, the other variable (e.g., the independent). Rho measures linear relationships only. It cannot measure nonlinear or curvilinear relationships. For example, a rho of zero can indicate either no relationship or a curvilinear relationship.

Chi-squared has two different uses. It can be used as a measure of association in descriptive statistics like the others listed here, or in inferential statistics. Inferential statistics are briefly described next. As a measure of association, chi-squared can be used for nominal and ordinal data. It has an upper limit of infinity and a lower limit of zero, meaning no association.

Summary of Measures of Association

Measure	Greek Symbol	Type of Data	High Association	Independence
Lambda	λ	Nominal	1.0	0
Gamma	γ	Ordinal	+1.0, −1.0	0
Tau (Kendall's)	τ	Ordinal	+1.0, −1.0	0
Rho	ρ	Interval, ratio	+1.0, −1.0	0
Chi-square	χ^2	Nominal, ordinal	Infinity	0

indicating a negative relationship and positive numbers a positive relationship. A measure of 1.0 means a 100 percent reduction in errors, or perfect prediction.

MORE THAN TWO VARIABLES

Statistical Control

Showing an association or relationship between two variables is not sufficient to say that an independent variable *causes* a dependent variable. In addition to temporal order and association, a researcher must eliminate alternative explanations—explanations that can make the hypothesized relationship spurious. Experimental researchers do this by choosing a research design that physically controls potential alternative explanations for results (i.e., that threaten internal validity).

In nonexperimental research, a researcher controls for alternative explanations with statistics. He or she measures possible alternative explanations with *control variables,* then examines the control variables with multivariate tables and statistics that help him or her decide whether a bivariate relationship is spurious. They also show the relative size of the effect of multiple independent variables on a dependent variable.

A researcher controls for alternative explanations in multivariate (more than two variables) analysis by introducing a third (or sometimes a fourth or fifth) variable. For example, a bivariate table shows that taller teenagers like sports more than shorter ones do. But the bivariate relationship between height and attitude toward sports may be spurious because teenage males are taller than females, and males tend to like sports more than females. To test whether the relationship is actually due to sex, a researcher must *control for* gender; in other words, effects of sex are statistically *removed.* Once this is done, a researcher can see whether the bivariate relationship between height and attitude toward sports remains.

A researcher controls for a third variable by seeing whether the bivariate relationship persists within categories of the control variable. For example, a researcher controls for sex, and the relationship between height and sports attitude persists. This means that tall males and tall females both like sports more than short males and short females do. In other words, the control variable has no effect. When this is so, the bivariate relationship is not spurious.

If the bivariate relationship weakens or disappears after the control variable is considered, it means that tall males are no more likely than short males to like sports, and tall females are no more likely to like sports than short females. It indicates that the initial bivariate relationship is spurious and suggests that the third variable, sex, and not height, is the true cause of differences in attitudes toward sports.

Statistical control is a key idea in advanced statistical techniques. A measure of association like the correlation coefficient only suggests a relationship. Until a researcher considers control variables, the bivariate relationship could be spurious. Researchers are cautious in interpreting bivariate relationships until they have considered control variables.

The Elaboration Model of Percentaged Tables

Constructing Trivariate Tables. In order to meet all the conditions needed for causality, researchers want to "control for" or see whether an alternative explanation explains away a causal relationship. If an alternative explanation explains a relationship, then the bivariate relationship is spurious. Alternative explanations are operationalized as third variables, which are called *control variables* because they control for alternative explanation.

One way to take such third variables into consideration and see whether they influence the bivariate relationship is to statistically introduce control variables using trivariate or three-variable tables. Trivariate tables differ slightly from bivariate tables; they consist of multiple bivariate tables.

A trivariate table has a bivariate table of the independent and dependent variable for each category of the control variable. These new tables are called *partials*. The number of partials depends on the number of categories in the control variable. Partial tables look like bivariate tables, but they use a subset of the cases. Only cases with a specific value on the control variable are in the partial. Thus, it is possible to break apart a bivariate table to form partials, or combine the partials to restore the initial bivariate table.

Trivariate tables have three limitations. First, they are difficult to interpret if a control variable has more than four categories. Second, control variables can be at any level of measurement, but interval or ratio control variables must be grouped (i.e., converted to an ordinal level), and how cases are grouped can affect the interpretation of effects. Finally, the total number of cases is a limiting factor because the cases are divided among cells in partials. The number of cells in the partials equals the number of cells in the bivariate relationship multiplied by the number of categories in the control variable. For example, a control variable has three categories, and a bivariate table has 12 cells, so the partials have $3 \times 12 = 36$ cells. An average of five cases per cell is recommended, so the researcher will need $5 \times 36 = 180$ cases at minimum.

For three variables, three bivariate tables are logically possible. In the example, the combinations are: (1) gender by attitude, (2) age group by attitude, and (3) gender by age group. The partials are set up on the basis of the initial bivariate relationship. The independent variable in each is "age group" and the dependent variable is "attitude." "Gender" is the control variable. Thus, the trivariate table consists of a pair of partials, each showing the age/attitude relationship for a given gender.

A researcher's theory suggests the hypothesis in the initial bivariate relationship; it also tells him or her which variables provide alternative explanations (i.e., the control variables).

Thus, the choice of the control variable is based on theory.

The *elaboration paradigm* is a system for reading percentaged trivariate tables.[3] It describes the pattern that emerges when a control variable is introduced. Five terms describe how the partial tables compare to the initial bivariate table, or how the original bivariate relationship changes after the control variable is considered. The examples of patterns presented here show strong cases. More advanced statistics are needed when the differences are not as obvious.

The *replication pattern* is the easiest to understand. It is when the partials replicate or reproduce the same relationship that existed in the bivariate table before considering the control variable. It means that the control variable has no effect.

The *specification pattern* is the next easiest pattern. It occurs when one partial replicates the initial bivariate relationship but other partials do not. For example, you find a strong (negative) bivariate relationship between automobile accidents and college grades. You control for gender and discover that the relationship holds only for males (i.e., the strong negative relationship was in the partial for males, but not for females). This is specification because a researcher can specify the category of the control variable in which the initial relationship persists.

The control variable has a large impact in both the interpretation and explanation patterns. In both, the bivariate table shows a relationship that disappears in the partials. In other words, the relationship appears to be independence in the partials. The two patterns cannot be distinguished by looking at the tables alone. The difference between them depends on the location of the control variable in the causal order of variables. Theoretically, a control variable can be in one of two places, either between the original independent and dependent variables (i.e., the control variable is intervening), or before the original independent variable.

The *interpretation pattern* describes the situation in which the control variable intervenes between the original independent and dependent variables. For example, you examine a relationship between religious upbringing and abortion attitude. Political ideology is a control variable. You reason that religious upbringing affects current political ideology and abortion attitude. You theorize that political ideology is logically prior to an attitude about a specific issue, like abortion. Thus, religious upbringing causes political ideology, which in turn has an impact on abortion attitude. The control variable is an intervening variable, which helps you interpret the meaning of the complete relationship.

The *explanation pattern* looks the same as interpretation. The difference is the temporal order of the control variable. In this pattern, a control variable comes before the independent variable in the initial bivariate relationship. For example, the original relationship is between religious upbringing and abortion attitude, but now gender is the control variable. Gender comes before religious upbringing because one's sex is fixed at birth. The explanation pattern changes how a researcher explains the results. It implies that the initial bivariate relationship is spurious.

The *suppressor variable pattern* occurs when the bivariate tables suggest independence but a relationship appears in one or both of the partials. For example, religious upbringing and abortion attitude are independent in a bivariate table. Once the control variable "region of the country" is introduced, religious upbringing is associated with abortion attitude in the partial tables. The control variable is a suppressor variable because it suppressed the true relationship. The true relationship appears in the partials. (See Box 10.2 for a summary of the elaboration paradigm.)

Multiple Regression Analysis

Multiple regression is a statistical technique whose calculation is beyond the level in this book. Although it is quickly computed by the appropriate statistics software, a background in statistics is needed to prevent making errors in its calculation and interpretation. It requires interval- or ratio-level data. It is discussed here for two reasons. First, it controls for many alternative explanations and variables simultaneously (it is rarely possible to use more than one control variable at a time using percentaged tables). Second, it is widely used in sociology, and you are likely to encounter it when reading research reports or articles.

Multiple regression results tell the reader two things. First, the results have a measure called R-squared (R^2), which tells how well a set of variables explains a dependent variable. *Explain* means reduced errors when predicting the dependent variable scores on the basis of information about the independent variables. A good model with several independent variables might account for, or explain, a large percentage of variation in a dependent variable. For example, an R^2 of .50 means that knowing the independent and control variables improves the accuracy of predicting the dependent variable by 50 percent, or half as many errors are made as would be made without knowing about the variables.

Second, the regression results measure the direction and size of the effect of each variable on a dependent variable. The effect is measured precisely and given a numerical value. For example, a researcher can see how five independent or control variables simultaneously affect a dependent variable, with all variables controlling for the effects of one another. This is especially valuable for testing theories that state that multiple independent variables cause one dependent variable.

The effect on the dependent variable is measured by a standardized regression coefficient or the Greek letter beta (ß). It is similar to a correlation coefficient. In fact, the beta coefficient for two variables equals the r correlation coefficient.

Researchers use the beta regression coefficient to determine whether control variables have an effect. For example, the bivariate correlation between X and Y is .75. Next, the researcher statistically considers four control

BOX
10.2 **Summary of the Elaboration Paradigm**

Pattern Name	Pattern Seen When Comparing Partials to the Original Bivariate Table
Replication	Same relationship in both partials as in bivariate table.
Specification	Bivariate relationship is only seen in one of the partial tables.
Interpretation	Bivariate relationship weakens greatly or disappears in the partial tables (control variable is intervening).
Explanation	Bivariate relationship weakens greatly or disappears in the partial tables (control variable is before independent variable).
Suppressor variable	No bivariate relationship; relationship appears in partial tables only.

EXAMPLES OF ELABORATION PATTERNS

Replication

	Bivariate Table			Partials			
				Control = Low		Control = High	
	Low	High		Low	High	Low	High
Low	85%	15%	Low	84%	16%	86%	14%
High	15%	85%	High	16%	84%	14%	86%

Interpretation or Explanation

	Bivariate Table			Partials			
				Control = Low		Control = High	
	Low	High		Low	High	Low	High
Low	85%	15%	Low	45%	55%	55%	45%
High	15%	85%	High	55%	45%	45%	55%

Specification

	Bivariate Table			Partials			
				Control = Low		Control = High	
	Low	High		Low	High	Low	High
Low	85%	85%	Low	95%	5%	50%	50%
High	15%	15%	High	5%	95%	50%	50%

Suppressor Variable

	Bivariate Table			Partials			
				Control = Low		Control = High	
	Low	High		Low	High	Low	High
Low	54%	46%	Low	84%	16%	14%	86%
High	46%	54%	High	16%	84%	86%	14%

variables. If the beta remains at .75, then the four control variables have no effect. However, if the beta for X and Y gets smaller (e.g., drops to .20), it indicates that the control variables have an effect.

Consider an example of regression analysis with age, income, education, and region as independent variables. The dependent variable is a score on a political ideology index. The multiple regression results show that income and religious attendance have large effects, education and region minor effects, and age no effect. All the independent variables together have a 38 percent accuracy in predicting a person's political ideology (see Box 10.3). The example suggests that high income, frequent religious attendance, and a southern residence are positively associated with conservative opinions, whereas having more education is associated with liberal opinions. The impact of income is more than twice the size of the impact of living in a southern region. We have been examining descriptive statistics (see Table 10.4); next, we look at a different type: inferential statics.

BOX 10.3 Example of Multiple Regression Results

Dependent Variable Is Political Ideology Index (High Score Means Very Liberal)

Independent Variable	Standardized Regression Coefficients
Region = South	−.19
Age	.01
Income	−.44
Years of education	.23
Religious attendance	−.39
$R^2 = .38$	

INFERENTIAL STATISTICS

The Purpose of Inferential Statistics

Researchers often want to do more than describe; they want to test hypotheses, know whether sample results hold true in a population, and decide whether differences in results (e.g., between the mean scores of two groups) are big enough to indicate that a relationship really exists. Inferential statistics use probability theory to test hypotheses formally, permit inferences from a sample to a population, and test whether descriptive results are likely to be due to random factors or to a real relationship.

This section explains the basic ideas of inferential statistics but does not deal with inferential statistics in any detail. This area is more complex than descriptive statistics and requires a background in statistics.

Inferential statistics rely on principles from probability sampling, where a researcher uses a random process (e.g., a random number table) to select cases from the entire population. Inferential statistics are a precise way to talk about how confident a researcher can be when inferring from the results in a sample to the population.

You have already encountered inferential statistics if you have read or heard about "statistical significance" or results "significant at the .05 level." Researchers use them to conduct various statistical tests (e.g., a t-test or an F-test). Statistical significance is also used in formal hypothesis testing, which is a precise way to decide whether to accept or to reject a null hypothesis.[4]

Statistical Significance

Statistical significance means that results are not likely to be due to chance factors. It indicates the probability of finding a relationship in the sample when there is none in the population. Because probability samples involve a random process, it is always possible that sample results will differ from a population parameter. A researcher wants to estimate the odds that sample

TABLE 10.4 Summary of Major Types of Descriptive Statistics

Type of Technique	Statistical Technique	Purpose
Univariate	Frequency distribution, measure of central tendency, standard deviation, z-score	Describe one variable.
Bivariate	Correlation, percentage table, chi-square	Describe a relationship or the association between two variables.
Multivariate	Elaboration paradigm, multiple regression	Describe relationships among several variables, or see how several independent variables have an effect on a dependent variable.

results are due to a true population parameter or to chance factors of random sampling. Statistical significance uses probability theory and specific statistical tests to tell a researcher whether the results (e.g., an association, a difference between two means, a regression coefficient) are produced by random error in random sampling.

Statistical significance only tells what is likely. It cannot prove anything with absolute certainty. It states that particular outcomes are more or less probable. Statistical significance is *not* the same as practical, substantive, or theoretical significance. Results can be statistically significant but theoretically meaningless or trivial. For example, two variables can have a statistically significant association due to coincidence, with no logical connection between them (e.g., length of fingernails and ability to speak French).

Levels of Significance

Researchers usually express statistical significance in terms of levels (e.g., a test is statistically significant at a specific level) rather than giving the specific probability. The *level of statistical significance* (usually .05, .01, or .001) is a way of talking about the likelihood that results are due to chance factors—that is, that a relationship appears in the sample when there is none in the population. If a researcher says that results are significant at the .05 level, this means the following:

- Results like these are due to chance factors only 5 in 100 times.
- There is a 95 percent chance that the sample results are not due to chance factors alone, but reflect the population accurately.
- The odds of such results based on chance alone are .05, or 5 percent.
- One can be 95 percent confident that the results are due to a real relationship in the population, not chance factors.

These all say the same thing in different ways. This may sound like the discussion of sampling distributions and the central limit theorem in the chapter on sampling. It is not an accident. Both are based on probability theory, which researchers use to link sample data to a population. Probability theory lets us predict what happens in the long run over many events when a random process is used. In other words, it allows precise prediction over many situations in the long run, but not for a specific situation. Since we have one sample and we want to infer to the population, probability theory helps us estimate the odds that our particular sample represents the population. We cannot know for certain unless we have the whole population, but probability theory lets us state our confidence—how likely it is that the sample shows one thing while something else is true in the population. For example, a sample shows that college men and women differ in how many hours they study. Is the result due to an unusual sample, and there is really no difference in the population, or does it reflect a true difference between the sexes in the population?

Type I and Type II Errors

If the logic of statistical significance is based on stating whether chance factors produce results. Why use the .05 level? It means a 5 percent chance that randomness could cause the results. Why not use a more certain standard—for example, a 1 in 1,000 probability of random chance? This gives a smaller chance that randomness versus a true relationship caused the results.

There are two answers to this way of thinking. The simple answer is that the scientific community has informally agreed to use .05 as a rule of thumb for most purposes. Being 95 percent confident of results is the accepted standard for explaining the social world.

A second, more complex answer involves a trade-off between making Type I and Type II errors. A researcher can make two kinds of logical errors. A *Type I error* occurs when the researcher says that a relationship exists when in fact none exists. It means falsely rejecting a null hypothesis. A *Type II error* occurs when a researcher says that a relationship does not exist, when in fact it does. It means falsely accepting a null hypothesis (see Table 10.5). Of course, researchers want to avoid both errors. They want to say that there is a relationship in the data only when it does exist and that there is no relationship only when there really is none, but they face a dilemma: As the odds of making one type of error decline, the odds of making the opposite error increase.

The idea of Type I and Type II errors may seem difficult at first, but the same logical dilemma appears outside research settings. For example, a jury can err by deciding that an accused person is guilty when in fact he or she is innocent. Or the jury can err by deciding that a person is innocent when in fact he or she is guilty. The jury does not want to make either error. It does not want to jail the innocent or to free the guilty, but the jury must make a judgment using limited information. Likewise, a pharmaceutical company has to decide whether to sell a new drug. The company can err by stating that the drug has no side effects when, in fact, it has the side effect of causing blindness. Or it can err by holding back a drug because of fear of serious side effects when in fact there are none. The company does not want to make either error. If it makes the first error, the company will face lawsuits and injure people. The second error will prevent the company from selling a drug that may cure illness and produce profits.

Let us put the ideas of statistical significance and the two types of error together. An overly cautious researcher sets a high level of signifi-

TABLE 10.5 Type I and Type II Errors

What the Researcher Says	True Situation in the World	
	No Relationship	Causal Relationship
No relationship	No error	Type II error
Causal relationship	Type I error	No error

cance and is likely to make one kind of error. For example, the researcher might use the .0001 level. He or she attributes the results to chance unless they are so rare that they would occur by chance only 1 in 10,000 times. Such a high standard means that the researcher is most likely to err by saying results are due to chance when in fact they are not. He or she may falsely accept the null hypothesis when there is a causal relationship (a Type II error). By contrast, a risk-taking researcher sets a low level of significance, such as .10. His or her results indicate a relationship would occur by chance 1 in 10 times. He or she is likely to err by saying that a causal relationship exists, when in fact random factors (e.g., random sampling error) actually cause the results. The researcher is likely to falsely reject the null hypothesis (Type I error). In sum, the .05 level is a compromise between Type I and Type II errors.

The statistical techniques of inferential statistics are precise and rely on the relationship between sampling error, sample size, and central limit theorem. The power of inferential statistics is their ability to let a researcher state, with specific degrees of certainty, that specific sample results are likely to be true in a population. For example, a researcher conducts statistical tests and finds that a relationship is statistically significant at the .05 level. He or she can state that the sample results are probably not due to chance factors. Indeed, there is a 95 percent chance that a true relationship exists in the social world.

Tests for inferential statistics are limited. The data must come from a random sample, and tests only take into account sampling errors. Nonsampling errors (e.g., a poor sampling frame or a poorly designed measure) are not considered. Do not be fooled into thinking that such tests offer easy, final answers. Many computer programs quickly do the calculation for inferential and descriptive statistics (see Box 10.4).

BOX 10.4

Statistical Programs on Computers

Almost every social researcher who needs to calculate many statistics does so with a computer program, often using a basic spreadsheet program, such as Excel. Unfortunately, spreadsheets are designed for accounting and bookkeeping functions. They include statistics, but are clumsy and limited for that purpose. There are many computer programs designed for calculating general statistics. The marketplace can be confusing to a beginner, for products evolve rapidly with changing computer technology.

In recent years, the software has become less demanding for a user. The most popular programs in the social sciences are Minitab, Microcase, and SPSS (Statistical Package for the Social Sciences). Others include SAS (Statistical Analysis System), STATISTICA by StratSoft, and Strata. Many began as simple, low-cost programs for research purposes.

The most widely used program for statistics in the social sciences in SPSS. Its advantages are that social researchers used it extensively for over three decades, it includes many ways to manipulate quantitative data, and it contains most statistical measures. A disadvantage is that it can take a long time to learn because of its many options and complex statistics. Also, it is expensive to purchase unless the user gets an inexpensive, "stripped down" student version included with a textbook or workbook.

As computer technology makes using a statistics program easier, the danger increases that some people will use the programs, but not understand statistics or what the programs are doing. They can easily violate basic assumptions required by a statistical procedure, use the statistics improperly, and produce results that are pure nonsense but that look very technically sophisticated.

CONCLUSION

You learned about organizing quantitative data to prepare them for analysis, and analyzing them (organizing data into charts or tables, or summarizing them with statistical measures). Researchers use statistical analysis to test hypotheses and answer research questions. You saw how data must first be coded and then analyzed using univariate or bivariate statistics. Bivariate relationships might be spurious, so control variables and multivariate analysis are often necessary. You also learned some basics about inferential statistics.

Beginning researchers sometimes feel their results should support a hypothesis. *There is nothing wrong with rejecting a hypothesis.* The goal of scientific research is to produce knowledge that truly reflects the social world, not to defend pet ideas or hypotheses. Hypotheses are theoretical guesses based on limited knowledge; they need to be tested. Excellent-quality research can find that a hypothesis is wrong, and poor-quality research can support a hypothesis. Good research depends on high-quality methodology, not on supporting a specific hypothesis.

Good research means guarding against possible errors or obstacles to true inferences from data to the social world. Errors can enter into the research process and affect results at many places: research design, measurement, data collection, coding, calculating statistics and constructing tables, or interpreting results. Even if a researcher can design, measure, collect, code, and calculate without error, another step in the research process remains. It is to interpret the tables, charts, and statistics, and to answer the question: What does it all mean? The only way to assign meaning to facts, charts, tables, or statistics is to use theory.

Data, tables, or computer output cannot answer research questions. The facts do not speak for themselves. As a researcher, you must return to your theory (i.e., concepts, relationships among concepts, assumptions, theoretical definitions) and give the results meaning. Do not lock yourself into the ideas with which you began.

There is room for creativity, and new ideas are generated by trying to figure out what results really say. It is important to be careful in designing and conducting research so that you can look at the results as a reflection of something in the social world and not worry about whether they are due to an error or an artifact of the research process itself.

Before we leave quantitative research, there is one last issue. Journalists, politicians, and others increasingly use statistical results to make a point or bolster an argument. This has not produced greater accuracy and information in public debate. More often, it has increased confusion and made it more important to know what statistics can and cannot do. The cliché that you can prove anything with statistics is false; however, people can and do *misuse* statistics. Through ignorance or conscious deceit, some people use statistics to manipulate others. The way to protect yourself from being misled by statistics is not to ignore them or hide from the numbers. Rather, it is to understand the research process and statistics, think about what you hear, and ask questions.

We turn next to qualitative research. The logic and purpose of qualitative research differ from those of the quantitative, positivist approach of the past chapters. It is less concerned with numbers, hypotheses, and causality and more concerned with words, norms and values, and meaning.

Key Terms

bar chart
bivariate statistics
body of a table
cell of a table
code sheets
codebook
contingency cleaning
contingency table
control variable
covariation

THE RESEARCH REPORT

INTRODUCTION

In the previous chapters, we have looked at how to design studies, gather data, and analyze the data. Yet, a research project is not complete until the researcher shares the results with others. Communicating results and how a study was conducted with others is a critical last step in the research process. It is usually in the form of a written report. In Chapter 1, we saw how the scientific community emphasizes that researchers make public how they conducted their research and their findings. In this chapter, you will learn about writing a report on one's research.

THE RESEARCH REPORT

Why Write a Report?

After a researcher completes a project or a significant phase of a large project, it is time to communicate the findings to others through a research report. One can learn a lot about writing a research report by reading many reports and taking a course in scientific and technical writing.

A *research report* is a written document (or oral presentation based on a written document) that communicates the methods and findings of a research project to others. It is more than a summary of findings; it is a record of the research process. A researcher cannot wait until the research is done to think about the report; he or she must think ahead to the report and keep careful records while conducting research. In addition to findings, the report includes the reasons for initiating the project, a description of the project's steps, a presentation of data, and a discussion of how the data relate to the research question or topic.

The report tells others what you, the researcher, did, and what you discovered. In other words, the research report is a way of disseminating knowledge. As you saw in Chapter 1, the research report plays a significant role in binding together the scientific community. Other reasons for writing a report are to fulfill a class or job assignment, to meet an obligation to an organization that paid for the research, to persuade a professional group about specific aspects of a problem, or to tell the general public about findings. Communicating with the general public is rarely the primary method for communication of scientific results; it is usually a second stage of dissemination.

The Writing Process

Your Audience. Professional writers say: Always know for whom you are writing. This is because communication is more effective when it is tailored to a specific audience. You should write a research report differently depending on whether the primary audience is an instructor, students, professional social scientists, practitioners, or the general public. It goes without saying that the writing should be clear, accurate, and organized.

Instructors assign a report for different reasons and may place requirements on how it is written. In general, instructors want to see writing and an organization that reflect clear, logical thinking. Student reports should demonstrate a solid grasp of substantive and methodological concepts. A good way to do this is to use technical terms explicitly *when appropriate;* they should not be used excessively or incorrectly.

When writing for students, it is best to define technical terms and label each part of the report. The discussion should proceed in a logical, step-by-step manner with many specific examples. Use straight-forward language to explain how and why you conducted the various steps of the research project. One strategy is to begin with the research question, then structure the report as an answer.

Scholars do not need definitions of technical terms or explanations of why standard procedures (e.g., random sampling) were used. They are interested in how the research is linked to abstract theory or previous findings in the literature. They want a condensed, detailed description of research design. They pay close attention to how variables are measured and the methods of data collection. Scholars like a compact, tightly written, but extensive section on data analysis, with a meticulous discussion of results.

Practitioners prefer a short summary of how the study was conducted and results presented in a few simple charts and graphs. They like to see an outline of alternative paths of action implied by results with the practical outcomes of pursuing each path. Practitioners must be cautioned not to overgeneralize from the results of one study. It is best to place the details of research design and results in an appendix.

When writing for the general public, use simple language, provide concrete examples, and focus on the practical implications of findings for social problems. Do not include details of research design or of results, and be careful not to make unsupported claims when writing for the public. Informing the public is an important service, which can help nonspecialists make better judgments about public issues.

Style and Tone. Research reports are written in a narrow range of styles and have a distinct tone. Their purpose is to communicate clearly the research method and findings.

Style refers to the types of words chosen by the writer and the length and form of sentences or paragraphs used. *Tone* is the writer's attitude or relation toward the subject matter. For example, an informal, conversational style (e.g., colloquial words, idioms, clichés, and incomplete sentences) with a personal tone (e.g., these are my feelings) is appropriate for writing a letter to a close friend, but not for research reports. Research reports have a formal and succinct (saying a lot in few words) style. The tone expresses distance from the subject matter; it is professional and serious. Field researchers sometimes use an informal style and a personal tone, but this is the exception. Avoid moralizing and flowery language. The goal is to inform, not to advocate a position or to entertain.

A research report should be objective, accurate, and clear. Check and recheck details (e.g., page references in citations) and fully disclose how you conducted the research project. If readers detect carelessness in writing, they may question the research itself. The details of a research project can be complex, and such complexity means that confusion is always a danger. It makes clear writing essential. Clear writing can be achieved by thinking and rethinking the research problem and design, explicitly defining terms, writing with short declarative sentences, and limiting conclusions to what is supported by the evidence.

Organizing Thoughts. Writing does not happen magically or simply flow out of a person when he or she puts pen to paper (or fingers to keyboard) although many people have such an illusion. Rather, it is hard work, involving a sequence of steps and separate activities that result in a final product. Writing a research report is not radically different from other types of writing. Although some steps differ and the level of complexity may be greater, most of what a good writer does when writing a long letter, a poem, a set of instructions, or a short story applies to writing a research report.

First, a writer needs something about which to write. The "something" in the research report includes the topic, research question, design and measures, data collection techniques, results, and implications. With so many parts to write about, organization is essential. The most basic tool for organizing writing is the outline. Outlines help a writer ensure that all ideas are included and that the relationship between them is clear. Outlines are made up of topics (words or phrases) or sentences. Most of us are familiar with the basic form of an outline (see Figure 14.1).

Outlines can help the writer, but they can also become a barrier if they are used improperly. An outline is simply a tool to help the writer organize ideas. It helps (1) put ideas in a

FIGURE 14.1 Form of Outline

I. First major topic	One of the most important
A. Subtopic of topic I	Second level of importance
1. Subtopic of A	Third level of importance
a. Subtopic of 1	Fourth level of importance
b. Subtopic of 1	"
(1) Subtopic of b	Fifth level of importance
(2) Subtopic of b	"
(a) Subtopic of (2)	Sixth level of importance
(b) Subtopic of (2)	"
i. Subtopic of (b)	Seventh level of importance
ii. Subtopic of (b)	"
2. Subtopic of A	Third level of importance
B. Subtopic of topic I	Second level of importance
II. Second major topic	One of the most important

sequence (e.g., what will be said first, second, and third); (2) group related ideas together (e.g., these are similar to each other, but differ from those); and (3) separate the more general, or higher-level, ideas from more specific ideas, and the specific ideas from very specific details.

Some students feel that they need a complete outline before writing, and that once an outline is prepared, deviations from it are impossible. Few writers begin with a complete outline. The initial outline is sketchy because until you write everything down, it is impossible to put all ideas in a sequence, group them together, or separate the general from the specific. For most writers, new ideas develop or become clearer in the process of writing itself.

A beginning outline may differ from the final outline by more than degree of completeness. The process of writing may not only reveal or clarify ideas for the writer, but also stimulate new ideas, new connections between ideas, a different sequence, or new relations between general and the specific. In addition, the process of writing may stimulate reanalysis or a reexamination of the literature or findings. This does not mean beginning all over again. Rather, it means keeping an open mind to new insights and being candid about the research project.

Back to the Library. Few researchers finish their literature review before completing a research project. The researcher should be familiar with the literature before beginning a project, but will need to return to the literature after completing data collection and analysis, for several reasons. First, time has passed between the beginning and the end of a research project, and new studies may have been published. Second, after completing a research project, a researcher will know better what is or is not central to the study and may have new questions in mind when rereading studies in the literature. Finally, when writing the report, researchers may find that notes are not complete enough or a detail is missing in the citation of a reference source (see Box 14.1). The visit to the library after data collection is less extensive and more selective or focused than that conducted at the beginning of research.

When writing a research report, researchers frequently discard some of the notes and sources that were gathered prior to completing the

BOX 14.1 Formats for Reference Lists, Using American Sociological Association Style

Books

First-Edition Books
Eliasoph, Nina. 1998. *Avoiding Politics: How Americans Produce Apathy in Everyday Life.* New York: Cambridge University Press.
Glynn, Carroll J., Susan Herbst, Garrett J. O'Keefe and Robert Y. Shapiro. 1999. *Public Opinion.* Boulder, CO: Westview Press.

Later Editions of Books
Portes, Alejandro and Ruben G. Rumbaut. 1996. *Immigrant America: A Portrait, 2d ed.* Berkeley: University of California Press.

[Abbreviations are 2d ed., 3d ed., Rev. ed., 2 vols.]

One Volume of Multivolume Book
Marx, Karl. [1887] 1967. *Capital: Critique of Political Economy, Volume 1, The Process of Capitalist Production.* Translated by Frederick Engles. Reprint. New York: International Publishers.

Translated Books
Durkheim, Emile. 1933. *The Division of Labor in Society.* Translated by George Simpson. New York: Free Press.
Weber, Max. 1958. *The Protestant Ethic and the Spirit of Capitalism.* Translated by Talcott Parsons. New York: Charles Scribner's Sons.

Edited Books
Danziger, Sheldon and Peter Gottschalk, eds. 1993. *Uneven Tides: Rising Inequality in America.* New York: Russell Sage Foundation.

Republished Books
Mason, Edward S. [1957] 1964. *Economic Concentration and the Monopoly Problem.* Reprint. New York: Atheneum.

Articles from Books or Scholarly Journals

Wright, Erik Olin. 1997. "Rethinking, Once Again, the Concept of Class Structure." Pp. 41–72 in *Reworking Class*, edited by J. Hall. Ithaca: Cornell University Press.

Pattillo-McCoy, Mary. 1998. "Church Culture as a Strategy of Action in the Black Community." *American Sociological Review* 63:767–784.

[*Note:* Omit issue number except when each issue is renumbered beginning with page 1. Then give volume(issue):pages—for example, 45(1):22–33.]

Articles from Popular Magazines and Newspapers

Janofsky, Michael. "Shortage of Housing for Poor Grows in the U.S." *New York Times* (April 29, 1998), p. A14.
Nichols, John. 1998. "How Al Gore Has It Wired" *Nation* 267 (July 20, 1998):11–16.

[It is not always necessary to include page numbers for newspapers].

Book Reviews

Academic Journals
Bergen, Raquel Kennedy. 1998. Review of *A Woman Scorned: Acquaintance Rape on Trial*, by Peggy Reeves Sanday. *Contemporary Sociology* 27:98–99.

Popular Magazines
Wolfe, Alan. 2001. Review of *Heaven Below: Early Pentacostals and American Culture*, by Grant Wacker. *New Republic*, 225 (September 10):59–62.

Government Documents

U.S. Bureau of Census. 1994. *Statistical Abstract of the United States, 114th ed.* Washington DC: U.S. Government Printing Office.

Doctoral Dissertations and Theses

King, Andrew J. 1976. "Law and Land Use in Chicago: A Pre-History of Modern Zoning." Ph.D. dissertation, Department of Sociology, University of Wisconsin, Madison, WI.

Unpublished Papers, Policy Reports and Presented Papers

Haines, Herbert H. 1980. "Ideological Distribution and Racial Flank Effects in Social Movements"

Continued

Presented at the annual meeting of the American Sociological Association, August, New York City.

Internet Sources

[*Note:* The date retrieved is the date that the reader located and read the work on the Internet.]

Announcement or Personal Home Page
American Sociological Association 1999. *Journals and Newsletters*. Retrieved January 16, 1999. http://www.asanet.org/Pubs/publicat.html

On-Line Journal Article
Sosteric, Mike, Mike Gismondi and Gina Ratkovic. 1998. "The University, Accountability, and Market Discipline in the Late 1990s." *Electronic Journal of Sociology* April 1988, Vol. 3. Retrieved January 16, 1999. http://www.sociology.org/content/vol003.003/sosteric.html

Newspaper Article
Lee, Don. 1999. "State's Job Growth Hits Unexpected Cold Spell." *Los Angeles Times* (January 16). Retrieved January 16, 1999. http://www.latimes.com/HOME/BUSINESS/topstory.html

Journal Abstract or Book Review
Grills, Steven. 1999. Review of *Missing Persons: A Critique of Personhood in the Social Science* by Mary Douglas and Steven Ney. *Canadian Journal of Sociology* on line. Retrieved January 16, 1999. http://www.alberta.ca/flcjscopy/reviews/persons.html

research project. This does not mean that the initial library work and literature review were a waste of time and effort. Researchers expect that some of the notes (e.g., 25 percent) taken before completing the project will become irrelevant as the project gains focus. They do not include notes or references in a report that are no longer relevant, for they distract from the flow of ideas and reduce clarity.

Returning to the library to verify and expand references focuses ideas. It also helps avoid plagiarism. *Plagiarism* is a serious form of cheating, and many universities expel students caught engaging in it. If a professional ever plagiarizes in a scholarly journal, it is treated as a very serious offense. Take careful notes and identify the exact source of phrases or ideas to avoid unintentional plagiarism. Cite the sources of both directly quoted words and paraphrased ideas. For direct quotes, include the location of the quote with page numbers in the citation.

Using another's written words and failing to give credit is wrong, but paraphrasing is less clear. *Paraphrasing* is not using another's exact words; it is restating another's ideas in your own words, condensing at the same time. Researchers regularly paraphrase, and good paraphrasing requires a solid understanding of what is being paraphrased. It means more than replacing another's words with synonyms; paraphrasing is borrowing an idea, boiling it down to its essence, and giving credit to the source.

Steps in Writing

Writing is a process. The way to learn to write is by writing. It takes time and effort, and it improves with practice. There is no single correct way to write, but some methods are associated with good writing. The process has three steps:

1. *Prewriting.* Prepare to write by arranging notes on the literature, making lists of ideas, outlining, completing bibliographic citations, and organizing comments on data analysis.

2. *Composing.* Get your ideas onto paper as a first draft by freewriting, drawing up the bibliography and footnotes, preparing data for presentation, and forming an introduction and conclusion.

3. *Rewriting.* Evaluate and polish the report by improving coherence, proofreading for mechanical errors, checking citations, and reviewing voice and usage.

Many people find that getting started is difficult. Beginning writers often jump to the second step and end there, which results in poor-quality writing. *Prewriting* means that a writer begins with a file folder full of notes, outlines, and lists. You must think about the form of the report and audience. Thinking time is important. It often occurs in spurts over a period of time before the bulk of composing begins.

Some people become afflicted with a strange ailment when they sit down to compose writing. It is known as *writer's block*—a temporary inability to write. It comes when the mind goes blank, the fingers freeze, and panic sets in. Writers from beginners through experts occasionally experience it. If you experience it, calm down and work on overcoming it.

Numerous writers begin to compose by *freewriting,* a process of sitting down and writing down everything you can as quickly as it enters into your mind. Freewriting establishes a link between a rapid flow of ideas in the mind and writing. When you freewrite, you do not stop to reread what you wrote, you do not ponder the best word, you do not worry about correct grammar, spelling, or punctuation. You just put ideas on paper as quickly as possible to get and keep the creative juices or ideas flowing. You can later clean up what you wrote.

Writing and thinking are so intertwined that it is impossible to know where one ends and the other begins. This means that if you plan to sit and stare at the wall, the computer output, the sky, or whatever until all thoughts become totally clear before beginning, you will rarely get anything written. The thinking process can be ignited during the writing itself.

Rewriting. Perhaps one in a million writers is a creative genius who can produce a first draft that communicates with astounding accuracy and clarity. For the rest of us mortals, writing means that rewriting—and rewriting again—is necessary. For example, Ernest Hemingway is reported to have rewritten the end of *Farewell to Arms* 39 times. It is not unusual for a professional researcher to rewrite a report a dozen times. Do not become discouraged. If anything, rewriting reduces the pressure; it means you can start writing soon and get out a rough draft that you can polish later. Plan to rewrite a draft at least three or four times. A draft is a complete report, from beginning to end, not a few rough notes or an outline.

Rewriting helps a writer express himself or herself with a greater clarity, smoothness, precision and economy of words. When rewriting, the focus is on clear communication, not pompous or complicated language.

Rewriting means slowly reading what you have written and, if necessary, out loud to see whether it sounds right. It is a good idea to share your writing with others. Professional writers have others read and criticize their writing. New writers soon learn that friendly, constructive criticism is very valuable. Sharing your writing with others may be difficult at first. It means exposing your written thoughts and encouraging criticism. Yet, the purpose of the criticism is to clarify writing, and the critic is doing you a favor.

Rewriting involves two processes: revising and editing. *Revising* is inserting new ideas, adding supporting evidence, deleting or changing ideas, moving sentences around to clarify meaning, or strengthening transitions and links between ideas. *Editing* means cleaning up and tightening the more mechanical aspects of writing, such as spelling, grammar, usage, verb tense, sentence length, and paragraph organization. When you rewrite, go over a draft and revise it brutally to improve it. This is easier if some time passes between a draft and rewriting. Phrases that seemed satisfactory in a draft may look fuzzy or poorly connected after a week or two (see Figure 14.2).

Even if you have not acquired typing skills, it is a good idea to type and print out at least one draft before the final draft. This is because it is easier to see errors and organization problems in a clean, typed draft. Feel free to cut and paste, cross out words, or move phrases on the printed copy.

Good keyboarding skills and the ability to use a word processor are extremely valuable when writing reports and other documents. Serious professionals find that the time they invest into building keyboard skills and learning to use a word processor pays huge dividends later. Word processors not only make editing much easier but they also check spelling and offer synonyms. In addition, there are programs that check grammar. You cannot rely on the computer program to do all the work, but it makes writing easier. The speed and ease that a word processor offers is so dramatic that few people who become skilled at using one ever go back to writing by hand or typing.

One last suggestion: Rewrite the introduction and title after completing a draft so that they accurately reflect what is said. Titles should be short and descriptive. They should communicate the topic and the major variables to readers. They can describe the type of research (e.g., "An experiment on . . . ") but should not have unnecessary words or phrases (e.g., "An investigation into the . . . ").

The Quantitative Research Report

The principles of good writing apply to all reports, but the parts of a report differ depending on whether the research is quantitative or qualitative. Before writing any report, read reports on the same kind of research for models.

We begin with the quantitative research report. The sections of the report roughly follow the sequence of steps of a research project.

Abstract or Executive Summary. Quantitative research reports usually begin with a short summary or abstract. The size of an abstract varies; it can be as few as 50 words (this paragraph has 90 words) or as long as a full page. Most scholarly journal articles have abstracts that are printed on the first page of the article. The abstract has information on the topic, the research problem, the basic findings, and any unusual research design or data collection features.

Reports of applied research that are written for practitioners have a longer summary called the *executive summary.* It contains more detail than an article abstract and includes the implications of research and major recommendations made in the report. Although it is longer than an abstract, an executive summary rarely exceeds four or five pages.

Abstracts and executive summaries serve several functions: For the less interested reader, they tell what is in a report; for readers looking for specific information, they help the reader determine whether the full report contains important information. Readers use the abstract or summary to screen information and decide whether the entire report should be read. It gives serious readers who intend to read the full report a quick mental picture of the report which makes reading the report easier and faster.

Presenting the Problem. The first section of the report defines the research problem. It can be placed in one or more sections with titles such as "Introduction," "Problem Definition," "Literature Review," "Hypotheses," or "Background Assumptions." Although the subheadings vary, the contents include a statement of the research problem and a rationale for what is being examined. Here, researchers explain the significance of and provide a background to the research question. They explain the significance of the research by showing how different solutions to the problem lead to different applications or theoretical conclusions. Introductory sections frequently include a context literature review and link the problem to theory. Introductory

FIGURE 14.2 Suggestions for Rewriting

1. *Mechanics.* Check grammar, spelling, punctuation, verb agreement, verb tense, and verb/subject separation with each rewrite. Remember that each time new text is added, new errors can creep in. Mistakes are not only distracting but they also weaken the confidence readers place in the ideas you express.

2. *Usage.* Reexamine terms, especially key terms, when rewriting to see whether you are using the exact word that expresses your intended meaning. Do not use technical terms or long words unnecessarily. Use the plain word that best expresses meaning. Get a thesaurus and use it. A *thesaurus* is an essential reference tool, like a dictionary, that contains words of similar meaning and can help you locate the exact word for a meaning you want to express. Precise thinking and expression requires precise language. Do not say *average* if you use the *mean*. Do not say *mankind* or *policeman* when you intend *people* or *police officer*. Do not use *principal* for *principle*.

3. *Voice.* Writers of research reports often make the mistake of using the passive instead of the active voice. It may appear more authoritative, but passive voice obscures the actor or subject of action. For example, the passive, *The relationship between grade in school and more definite career plans was confirmed by the data* is better stated as the active, *The data confirm the relationship between grade in school and more definite career plans.* The passive, *Respondent attitude toward abortion was recorded by an interviewer* reads easier in the active voice: *An interviewer recorded respondent attitude towards abortion.* Also avoid unnecessary qualifying language, such as *seems to* or *appears to*.

4. *Coherence.* Sequence, steps, and transitions should be logically tight. Try reading the entire report one paragraph at a time. Does the paragraph contain a unified idea? A topic sentence? Is there a transition between paragraphs within the report?

5. *Repetition.* Remove repeated ideas, wordiness, and unnecessary phrases. Ideas are best stated once, forcefully, instead of repeatedly in an unclear way. When revising, eliminate deadwood (words that add nothing) and circumlocution (the use of several words when one more precise word will do). Directness is preferable to wordiness. The wordy phrase, *To summarize the above, it is our conclusion in light of the data that X has a positive effect of considerable magnitude on the occurrence of Y, notwithstanding the fact that Y occurs only on rare occasions,* is better stated, *In sum, we conclude that X has a large positive effect on Y, but Y occurs infrequently.*

6. *Structure.* Research reports should have a transparent organization. Move sections around as necessary to fit the organization better, and use headings and subheadings. A reader should be able to follow the logical structure of a report.

7. *Abstraction.* A good research report mixes abstract ideas and concrete examples. A long string of abstractions without the specifics is difficult to read. Likewise, a mass of specific concrete details without periodic generalization also loses readers.

8. *Metaphors.* Many writers use metaphors to express ideas. Phrases like *the cutting edge, the bottom line,* and *penetrating to the heart* are used to express ideas by borrowing images from other contexts. Metaphors can be an effective method of communication, but they need to be used sparingly and with care. A few well-chosen, consistently used, fresh metaphors can communicate ideas quickly and effectively; however, the excessive use of metaphors, especially overused metaphors (e.g., the *bottom line*), is a sloppy, unimaginative method of expression.

sections also define key concepts and present conceptual hypotheses.

Describing the Methods. The next section of the report describes how the researcher designed the study and collected the data. It goes by several names (e.g., "Methods," "Research Design," or "Data") and may be subdivided into other parts (e.g., "Measures," "Sampling," or "Manipulations"). It is the most important section for evaluating the methodology of the project. The section answers several questions for the reader:

1. What type of study (e.g., experiment, survey) was conducted?
2. Exactly how were data collected (e.g., study design, type of survey, time and location of data collection, experimental design used)?
3. How were variables measured? Are the measures reliable and valid?
4. What is the sample? How many subjects or respondents are involved in the study? How were they selected?
5. How were ethical issues and specific concerns of the design dealt with?

Results and Tables. After describing how data were collected, methods of sampling, and measurement, you then present the data. This section presents—it does not discuss, analyze, or interpret the data. Researchers sometimes combine the "Results" section with the next section, called "Discussion" or "Findings."

Researchers make choices in how to present the data. When analyzing the data, they look at dozens of univariate, bivariate, and multivariate tables and statistics to get a feel for the data. This does not mean that every statistic or table is in a final report. Rather, the researcher selects the minimum number of charts or tables that fully inform the reader and rarely present the raw data itself. Data analysis techniques should summarize the data and test hypotheses (e.g., frequency distributions, tables with means and standard deviations, correlations, and other statistics).

A researcher wants to give a complete picture of the data without overwhelming the reader—not provide data in excessive detail nor present irrelevant data. Readers can make their own interpretations. Detailed summary statistics belong in appendixes.

Discussion. In the discussion section, researchers give the reader a concise, unambiguous interpretation of its meaning. The discussion is not a selective emphasis or partisan interpretation; rather, it is a candid discussion of what is in the results section. The discussion section is separated from the results so that a reader can examine the data and arrive at different interpretations.

Beginning researchers often find it difficult to organize a discussion section. One approach is to organize the discussion according to hypotheses, discussing how the data relate to each hypothesis. In addition, researchers should discuss unanticipated findings, possible alternative explanations of results, and weaknesses or limitations.

Drawing Conclusions. Researchers restate the research question and summarize findings in the conclusion. Its purpose is to summarize the report, and it is sometimes titled "Summary."

The only sections after the conclusion are the references and appendixes. The references section contains only sources that were referred to in the text or notes of the report. Appendixes, if used, usually contain additional information on methods of data collection (e.g., questionnaire wording) or results (e.g., descriptive statistics). The footnotes or endnotes in quantitative research reports expand or elaborate on information in the text. Researchers use them sparingly to provide secondary information that clarifies the text but might distract from the flow of the reading.

The Qualitative Research Report

Compared to quantitative research, it is more difficult to write a report on qualitative social research. It has fewer rules and less structure. Nevertheless, the purpose is the same: to clearly communicate the research process and the data collected through the process.

Quantitative reports present hypotheses and evidence in a logically tight and condensed style. By contrast, qualitative reports tend to be longer, and book-length reports are common. The greater length is for five reasons:

1. The data in a qualitative report are more difficult to condense. Data are in the form of words, pictures, or sentences and include many quotes and examples.

2. Qualitative researchers try to create a subjective sense of empathy and understanding among readers in addition to presenting factual evidence and analytic interpretations. Detailed descriptions of specific settings and situations help readers better understand or get a feel for settings. Researchers attempt to transport the reader into the subjective world view and meaning system of a social setting.

3. Qualitative researchers use less standardized techniques of gathering data, creating analytic categories, and organizing evidence. The techniques applied may be particular to individual researchers or unique settings. Thus, researchers explain what they did and why, because it has not been done before.

4. Exploring new settings or constructing new theory is a common goal in qualitative research. The development of new concepts and examination of relationships among them adds to the length of reports. Theory flows out of evidence, and detailed descriptions demonstrate how the researcher created interpretations.

5. Qualitative researchers may use more varied and literary writing styles, which increases length. They have greater freedom to employ literary devices to tell a story or recount a tale.

Field Research. Field research reports rarely follow a fixed format with standard sections, and theoretical generalizations and data are not separated into distinct sections. Generalizations are intertwined with the evidence, which takes the form of detailed description with frequent quotes.

Researchers balance the presentation of data and analysis to avoid an excessive separation of data from analysis, called the *error of segregation.* This occurs when researchers separate data from analysis so much that readers cannot see the connection.[1]

The tone of field research reports is less objective and formal, and more personal. Field research reports may be written in the first person (i.e., using the pronoun *I*) because the researcher was directly involved in the setting, interacted with the people studied, and was the measurement "instrument." The decisions or indecisions, feelings, reactions, and personal experiences of the researcher are parts of the field research process.

Field research reports often face more skepticism than quantitative reports do. This makes it essential to assess an audience's demands for evidence and to establish credibility. The key is to provide readers with enough evidence so that they believe the recounted events and accept the interpretations as plausible. A degree of selective observation is accepted in field research, so the critical issue is whether other observers could reach the same conclusion if they examined the same data.

Field researchers face a data reduction dilemma when presenting evidence. Most data are in the form of an enormous volume of field notes, but a researcher cannot directly share all the observations or recorded conversations with the readers. For example, in their study of medical students, *Boys in White,* Becker and colleagues (1961) had about 5,000 pages of single-spaced field notes. Field researchers only include about 5 percent of their field notes in a report as quotes. The remaining 95 percent is not wasted; there is just no room for it. Thus, writers select quotes and indirectly convey the rest of the data to readers.

There is no fixed organization for a field research report, although a literature review often appears near the beginning. There are many acceptable organizational forms. Lofland (1976) suggests the following:

1. Introduction
   a. Most general aspects of situation
   b. Main contours of the general situation
   c. How materials were collected
   d. Details about the setting
   e. How the report is organized
2. The situation
   a. Analytic categories
   b. Contrast between situation and other situations
   c. Development of situation over time
3. Strategies
4. Summary and implications

Devices for organizing evidence and analysis also vary a great deal. For example, writers can organize the report in terms of a *natural history*, an unfolding of events as you discovered them, or as a chronology, following the developmental cycle or career of an aspect of the setting or people in it. Another possibility is to organize the report as a *zoom lens*, beginning broadly and then focusing increasingly narrowly on a specific topic. Statements can move from universal statements about all cultures, to general statements about a specific cultures, to statements about a specific cultural scene, to specific statements about an aspect of culture, to specific statements about specific incidents.

Field researchers also organize reports by themes. A writer chooses between using abstract analytic themes and using themes from the categories used by the people who were studied. The latter gives readers a vivid description of the setting and displays knowledge of the language, concepts, categories, and beliefs of those being written about.[2]

Field researchers discuss the methods used in the report, but its location and form vary. One technique is to interweave a description of the setting, the means of gaining access, the role of the researcher, and the subject/researcher relationship into the discussion of evidence and analysis. This is intensified if the writer adopts what Van Maanen (1988:73) called a "confessional" style of writing.

A chronological, zoom lens, or theme-based organization allows placing the data collection method near the beginning or the end. In book-length reports, methodological issues are usually discussed in a separate appendix.

Field research reports can contain transcriptions of tape recordings, maps, photographs, or charts illustrating analytic categories. They supplement the discussion and are placed near the discussion they complement. Qualitative field research can use creative formats that differ from the usual written text with examples from field notes. Harper's (1982) book contains many photographs with text. The photographs give a visual inventory of the settings described in the text and present the meanings of settings in the terms of those being studied. For example, field research articles have appeared in the form of all photographs, a script for a play, or a documentary film.[3]

Direct, personal involvement in the intimate details of a social setting heightens ethical concerns. Researchers write in a manner that protects the privacy of those being studied and helps prevent the publication of a report from harming those who were studied. They usually change the names of members and exact locations in field reports. Personal involvement in field research leads researchers to include a short autobiography. For example, in the appendix to *Street Corner Society* the author, William Foote Whyte (1955), gave a detailed account of the occupations of his father and grandfather, his hobbies and interests, the jobs he held, how he ended up going to graduate school, and how his research was affected by his getting married.

Historical-Comparative Research. There is no single way to write a report on historical-comparative research. Most frequently, researchers "tell a story" or describe details in general analytic categories. The writing usually goes beyond description and includes limited generalizations and abstract concepts.

Historical-comparative (H-C) researchers rarely describe their methods in great detail. Explicit sections of the report or an appendix that describes the methods used are unusual. Occasionally, a book-length report contains a bibliographic essay that discusses major sources used. More often, numerous detailed footnotes or endnotes describe the sources and evidence. For example, a 20-page report on quantitative or field research typically has 5 to 10 notes, whereas an H-C research report of equal length may have 40 to 60 notes.

Historical-comparative reports can contain photographs, maps, diagrams, charts, or tables of statistics throughout the report and in the section that discusses evidence that relates to them. The charts, tables, and so forth supplement a discussion or give the reader a better feel for the places and people being described. They are used in conjunction with frequent quotes as one among several types of evidence. Historical-comparative reports rarely summarize data to test specific hypotheses as quantitative research does. Instead, the writer builds a web of meaning or descriptive detail and organizes the evidence itself to convey interpretations and generalizations.

There are two basic modes of organizing historical-comparative research reports: by topic and chronologically. Most writers mix the two types. For example, information is organized chronologically within topics, or organized by topic within chronological periods. Occasionally other forms of organization are used—by place, by individual person, or by major events. If the report is truly comparative, the writer has additional options, such as making comparisons within topics. Figure 14.3 provides a sample of some techniques used by historical-comparative researchers to organize evidence and analysis.

Some H-C researchers mimic the quantitative research report and use quantitative research techniques. They extend quantitative research rather than adopt a distinct historical-comparative research method. Their reports follow the model of a quantitative research report.

You learned about the narrative strategy of qualitative data analysis in Chapter 13. Researchers who use this strategy often adopt a narrative style of report writing. Researchers who use the narrative style organize their data chronologically and try to "tell a story" around specific individuals and events.

The Research Proposal

What Is the Proposal? A research *proposal* is a document that presents a plan for a project to reviewers for evaluation. It can be a supervised project submitted to instructors as part of an educational degree (e.g., a master's thesis or a Ph.D. dissertation) or it can be a research project proposed to a funding agency. Its purpose is to convince reviewers that you, the researcher, are capable of successfully conducting the proposed research project. Reviewers have more confidence that a planned project will be successfully completed if the proposal is well written and organized, and if you demonstrate careful planning.

The proposal is similar to a research report, but it is written before the research project begins. A proposal describes the research problem and its importance, and gives a detailed account of the methods that will be used and why they are appropriate.

The proposal for quantitative research has most of the parts of a research report: a title, an abstract, a problem statement, a literature review, a methods or design section, and a bibliography. It lacks results, discussion, and conclusion sections. The proposal has a plan for data collection and analysis (e.g., types of statistics). It frequently includes a schedule of the steps to be undertaken and an estimate of the time required for each step.

**FIGURE 14.3 Ten Features to Consider When Writing a Report
on Historical-Comparative Research**

1. *Sequence.* Historical-comparative researchers are sensitive to the temporal order of events and place a series of events in order to describe a process. For example, a researcher studying the passage of a law or the evolution of a social norm may break the process into a set of sequential steps.

2. *Comparison.* Comparing similarities and differences lies at the heart of comparative-historical research. Make comparisons explicit and identify both similarities and differences. For example, a researcher comparing the family in two historical periods or countries begins by listing shared and nonshared traits of the family in each setting.

3. *Contingency.* Researchers often discover that one event, action, or situation depends on or is conditioned by others. Outlining the linkages of how one event was contingent on others is critical. For example, a researcher examining the rise of local newspapers notes that it depended on the spread of literacy.

4. *Origins and consequences.* Historical-comparative researchers trace the origins of an event, action, organization, or social relationship back in time, or follow its consequences into subsequent time periods. For example, a researcher explaining the end of slavery traces its origins to many movements, speeches, laws, and actions in the preceding fifty years.

5. *Sensitivity to incompatible meaning.* Meanings change over time and vary across cultures. Historical-comparative researchers ask themselves whether a word or social category had the same meaning in the past as in the present or whether a word in one culture has a direct translation in another culture. For example, a college degree had a different meaning in a historical era when it was extremely expensive and less than 1 percent of the 18- to 22-year-old population received a degree compared to the late twentieth century, when college became relatively accessible.

6. *Limited generalization.* Overgeneralization is always a potential problem in historical-comparative research. Few researchers seek rigid, fixed laws in historical, comparative explanation. They qualify statements or avoid strict determination. For example, instead of a blanket statement that the destruction of the native cultures in areas settled by European Whites was the inevitable consequence of advanced technological culture, a researcher may list the specific factors that combined to explain the destruction in particular social-historical settings.

7. *Association.* The concept of association is used in all forms of social research. As in other areas, historical-comparative researchers identify factors that appear together in time and place. For example, a researcher examining a city's nineteenth-century crime rate asks whether years of greater migration into the city are associated with higher crime rates and whether those arrested tended to be recent immigrants.

8. *Part and whole.* It is important to place events in their context. Writers of historical-comparative research sketch linkages between parts of a process, organization, or event and the larger context in which it is found. For example, a researcher studying a particular political ritual in an eighteenth-century setting describes how the ritual fit within the eighteenth-century political system.

9. *Analogy.* Analogies can be useful. The overuse of analogy or the use of an inappropriate analogy is dangerous. For example, a researcher examines feelings about divorce in country X and describes them as "like feelings about death" in country Y. This analogy requires a description of "feelings about death" in country Y.

10. *Synthesis.* Historical-comparative researchers often synthesize many specific events and details into a comprehensive whole. Synthesis results from weaving together many smaller generalizations and interpretations into coherent main themes. For example, a researcher

FIGURE 14.3 Continued

studying the French Revolution synthesizes specific generalizations about changes in social structure, international pressures, agricultural dislocation, shifting popular beliefs and problems with government finances into a compact, coherent explanation. Researchers using the

narrative form summarize the argument in an introduction or conclusion. It is a motif or theme embedded within the description. Thus, theoretical generalizations are intertwined with the evidence and appear to flow inductively out of the detailed evidence.

Proposals for qualitative research are more difficult to write because the research process itself is less structured and preplanned. The researcher prepares a problem statement, literature review, and bibliography. He or she demonstrates an ability to complete a proposed qualitative project in two ways. First, the proposal is well written, with an extensive discussion of the literature, significance of the problem, and sources. This shows reviewers familiarity with qualitative research and the appropriateness of the method for studying the problem. Second, the proposal describes a qualitative pilot study. This demonstrates motivation, familiarity with research techniques, and ability to complete a report about unstructured research.

Proposals to Fund Research. The purpose of a research grant is to provide the resources needed to help complete a worthy project. Researchers whose primary goal is to use funding for personal benefit or prestige, to escape from other activities, or to build an "empire" are less successful. The strategies of proposal writing and getting grants has become an industry called *grantsmanship.*

There are many sources of funding for research proposals. Colleges, private foundations, and government agencies have programs to award grants to researchers. Funds may be used to purchase equipment, to pay your salary or that of others, for research supplies, for travel to collect data, or for help with the publication of results. The degree of competition for a grant

varies a great deal, depending on the source. Some sources fund more than 3 out of 4 proposals they receive, others fund fewer than 1 in 20.

The researcher needs to investigate funding sources and ask questions: What types of projects are funded—applied versus basic research, specific topics, or specific research techniques? What are the deadlines? What kind (e.g., length, degree of detail, etc.) of proposal is necessary? How large are most grants? What aspects (e.g., equipment, personnel, travel, etc.) of a project are or are not funded? There are many sources of information on funding sources. Librarians or officials who are responsible for research grants at a college are good resource people. For example, private foundations are listed in an annual publication, *The Foundation Directory. The Guide to Federal Funding for Social Scientists* lists sources in the U.S. government. In the United States, there are many newsletters on funding sources and two national computerized databases, which subscribers can search for funding sources. Some agencies periodically issue *requests for proposals (RFPs)* that ask for proposals to conduct research on a specific issue. Researchers need to learn about funding sources, because it is essential to send the proposal to an appropriate source in order to be successful.

Researchers need to show a track record of past success in the proposal, especially if they are going to be in charge of the project. The researcher in charge of a research project is the *principal investigator (PI)* or project director.

Proposals usually include a curriculum vitae or academic resumé, letters of support from other researchers, and a record of past research. Reviewers feel safer investing funds in a project headed by someone who already has research experience than in a novice. One can build a track record with small research projects or by assisting an experienced researcher before seeking funding as a principal investigator.

The reviewers who evaluate a proposal judge whether the proposal project is appropriate to the funding source's goals. Most funding sources have guidelines stating the kinds of projects they fund. For example, programs that fund basic research have the advancement of knowledge as a goal. Programs to fund applied research often have improvements in the delivery of services as a goal. Instructions specify page length, number of copies, deadlines, and the like. Follow all instructions exactly.

Proposals should be neat and professional looking. The instructions usually ask for a detailed plan for the use of time, services, and personnel. These should be clearly stated and realistic for the project. Excessively high or low estimates, unnecessary add-ons, or omitted essentials will lower how reviewers evaluate a proposal. Creating a budget for a proposed project is complicated and usually requires technical assistance. For example, pay rates, fringe benefit rates, and so on that must be charged may not be easy to obtain. It is best to consult a grants officer at a college or an experienced proposal writer. In addition, endorsements or clearances of regulations are often necessary (e.g., IRB approval). Proposals should also include specific plans for disseminating results (e.g., publications, presentations before professional groups, etc.) and a plan for evaluating whether the project met its objectives.

The proposal is a kind of contract between researcher and the funding source. Funding agencies often require a final report, including details on how funds were spent, the findings, and an evaluation of whether the project met its objectives. Failure to spend funds properly, complete the project described in the proposal, or file a final report may result in a researcher being barred from receiving future funding or facing legal action. A serious misuse of funds may result in the banning of others at the same institution from receiving future funding.

The process of reviewing proposals after they are submitted to a funding source takes anywhere from a few weeks to almost a year, depending on the funding source. In most cases, reviewers rank a large group of proposals, and only highly ranked proposals receive funding. A proposal often undergoes a peer review in which the reviewers know the proposer from the vitae in the proposal, but the proposer does not know the reviewers. Sometimes a proposal is reviewed by nonspecialists or nonresearchers. Instructions on preparing a proposal indicate whether to write for specialists in a field or for an educated general audience.

If a proposal is funded, celebrate, but only for a short time. If the proposal is rejected, which is more likely, do not despair. Most proposals are rejected the first or second time they are submitted. Many funding sources provide written reviewer evaluations of the proposal. Always request them if they are provided. Sometimes, a courteous talk on the telephone with a person at the funding source will reveal the reasons for rejection. Strengthen and resubmit a proposal on the basis of the reviewer's comments. Most funding sources accept repeated resubmissions of revised proposals, and proposals that have been revised may be stronger in subsequent competitions.

If a proposal has been submitted to an appropriate funding source and all instructions are followed, reviewers are more likely to rate it high when:

1. It addresses an important research question. It builds on prior knowledge and represents a substantial advance of knowledge for basic research. It documents a major social problem and holds promise for solutions for applied research.

2. It follows all instructions, is well written, and is easy to follow, with clearly stated objectives.
3. It completely describes research procedures that include high standards of research methodology, and it applies research techniques that are appropriate to the research question.
4. It includes specific plans for disseminating the results and evaluating whether the project has met its objectives.
5. The project is well designed and shows serious planning. It has realistic budgets and schedules.
6. The researcher has the necessary experience or background to complete the project successfully.

CONCLUSION

Clearly communicating results is a vital part of the larger scientific enterprise, as are the ethics and politics of social research.

I want to end this chapter by urging you, as a consumer of social research or a new social researcher, to be self-aware. Be aware of the place of the researcher in society and of the societal con-text of social research itself. Social researchers, and sociologists in particular, bring a unique perspective to the larger society.

Key Terms

editing
error of segregation
executive summary
free writing
grantsmanship
paraphrasing
plagiarism
prewriting
principal investigator
request for proposals (RFPs)
revising
rewriting
zoom lens

Endnotes

1. The error of segregation is discussed in Lofland and Lofland (1984:146).
2. See Van Maanen (1988:13).
3. See Becker and associates (1989), Dabbs (1982), and Jackson (1978).